A Peculiar Kind of Mission

In memoriam
Sister M. Hugh Shayler (1916–2005)
Father Jonathon Fleetwood (1926–2011)
true Dominicans – true friends

A Peculiar Kind of Mission

The English Dominican Sisters, 1845–2010

Anselm Nye

Gracewing

First published in 2011

Gracewing
2 Southern Avenue, Leominster
Herefordshire HR6 0QF

UK ISBN 978 085244 763 5

Typeset by
Action Publishing Technology Ltd, Gloucester, GL1 5SR

Printed in England by
MPG Books Group, Bodmin and King's Lynn

Contents

List of Illustrations

All illustrations within the text, with the exception of Fig. 5, have been reproduced from the Stone Archives, with permission.

List of Plates

A Note on Names

Like members of many religious congregations, the English Dominican Sisters normally prefixed their names in religion with that of Mary, generally abbreviated to 'M.' in written form. The practice has been retained in this book with the exception of double-barrelled names, such as Rose Columba. At the Special General Chapter in 1967 sisters were given the option to revert to their baptisimal names or to a feminine form of a masculine religious name, several did so then or subsequently. The old or new name has generally been indicated in the text, name changes of all sisters are given in the index.

Until after the Second Vatican Council, members of the General Council, former Prioresses General, local prioresses and novice mistresses were addressed as 'Mother'. I have generally used the title only for those who were major superiors when referring to them during their term of office.

The terms 'nuns' and 'sisters' are used interchangeably in modern parlance. Apart from the introduction, or when making citations, I have endeavoured to adhere to the proper canonical usage, reserving the term 'nuns' for contemplative religious bound to enclosure and 'sisters' for members of active congregations.

Foreword

It is a privilege and a pleasure to write this foreword to 'our book' with the intriguing title: *A Peculiar Kind of Mission*. Its pages contain the history of our Congregation, or rather the histories of five individual streams which joined together in 1929 forming *The Dominican Sisters of the English Congregation of Saint Catherine of Siena*. The author, Anselm Nye, has traced the sources of each stream originating in different parts of England, describing the period of confluence and its flow through the decades until the present time. Relying on meticulous research but also on interviews with present members of the Congregation, Anselm is presenting our story in an accessible style and with palpable warmth and insight. During the period of writing, individual chapters were read and discussed with the author by a critical team, that is, the members of the General Council. It was a fruitful and enjoyable period of collaboration for which I would like to thank Anselm and my fellow councillors.

A Peculiar Kind of Mission does not contain mere historical facts. Underlying the historian's presentation is a love of Dominican preaching which inspired our sisters in the past and is still the main force behind our apostolic engagements today. We may ask: Why this desire to preach? Where did they and where do we get our motivation from? As Dominican Sisters we follow the inspiration of St Dominic, St Catherine and all our saints who were filled with the love of God and wanted to bring the good news of Jesus Christ to all people. Following in their footsteps we are sustained by prayer, common life and study so that we too may be filled with God's love and can engage in direct work for the good of our neighbour. This may be shown by teaching, lecturing, caring for the sick, visiting the lonely, and accompanying the dying. Whatever form or expression the apostolate takes – it is always motivated by the one goal – which is to bring a word of faith, encouragement and healing. And it is through our way of life that we become and are sustained as Dominican preachers.

It seems to me that Anselm has managed to tell our story truthfully with many edifying features but not avoiding rough sailings, obstacles, and peculiarities. In the past our sisters took on the hardships of new foundations, but many times they faced changes in the form of different kinds of apostolic engagements or, what is always painful, closure of institutions and houses. Whatever they have done or suffered has contributed to the history of Dominican life in Britain which, I am sure, will inspire us, the present members, to trust that everything we do or suffer now will add to Dominican life of the twenty-first century. With other religious orders and congregations in the West we are experiencing a lack of vocations. This means that the time for expansion and running big institutions has almost gone. In future more flexibility may be asked of our sisters, for example when called to collaborate with different branches of the Dominican Order or other religious in new missions. In the past as also today it takes women armed with courage and commitment to preach and witness to the kingdom of God in changing circumstances, especially in the increasing secular world of today. Anselm Nye concluded our book by saying that

> *There is no question that this particular expression of Dominican life deserves to survive, but no certainty that it will. What is certain is that, as long as they are able, the Sisters of the English Dominican Congregation will keep on preaching, praising and blessing and continue that 'peculiar kind of mission' that has been theirs from the beginning.*

I can only second this. Once more I would like to express my gratitude to Anselm for his work with and for our sisters. Our meetings with Anselm and many interviews took place in our convent in Stone. Here I would like to take the opportunity to thank the Prioress and the members of the Stone community for kind hospitality rendered on these occasions as well as on many others. Anselm also visited other houses and there has been cooperation all round which I would like to acknowledge gratefully. Moreover, I would also like to extend sincere thanks to innumerable lay people who have been associated with the sisters over the years in all our houses and have worked alongside us. Their particular involvement and participation in our mission would need an extra book.

Lastly let us utter a heartfelt DEO GRATIAS together for everything written but also for things unwritten and forgotten which have made up our story, and let us walk confidently into the future!

Sister Mary Pauline Bürling, OP
Prioress General

Introduction

Ther was also a Nonne, a prioresse
That of hir smyling was ful simple and coy ...
And sikerly she was of greet desport,
And ful plesaunt, and amyable of port.
Geoffrey Chaucer, *The Canterbury Tales*[1]

They were turning the corner into Peraki Street; two in front and one behind. My brothers ran back and forth between the front door and the gate of my grandmother's house in a small town north of Christchurch, New Zealand, with frenzied shrieks: 'The witches are coming, the witches are coming!' Of course we knew quite well they were not witches, but nuns who inhabited the world of our Catholic cousins, a world which would very soon become our own. I stood by the gate as the swish of black serge and blue braiding approached, the starched white linen lining to the veils bouncing against their shoulders as they walked. My brothers stopped their shrieking and one of them swung onto the gate, informing the passing trio with enormous self confidence; 'We're just going to have a cup of tea.' The creatures smiled down benevolently and passed on silently. I was not quite five years old at the time, but the impression remains so strong in every detail – my first memory of women religious.

Three years later my brothers and I, duly instructed and conditionally baptized along with our parents, were being taught by the Sisters of Mercy in our local parish school. In neighbouring parishes our peers were being taught by the Irish and Canadian nuns with the small pie-crust bonnets; or the 'posh' nuns with the larger pie-crust bonnets and gossamer-thin veils who had actually deigned to open a day school in the city; or the Irish nuns with widow's-peak coifs beneath bus-shelter-sized veils. If our mother had carried out her oft' repeated but never believed threat and actually 'had enough and walked out' we would doubtless have been placed in the children's home run by other nuns in black with blue braiding who wore large medals dangling on long chains and long leather belts. Elderly Catholics who could no longer care for themselves went to the home for the aged run by the same nuns; operations were performed and Catholic babies were born in the hospital run by the nuns with the pale blue veils. My aunt acted as driver for the blue- and black-clad nuns who managed domestic arrangements at the seminary; whereas the brown-clad sisters in the newly founded neighbouring parish, who lived in an ordinary little house, drove themselves about visiting parishioners. On the other side of the city, down next to the psychiatric hospital so cheeringly named Sunnyside, lived the enclosed nuns who never went out but prayed day and night behind their grilles.

The sisters, whatever the hue or style of their raiment, were everywhere. We patronized the concerts and fêtes they organized to raise funds for the missions. We saw them in the street visiting the sick and the lonely, when we went to church, even when we went shopping. We marched with them in the annual Christ the King procession. We saw the external changes in their lives as the 1960s merged into the 1970s, the 'new look' habits, the first experiments with secular dress, and our mothers questioned their 'opting out' of the schools and taking up new apostolates. By this time we might run into them rather self-consciously at the cinema or the beach, or on an anti-Vietnam war demonstration – oh, the letters to the Catholic press that produced! – or even see one or two of them locked in a cage in Cathedral Square symbolically sharing the plight of political prisoners.

In the late 1970s, when I was a religious myself, reading theology in Melbourne, I followed a course in local church history. I had wanted to write my essay on the role that religious sisters had played in keeping the faith alive in the rural areas of Australia and New Zealand. But when I consulted the works on national and diocesan history the nuns, so ubiquitous in my own experience of Catholic life, were almost completely absent, or relegated to footnotes. After arriving in Britain I learned that this was not an exclusively antipodean phenomenon. Across the globe, academic interest in women religious seemed to have stopped stock still with the end of the Middle Ages, or the dissolution of the religious houses at the Reformation and the French Revolution. It was not until I discovered the magisterial work of Claude Langlois, *Le Catholicisme au féminin* on the shelves of the FNAC bookshop in Strasbourg in 1987, that I realized that women religious of more recent times were indeed suitable matter for serious, academic study.

The renewal of religious life after the Second Vatican Council, based on a return to the values of the Gospel and the founding charism of the institute, resulted in a plethora of publications. Almost without exception these concentrated on the adaptation of religious life to the modern world, or a re-evaluation of its fundamental principles. Almost no attention was paid, at least in commercially published works, to serious evaluation of the historical aspects of renewal. Many religious, especially women, remained relatively unaware of their own historical significance. Neither has the role played by women, and religious sisters in particular, in British Catholic life received the critical historical attention it deserves. Joyce Sugg, by exception, shows in her work just how important the mutual interaction was between Newman and his female friends. While the newly appointed bishops governed, it was often women – sometimes their mothers – who brought needs to light, who networked with other women to raise funds, got the churches built and helped establish the schools, orphanages and refuges. Women religious played their part in funding, maintaining and staffing these institutions and also engaged in a wide range of non-institutional works. They continue to do so.

Over the last twenty years or so, beginning with the articles of Susan O'Brien, interest has mounted, slowly but surely, in the history of women religious in Britain, with an increasing amount of research at doctoral level. Excellent biographical works on Cornelia Connelly, founder of the Society of the Holy Child Jesus, and Elizabeth Prout, founder of the Sisters of the Cross and Passion, have been published. There have also been excellent studies of several communities of the Sisters of Mercy by Maria McClelland, Penny Roker and Jean Maynard, and of the Glasgow Franciscan Sisters by John Watts, all of which have made an important contribution to understanding the interaction of religious sisters with local Catholic communities. Perhaps even more important have been the works of Barbara Walsh and Carmen Mangion which have placed the history of women religious in the broader context of social and feminist history.[2] The current work is offered in the hope of adding a significant story to this growing corpus, in a style sufficiently accessible to the general reader, while satisfying the appetite of the more academic.

The research for this book began as work towards a doctorate which, for a number of reasons, was never completed. My visits to the archives at Stone more or less ceased until the late Sister M. Hugh Shayler, archivist at the time, asked her sister Esmé to call me and let me know how much my visits were missed! Subsequently Sister Angela Mary Leydon, during her term as Prioress General, put my research to good use by asking me to present two entire days of congregational history in 2004 and 2005. The Acts of the General Chapter of 2007 ordained that a history of the English Dominican Congregation, and the five groups from which it was formed in 1929, should be written and I was delighted to be asked to undertake the task.

To the present Prioress General, Sister M. Pauline Bürling and her Council: Sisters Anna Mary House, M. Jadwiga Świątecka, M. Cecily Boulding and M. Teresa Billington, I owe an enormous debt of gratitude. Generosity is nothing new to the English Dominican Sisters, but I wish to acknowledge theirs to me, in providing the financial support which enabled me to spend the last twelve months completing the project full time. I must likewise acknowledge the generosity of Emma Bull, Director of Library Services at Queen Mary, University of London, for supporting my application for a year's leave at a particularly difficult juncture in the library's development. Working with the General Council has been tremendously enjoyable, learning from their insights and experience, pooling our mutual enthusiasm, reminiscing and laughing together, responding to their suggestions and their insistent prodding if I fell behind deadline. I thank them for having maintained their confidence in me. They have been every bit as 'full pleasant and amiable' as Chaucer's Prioress!

Over a considerable number of years, the sisters of the congregation have welcomed me to share their meals and choral prayer, their celebrations, professions and funerals. At Stone and elsewhere the sisters have given me their friendship and their trust, and each has contributed something to my understanding of the history of their congregation. In thanking them, my only concern is that I may have become too fond of them to write objectively. And at Stone thanks are due not only to the sisters, but to those who work with them to ensure that my room is prepared and I am well fed.

Thanks must also be acknowledged to others. In the first instance to all those sisters who elicited my curiosity, who gave me my first education in the faith, who taught me, studied with me, offered me their friendship and in various ways influenced my life. I owe a great deal to my friend Gareth Hughes who was the first to encourage me to apply my almost obsessive interest and knowledge to academic research and who, despite a Welsh Calvinist heritage, has always been willing to read and provide informed and objective criticism. Judith Champ was most encouraging during the early years of my research as my supervisor, before her departure from King's College London. Her biography of Archbishop Ullathorne is most important in acknowledging the influence of women on its subject, and highlighting in particular Ullathorne's relationship with Mother Margaret Hallahan, founder of the first congregation of Dominican Sisters in England.

The Dominican brethren have also welcomed me and given their help and advice. Father Bede Bailey, during his time as archivist of the English Dominican Province welcomed me most kindly to the provincial archives of the friars some years ago; while Father Lazaro Sastre Varas did the same with good humour and real interest at the General Archives of the Order, at Santa Sabina in Rome, more recently. Father Jonathan Fleetwood, chaplain at Stone 2002–11, proved an excellent sounding board during our Monday evening visits to The Poste of Stone. Brother Lawrence Lew of Blackfriars, Oxford, very kindly provided some of his excellent photographs to illustrate this work.

To the archivists and their support staff at the Archdioceses of Westminster and Birmingham, the Dioceses of Arundel & Brighton, Brentwood, Clifton, Hexham & Newcastle, Nottingham, Plymouth and Southwark I am also indebted. While in Rome, visits to the archives of *Propaganda Fide* at the Pontifical University Urbaniana and those of the Sacred Congregation for Institutes of Consecrated Life and Societies of Apostolic Life – to give its full current title to the Vatican Department which deals with religious institutes – although they yielded little useful material, were certainly intriguing. The welcome received in many of these places was facilitated by my involvement with the Catholic Archives Society, membership of which has been a constant source of support for many years. Likewise, membership in the History of Women Religious networks and attendance at their conferences, both those of the US-based group and that for Great Britain & Ireland, has brought me many enriching contacts and friendships.

Finally, sincere thanks must go to the staff of Gracewing Publishing for their work of editing and production, particularly to the copy editor, Jo Whale, who was quick to send calming and helpful e-mails. Publishers impose a word limit, and this work tells only part of the story. If the huge archival holdings of the English Dominican Sisters, and the interviews I have recorded with them, were exploited fully, the world itself, as John the Evangelist tells us about the saying and doings of Jesus,[3] would hardly have enough space for all the books!

Notes

1. Chaucer, *The Canterbury Tales*, from 'The General Prologue', p. 8.
2. Details of the works mentioned in this introduction are all listed in the Bibliography.
3. John 21:25.

Chapter One

Taking to the road: a Dominican mission

From the beginning Dominic gathered together a family of preachers, men and women, lay and religious, contemplatives and preachers, who took to the road. Fr Timothy Radcliffe, OP[1]

Introduction: two souls, one vision

Disheartened and discouraged, from his vantage point on a rocky outcrop in the hill town of Fanjeaux, Dominic Guzmán looked out across the plain of Lauragais to the northeast. There, above the dilapidated hamlet and chapel of Our Lady at Prouilhe, it seemed he saw a ball of fire descending. This spiritual experience was to be the turning point, the sign from God that he should continue his work of apostolic preaching, and the place itself became known in the Occitan dialect as *Seignadou*. This event, an oral tradition long before it was first documented almost a century later, is thought to have taken place in the latter half of 1206.[2] St Dominic's first response to the sign from God was to gather a group of women into the first House of Holy Preaching, as it came to be called, at Prouilhe, the beginning of his Order of Preachers.

More than 600 years later, on an April day in 1842, a woman in the prime of life was setting out on the journey across the Channel, returning to her native England. For most expatriates returning home after a long absence, two emotions come to the fore: anticipation and anxiety. Despite having spent twelve years in Belgium, Margaret Hallahan does not seem to have suffered from sentiments of nostalgia for her homeland. On the contrary, the prospect of returning filled her with dread, it would be 'like going to hell' and a route she took only under obedience, which was for her the sign from God. Despite this initial reluctance, Margaret would play a significant role in the transformation of 'this heretical country'.[3] Through her profession as a secular tertiary, she was already a member of Dominic's Order and shared his vision; her means of winning souls and propagating the Catholic faith would be the foundation of the first congregation of Dominican Sisters in Britain.

Though Dominic and Margaret were united by a single vision, the form of life adopted by the Dominican communities of women founded in Britain during the nineteenth century differed greatly from that of the first Dominicans at Sainte-Marie de Prouilhe. Understanding the developments in the history of Dominican women, from the first House of Holy Preaching to the growth of congregations of what became known as the Third Order Regular, requires a brief historical overview. Although thirteenth-century Languedoc and nineteenth-century Britain were both arenas of religious controversy, there is little else in common between the environment which first produced the Order of Preachers, and that which both called forth and shaped Margaret Hallahan's congregation and those like it. For this reason, a summary of the situation of the Catholic community to which she returned is also provided.

Dominic's sisters: the development of the Third Order regular

Dominic Guzmán was a Spaniard and had been an Augustinian Canon of the cathedral church at Osma in Castile. In 1203 his bishop, Diego, was sent on a diplomatic mission to Denmark by King Ferdinand VIII, and asked Dominic to accompany him. It was while passing through the south of France that he first encountered the Cathars, and on his return from the north that he began his preaching mission amongst them. The members of this sect were convinced dualists believing in the goodness of spirit and the evil of matter, to whom the central and consoling mystery of the incarnation, God's assuming flesh and sharing our human condition, was considered an illusion and an absurdity. Their preachers lived a life of utter austerity, while lesser mortals might live as they pleased, hoping for redemption through the deathbed sacrament, the *consolamentum*.

Dominic realized, unlike the Cistercian abbots with their worldly retinues, commissioned by the Pope to convert the Cathars, that the best way to combat their teaching was to form a body of preachers living a lifestyle of irreproachable sanctity and asceticism. It was, in fact, to be modelled on Christ's commission to his disciples recorded in the tenth chapter of Matthew's gospel, so beloved of the saint. Dominic's organizational genius bequeathed to the

Church a new type of religious life where the accent was not on stability to a local community, as with monks and canons, but upon mobility for mission. The mission of preaching was to be nourished by the regular observance of choral and private prayer, penance and assiduous study.

The Cathar preachers also gathered together groups of women who lived a similarly austere life, and converts from amongst their number made up part of the first community at Prouilhe. The house served as a base for the preaching expeditions of Dominic and the companions who began to join him. It would remain the only house of the Preaching Friars until that of Toulouse was established in 1215. Once the Order of Preachers began to spread, other houses of Dominican women were established or incorporated into the Order, beginning with that of San Sisto in Rome. Within a few years the women at Prouilhe were already being referred to as *sorores inclusae*, cloistered sisters. Their mission was to support by their prayer and penance the work of the Preaching Friars.

The twelfth and thirteenth centuries saw the development of a great number of virtuoso lay movements within the Church. In northern Europe there were the Brothers and Sisters of the Common Life, the beghards and their female counterparts the beguines. The beguines established female precincts, the beguinages, whose members engaged in cooperative industries such as spinning, weaving or lacemaking, often having a considerable impact on the development of local economies.[4] Supported by their own labour rather than endowments, these communities, unlike most monastic houses of women, were accessible to those of humbler origin. In the south, more disparate groups such as the Humiliati and the Brothers and Sisters of Penance developed.[5] The members of these groups sometimes lived lives of extreme asceticism and engaged in popular preaching or exhortation; some were itinerant, others lived in their own homes or in community.

The hierarchy was concerned that these groups should be contained, lest they fall into the dangers of unbridled enthusiasm or doctrinal heterodoxy. On numerous occasions church councils called upon all those living in community to adopt an established rule or else disband. Many of these groups attached themselves to the religious orders, particularly the Franciscans and Dominicans, profiting from their guidance and adopting their spirituality and mission. Within a century of St Dominic's death, his Order had developed a tripartite form: the First Order of friars, the Second Order of nuns, and the Third Order of Penance. The Third Order comprised secular tertiaries living in their homes, though often affiliated to a house of the friars, and regular tertiaries, usually women, living a conventual life in community.

Exactly how the lifestyle of these houses of Dominican women differed from those of the Second Order nuns is not entirely clear. Certainly, the rule prepared for the Sisters of Penance by Munio of Zamora, Master of the Order of Preachers from 1285 until 1291, has much in common with that of the nuns. As early as 1255 there is evidence of Dominican women being involved in education when a convent, which included a school, was founded at Vercelli by Blessed Aemilia Bicchieri. The Sisters of the convent established at Perugia in 1490 by Blessed Columba of Rieti participated in public processions, nursed the sick and took some part in the political life of the town.[6] Although she was a secular tertiary, the fame of St Catherine of Siena and the approval of Munio's Rule by the Pope in 1405 both stimulated the development of the Third Order Regular, while the general chapters of the friars encouraged the communities of sisters to conform their varied lifestyles as much as possible to that of the Second Order nuns.[7] The decree *Periculoso* issued by Boniface VIII in 1298 reinforced this tendency by declaring cloister obligatory for all women religious, though it is highly likely that many houses of the Third Order continued to exercise at least a limited apostolate beyond the convent walls.

In 1566 the Council of Trent, reacting against the laxity of some religious houses which had so scandalized the Protestant reformers, issued the decree *Circa pastoralis* which recognized as true religious only those who took solemn vows and observed cloister. Most houses of the Third Order Regular adopted both, even if they retained a limited teaching apostolate within the enclosure. But new types of consecrated life also came into existence in the post-Tridentine era whose members deliberately distanced themselves from the lifestyle of 'real religious' in a conscious effort to avoid enclosure and preserve an active, social apostolate. Perhaps the most famous of these foundations was the Daughters of Charity of St Vincent de Paul, founded in Paris in 1633, though there were numerous others.

One of these communities of *filles séculiaires*, as they were called, was founded at Sainville near Tours in 1696 by Marie Poussepin. The founder had been a member of the Rosary Confraternity and her Sisters of Charity of the Presentation continued to benefit from the guidance of the Dominican friar François Mespolié who had directed the confraternity. A definite Dominican flavour may be discerned in the constitutions Marie Poussepin prepared for the community, and in 1712 approval was granted by Antonin Cloche,

Master of the Order, for the vicar of Sainville to receive novices into the Third Order in the absence of a friar. Like the friars, these sisters went on mission, teaching and providing nursing care in the towns and villages of Touraine. However, maintaining links with the Order after the deaths of the founders proved virtually impossible and it was not until the late nineteenth century that the congregation began to rediscover its Dominican roots, and even later before it was officially aggregated to the Order.[8] Nonetheless, Marie Poussepin's sisters were the prototype of the modern congregations of Dominican Sisters.

The rise of rationalism in the eighteenth century, together with an increasing government control exercised over the Church, proved unfavourable to the development of religious life. The French Revolution swept away the entire ecclesiastical structure of France and, to a lesser degree, those countries which became part of the First Empire. The Order of Preachers was numerically decimated, suffering from serious challenges to its central authority. It suffered further decline following the independence of the Spanish colonies in Latin America and the rise of liberal, anti-clerical regimes in Spain and Portugal. The houses of women, whether of the Second or Third Order fared no better.

Although the friars and the nuns would never again match their pre-revolutionary numbers, the nineteenth century was to see a spectacular growth of congregations of Third Order sisters. A combination of factors contributed to this. Despite the Tridentine legislation, Rome itself was becoming more tolerant of religious in simple vows, and began granting approval to new institutes and their constitutions. The desire to reconstruct Catholic society after the revolutionary period, particularly through education, gave impetus to the development of congregations of women in simple vows, as did the crying social needs stemming from industrialization and urbanization. The religious congregation, governed by a superior general, having jurisdiction over dependent branch houses, became the predominant model. More than 400 congregations of this type were founded in France between 1800 and 1880.[9] A similar pattern of development obtained in other European countries as the century progressed.

Just as the reform movements within the Order of Preachers during the Middle Ages often began with the houses of women,[10] so the regeneration of the Order in the nineteenth century began, in many places, with the establishment of congregations of Dominican Sisters. In an age when literature, art and architecture were increasingly finding their models in a romanticized view of medieval

Catholic culture, it is no surprise to find a similar preoccupation amongst many founders of religious institutes. For Dominicans, both male and female, fidelity to the traditions of the past was part and parcel of the revival. An eagerness to adopt the established traditions and observances of the Order, as legislated and documented by the friars and the nuns, is easily detected in the history of congregations of Dominican Sisters.

The majority of the hundred or more congregations of Dominican Sisters founded in the nineteenth century began as local initiatives, frequently founded by women who were already members of the Third Order secular. Some congregations were founded by friars. Missionary bishops, particularly from the United States and southern Africa, sometimes approached monasteries of nuns in Europe, asking them to make foundations abroad. The particular circumstances of the Church in these countries meant that the new foundations eventually developed as congregations of Third Order sisters, the process often beginning with a mitigation of the rules of enclosure and giving up the Divine Office for the shorter Little Office of Our Lady. Such transformations were seldom free from tension. Even houses which had always considered themselves members of the Second Order, such as those in Ireland, might eventually have to content themselves with Third Order status as Rome, taking into consideration similar changes in their way of life, declared their vows to be simple rather than solemn.

New Dominican congregations could also arise through a process of fragmentation or secession. So long as the status of women in simple vows remained ambiguous under canon law, many bishops were unwilling to have religious houses in their own diocese which depended on a motherhouse in another. There are frequent instances of bishops forming such houses, whether of Dominicans or other sisters, into new congregations under their direct jurisdiction. Internal tensions, for instance over the balance between external activity and regular observance, could also result in groups of sisters seceding from a congregation and forming their own. Finally, there are several instances of congregations which had no association with the Order at all finding, sometimes after many years of existence, an attraction to the Dominican way of life.

The foundation of congregations of Dominican women in England is part of this larger picture. They developed in different circumstances, each having its own foundation dynamic, each influenced by the currents of revival within the Order as a whole, and within the local Church.

The return of the native: Margaret Hallahan's England

Twenty years after her return to England, when the prospect of placing her schools under government inspection was considered, Mother Margaret Hallahan wrote to one of her sisters that the British government 'could never mean any good to the Catholic Church'.[11] This judgement was perhaps a little harsh. After the 1760s, prosecutions under the penal code were almost unknown and Catholicism was being practised quite openly, particularly in the northwest, before the Relief Act of 1778. Within years of the Gordon Riots of 1780, the British government welcomed some 5500 émigré priests, refugees from revolutionary France, providing state pensions for many of them. A deep-seated suspicion of Catholicism and its doctrines would certainly maintain its hold on English popular imagination and the rabble could still be roused, though its anger would more often be expressed in vehement polemic than violent action. There was no widespread recurrence of rioting following the passage of the Catholic Relief Act which received royal assent only six months before Margaret left England for Bruges in 1829. Although those voting in favour of the Act may have had little love of Catholicism they did have, as reasonable and educated Englishmen, an attachment to the principle of civil liberties.[12]

The Church was experiencing considerable growth in numbers even before Emancipation. Margaret Hallahan's parents had been part of a wave of Irish immigration to England, both seasonal and permanent, which accounted for the greater part of this increase. Although statistics for this period are unreliable, there were almost 300,000 Irish-born residents of England and Wales recorded in the 1841 census, the figure increasing by a further eighty per cent in the following ten years, by which time the total number of Catholics probably exceeded four per cent of the total population. As a response to this growth the number of ecclesiastical jurisdictions in England and Wales was doubled in 1840 from four to eight. While agricultural labour and canal building had been the early areas of employment, Irish migrants turned increasingly to the industrial towns in their search for work. The image of the poor 'bog-Irish' labourer may have become the normative image of Catholicism in the country, but the recent historian of the Archdiocese of Liverpool suggests that the existence of a strong, well-organized church structure in Lancashire assisted integration and encouraged social promotion.[13]

As the Catholic population grew and became increasingly urban, the centre of gravity moved away from the rural missions under the patronage of the local Catholic gentry, to the city chapels. This posed new challenges in terms of providing the infrastructure required to support Catholic life and worship and also in combating defection from the Church. The social dislocation which accompanied the move from rural settings, whether English or Irish, to the developing industrial centres, could precipitate a decline in religious practice. The anonymity of the city, the lack of peer pressure, the compulsion to work long hours and a level of poverty which could not ensure respectable attire are all noted as reasons for the decline in church attendance amongst the working classes of all faiths in nineteenth-century England.[14] The provision and upkeep of churches, poor schools and other works depended financially upon a small pool of wealthy Catholics. Until the influx of Anglican converts in the 1840s and beyond, English Catholicism was a social anomaly, lacking a solid middle class.[15]

The publication of *Tracts for the Times* began in 1833. In these tracts Newman, Froude, Pusey and others propagated the theory that the Church of England, along with the Orthodox and Roman communions, was a branch of the Catholic Church. A renewed interest in the Catholic origins of Anglicanism, in patristics and liturgy, absorbed them. Amongst both writers and readers of the tracts, many began to question the nature of authority in the Established Church and by the time Margaret Hallahan returned to England a number of prominent Tractarians had already converted to Catholicism. Newman's conversion in 1845 was particularly influential in increasing this flow of converts. In 1850, Bishop Philpotts of Exeter had attempted to prevent George Gorham from taking up a living in his diocese, on the grounds that he rejected the doctrine of baptismal regeneration. The case went to the Privy Council which found against the Bishop. The Gorham judgment was to highlight the question of authority in the Church of England, convincing many Anglicans that the state rather than the episcopacy was now the arbiter of doctrine, and this led to another series of prominent conversions, including that of Henry Manning.[16]

However, the Church into which these new converts were received was not an entirely united one. The Vicars Apostolic had acted quite independently within their districts, and while there were strong and effective figures such as John Milner and William Poynter, others had difficulty in dealing with lay trustees or administering finances. Amongst the clergy ancient rivalries between the seculars and regulars could resurface. To this day the elegant churches of St Mary and St John, the former built for the secular clergy, the latter for the Jesuits, stand within spitting distance on the Standishgate in Wigan as a memorial to the division of local loyalties which Bishop William Gibson was not able to contain.[17] Even after the restoration of the Hierarchy in 1850 the diocesan bishops would defend their independence of thought and action, many of them wary of the Romanizing and centralizing tendencies of Nicholas Wiseman, the first Archbishop of Westminster. There was no guarantee that the new converts would feel entirely at home with their new co-religionists. Members of the old Catholic families, having lived so long at a remove from their non-Catholic peers, often lacked the intellectual training, social awareness and political sensitivity of the converts who had, in many instances, been prominent personalities as Anglicans.[18] Neither group could have felt much in common with the humble Irish Catholics.

Nevertheless, there were certainly grounds for optimism. Less than a year before Margaret Hallahan's arrival in Coventry, the Church of St Chad in Birmingham, clearly designed by Pugin to serve as a cathedral, had been opened and consecrated on 21 June 1841. 'God's architect' as his recent biographer calls him, was involved in the planning or building of more than a dozen other churches at the time.[19] The relentless advance of bricks and mortar gathered pace with the century and proved to be something of a unifying factor since all classes of Catholics supported it according to their means. Two other factors played a major part in moulding together the Catholic community: a shared devotional life and a monumental effort in providing education for all levels of society. Recent study suggests that there was a significant continuity in devotional practice during the pre- and post-emancipation eras and stresses the enduring popularity of the rosary and benediction of the Blessed Sacrament. By the end of the nineteenth century a far greater proportion of Catholics attended Mass, received communion, attended missions and retreats and enrolled in confraternities, sodalities and guilds than fifty years before.[20] Margaret Hallahan's role in promoting Marian and other devotions is widely acknowledged, but she also gave encouragement to the preaching of missions, not only by the Dominican friars, but particularly by members of the recently arrived Italian congregations, the Passionists and Rosminians.

Where the provision of education was concerned, the bishops emphasized the responsibility of all Catholics, no matter what their social status, for the educational welfare of their community. They were quick to call the gentry and middle classes to account if their efforts in providing for the poor were considered inadequate.[21] For the remainder of the century, the religious congregations of women were to play a leading part, not only in directing Catholic elementary education, but after the opening of Notre Dame Training College at Liverpool in 1855, of ensuring an adequately trained supply of Catholic lay teachers to staff the schools. Convent secondary schools, industrial schools, and later on schools for those with special needs broadened the scope of provision. Both the hierarchy and prominent laymen kept the education question on the political agenda. Just fifty years after the first Westminster synod, and five years after the foundation of the last of the five Dominican foundations whose history is recorded here, the 1902 Education Act was passed. This offered Catholic schools a level of financial support and a guarantee of their religious integrity which, though it might fall short of the optimum, was far beyond what might have been hoped for in 1852.

The Catholic Church in England was predominantly a church of the poor during the nineteenth century. The willingness of its clergy and religious to engage with the poor also contributed to improving the public image and acceptance of Catholicism. During the typhoid and dysentery epidemics in Liverpool in 1847, ten of the twenty-four priests in the city died after contracting infection while ministering to the dying.[22] The Sisters of Mercy would show similar devotion to duty nursing the victims of asiatic cholera in Bermondsey, or the casualties of war in the Crimea. Caring for the poor would become a major focus of the religious congregations, Dominican and otherwise, with an increasing network of orphanages, hospitals, homes for the aged, soup kitchens, night shelters, employment bureaux, refuges and reformatories. Some institutes were dedicated exclusively to home nursing and other forms of social welfare, and many engaged in the work of parish visiting and relief of the poor once their teaching and domestic work was done.

When Margaret Hallahan arrived in Coventry in 1842, the friars of the English Province of the Order were in a sad state of decline. Having fled before the French revolutionary forces from their house at Bornhem in Flanders, they had first established themselves at Carshalton in Surrey. The departure of half their number for the United States early in the nineteenth century, and the ensuing dispute over the division of their assets, further weakened the group, which numbered only nine in 1832.[23] Soon after his reception into the Catholic Church, John Henry Newman, referring to the Order of Preachers in a letter to his friend John Dalgairns, wondered 'whether it was not a great idea extinct'.[24]

This judgement was perhaps premature. By the time Newman preached his 'Second Spring' sermon, Mother Margaret's community would number more than twenty women and soon its register of clothing and profession would record the names of many of the old Catholic families and Tractarian converts. The revival of the First Order would follow on the fortunes of the Third.

When Margaret's first three companions received the Dominican habit and began their noviciate at Coventry in 1844, there were only twenty-nine religious houses of women in England and Wales – eight of which had been founded since her return from Belgium – and one in Scotland. Almost half of these houses belonged to enclosed, contemplative communities, most of them having been founded in Flanders during the penal days and taken refuge in England during the revolutionary turmoil sixty years before. By 1891 there were close to five hundred religious houses of women in Great Britain with a membership of about 7500.[25]

The Dominicans of Stone, Stroud, Leicester, Harrow and Portobello Road all contributed to this growth of Catholic life and culture, responding to needs and adapting to circumstances. By the time the last of these Dominican congregations was established, the pioneering phase for women religious in Britain had given way to one of consolidation. The religious sister had very much become the public face of the Church. Not only had the Catholic community come to expect the presence of sisters but they had also gained the acceptance of society at large.

Notes

1. Radcliffe, 'The Mission of the Dominican Family' in *To Praise, to Preach, to Bless*, p. 490.
2. According to the most scholarly biography of St Dominic, there is no authentic source for the event though it was certainly recounted by the end of the thirteenth century. Vicaire, *Saint Dominic and his Times*, p. 475.
3. Stone, T757/2, *Memoranda of our beloved Mother by our beloved Father and Superior the Rt Rev. Bishop Ullathorne*.
4. McNamara, *Sisters in Arms*, p. 283.
5. Ranft, *Women and the Religious Life*, pp. 64, 85.
6. *Congrégations Dominicaines*, p. 17.
7. Ashley, *Dominicans*, p. 94.
8. Préteseille, *Marie Poussepin*, p. 138.
9. Langlois, *Catholicisme au féminin*, p. 203.

10. Hinnebsuch, *Dominicans*, p. 76.
11. Stone T977, Mother Margaret Hallahan to 'My dear Sister', undated, *c.*1861.
12. Norman, *English Catholic Church*, p. 22.
13. Doyle, *Mitres & missions*, p. 47.
14. McLeod, *Religion and society in England*, p. 114.
15. Newsome, *Victorian World Picture*, p. 66.
16. Norman, *English Catholic Church*, p. 147.
17. Doyle, *Mitres & Missions*, p. 34.
18. McClelland, 'Formative Years, 1850–92', in *From out the Flaminian Gate*, p. 15.
19. Hill, *God's architect*, p. 288.
20. Heimann, *Catholic devotion*, p. 35.
21. Whitehead, 'View from the Bridge', in *From out the Flaminian Gate,* p. 219.
22. Doyle, *Mitres & missions,* p. 74.
23. Gaine, *Obituary notices*, p. 8.
24. John Henry Newman to John Dalgairns, 6 July 1846 in Dessain (ed.), *Letters and Diaries*, vol. 11, p. 195.
25. These figures are based on my own collation of returns for religious houses of women in the 1891 census, in many cases verified against other data supplied by the orders and congregations themselves.

Chapter Two

Almost an irregular affection: Margaret Hallahan and her congregation

I have always loved the Order, it has almost been an irregular affection with me . . . and I desired to see it flourish.

Mother Margaret Hallahan[1]

Introduction

Margaret Hallahan is the only English Dominican founder for whom we have a large collection of documentary sources. Mother Francis Raphael Drane's *Life*, published within a year of Mother Margaret's death in 1868, still provides a sound starting point for understanding her. The book was written with the clear agenda of promoting the founder's sanctity and is typical of the nineteenth-century hagiographical genre. The *Life* was reprinted in 1929 and several shorter accounts, all clearly derivative, appeared subsequently. It was not until 1997 that a critical study of the first forty years of Margaret's life, dealt with in only a cursory manner in Mother Francis Raphael's work, appeared and corrected many unverified claims in the biography, adding valuable information through a more critical examination of the sources.[2]

A long and difficult apprenticeship

Margaret Hallahan was born in London on 23 January 1802, the only surviving child of Edmund Hallahan and Catherine O'Connor, and was baptized in the Sardinian Embassy Chapel four days later. Her father had come from County Clare some years before and worked in Southwark before moving across the river to St Giles's about the time of his marriage to Catherine in 1800. In common with so many of the Irish immigrants crowded into the lanes and courts of St Giles's, Edmund Hallahan's life was not a success. He rented and sub-let a row of cottages, worked as a porter for a wine merchant and as a general labourer, the family fortunes becoming ever more straitened and unhappy as his health was undermined by drink and tuberculosis. This fatal combination saw him to an early grave in June 1813 at the age of thirty-five. Nothing is recorded of Margaret's mother, other than that she had a relative (a Dominican friar) in Cork, and that she died several months after her husband.

Margaret was for some time a pupil at the mission schools founded by the Abbé Carron, attached to St Aloysius' chapel at Somers Town. Her formal education was interrupted by illness and even before she was orphaned, Margaret was sent to live with in-laws in Kilburn. From here, on the recommendation of the mission priest at Moorfields, Rev. Joseph Hunt, Margaret went to live with Sarah Caulier, the childless wife of a French lace merchant who lived near Cheapside. It appears that she was taken on as much for companionship as service, though Madame Caulier was initially a severe mistress to Margaret who appeared careless, untidy and clumsy. By the time she attained her majority, Margaret had acquired a sufficient grounding in household management to take up a situation with a Dr Morgan in Lambeth Terrace. Morgan was a widower whose extended family of children and grandchildren lived either in his own household or nearby. After his death in 1824 Margaret continued in service to his daughter Clara, who was married to George Thompson, and lived for a time in Margate.

The Thompsons' eldest daughter, Matilda, attended the school run by the Benedictine nuns at Winchester and it was on a visit to this house that Margaret Hallahan first developed a consciousness of her religious vocation. Towards the end of her life she would write to the Dominican Father Austin Maltus: 'My nature has ever been independent, I could never have married from this very feeling, to be subject to a man was my abhorrence and I fear much of it remains.'[3] She also mentioned to Mother M. Imelda Poole that the difficulties between her parents had given her a horror of marriage, 'for my father broke my mother's heart'.[4] Apparently Margaret declined two proposals of marriage, and Bishop Ullathorne in his *Interior Life* quotes her as saying 'there was someone after me'. Perhaps it was this man who 'pressed his claim too far' at some point, an incident which impressed itself so potently upon the young woman that, kneeling on a chair in the kitchen, she made a private vow of chastity. [5]

It was about five years after this incident, in October 1829, that the Thompson family moved to Bruges. Here there was a thriving English Catholic community attracted by the lower cost of living, particularly that of educating their children. Matilda now attended school at the English Convent of the Augustinian Canonesses and it was here that Margaret was received as a postulant, leaving within a week when it became clear to her that as a lay postulant she would not pray the Divine Office. On her arrival in Bruges Margaret had presented herself at the confessional of one of the two English speaking confessors in the city, the Abbé Bruno Versavel, Rector of the Church of St Walburga and chaplain to the famous Béguinage. The Abbé Versavel's wise direction mitigated his penitent's tendency towards scruples and corporal penances, and encouraged her to deepen her spiritual reading and her active involvement in works of charity. Only when he deemed her absolutely ready did he allow Margaret to follow her ardent desire to be received as a Dominican tertiary in January 1834. She made her profession on the feast of St Catherine of Siena, 30 April 1835, in the hands of the Abbé Louis Capron, parish priest of the Church of St James, and himself a Dominican tertiary.

In the years immediately after Belgium gained independence from the Netherlands in 1830, Bruges was enjoying a magnificent religious revival, and Margaret's spiritual development was deeply affected by the intense devotional life of the city. She also witnessed at first hand the work of apostolic women religious. After ten years in Belgium her health gave way completely and Margaret spent some months as a patient in the hospital for incurables run by the Sisters of Charity of Jesus and Mary. These religious had been founded by Canon Pierre Triest in Lovendegem, near Ghent, in 1803, with the intention of combining the contemplation of St Bernard with the charity of St Vincent de Paul.[6] Their life and work, viewed at such close quarters, must surely have opened up to Margaret new possibilities for service. Having recovered, instead of returning to the Thompsons, she attempted to set up a community of regular tertiaries, with the sanction of the vicar-provincial of the Dominican friars in Belgium. Despite her enthusiasm, the lack of suitable collaborators and financial support undermined the project. So did the opposition of the Abbé Versavel, who doubted whether Margaret's impetuosity and lack of prudence in matters of asceticism would fit her for the role of founder and superior. It seemed to Margaret that her dream was not to be realized, and she was forced to take in lodgers for her support while continuing her work amongst the poor.

The Thompsons were connected to a number of Catholic families who had served in the East India Company, including the Amhersts of Kenilworth. Mary Louisa Amherst, mother of the future bishop of Northampton, was a benefactor of several Catholic missions in the Midlands and known personally to Margaret Hallahan. Although there was talk of sending her to a Dominican convent in Paris or even to the United States, the Abbé Versavel was now encouraging Margaret to return to England, and it was to Mrs Amherst that she addressed herself in order to find a situation. Mrs Amherst's first thought was of the Uttoxeter mission, but in the end she recommended Margaret to the rector of the mission at Coventry, the Benedictine William Bernard Ullathorne, recently returned from New South Wales. Margaret crossed the channel on 30 April 1842 and after a brief stay at Kenilworth, arrived at Coventry early in May. Ullathorne described his first meeting with the tall, solid woman, possessed of an unquestionable grace of presence: 'her large eyes beaming with a smile that was not unchecked by an expression of shyness that ... [in] no wise ruffled her pale and tranquil face'.[7]

The greatest privilege of my life

The priest upon whom Margaret Hallahan made such an impression that spring morning in Coventry was a Yorkshire man. William Ullathorne was born at Pocklington in the East Riding on 7 May 1806, eldest of the ten children of William Ullathorne and Hannah Longstaff. When the younger William was ten the family moved to Scarborough where his father established a grocer's and general trading company. As a youth the future bishop was awkward, bookish and given to daydreaming to such an extent that his father eventually took him out of school at the age of fifteen and allowed him to follow his passion for the sea by enlisting on a merchant vessel.[8] Although not particularly pious, after little more than a year at sea William attended Mass in the Baltic port of Memel[9] which resulted in a conversion experience leading him to enter the Benedictine priory of Downside, where he made profession as Dom Bernard on 5 April 1825.

Dom Bernard was not to enjoy the cloistered life for long. No sooner was he ordained priest in 1832 than he was appointed vicar general of the Catholics in the Australian colonies, and set out, somewhat reluctantly, for Sydney. At this time Australia still formed part of the enormous Vicariate Apostolic of the Cape of Good Hope, whose bishop resided in Mauritius. In the isolation of New

South Wales Ullathorne matured from an inexperienced young priest, too keen to stand on the dignity of his office, into a man of compassion and sound judgement. This change was effected in part by his interactions with strong, independent women from both ends of the social spectrum: the female convicts of the Parramatta factory and Norfolk Island, and the more refined Irish Sisters of Charity who had accompanied Bishop Polding to Australia in 1833.[10] It is clear that both types of women impressed him deeply, and perhaps these experiences gave him an ease in his relationships with women that was not always evident in other members of the English hierarchy. After the harsh realities of the colonial mission, Ullathorne would always remain something of a radical, keen on innovative approaches to the church's engagement in mission and a strong supporter of cooperation between clergy and laity, particularly women.[11]

After seven years in the colony Ullathorne's health broke down and in an attempt to avoid appointment as bishop of the newly erected dioceses of Hobart or Adelaide, he returned to Downside where he taught for a brief period in the school. In November 1841 he was appointed to the impoverished mission of Coventry. Although the centre of economic gravity for the county of Warwickshire had long since moved to Birmingham, Coventry still remained an important centre for the manufacture of cloth – ribbon in particular – and also for watch and clock making. By the time Ullathorne arrived it was a congested city of nearly 40,000 inhabitants boasting gas lighting and a railway station, but plagued with all the social problems consequent on industrialization. Though the master manufacturers grew rich, the journeymen and unskilled labourers were 'kept in a most demoralising uncertainty between the loom-shop and the workhouse'.[12] There was ample work for the new mission priest and his newly recruited helper.

Margaret set to work at once, insisting that she had come, not to be paid, but to work for God. She soon had the chance to prove her mettle as Ullathorne left for Rome two weeks after her arrival in a further attempt to avert his appointment to an antipodean diocese. Margaret began teaching in the school attached to the mission, which within a year averaged an attendance of almost 100 girls. She also set up evening classes for the ribbon weavers and other factory workers, visited the sick and managed the household. When he returned, Ullathorne found that her name had already become a household word in Coventry. Once a week he invited her into his parlour for an hour or so of conversation and during these exchanges their friendship deepened.[13]

Bishop Thomas Walsh, Vicar Apostolic of the Midland District, took an interest in Margaret, and since she was living the life of a religious in all but name, offered to get her into a convent of the Sisters of Mercy. She declined with great indignation saying she would live and die a Dominican despite the bishop's insistence that this would mean continuing alone. 'Then I must remain alone, but a Dominican I shall always be.'[14] Gradually several women began to assist Margaret in her work: the Roby sisters, Ann and Maria, whose father was a watchmaker with a business in Holyhead Street; Harriet Goode who had recently arrived from London[15] and a recent convert, Charlotte Gittens, who had been introduced to Ullathorne while he was giving a mission in Worcester.[16] Although she felt a natural repugnance for governing others, Margaret was encouraged by Ullathorne to form this group into a religious community.

Early in 1844 Margaret made a visit to Belgium. Although the main reason was to raise funds amongst the English community there towards the cost of the new church of St Osburg being built at Coventry by Charles Hansom, it was also a fact finding tour in support of the proposed foundation. Both aims met with success, for Margaret returned with a substantial donation from Charles Eyre[17] and also consulted with Father Bernard Moulaert, prior of the Dominican house at Tienen, who was well versed in the history of the Third Order regular. It was probably from him that Margaret obtained copies of the constitutions of the Dominican nuns, in French, and of the secular Tertiaries, in Flemish. Moulaert would also be influential in allaying Bishop Walsh's anxieties concerning the establishment of a Dominican community that would not be bound to enclosure. On 27 March 1844 the women moved into a house in Spon Street where Ullathorne had been residing since the clergy house in Hill Street had been demolished to make way for the new church. In May the Rosminian, Luigi Gentili, came to preach a mission in Coventry and this became the occasion for what might well have been the first public Marian procession in England since the Reformation. Margaret's own statue of the Blessed Virgin was carried in procession round the church, not only as an added attraction to attend the mission but also to entice people away from the more worldly attraction of the Lady Godiva procession![18]

Having obtained permission from the Dominican provincial, Father Thomas Nickolds, the three postulants were clothed as Sisters M. Rose Goode, M. Gertrude Roby and M. Osburg Gittens on 11 June that year. Their noviciate began in earnest with regular instruction from Ullathorne not only in the duties of their state, but also in the rudiments of *Cobbett's Grammar*. Two words were banned from the vocabulary of the nascent community: 'uncomfortable' and 'impossible'.[19] Life was certainly frugal though, like generations of novices after them, the first sisters found themselves giving way to fits of uncontrollable laughter at the most inappropriate times. Margaret herself was not excluded, though she wrote to Ullathorne expressing her sense of shame at not being able to correct this failing with firmness:

> The natural cheerfulness of my inclination has often been a source of anxiety to me because I am so easily inclined to laugh when I see another do it and now it is a real cross although I do not give way to it to the same extent as the others.[20]

Margaret set about compiling the first rule of life for the community, laid out in twenty-nine brief articles. It shows that she was well acquainted with the Rule of St Augustine, the two books of constitutions already mentioned, the life of St Dominic and perhaps with the Benedictine Rule as well. There is almost a Vincentian tone to article 11 which stipulates the time for retiring as 10:30 p.m. but admits that 'as God has called us to work for our neighbour in all kinds of ways, the hour must depend on our occupations'.[21] There was a strong emphasis on the common life and a firm injunction to attend recreation together. Despite the influence of the Abbé Versavel there is also a strong emphasis on the ascetical life, including corporal penances.

In September 1845 the new church was opened by Bishop Wiseman and on 8 December that year Margaret Hallahan renewed her profession, and the three novices made their vows, in the hands of the Dominican, Father Dominic Aylward, who had come across from Nuneaton to represent the Provincial. That month, Michael Roby allowed his younger daughter Maria, already in the last stages of tuberculosis, to join her sister at Spon Street, where she was professed on her deathbed as Sister M. Catherine on New Year's Eve. Sarah Muston, sent by the Dominican friars at Hinckley, had entered the community in April 1845 and received the habit and the name Dominica a year later.

Although the poor appreciated the community's work, the sisters did not receive unreserved approbation in all quarters. Two Benedictines visiting Coventry for the opening of the church dismissed them as 'a few poor girls'; others discouraged prospective candidates by insisting the community was not for respectable ladies and that Sister Margaret was an imposter. Even on the first profession day a cleric was heard to quip: 'Look at those wenches, they make as much fuss as if they were nuns at Princethorpe!'[22] But the wenches were not long for Coventry. Unable to persuade him to take up episcopal office in the southern hemisphere, Rome now appointed William Bernard Ullathorne Vicar Apostolic of the Western District. He was consecrated bishop in St Osburg's with the titular See of Hetelonia on 21 July 1846. The nascent Dominican community, anxious to continue under the Bishop's guiding hand, followed him to Bristol in November.

The bond which had developed between the new bishop and Mother Margaret during the four years they worked together in Coventry was to endure. The frank and impetuous Margaret trusted him implicitly: 'No person knows my nature so well and no other person will or does work for my perfection but yourself.'[23] The respect and affection was entirely mutual and at the time of Margaret's death Ullathorne was unrestrained in his expressions of grief, acknowledging that 'The greatest privilege of my life has been the twenty-five years of her friendship and confidence, of which I always thought myself unworthy.'[24] Just how strong this bond was is evident in Ullathorne's choice of burial place for he chose to be buried not in St Chad's Cathedral, but in a side chapel of the church at Stone a short distance from his great friend.

Clifton: defining Dominican identity

Bristol at mid-century was three times more populous than Coventry though, having grown prosperous on the Atlantic trade, particularly the slave trade, it had a much less developed industrial base. By the time of Margaret Hallahan's arrival the city was economically depressed. The development of Jessop's floating harbour was a public work undertaken at enormous cost but much too late to challenge the fast developing deep water port of Liverpool.[25] The finances of the Western District were in no less parlous a state. During his twenty years as Vicar Apostolic the former Ampleforth monk, Bishop Peter Baines, had instituted one grandiose scheme after another, including the purchase of Prior Park near Bath, and the building of a vast cathedral at Clifton designed in the classical style by Henry Goodridge.

Margaret's community took up residence in Queen Square and began teaching in the mission schools attached to St Mary's-on-the-Quay, visiting the poor and also the Bristol Infirmary. They also brought with them from Coventry two destitute elderly women and three or four orphans who had recently come into their care. To help support these dependents a fee-paying school was also begun. The new Vicar Apostolic's initial concern was to liquidate the debt on the pro-cathedral and to have it roofed, and he turned to Charles Hansom to undertake the work. Part of the cost was to be covered by Mother Margaret purchasing the old chapel and mission house, and enlarging the premises for use as a convent. It is not entirely clear from what source the money came, though the community had already been befriended by wealthy and influential Catholics such as the Du Bary and Knight families. Several postulants, not all of whom persevered, entered at Queen Square and on 27 April 1847, Sister M. Dominica Munston made her profession of vows in St Mary's church before a crowd so pressing that, much to Mother Margaret's displeasure, the mission priest issued tickets to keep order.[26]

Building the convent at Clifton was no easy task, partly because of the steep terrain, the constraints of the existing buildings, and also because Mother Margaret insisted on a regular conventual building with a cloister round a small central garth. The old mission church was enlarged as a chapel, but the only way of accommodating a choir for the sisters was to have it in a gallery, an arrangement which would become the source of unimagined difficulties a few years later. The same constraints of space meant that the chaplain's room opened onto a passageway which was used by the sisters as they moved between the convent proper, the orphanage and the schools. The buildings were nearing completion in March 1848 when the community moved in, together with the elderly women and orphans, who were accommodated in what had been the choir loft and sacristy of the old chapel.

Immediately Margaret set about strengthening the Dominican character of the establishment. Until this time, the Little Office of Our Lady had been recited in English, but while still at Queen Square the sisters were receiving instruction in its proper recitation in Latin. A year after the move to Clifton, Father Bernard Moulaert visited from Belgium and spent some time initiating the community in Dominican observance and ritual, teaching them the Dominican rite *Salve Regina* and the anthem to St Dominic, *O Lumen Ecclesiae,* also sung after the office of Compline. During Holy Week of 1851 the full Dominican liturgy was sung for the triduum, though the annalist admits that the litany on Holy Saturday morning was not well sung.[27]

The Dominican provincial, consulted on the matter of enclosure, assured Margaret that 'being all walled-up ... would defeat the end you have in view'.[28] There was also the question of jurisdiction to sort out. In July 1848 Bishop Ullathorne had been transferred back to the Midland District to replace Bishop Walsh, who had been transferred as Vicar Apostolic of the London District. When the hierarchy was re-established in 1850, Ullathorne was named first bishop of Birmingham and his successor in the Western District, the Franciscan Joseph Hendren, became first bishop of Clifton. In 1847 the Master of the Dominican Order, Vincent Ajello, had granted Ullathorne jurisdiction over the community, and the sisters were keen for this to continue, despite the fact that Ullathorne was now bishop of another diocese. Rome sanctioned the continuation of this arrangement.[29] Plans were made for a foundation in the Diocese of Birmingham and the subsequent events at Clifton show how wise this move would be.

Although women from more modest backgrounds continued to enter the community, once they moved to Clifton an increasing number of postulants came from the better heeled and better educated ranks of both the established Catholic families and those of the recent converts. In fact, the register of clothings and professions during this period reads something like a contemporary Catholic *Who's Who*. The strong communication network amongst the more comfortable English Catholics and the limited number of active communities must have facilitated this growth. Certainly by the time Margaret Anna Cusack, later famous as the Nun of Kenmare and founder of the Sisters of St Joseph of Peace, tried her vocation in the noviciate at Stone in 1857, there was no question of confusing recruits with 'wenches'. In the last of her autobiographical works, despite expressing generally negative attitudes towards convents, Margaret Cusack states: 'this at least must be said of the nuns at Stone, they were ladies'.[30]

By December 1855, just ten years after the first ceremony of profession of vows, the congregation numbered thirty-seven professed sisters, one novice and eight postulants. At least seventy-six women had entered the community, though not all had persevered, and five had already died.[31] Some of those who entered brought substantial dowries: Lucy (Sister M. Columba) and Maria Poole (Sister M. Imelda), the former to die prematurely of tuberculosis, the second to succeed Mother Margaret, were gifted linguists with fine voices who also brought almost £3000 a piece. Agnes Salvin (Sister M. Philip) brought twice this amount and Agnes Berkeley (Sister M. Philomena) almost as much. While these huge sums would eventually allow the congregation to support and

Fig. 1 Initiation at Clifton; 'The new postulant is discovered by Sister M. Theresa Williams toasting with the carving knife, recently ground.'

Fig. 2 Initiation at Clifton; 'The new postulant, with much pains and labour, sweeps out her room, & wonders why the dust flies about so.'

expand its apostolic works, the human gifts, the culture and polish, were just as much valued and all directed to enhancing the Dominican identity of the community.

Mother Margaret remained egalitarian in her views of recruitment. She wrote to Father Dominic Aylward in 1850 after a preliminary visit to consider making a foundation at Longton in the Potteries:

> It seems to me that Our Lord will make use of our Order to break through that custom which has crept into England, that scarcely any were able to enter religion but the aristocracy ... I smile to myself in looking on some here and hope to have some sisters – and saints – out of this 'potter's clay'. I know it will be thought very presumptuous by many that I should dare to give the habit of religion to a potter but ... I hope I shall get one of the colliers to be a Dominican.[32]

It shows something remarkable about her character that Mother Margaret was able to attract women of such diverse backgrounds and talents, and govern them in such a way that they lived together harmoniously. After her death Newman would refer to her 'singular powers of influence' and her 'tenderness towards myself, her sympathy and interest in one who, in all his habits and circumstances, his ways of thought and his history, was so unlike what she was'.[33] This appears to have been one of her greatest gifts, that with her direct and unaffected approach she could identify with, and win the respect and affection, of almost anyone.

The first great trial: the dispute with Archbishop Errington

Almost everyone! In 1854, after the death of Bishop Thomas Burgess, the Diocese of Clifton was placed under the jurisdiction of George Errington, coadjutor – with the right of succession – to Cardinal Wiseman at Westminster. Errington had once been Wiseman's deputy rector in Rome. He was from an old Catholic family with little apparent sympathy for the recent wave of English converts, and a suspicion of the ultramontane tendencies so many of them displayed. He was also an accomplished canonist and a man of rigid principles though, like many men of principle, he did not always play a good hand in tact. He fell out with Wiseman by criticising his administration and supporting the cathedral chapter against him. Mother Margaret's dealings with him lead her to exclaim that 'It is difficult to believe that he has ever had a mother.'[34]

In October 1855 the *Records* compiled by Mother M. Imelda Poole note that Archbishop Errington had expressed his disapproval of the custom of the sisters receiving communion in the choir before Mass.[35] He also refused to sanction the appointment, already confirmed by Ullathorne, of the Abbé Paterne Miot as resident chaplain, on the grounds that his proposed quarters were not sufficiently separated from those of the religious. The former objection would hardly seem sufficiently grave matter to begin a dispute which would take two years to resolve.

It would take more than architecture to cause a dispute of this intensity, even with George Errington. The dispute was much more about the vision which Mother Margaret and her sisters shared of their own vocation and apostolate. Ten years later she would write to the Dominican Provincial, Father Austin Maltus, that 'we could not fulfil our state did we not burn with zeal to save souls by all manner of means that are in our power'.[36] One of the chief means at their disposal was to incite religious feeling through the propagation of a rich devotional life, like that which Mother Margaret had experienced in Bruges. The liturgical celebrations in the conventual churches were made as solemn and attractive as possible, though she did not wish to raise the faithful on a diet of sentiment and emotion alone. Not everyone, particularly not a cleric of Errington's background, could appreciate the idea of women religious having a direct role to play in the apostolic and missionary endeavour of the Church in England as it emerged from centuries of hidden activity. In December the Archbishop refused the sisters permission to hold the *Forty Hours* devotion in the convent church on the solemnity of the Immaculate Conception.

Mother Margaret, who was establishing the new convent at Stone by this time, was deeply wounded by Archbishop Errington's attitude and the restraints he seemed bent on imposing. She commissioned Sister M. Imelda Poole to draw up a letter explaining in detail their understanding of the mission of the community, obtaining Bishop Ullathorne's approval of the text before it was sent. It is a magnificent combination of the frank, straightforward approach of Mother Margaret and the measured eloquence of Sister M. Imelda.

> To make every sacrifice of expense, time, and labour in order to advance faith and devotion amongst the people, by the adornment of the house of God, and the public service of our Churches, has been

> one main principle on which our religious Community has been formed, and then we find these efforts thwarted and discouraged in the very quarters from whence we might have most expected encouragement and support, we cannot but feel that our efficiency is paralysed, and that our mission for the good of England is in great measure frustrated.

After reaffirming the disinterest the community had shown by purchasing the land on which the convent was built, the letter continues to expound the charism of the community as perceived by its founder.

> Wherever we may be established, the object of our Order is, not only to devote ourselves to the service of the poor but to the utmost extent of our means & even beyond them, to meet the crying needs of this miserable country by building Churches for the people, and supporting Priests to labour among them out of our own resources, without being in any way burdensome to the Diocese.[37]

All they asked of the Archbishop was encouragement. Errington did not reply himself but through his secretary, Rev. Frederick Neve. One wonders how enthusiastic this priest was in putting pen to paper as he was one of the community's principal benefactors, having given £2000 towards the conventual church. The tone is succinct and almost sarcastic:

> The Archbishop ... will be better able to judge of [your letter's] general tendency when he shall have had an opportunity of conversing with your V[er]y Rev. Eccl[esiastical] Superior on the peculiar kind of mission your letter seems to suppose your Community to have received for this country ... his Grace can scarcely believe [it] to represent the judgement of the Rev. M[othe]r Prioress.[38]

The real cause of the dispute is here revealed and it mirrors very closely the first great crisis the Dominican Order faced in the thirteenth century, commonly referred to as the pastoral crisis. St Dominic's dispersal of the brethren to the great cities of Europe had aroused the suspicion and jealousy of the local clergy and bishops who saw their churches deserted for those of the Preaching Friars – and their revenues decline.[39] At Clifton the sisters had always ensured that the times of their services did not conflict with those of 'the Great Church' next door and some of them even attended the High Mass there on a Sunday with the children of the poor schools.

A meeting took place at the Dominican Priory at Woodchester, near Stroud, on 10 January 1856 between Errington, Ullathorne and Father Dominic Aylward. The Archbishop wanted to have the chapel at Clifton closed to the public and declared his abhorrence at the sisters' claim to be missionaries, making the counter-claim that they were 'disarranging the Clifton mission awfully'. He had no interest in the sisters exercising an independent ministry but required them to be his auxiliaries, supplying the staff for the poor schools and visiting the sick.[40] The other parties to the meeting argued quite firmly against this. The following month Errington forbade the public recitation of the rosary in the conventual church but Mother Margaret, visiting Clifton and finding the church 'desolate and deserted' insisted it be recited in the choir in order to fulfil the obligations of the Rosary Confraternity. Making open demonstration of the equivocal position he held between the community and his superior, Frederick Neve attended as one of the congregation. On a subsequent visit Mother Margaret arrived only moments before Errington came to the door demanding an interview during which, for more than two hours, he berated her for her stubborn attitude and reiterated his intention of stopping all public services in the convent.[41]

Frederick Neve was not the only subject of the Archbishop to take an equivocal position. The case was brought before the secretary of the Propaganda, Cardinal Barnabò, in April and surprisingly, Errington did not attend in person but sent William Clifford, who was acting as his agent in Rome. Clifford was clearly uncomfortable with the Archbishop's attitude to certain points in dispute. He records in his report the exasperation of Cardinal Barnabò and the general feeling that the Pope, who had expressed his interest in the matter, would decide in favour of the sisters.

Meanwhile the stress was taking its toll on the community at Clifton. The prioress, Sister M. Osburg Gittens, asked to resign and there was a considerable change of personnel. The quarrel with Errington also contributed to the rejection of a plan to take on an important new apostolic venture in London. Mother Margaret had been asked to undertake the administration of a proposed hospital for incurables at Great Ormond Street but the fact that Errington had the right to succeed Wiseman at Westminster heightened her anxiety and she turned down the offer. By June, Errington appeared more conciliatory, granting the sisters permission to hold exposition of the Blessed Sacrament on the feast of the Sacred Heart, though only if there were a priest and two acolytes present for the duration.[42]

Mother Margaret had mounted her own campaign to obtain an amelioration of the state of affairs. She set the novices to pray for one of her 'special intentions' and pray they did. In March news was received that the Pope had refused a rescript allowing the sisters in Clifton to receive communion in the choir [43] but they also learned that Mother Margaret's special intention had been answered. William Clifford was appointed Bishop of Clifton and Archbishop Errington returned to Westminster where he was to fall out with Cardinal Wiseman once again, and be passed over as his successor in favour of Manning. For another twenty years the community remained in Clifton, enjoying excellent relations with their new bishop.

The 'pastoral crisis' at Clifton shows how easily a community with a strong vision of its place in the Church could come into conflict with authority and be drawn into the political dynamic. But the centre of operations of this young Dominican community had now moved to the Midlands under Ullathorne's jurisdiction. He was quick to defend the Dominican Sisters in the public forum of the press when they were accused of taking it upon themselves to direct the missions where they were established, to give guidance to the clergy and even preach to the people.[44] The dispute, as much as Ullathorne's support , would reaffirm this 'peculiar kind of mission' which would be Mother Margaret's legacy to her community; not a legacy she would claim as her own, however, but merely a sharing in that of the Order of which she considered herself first and foremost a member.

A period of foundations

The first branch house of the congregation was founded at Bridgewater in Somerset at the beginning of July 1850 with Sister M. Francis Lynch as superior. The mission was served by Abbé de Blon, a French émigré, who could read, but hardly speak English, and this left ample scope for the sisters to give instruction and invigorate local Catholic life.[45] Since it was considered that the full regular life could not be lived with a community of only four, it was decided that no sister should stay long at the new foundation before being re-immersed in the atmosphere of regular observance maintained at Clifton. Mother Margaret tried to persuade Bishop Hendren to transfer the diocesan orphanage to the town to ensure sufficient work to maintain a larger community but he did not fall in with her plan.[46] By April 1851, since no other scope for development seemed possible, it was decided to withdraw from Bridgewater and consolidate the new foundation at Longton.

Longton in the Potteries certainly offered endless opportunities for development when the community was established in January 1851. Sister M. Francis Lynch was once again appointed foundation superior in this crowded, industrial town crisscrossed with kilns, foundries and mines, a collection of dust heaps which Mother Margaret considered the 'fag end of the world'. A house known as The Foley was rented from the railway company and here the community made its home along with an enormous number of rats and a garden full of frogs. Day and night schools were opened and on Sundays the children stayed all day with the sisters. Unfortunately tensions developed between the community and the mission priest, Edward Daniel. He appeared to be jealous of the sisters' chaplain and increasingly uneasy as more and more people flocked to the services in the convent chapel. The divisions became so acute between those supporting and opposing the community that Bishop Ullathorne had to undertake a visitation to resolve matters.[47] The decision to leave was taken after little more than three years.

The quiet Staffordshire market town of Stone was the location of the next foundation, soon to become the mother house and noviciate of the congregation. Nearby Aston Hall, once the home of the Heveningham family, had been a centre of Catholic activity throughout the penal days and in the early years of the nineteenth century had been occupied at times by Franciscan friars and Bridgettine nuns. In 1842 the first English foundation of the Passionists was made at Aston under the leadership of Blessed Dominic Barberi and two years later the chapel of St Anne, designed by Augustus Pugin, was built in the town of Stone. In 1853, James Beech of Longton, five of whose granddaughters were to become Dominicans, offered a small house in Stone to Mother Margaret. Sisters began to stay in the less than ideal dwelling, which they nicknamed Job's, and taught in the mission school, returning to Longton at the weekend.[48]

Despite the huge debt outstanding at Clifton, Bishop Ullathorne commanded Mother Margaret to build. Hansom was again pressed into service and the first wing of the new convent was sufficiently ready for occupation, though incomplete, by 28 July 1853 when seven professed sisters and four novices arrived. At once they began instructing converts and seeking out lapsed Catholics in the town. Over the next three years, work on the extensive conventual buildings and attached church went on apace. The community became accustomed to the inconvenience of having the cloisters and main rooms on the ground floor given over to all sorts of activities and being constantly thronged with people. These early days are recorded in a wonderful series of cartoons by Mother Francis Raphael Drane, who also depicts the involvement of the sisters in the mission undertaken at Newcastle-under-Lyme, featuring magnificently sketched urchins and large, rough looking women.[49] Here the sisters were involved in instructing hundreds of Catholics in the rudiments of their faith and the annalist remarks on the evident success of their labours and enduring effect of the work.

Some of the elderly women who had resided at the convent in Clifton came to Stone and in 1857 a house was taken in Newcastle Road to accommodate them. They were soon joined by local destitute, elderly and disabled women who became the first patients of what developed into St Mary's Hospital. One of the first of these was the orphan Mary Loftus, nicknamed Polly Providence, who was found begging and sleeping on the street, and whom Mother Margaret adopted and sent to the orphanage at Clifton. Soon afterwards she developed tuberculosis and returned to Stone, dying in the hospital in 1862. The early pages of the register of St Mary's lists women suffering from scrofula, dropsy, cancer, and paralysis, an amputee, another who was deaf and mute and several others who had suffered reverses of fortune and had no one to care for them. In 1861 the Hand & Trumpet public house was acquired and ten years later neighbouring Elmhurst House, by which time more than fifty women were being cared for. In 1893 a spacious new building was erected on the corner of Station Street and Margaret Street and did duty for over eighty years.[50]

William Bush, a small boy almost crippled in an accident, was taken in by the community in 1856 and for several years a home for orphan and destitute boys named St Vincent's was maintained at Stone. Perhaps recalling her own sensitivities as a child, Mother Margaret wanted her orphans, whether in Clifton, Stone or later at St Marychurch, cared for with tenderness and consideration, with nothing that 'gave them the stamp of pauperism'; though she insisted they be trained to earn their own living.[51] The education given in the mission schools was also to be geared towards the immediate needs of the working classes. One of Mother Margaret's fears in educating girls, in particular, was that they might develop refined tastes that would make them ashamed of their background and dissatisfied with their lot in life. She also had a dread of any sort of government intervention in the schools, refusing to allow those in which her sisters taught to be placed under the jurisdiction

Fig. 3 The Mission at Newcastle-under-Lyme; 'We sit in profound recollection.'

Fig. 4 The Mission at Newcastle-under-Lyme; 'group during second Mass'.

of the Education Boards. Not that she wanted her children to be at a disadvantage:

> Do not think from this that I would like our own humbler classes to be less educated than others; no, I should like them to be superior to other people in every way and everything – as they are in reality superior to them by the blessing of faith.[52]

Although Mother Margaret could not be induced to believe the government harboured any good will towards the Catholic Church or its schools, she did concede that the prospect of government grants had provided an incentive to improve the education offered in her own schools. Another educational work undertaken from the time that the sisters arrived in Stone was Blessed Imelda's Pension School which opened under the direction of Sister M. Gabriel Du Boulay. Although it never grew beyond twenty-five pupils during the nineteenth century, the school was to be a rich source of vocations to the congregation.

A return was made to the Potteries in 1857 when a house was founded at Stoke-on-Trent. Sister M. Rose Goode led the first group to the convent which was to become a miniature version of Stone in terms of the works undertaken: teaching in the mission schools – gratis for many years – a small boarding school, and in 1864 St Margaret's Hospital was opened. From 1859 until 1881 the mission was staffed by the Dominican friars and, as at Stone, the community maintained them. The work of visiting and relieving the poor was undertaken with great zeal, the casual nature of employment in the town being a cause of hardship to many families.[53]

Two foundations of short duration followed. The first was made at Leicester on 13 February 1860 at the invitation of the Dominican friars and with the financial support of a local manufacturer by the name of Worswick. Father Thomas Nickolds, prior of Leicester at the time, decided to sell off part of the land adjacent to the house the sisters occupied for use as a drill yard which, apart from the problem of noise, would make it difficult for the work to expand. When Father Thomas was elected prior of Woodchester reports circulated that it was the influence of the sisters which had precipitated his removal. The situation became quite unpleasant and the community withdrew in August. Although Sister M. Philippa Dunsford returned with a small group of sisters in November, the work did not prosper and a final departure was made in August 1861.[54] A foundation at Rhyl on the north coast of Wales was made in June 1864 but it was soon evident that the town was too small to offer either enough scope for the usual works or sufficient means to support them. The house was closed in August 1866.[55]

In the same year as the foundation at Rhyl, Mother Margaret's attentions were directed southwards where several invitations were made. Eventually she accepted the offer made by Bishop William Vaughan of Plymouth and a community led by Mother Rose Columba Adams set out for St Marychurch, near Torquay in Devon, in August 1864. Two benefactors secured the future of the Devon house, Lilias Bonar, a sister of the Duchess of Argyle, and William Denis Potts Chatto who gave £10,000 towards the building and maintenance of the church. The building work began at once with the community giving a hand in the evenings digging the trenches. It was not until 1881 that the Church of Our Lady and St Denis with its magnificent spire and the neighbouring conventual buildings were completed.

In the meantime the sisters made their home in Southampton Villa. Although the sisters made the journey to Torquay by foot in all weathers to teach in the mission school there, they also opened fee paying schools for boarders and day pupils and established an orphanage.[56] In 1873 the director of the terracotta works at Watcombe offered work to the orphanage and several of the older girls who showed talent for drawing were selected to work, painting in the lined patterns stamped on the chinaware under the expert eye of Sister Francis Philomena Ullathorne.[57] Evening classes in drawing and painting were also given by Sister Francis Philomena and were attended by a larger number of young women from the town, who also worked on the china painting. Unfortunately, the sisters' connection with the pottery works aroused the ire of a Protestant clergyman who was anxious about the number of younger members of his flock who were frequenting the convent. He put pressure on the owner and the scheme came to an end. Although the sisters had been subjected to some verbal abuse and threatening behaviour when they first arrived in Devon, their devoted nursing of those suffering from a virulent fever epidemic in 1875 reversed these anti-Catholic attitudes. In some cases the sisters nursed sufferers when clergy and district visitors would not do so for fear of contagion.[58]

Soon after the house at Rhyl was closed, Mother Margaret accepted what was to be her final foundation. Archbishop Manning invited her to establish an orphanage for Catholic children who might otherwise be placed in the workhouse and be lost to the faith. A large house in Walthamstow on the outskirts of London, capable

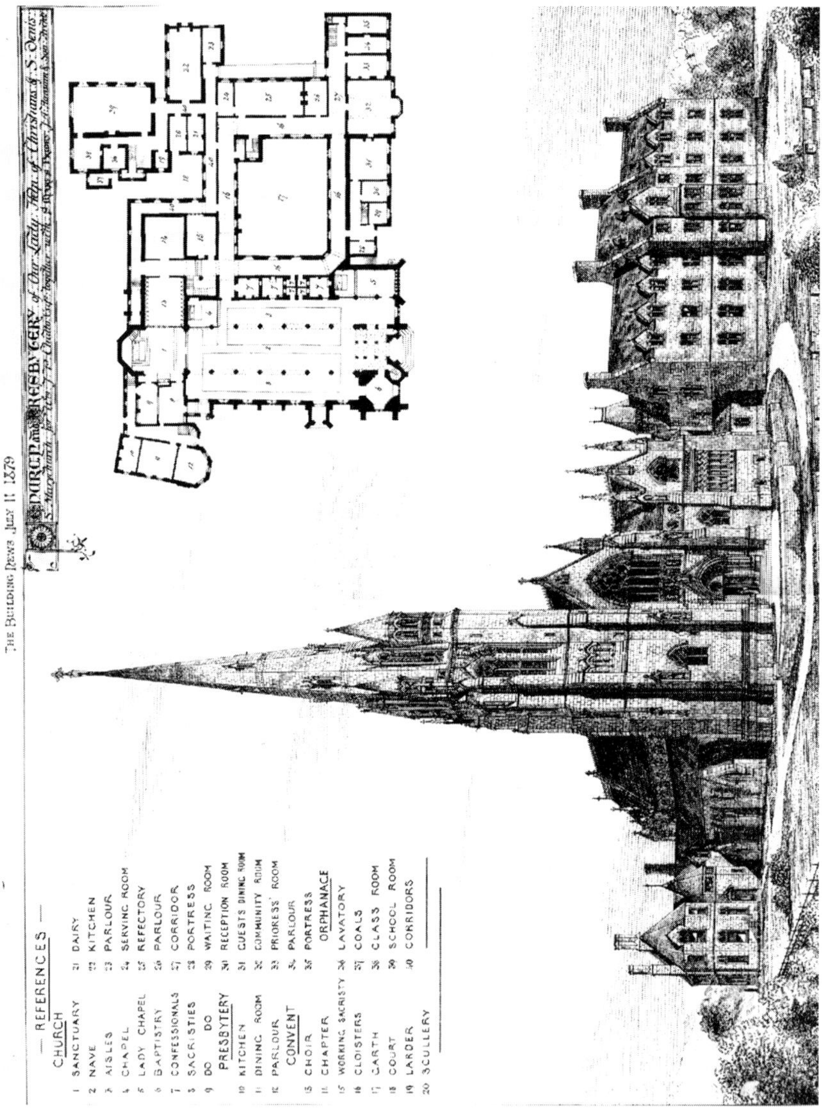

Fig. 5 Plan of St Mary's Priory, St Marychurch.

of accommodating 100 children, was offered. On her way to inspect the house and conclude the negotiations Mother Margaret and her companion passed through the East End where she was struck by the destitution of the local populace. The contrast with the semi-rural idyll of Walthamstow House caused her to ask the Archbishop, 'Can't you send us to some dirty place?'[59]

Diffiulties with the Poor Law Authorities prevented the work at Walthamstow from developing but by this time the founder's sights were already set on Bow, a newly established mission in the East End. It was only several months after her death that a house in Clarendon Terrace was rented while the purchase of Alfred House on Bow Road was arranged. The remaining sisters left Walthamstow in December 1868 and the following March the Convent of St Catherine was erected with Mother M. Hyacinth Stone as vicaress. A convent with steep Flemish gables and tall Tudor-style chimneys was erected, along with a church to serve the mission. The sisters began teaching in the mission schools, not accepting a salary until 1870 when they were placed under government inspection and received a grant. In 1872 a private school was opened under Sister M. Aimée Beech. From the start a number of the sisters at Bow began visiting the poor and sick, and guilds were set up to benefit the girls and young women, both works continuing to be of major importance for this house.[60]

In little over twenty years Margaret Hallahan's role had changed from parish worker to superior general of a religious congregation, approved at Rome, comprising five houses and ninety-three professed religious. But though her role had been transformed she had lost nothing of the simplicity, directness or self-effacement of those early years. She died on 11 May 1868 after a long and painful illness which probably had its origins in the tubercular infection to which she had been exposed as a child. Her followers were plunged into sadness. When Mary Mostyn arrived at Stone as a postulant shortly before Mother Margaret's death, observing the constant recourse to tears amongst the sisters, she understood that weeping was part of the rule!

Disciples become leaders: Mother Margaret's successors

It was no surprise that Mother M. Imelda Poole, who had been Margaret's able assistant since Clifton days, should be appointed by the Master of the Order to succeed her as Prioress Provincial, or that she was later elected to continue in office at the chapter of

1871. Maria Poole, called Minnie in the family, was born on 31 July 1815 at Westbury in Somerset, the daughter of a solicitor, Joseph Spencer Ruscombe Poole and his wife Elizabeth Stone. As a child she was something of a tomboy with a love of outdoor pursuits, but she also developed into something of a bluestocking, mastering Greek and Latin as well as several European languages.

When Minnie was a young woman, the whole family came under the influence of Pusey and at one point he tried to persuade her to become a member of his Park Village sisterhood. Along with her widowed sister Elizabeth Anstice, she read Newman's tracts and both preceded him into the Roman Church. Later, Minnie was to meet Newman and to correspond with him for the rest of her life. Another of her sisters, Susannah, was married to an Anglican cleric, James Spencer Northcote who also became a Catholic and visited Coventry soon after his conversion. Here he was introduced to Mother Margaret and it was through him that Minnie became aware of the community. She came to Clifton with her older sister Lucy and both were received as novices on 11 July 1849.

Sister M. Imelda became utterly devoted to Mother Margaret who prized her highly. Certainly, she complemented the founder's vision and charisma with her own arsenal of intellectual and social gifts. In the early days at Clifton it was she who ensured that new members of the community were sufficiently instructed in Latin to pray the Divine Office with devotion and spiritual benefit. As a schoolteacher she was less of a success for although she had ability, like many intellectuals she sometimes lacked the imagination to convey her enthusiasm to others. It was she who worked on the first draft of the constitutions and assisted in their completion and revision when Prioress Provincial. During Mother Margaret's lifetime, Sister M. Imelda took in hand the major part of the official correspondence, her literary ability, forethought and tact standing her in good stead. She also undertook a considerable part of the administration of the congregation's temporal affairs. Despite her devotion to Mother Margaret she was not afraid to institute changes and her tenure of office, which ended with her death on 14 October 1881, would herald organizational change, just as it preserved institutional stability.

Mother M. Imelda was succeeded in office by Mother Francis Raphael, who was born Augusta Theodosia Drane at Bromley-by-Bow on 28 August 1823. Her father, Thomas, was a managing partner in an East India mercantile house who had travelled widely and amassed a large library and collection of curiosities. Augusta was a precocious reader and developed a love of the natural sciences. By the time she was twelve she had exploited her father's library and, amongst other titles, had read Holinshed's *Chronicles*, Spenser, Milton, Homer, Hume's *History of England*, Sully's *Memoirs* and Walton's *Compleat Angler*. Perhaps it was this eclectic taste in reading matter which also developed a broadness of vision not often associated with conventual life. In the late 1840s the family moved to Devon and Augusta came under the influence of the Oxford Movement, being received into the Catholic Church at Tiverton on 2 June 1850.

Barely a month after her conversion she first made the acquaintance of Mother Margaret and her community at Clifton and was immediately attracted to the founder and the sisters' way of life. After spending more than a year in Rome, Augusta entered the community on 4 October 1852, receiving the habit and the name Francis Raphael on 7 December. Margaret Hallahan was determined to develop whatever natural abilities her novices might have, but she was equally committed to the principle of all working for the common good. On one occasion she remarked of Sister Francis Raphael, 'Why, you don't suppose I would have had her for her books, if she wouldn't peel potatoes?'[61] As a young religious, there was little danger of Sister Francis Raphael suffering from intellectual pride as she was being constantly changed from one occupation to another. From this she assumed she was good for nothing but, in fact, her superior wisely left her as a stop-gap in order that she might devote more of her time to intellectual pursuits. In 1860 Francis Raphael Drane was appointed novice mistress and three years later mistress of studies.

Before she entered the community Sister Francis Raphael had already written a number of apologetical tracts. In 1855 she produced a series of legends and stories for *The Lamp* and two years later her first book, *The Life of Saint Dominic with a Sketch of the Dominican Order* was published by Burns and Lambert. Between 1858 and her appointment as conventual prioress at Stone in 1872, nine further works came off the press, including a *History of England* which went through six editions; her masterpiece *Christian Schools and Scholars* and *The life of Mother Mary Margaret Hallahan,* which appeared within months of the founder's death. She also engaged in a considerable amount of translation work, always at a prodigious rate. Her English translation of Père Chocarne's biography of Henri-Dominique Lacordaire, the reviver of the French Dominican province, was made in a matter of months while supervising the evening study of the girls in the pension school at Stone.

During her term as Prioress at Stone, Mother Francis Raphael's administrative obligations limited her to a single volume of poetry, an article in the *Irish Monthly* and in 1880, for the 500th anniversary of the saint's death, *The History of St Catherine of Siena and her Companions*. The following year she succeeded Mother M. Imelda Poole as Provincial, a post she held until shortly before her death on 29 April 1894. Responsibility for some 150 religious in four communities engaged in a wide variety of works, did nothing to hinder Mother Francis Raphael's literary and intellectual curiosity. She still found time for several works of fiction, compiled a series of school readers, a second biography of St Dominic and edited Archbishop Ullathorne's autobiography and letters.

Several notebooks of instructions given to the community, circular letters to the various convents and hundreds of letters to individual sisters are preserved in the archives at Stone. To some Mother Francis Raphael seemed a formidable figure, however, in her letters there is not only spiritual insight, but curiosity about people and an ample measure of human warmth. She was equally at ease discussing contemporary literature, saying of Shelley's *Lament*: 'I think he was a glorious poet and the meanest and most selfish of men: that is what is so disappointing, that a man can be so inspired and at the same time so debased.'[62] She was also curious to know about George Eliot and ploughed through the three volumes of journals and letters edited by Cross and published in 1885. Despite being unable to 'discover what principles she taught, or what is the object aimed at in her books'[63] Mother Francis Raphael clearly recognized Eliot's genius. Her wonderful gift for sketching and caricature has already been mentioned, but besides the illustrated annals there is also a hagiographical spoof on Sister Catherine of the 4th Order of Preachers, a cat who was turned out of the convent for being a Pusseyite; a lecture on postulantology and much else besides.

In terms of her published work, Francis Raphael Drane was more prolific than any of the friars of the English Province who were her contemporaries. Admittedly, her work was not particularly speculative and it must be kept in mind that the study of history was not recognized as an academic discipline in the universities until towards the end of the nineteenth century. Amongst the brethren of this era, Augustine Proctor compiled two brief catechisms for those preparing for first confession and communion, a short book on the rosary and published a series of lectures. Dominic Aylward, 'a most learned and cultured man' according to Walter Gumbley's *Obit Book*, like Mother Francis Raphael, published a good deal of poetry and provided articles for many Catholic periodicals, while

Austin Maltus published several devotional works. But it was not until considerably later that the first great historians of the province, Raymond Palmer and Bertrand Willberforce came into their own, the latter publishing his *Memoir of Mother Francis Raphael* in 1895.[64]

From this it may be argued that the revival of Dominican intellectual life in Britain was lead by the sisters rather than the friars. However, there is little evidence to support any idea of a corporate approach to learning. In her own work, *The Daily Life of a Religious*, there is a chapter devoted to study and teaching in which the first source Mother Francis Raphael quotes is not St Thomas Aquinas but de Rancé, the austere reformer of La Trappe. Her first concern is that intellectual work can open the mind to attacks of vanity and pride and that it can dry up the soul. Although there is mention of St Augustine, the Franciscan St Bonaventure, and quite a long passage from a treatise written for Ursuline novices, the only Dominican authority resorted to is St Vincent Ferrer. It is quite probable that Mother Francis Raphael is speaking from her own experience in proffering St Vincent's advice that study ought always to be seasoned with prayer. She states 'even when quite innocently pursued, it produces a certain degree of aridity. Mental fatigue always results in dryness'.[65] On the contrary, the action of the heart never wears one out. Perhaps this was the secret of her productivity. Mother Francis Raphael may not have had the common touch of Mother Margaret or the affectionate nature of Mother Imelda but she was certainly an impressive woman and an impressive Dominican.

Innovation and change: can the spirit be maintained?

The first General Chapter following the election of Mother M. Imelda, which was convened at Stone in May 1873, instituted several profound changes in the life of the congregation. It drew attention to the congregation's precarious financial state; noting that expenditure continued to outrun income and that rigorous measures would have to be introduced, particularly at Stone and Clifton.[66] Two causes of the problem at Stone were the maintenance of the mission clergy in the convent and the large number of dependents who had been received gratis into the institutions run by the congregation.[67] As a consequence, an agreement was drawn up with the clergy by which they were to maintain their own residence and receive the revenue of the church in exchange. A decision was also made not to accept anyone into the institutions of the congregation without adequate maintenance, and to make every attempt to send those not so provided for to relatives or friends. At Clifton the situation was deemed serious enough for immediate moves to be made to dispose of the property. The sale of the convent could not be concluded until 1876 when Bishop Clifford purchased it for £2000. He then leased it to a Mrs Mathews who ran it as a successful boarding house, though after some years it became home to Franciscan friars expelled from France and later still welcomed back a community of Dominican sisters.[68]

There was also a strengthening of the executive power of the General Council. The constitutions printed in 1853 were, in reality, only one half of the required work, since they lacked a section dealing with the government of the congregation. The General Chapter of 1873 called for the revision of the first part and the preparation of the second, and the Extraordinary Chapter of the following year commissioned Sister M. Angela Northcote to undertake the work. In the meantime norms were laid down for the composition of Council and General Chapter and the right of election of prioresses was withdrawn from the local communities, appointments in future being made by the General Council. This was a novel departure from the traditions of the Order, at least insofar as it was practised by contemplative Dominican women. However, the practice of modern congregations governed by a superior general, encouraged by Rome, was of concentrating authority and appointing local superiors. A century would pass before English Dominican Sisters again elected their local prioresses.

The decision was also made at the chapter of 1873 to introduce a second class of religious into the congregation. The decrees of the chapter state:

> We are of the opinion that the employment of secular domestics in our Convents is attended with many grave inconveniences, we therefore deem it expedient that with the view of supplying their services, the class of Sisters be increased in our Congregation, who, being in all aspects equal in rank with the other religious, are yet exempt from choir and devoted to domestic service, such Sisters not enjoying the active or passive voice. [69]

The division of communities into choir and lay members developed amongst the Cistercians in the twelfth century and was adopted by most communities of nuns. Many congregations founded in the nineteenth century, including most Dominican groups, had lay sisters from the beginning or introduced them after a time.

Although most lay sisters were from a lower social class than their choir counterparts, and their energies were generally directed towards household duties and manual work, the great distinction between the two was that lay sisters enjoyed neither active nor passive voice in the affairs of the community: they could not vote in chapter, neither could they be elected to any office, they had no say in the business of the community.

Having spent most of her adult life in domestic service would hardly have fitted Mother Margaret for the duties of a choir sister in most existing communities and it had been as a lay sister that she made her first trial of religious life. In his account of Mother Margaret's spiritual life, Ullathorne relates their common attitude towards the division of the community into choir and lay members:

> From the first ... we were both strongly of the opinion that it would be much the best not to receive lay sisters. We thought it would greatly contribute as well to the vigour as to the unity of the community if there was only one grade in it, if the sisters never had to look down, as it were, on their habit as it clothed other Sisters holding an inferior position; and experience has proved that this limitation of the communities to one class of Sisters has greatly contributed to humility as well as to vigour and to a complete unity of spirit.[70]

Despite the entrance of women from well-to-do families after the move to Clifton, all the postulants, whether they were lineal descendants of Edward III – of whom there were three in the noviciate at one time – or the daughters of tradesmen, took their share of work in the household and this often included extremely heavy work at the time of new foundations. By the time the foundation at Stone was made in 1853 servants were also being employed, drawn mainly from amongst the orphan girls in the sisters' care.

Notwithstanding the founder's antipathy to the notion of lay sisters, the first printed constitutions of the congregation did make provision for them. Chapter 13 of the 1853 constitutions, entitled *Of those who shall be received* states: 'It is permitted also to receive some lay sisters when it is thought expedient, but in moderate number, according as the other sisters need their service and their assistance.'[71] However, an explanatory note makes it clear that this article is included so that the legislation of the Order may be observed, but that 'it is much to be desired that the original intention of this Institute of having no lay sisters should be adhered to, in order to avoid all distinction of rank between the religious'.

Perhaps there was also some concern about the possibility of exempting some sisters who had little education from recitation of the Latin office. It is possible that Mother Margaret's egalitarian views were already beginning to change as a consequence of having servants working in the convents. Not having bound themselves to a life of monastic discipline, paid servants could not possibly be expected to conduct themselves in the same manner as the sisters; neither could it have been easy to exert moral pressure upon them to do so. Though the chapter legislated not for lay sisters so called, but for sisters exempt from choral office, they would not enjoy active or passive voice. Aware of the novelty of the situation, it was decided not to dismiss the domestic servants until the prospective candidates had been trained to their work. The first three postulants for the exempt sisters: Margaret Sutherland, Annie Tofts and Mary Jane King, arrived in July. They were joined two months later by Margaret Alcock.

From the first the new arrangement did not seem to be working out. Annie Tofts remained less than a month and Mary Jane King left in December. Three more postulants arrived the following year, but by the time the last of these entered at the beginning of August 1874, five of her predecessors had already left. Almost a year earlier the Council had rejected an application from Bridget Horton of Stoke-on-Trent on the grounds that 'her success appeared doubtful and it was considered undesirable under such circumstances to receive any more from Stoke'.[72]

There was also the difficulty of forming two distinct classes of religious in the same noviciate. At the time there were only three choir novices at Stone, but it is more than likely that the common instruction was geared to their needs rather than the more humble requirements of the exempt sisters. Ellen Barry, an Irish woman of thirty, who could not read and had been brought up to heavy farm work, would hardly appear to advantage against a niece of Bishop Ullathorne or the daughters of a solicitor and surgeon. The exempt sisters were to be 'in all aspects equal in rank', but their own social status and their position in the community made for a very spurious type of equality.

Whenever the Council received an application for admission as an exempt sister, and on the occasions when postulants stayed long enough to be considered for reception of the habit, the whole question was open again for discussion. Margaret Sutherland was beyond the normal term of postulancy, but the Mothers of Council were still inclined to prolong her initial probation until such time as the whole question of exempt sisters was settled. Would she, as the only exempt sister, come to feel resentment at the anomaly of wearing the white scapular but being deprived of a voice in chapter? In the months that followed her reception of the habit Margaret Sutherland's capability for reciting the choral office and her love for it were established, and eventually she was professed as a choir sister along with the solicitor's daughter. One condition was attached to her admission to the ranks of the choir sisters; she would still devote the major part of her time to domestic work, though in a supervisory role.

Ellen Barry was not so fortunate; she did not receive the necessary votes to proceed. In summing up the reasons for her failure the councillors admitted that the system was perhaps as much at fault as the individual:

> The failure of this postulant and of others received as exempt sisters had arisen from the difficult position in which they were placed and that they would have had a fair chance of success had they from the first been accepted as lay sisters.[73]

The experiment with hybrids had been a failure. On the advice of Bishop Ullathorne an extraordinary Provincial Chapter was convened in September 1874 at which the experiment with exempt sisters was evaluated and the proposal made to admit candidates as lay sisters. There was only one dissenting vote.[74] It was agreed that candidates for the lay sisters should be formed separately, with a mistress of their own, Sister M. Walburga Beech being nominated for the task. One of the dormitories was subdivided to accommodate this alternative noviciate; irony was not entirely absent in this, as the lay postulants' sleeping place was dedicated to the archangels while the choir novices had to content themselves with sleeping under the patronage of mere angels! Lest they should remain under any illusion during the day, however, the lay sisters' community room was dedicated to St Martha, patroness of servants.

On 22 January 1875 the first lay postulants, Cicely Exton and Louisa Nicholas, arrived at Stone. The following year they were clothed in the black scapular – ostensibly more practical for those engaged in manual work – and the white veil which would seem to mark them off as perpetual novices. They were given the religious names Stephana and Dominic which were not, as was the case with the choir religious, prefixed by Mary.[75] Even the ceremonial for their reception of the habit reinforced their different status. During the clothing of choir nuns the hymn *Veni Creator* was sung, while during that of the lay sisters it was merely recited.

So the egalitarian vision of Mother Margaret for her sisters was lost. In its somewhat formalized manner and coded vocabulary, the

Necrology tells something of how their lives were spent. Sister Blandina Dennett, for instance, spent forty years baking altar breads but could also put her hand to wood turning or erecting a rockery in the garden at Stone. Sister Pauline Wyatt is remembered as a great character with 'an utter absence of human respect' who, when invited to attend High Mass replied; 'No thank you, I never did care for the organ, the street kind or any other.' Sister Bridget Cain is remembered for her 'quiet dignity of manner accompanied with a good deal of fun'. [76] At times it must have been difficult to maintain either dignity or a sense of fun when constantly made aware of the inferior position one held in community.

It is true that in the Stroud congregation for many years lay candidates, unlike their choir counterparts, were first received as secular tertiaries and only after at least three years were they clothed in the habit. But in their Constitutions (1897)[77] and those of the London congregation (1913)[78] emphasis falls on the collaborative aspect of the lay sisters' work, freeing the choir nuns to devote themselves without interruption to intellectual and charitable works. In the somewhat harsher tones of the 1889 revision of the Stone Constitutions one is immediately aware of the scriptural allusion to the Fall: 'As the lay sisters are called to religion for bodily labour, and to eat their bread in the sweat of their brow, it is not necessary for them to be present in Choir.'[79] It was this wording which would later find its way into the constitutions of the amalgamated congregation. Bishop Brindle of Nottingham tried to induce the Leicester sisters, who were a much more socially homogenous group, to integrate the two classes of religious soon after the turn of the century, but their Council voted against the change.[80] What would have happened, one wonders, if the amalgamation had included one community without lay sisters?

On balance, it must be remembered that the lay sisterhood at Stone and elsewhere offered to many women of humble background the chance of living out a life of religious consecration which would otherwise have eluded them. For many, coming to the convent from positions in domestic service, it must have been merely an extension of the natural order of things. Certainly there was greater security in the sympathetic atmosphere of the convent; neither were women subjected to the physical or sexual abuse which was so often the lot of female domestic servants. Unfortunately, as the twentieth century progressed, religious congregations did not reflect the greater degree of social equality in the population at large. It must also be remembered that other congregations, admittedly not bound to the choral celebration of the Divine Office, retained a single class of sister and managed to survive with the assistance of 'dangerous domestics' as, indeed, the Dominicans of Stone were still obliged to do.[81]

Another aspect of conventual practice to which Mother Margaret's successors turned their attention was that of enclosure. It was clear from the beginning that both Mother Margaret and her early advisors wanted as little enclosure as possible, although the founder was quite prepared to submit to it as a necessary condition of being recognized as Dominicans. The reviver of Dominican life in France, Henri-Dominique Lacordaire, had not thought its lack an obstacle to the community being considered genuinely Dominican but, rather, extremely useful to the situation in England.[82] It is clear that a certain liberty was also envisaged in terms of dealings with outsiders. Although Bishop Ullathorne mentioned religious decorum during his canonical visitation at Clifton in 1849, he also insisted on the rights of novices to see their near relatives – though not strangers – without the presence of a professed sister.[83]

In 1877 Ullathorne emphasized, as Mother Margaret herself had done, that apostolic effectiveness is fed by a life of prayer and regular observance. He gives a picture of two different kinds of sister involved in the work of visiting the poor. A weak sister will have an idea of the work of the Order as going from home to home to save souls but having a tenacious attachment to her own judgement will waste time and be 'the veryest [sic] gossip, tattle tongue and bore to the poor' while the religious 'wisely chosen by the superiors enters the homes of the poor, carries with her a solidity of character ... which derives from conventual prayer and discipline ... [and] gives an unction and sanctity to her works and ways'.[84]

The work of visiting the sick continued and in the early years the sisters assisted in missions as that at Newcastle-under-Lyme already mentioned. But twenty years later the mood had changed somewhat. Writing to the community at Stoke after carrying out a visitation in 1874, Mother M. Imelda Poole informed them that, in future, the sisters would no longer be allowed to take part in public processions. The fact they had done so before was attributed to the exceptional state of Catholicity in the country as it came out of the penal era, when every help and encouragement was needed to raise the level of fervour and devotion.

> Our dear Father the bishop always told our dear Mother Margaret that these practices would some day be put down by Episcopal authority, but with his usual largeness of heart, his Lordship

> tolerated it at that time when but for the help of the religious the people could not have been taught to have processions at all in a decorous manner.[85]

About the same time, the Bishop of Plymouth stipulated that the Corpus Christi procession should not go outside the convent garden at St Marychurch and the rogation day processions were to be kept to the bottom end of the garden 'where they will be less conspicuous'. If the Catholics of Torquay were afraid of being conspicuous, then Mother Margaret would surely have believed them very much in need of the 'exceptions' she had been granted!

A similar tendency is seen in the visitation report from Bow in 1880. The door between the two sacristies was to be bolted from the nuns' side whenever the priests and servers were occupying the other room, and necessary communication should be held through the 'turn'.[86] Because the sacristan at the time was deaf, allowance was made for communicating at the open door! On the other hand, half an hour of outdoor exercise was required for the younger sisters because 'the works of charity depend on the general health of the communities being maintained'.[87] At St Marychurch the choir was to be arranged in such a way that sisters going in and out should not be seen by seculars. To secure this amount of privacy, whenever the sisters were assembled in choir the curtain at the end of the left-hand side had to be at least partially drawn. During public Mass and Benediction the right-hand curtain was also drawn, and whenever the priest and his attendants occupied seats exactly opposite the choir, the middle curtain would be drawn as well.[88]

There is no doubt that such legislation was instigated from the best of intentions and a desire for a more perfect living of religious and Dominican life. It also provides evidence of the tendency highlighted by Père Mainage in his biography of the founder of the French congregation of Etrépagny, of active sisters of the Third Order inclining towards the practices of enclosed nuns of the Second.[89] One wonders how the sisters coped with this dichotomy which saw them as enclosed nuns in some areas of their lives and as apostolic women going out to teach in schools and to visit the sick in homes and hospitals at others.

Another major organizational change took place in 1887 when the congregation was removed from the jurisdiction of the Order of Preachers. Since the 1860s several other congregations of Third Order sisters had already made this transition, conforming to the directives of the Congregation for Bishops and Regulars concerning women in simple vows. Some were very much opposed to the move.[90] This does not seem to have been the case at Stone where relations with the friars had sometimes been rather fraught. The sisters had been quite happy with the arrangement whereby Ullathorne acted as vicar for the Master of the Order and at a meeting of prioresses held in 1879 declared, that if this position could not be maintained, they would rather the jurisdiction of the Order be exercised by a tertiary – they named Doctor Northcote, brother-in-law of Mother M. Imelda and friend and advisor to the congregation – than by the Provincial.[91]

It is clear from a letter addressed to Bishop Ullathorne by the Master of the Order, Father Giuseppe Sanvito, in February that year, that certain of the friars in the English province, aware that a change in jurisdiction was imminent, were causing disquiet amongst the sisters. These friars implied that once the congregation was removed from the jurisdiction of the Order, the sisters would no longer be true Dominicans. Sanvito assured Ullathorne that the congregation had no need of affiliation to the province to assure its place in the Dominican family. [92] Despite these assurances one of the religious, Sister Lucy Raphael Allway, who had been professed almost twenty years, sought a dispensation from her vows of obedience and poverty as a consequence of this change.[93] She must subsequently have been dispensed from her vow of chastity, for she later married and went out to Australia. After several years as Mrs Otway she was widowed and entered the Dominican convent at North Adelaide, making profession once more in 1897. She lived to draw a large annuity and to celebrate her silver jubilee before dying in December 1922.[94]

The matter of jurisdiction was not discussed at the General Chapter of 1884, but three years later, when it was clear that Rome would impose the change, a petition was drawn up. The petition expressed the conviction that closer links with the local bishops were absolutely necessary for a congregation involved in various active works in several dioceses. Their being under the jurisdiction of the Order, exempt from that of the bishops, was specifically mentioned as an impediment to the development of their works. This was a strange argument as, having had their constitutions approved at Rome, the powers local bishops could exert over them were limited. At the same time it is stated clearly that the unity of the congregation must be guaranteed, along with the right of appeal to the Master of the Order as the interpreter of their Dominican constitutions. Perhaps more surprising is the statement that the spiritual welfare of the sisters would be better seen to under the care of the bishops. An extraordinary General Chapter was convoked to consider the matter and the proposition to transfer from the jurisdiction of the Order was carried by 103 votes to one.[95] By a strange anomaly the term 'Mother Provincial' was retained by the major superior of the Stone congregation though she neither governed nor belonged to a province!

Further afield: foundations in Australia and Scotland

In 1882 Christopher Reynolds, Bishop of Adelaide, wrote to Stone regarding a hospital in his diocese being financed by a Mrs Baker and her daughter. The Irish Dominican Sisters had made a foundation in Adelaide in 1868 but teaching was the only apostolic work which their constitutions allowed. Confident that he could find Australian recruits to form the nucleus of a new foundation in his diocese, Bishop Reynolds sought permission for them to be trained in the noviciate at Stone, and for several experienced sisters to come with them to Adelaide for three years once they were professed. Because South Australia was well beyond the territorial bounds of the English Province of the Order, the foundation could not be dependent upon Stone.[96]

Eventually it was decided to make a foundation at once and receive novices on arrival. Six sisters were chosen for the new venture under the leadership of Mother Rose Columba Adams, prioress at St Marychurch. Sophia Adams was born into a landed family at Woodchester, Gloucestershire, in 1832. Shortly after the arrival of the Dominicans in her home town in 1851, she followed her elder sister Cecilia into the Catholic Church; both were forced to leave home in consequence. Five years later Sophia entered at Stone making profession on 26 May 1857. In Mother Margaret she found a kindred heart and her biographer states with confidence that she was considered more like Mother Margaret than any other member of the congregation.[97] She was intellectually gifted without being formidable, relied as much on intuition as reason, spoke little but always to the point. Despite affluent origins, Mother Rose Columba was not above delousing the abject poor, and like Mother Margaret had a way of attracting people of every class and background and making each feel appreciated.

It was little surprise that such a religious should be appointed founding superior at St Marychurch, where she remained in office until her departure for Australia. Her competence as a local superior may not have been the only motive in her choice as leader of the

Australian expedition. An oral tradition maintained at North Adelaide, and not unknown at Stone, is that Rose Columba was seen as a focus of opposition to some of the changes introduced after Mother Margaret's death.[98] Brownlow in his *Memoir* is at pains to state that though her qualities might well attract, there was nothing of party spirit about her.[99] Was he protesting too much?

Only after their arrival in Adelaide did the sisters learn that they would be expected to nurse men in the proposed hospital whereas the Stone constitutions permitted them to nurse only children and women. The decision was made to open a school instead. None of the foundation sisters exercised her right to return to Stone, Mother Rose Columba governing the community until her death on 30 December 1891. North Adelaide always retained something of the Stone flavour, an exquisite chapel was erected and became the centre for perpetual adoration of the Blessed Sacrament, while the school long retained an English feel. At various times the question arose of becoming Second Order nuns but eventually in 1958 the community became part of the newly amalgamated Australian congregation.[100]

A Scottish foundation was made at Crieff near Stirling in 1889 by Mother M. Ignatius Elwes, a Newfoundlander, born of Scottish parents, who had entered at Stone as a widow in 1870. Though detailed conditions for the foundation are recorded, no overt reason, other than Mother M. Ignatius' desire to provide a home for her three half sisters, is mentioned. A school was opened but the community was too isolated to attract enough postulants or provide sufficient income. After Mother M. Ignatius' death on the last day of 1899 the community was disbanded, three of the seven remaining members being received into the noviciate at Stone.

Conclusion

Although she had worked with nothing short of zeal to make the congregation thoroughly Dominican in its legislation, prayer life and apostolic engagements, Mother Margaret never lost sight of the simplicity, breadth of vision and trust in providence which characterized the early years of the community. There is no question that the members of the Stone congregation were devoted to their founder and sought to propagate her spirit. The prompt publication of the *Life* so soon after her death is ample evidence of their devotion. But those who succeeded her in leadership, coming from a quite different social background, very soon enacted legislation that changed the character of the congregation quite considerably. Mother Margaret had left behind her a congregation that was self-confident and united. Although the bond of unity remained, the style of government and other structures had become more rigid, the lifestyle more formalized, the membership divided into two distinct classes. As it approached the new century with a solid record of achievement, self-confidence perhaps gave way to an increasing, and less healthy self assurance.

Notes

1. Stone, T782E, *Our Mother's Early Life, Spinal Complaint, Penances, Sickness*, p. 118.
2. Hancock, 'From Hagiography to History', in *Recusant History*, vol. 23, no. 3, May 1997, pp. 341–71.
3. Stone, T170, Mother Margaret Hallahan to Father Austin Maltus, 13 November 1866.
4. Stone, T763, Mother M. Imelda Poole, *My own reminiscences of our dearest Mother*, p. 14.
5. Stone, T756, William Bernard Ullathorne, *On the Interior Life of our beloved Mother*, p. 33.
6. Cnockaert, *Pierre-Joseph Triest*, p. 165 ff and p. 434 ff.
7. Stone, T756, *Interior Life*, p. 2.
8. Champ, *William Bernard Ullathorne*, p. 6 ff.
9. Now Klaipeda in Lithuania.
10. Champ, *William Bernard Ullathorne*, p. 58.
11. Ibid., pp. 186, 237.
12. Stephens (ed.), *History of the County of Warwick. Vol. 7*, p. 232.
13. Stone, T756, *Interior Life*, p. 44.
14. Stone, T764, Mother M. Imelda Poole, *Reminiscences suggested by the MS Life of our dearest Mother*, p. 27.
15. The only Harriet Goode born in London and recorded in the 1841 census was living in Bethnal Green with her mother Sarah, a laundress.
16. The only Charlotte Gittens recorded in the 1841 census resided with Sarah Griffiths at Claines near the city of Worcester. Both are listed as glove makers. We do know that Charlotte Gittens had a knowledge of French and that she brought the first dowry to the community.
17. Champ, *William Bernard Ullathorne*, p. 116.
18. Heiman, *Catholic Devotion*, p. 60.
19. Stone, T782C, *Beginnings of the Community*, p. 95.
20. Stone, T146, Mother Margaret Hallahan to Bishop Ullathorne, 18 June (1844).
21. Stone, T570, *Rules of [sic] Constitutions of Customs for the present Regulation of*

this Community ... etc, Article 11.
22. Stone, T782B, Mother M. Imelda Poole, *The Servant of God's Life at Coventry*, p. 3.
23. Stone, G/ULL/iv/2, Mother Margaret Hallahan to Bishop Ullathorne, 14 August 1859.
24. Quoted without citation in Champ, *William Bernard Ullathorne*, p. 349.
25. Foyle, *Bristol*, p. 24.
26. Stone, T862, Sister M. Francis Lynch, *Some little Account of the first Commencement at Bristol*, p. 20.
27. Stone, T864, *Records written by Sister M. Imelda Poole & Sister Francis Raphael Drane, 1850–1859*, p. 13.
28. Stone, T812, Father Dominic Aylward to Mother Margaret Hallahan, 14 February 1850.
29. Stone, T825, copy, bearing the date 15 August 1851, is preserved at Stone.
30. Cusack, *The Truth about Convent Life*, p. 38.
31. Stone, T864, *Records*, p. 99.
32. Stone, T507, Mother Margaret Hallahan to Father Dominic Aylward, 14 November 1850.
33. Stone, T773/1, John Henry Newman to Mother Francis Raphael Drane, 28 May 1869.
34. I have been unable to locate the original quotation which is cited by Philip Hughes, 'The English Catholics in 1850', in George Andrew Beck (ed.), *The English Catholics*, p. 77.
35. Stone, T864, *Records etc.*, p. 72.
36. Stone, T791/6, Mother Margaret Hallahan to Father Austin Maltus, no date.
37. Clifton, Misc. Files, Sister M. Imelda Poole to Archbishop George Errington, 5 December 1855.
38. Clifton, Misc. Files, Canon Frederick Neve to Sister M. Imelda Poole, 10 December 1855.
39. Hinnebusch, *Dominicans*, p. 25.
40. Clifton, Misc. Files, Archbishop Errington to Bishop Ullathorne, 31 December 1855.
41. Stone, T864, *Records etc*, p. 82–83.
42. Ibid.
43. Stone, T853 (copy).
44. Champ, *William Bernard Ullathorne*, p. 116.
45. Stone, T970, Father Bernard Morewood to Bishop Ullathorne, 11 July 1850.
46. Stone, T864, *Records etc*, p. 8.
47. Stone, T872, Pastoral Letter from Bishop Ullathorne to the faithful of the mission at Longton, 24 December 1853.
48. Boulding & Pearce, *Mother Margaret Hallahan in Staffordshire*, p. 13
49. Stone, G35, *Annals of the Congregation of S. Catherine of Siena: artistic and comic*.
50. Stone, S54, *St Mary's Hospital Stone*.
51. Drane, *Life*, p. 371.

52. Stone, T799, Mother Margaret Hallahan to an un-named Sister, undated but *c.*1858–61.
53. Stone, G15, *Register of the Branch Houses of the English Congregation of St Catherine of Siena of the Third Order of St Dominic*, pp. 27, 49.
54. Stone, T865, Drane, *Records 1859 to 1865*, p. 9.
55. Ibid., p. 35.
56. Stone, G15, *Register*, pp. 85–102.
57. Stone, STM18a, *Annals of St Mary's Priory from 1864*, p. 93.
58. Ibid., p. 130.
59. Drane, *Life*, p. 474.
60. Stone, G15, *Register,* p. 115–85.
61. Wilberforce, *Memoir of Mother Francis Raphael Drane,* p. lxxxii.
62. Unattributed letter quoted in ibid., p. 176.
63. Ibid.
64. Gumbley, *Obituary Notices,* pp. 218, 227.
65. Drane, *Daily Life*, p. 79.
66. Stone, G1b, 'Acts of the Second Provincial Chapter, 3–15th May 1873, nos. 1–6' in *Register of Documents*, p. 86.
67. Stone, T939, A *List of Names of those received gratis into Institutions founded by Mother Margaret Hallahan* gives the names of 78 persons maintained.
68. Harding, *Diocese of Clifton,* p. 40.
69. Stone, G1b, p. 86.
70. Stone, T756, Ullathorne, *Interior Life.,* pp. 36–7.
71. *Rule ... and Constitutions* (Stone, 1853), Chapter 13, section 5.
72. Stone, G1a, p. 81.
73. Ibid., 30 November 1874.
74. Ibid., p. 88.
75. This distinction was not uncommon in other congregations; many houses of the Sisters of Mercy adhered to it. Since the other four English Dominican foundations gave the prefix 'Mary' to all religious those who had been professed as lay sisters at Stone assumed it also at the amalgamation in 1929. However, reminders that the full form should be used for all, were still being sent out almost ten years later!
76. Stone, STM9(a), *Necrology drawn up for the Provincial Chapter 1924*.
77. *Rule ... and Constitutions* (Stroud, 1897), Chapter 26, no. 232 and Chapter 28, no. 240.
78. *Constitutions (*London, 1913), Chapter 25, no. 209.
79. *Rule ... and Constitutions* (Stone, 1889), Chapter 17, section 1, no. 370.
80. Stone, L16A2, *Council Book 1893–1917,* 12 April 1908. The Leicester Council Book gives ample evidence in the period after 1894 of lay sisters who were 'troublesome' or discontented with their lot.
81. The Sisters of Notre Dame de Namur where amongst these, though it would be interesting to know whether members who habitually carried out domestic and manual work were ever appointed to positions of authority. The census returns for the various convents, most of which number more than twenty-five sisters and a greater number of boarding pupils, always include paid servants in the returns.

82. Stone, T854, Henri-Dominique Lacordaire to Mother Margaret Hallahan, 23 November 1849.
83. Stone, C1/G/ULL/vi/30, *Report of Canonical Visitation of Clifton Convent, 31 May 1849*.
84. Stone, G/ULL/vi/23, Ullathorne, *Work in a community without lay Sisters*.
85. Stone, C7, *Register of Appointments & Acts of Visitation (1860–1877)*, p. 40.
86. The turn is a revolving cupboard, still used in some enclosed monasteries to pass things between the nuns and their visitors in the parlour or sacristy. It had a dividing panel preventing either side from seeing the other as it revolved.
87. Stone, C7, *Register*, p. 98.
88. Ibid., p. 123.
89. Mainage, *Mère Saint Dominique*, vol. 1, p. 230.
90. The sisters at St Catharine, Kentucky were even prepared to adopt enclosure and take solemn vows in order to remain under the jurisdiction of the Order; cf. Noonan, *Signadou*, p. 84.
91. Stone, G74/B, *Private Resolutions adopted by the Assembly of Prioresses*, May 1881.
92. Stone, G74/B, Giuseppe Sanvito to William Bernard Ullathorne, 6 February 1879.
93. Stone, G74/B, William Bernard Ullathorne to Mother M. Imelda Poole, 1 March 1879.
94. Burley, *Chapel, Cloister & Classroom*, p. 101.
95. Stone, G1b, *Register of Documents*, p. 109.
96. Ibid., p. 96.
97. Brownlow, *Memoir of Mother Rose Columba*, p. 62.
98. This opinion was first expressed to the author by the late Sisters M. Magdalen Hayman and M. Peter Broadley during a visit to St Dominic's Priory, North Adelaide, in August 1979.
99. Brownlow, *Memoir of Mother Rose Columba*, p. 166.
100. The Australian congregation was dissolved in 1988, the four constituent provinces, of which North Adelaide was one, becoming independent members of a federation.

Chapter Three

Everything wanting, save hope: new Dominican foundations

It was no child's play to have been a member of this community in its childhood, when almost everything was wanting, save hope.

Fr Vincent McNabb, OP[1]

Introduction

Considering Mother Margaret Hallahan had been appointed superior of all sisters of the Third Order Regular within the English Province, it is perhaps surprising that before the turn of the next century four other distinct groups of active Dominican women had been established in Britain.[2] They would have quite different patterns of development, but conform to the four major foundation dynamics for nineteenth-century communities of women religious: a group of lay women responding to local needs as at Stroud; secession from an established group as in the case of the community which eventually settled at Leicester; wholesale transfer from abroad with the arrival of the Ghent Dominicans at Harrow, and separation from a foreign mother house as in the case of the Portobello Road sisters in London.

The successful development of religious communities is dependent upon a variety of factors. In the first place, the founder must have a clear vision, which she is able to communicate to others and lead them towards. No community can be canonically established without ecclesiastical approval, and establishing good working relations with the clergy, though not necessarily the bishop in the first instance, is essential if formal recognition is to be granted. Some form of apostolate, which is compatible with the founder's vision and the capabilities of the members, has to be developed and sustained. The community has to be financially viable, whether revenue comes from the pooled resources of the membership, remuneration for the apostolic or other work undertaken, or from benefactors who are willing to support them. Finally, the future of a community is only secure if it attracts new members, amongst whom there must be some with the requisite spiritual and human qualities to assume leadership when the time comes. Each of the four new Dominican sisterhoods would develop its own characteristics and manner of living the Dominican life, while endeavouring to adhere to the spirit of the Order, but they would not all meet with the same measure of success.

Once they were established at Clifton, the sisters of Mother Margaret's congregation recorded their daily lives in the most minute detail in voluminous annals and other writings, both at the mother house and the branch convents. By contrast, sources for the early years of the other four groups of Dominican women are sparse. The Stroud congregation kept no formal annals until 1901; Harrow and its branch houses seem never to have kept any and Leicester only from 1892. This makes piecing together and filling out the history of these four groups a more difficult task, especially for the earlier periods. This chapter traces their history from the foundation until significant events for each early in the twentieth century: the golden jubilee and resignation of the second Superior General at Stroud in 1907; the move of the Leicester community to Dane Hills in 1906; the death of Mother Catherine Philip Bathurst at Harrow, also in 1907; and the separation of the Portobello Road house from the French parent congregation in 1910.

The Congregation of St Rose of Lima, Stroud

Stroud in Gloucestershire began as a small market town at the beginning of the fourteenth century but it soon developed as a manufacturing centre where cloth was produced from Cotswold wool. By the mid eighteenth century it had become one of the early centres of industrialization, its abundant water courses being harnessed to power the mills, while the development of the Stroudwater canal increased its importance as a centre of commerce. Since its population had been swelled by a sizeable Huguenot contingent in the seventeenth century, and it had also been one of the first towns to hear the preaching of Charles Wesley, Stroud might not have seemed a likely cradle for a Dominican congregation. However, two local converts were responsible for building a strong Catholic presence in the area.

The first of these was William Leigh, whose home, Woodchester Park, was a few miles from Stroud. In 1846 he invited the Passionist missionary, Blessed Dominic Barberi, to make a foundation in the vicinity. The community lived temporarily at Nailsworth while a monastery was built for them with plans by the architect Charles Hansom. Five years later, and only a year after the consecration of the church, the Passionists withdrew from Woodchester and were replaced by the Dominican friars. From 1850 until 1966 Woodchester Priory would serve as the noviciate for the English Province of the Order of Preachers and provide religious formation not only for hundreds of friars but for a number of influential lay Catholics, many of them converts.

Emily Sandys, the second of these converts, was the daughter of a colonel and the widow of an Anglican clergyman who had been killed in a train crash on the Great Western line. When Mrs Sandys, assisted by her maid Jane Daniels, who was a Dominican tertiary, opened a school in Albert Buildings on the London Road in Stroud in 1855, it immediately became a centre for Sunday Mass served by the friars from Woodchester.[3] Within a year Jane Daniels had died and her place in the household was taken by Elizabeth Corbett, whose mother ran a grocer's shop at Horsley. A third woman by the name of Hazelwood, about whom little else is known, joined the group soon after.

But the woman who would eventually emerge as the leader of the group was only the fourth to join. Elizabeth Matthews was born in 1815 at nearby Avening, the eldest daughter of a wool stapler and mill owner. In old age she still retained vivid memories of her early education in a dame school and at fourteen years of age she was to have been sent away to boarding school to complete her studies. By this time Elizabeth's mother was widowed and had allowed her brother to administer her savings, which were squandered by him in bad investments and gambling. This reversal of fortune brought an end to the project of further schooling and some time towards the end of the 1840s Elizabeth went to live with the family of a Stroud jeweller, Edwin Bucknall.

Elizabeth's religious affiliation at this time was with the Baptists, while the Bucknalls adhered to the tenets of Swedenborg's Church of the New Jerusalem. It is said that before her conversion Elizabeth's entire knowledge of Catholicism was gained from reading the Waverly novels aloud to Mr Bucknall, though we also know that the family kept up with religious debate and read some of the Oxford tracts. Edwin Bucknall also showed a reverence towards the Passionists of Woodchester and Elizabeth would long remember her first nervous glimpse of a Catholic priest when one of them stopped in the shop while engaged on a sick call. Three of

Bucknall's sons, including the youngest, Benjamin, who would become the architect of the new Woodchester mansion and St Rose's Convent, were received into the Catholic Church soon after and may well have influenced Elizabeth in this direction.[4] She was received into the Catholic Church by the Passionist Father Honorius Mazzini and was a convert of seven years' standing when she went to live in the house on the London Road.

At some point, probably in 1856, the date is not certain, Elizabeth had met Emily Sandys and offered to work for her. It was on the advice of Father Bernard Morewood, a Dominican from Woodchester, that the four women now residing in the house on London Road began living a simple communal life in the summer of 1857. Elizabeth Matthews had already been clothed as a Dominican tertiary under the name Teresa in February that year and Emily Sandys, Elizabeth Corbett and Miss Hazelwood were received into the Third Order on 8 December, becoming Sisters M. Catherine, M. Rose and M. Dominica respectively. The community's early years were marked with uncertainty, as it lacked the kind of dynamic leadership which Mother Margaret Hallahan's Dominicans enjoyed, and there was divergence of opinion as to the manner of living the Dominican life. The traditional version is that Emily Sandys provided the financial backing for the foundation but that she then retired from the scene, handing the work over to Mother M. Teresa Matthews. An examination of the archival material shows that the reality was not so straightforward. It seems certain that Mrs Sandys would have preferred the group to continue living together by mutual consent, with a minimum of structures; whereas Elizabeth Matthews was more attracted to a fully conventual style of life. There are several early accounts, the oldest of them begun by Sister M. Rose Corbett, but the sequence of events and dates do not always coincide.

In May 1858 Emma Langston joined the community. She had the distinction of having been superior of the first community of Anglican religious, the Park Village Sisterhood, founded some ten years previously in London. This community had been merged with the Society of the Holy Trinity in Devonport, ruled over by the redoubtable abbess Lydia Priscilla Sellon. Perhaps Father Bernard Morewood hoped to find a suitable and experienced superior in Sister Vincent Baptist, as she was called at Stroud; there is certainly evidence that she was a capable woman of considerable human warmth. Unfortunately, within a few months her health had broken down and she withdrew from the community.[5]

As early as September 1857, after the opening of the new church at Stoke-on-Trent, a meeting had been held between Bernard Morewood, the Dominican Provincial Thomas Nickolds and bishops Clifford of Clifton and Ullathorne of Birmingham, to discuss the question of affiliating the community at Stroud with Mother Margaret's congregation, then in the process of transferring its mother house from Clifton to Stone. It was already clear that there were differing opinions within the Stroud community as to how conventual its lifestyle should be and perhaps because of this tension no agreement was reached regarding a union with Mother Margaret's sisters. The records of Mother Margaret's council at Clifton show that she was asked to receive the women at Stroud as postulants and that:

> In the event of their profession any dowry brought by them should be applied to the foundation of a convent at Stroud, but that we could not promise that those individual sisters should be the ones selected for that convent. In answer to this proposal Fr Bernard [said] that the postulants do not wish to join the community at Stone, having imbibed a prejudice against it and thus the proposal was rejected contrary to the judgment of both bishops present.[6]

This decision may have been at the root of some bad feeling between the friars of the Province and Mother Margaret's sisters, as ten years later the annalist at Stone refers to the situation again. Father Dominic Aylward, in conversation with Mother Margaret while visiting St Marychurch, clearly blamed her for refusing to accept the women from Stroud, and claimed the foundation had been nothing to do with him but had been encouraged by Father Bernard Morewood against his will.[7] Clearly, the Provincial was on the defensive as his 'having nothing to do with' had certainly involved preaching at the clothing ceremony of Emily Sandys and her companions when he was sub-prior of Woodchester and continuing to support the Stroud sisters as we shall see!

The year 1859 brought several changes: Bernard Morewood ended his connection with the community and within four years had left the Order and the Church[8] and was replaced as director of the community by Father Dominic Aylward. At the same time, Emily Sandys began suffering financial difficulties, though after settling her outstanding liabilities she was still able to provide dowries for Sisters M. Rose Corbett and M. Teresa Matthews. Mention is made of unspecified 'distressing circumstances and difficulties' which confirmed her resolution to leave the community, and she retired to France where she died at Pau in 1878.[9]

However, it was not Sister M. Teresa Matthews who was appointed superior by Aylward after Emily Sandys' departure, but Sister M. Austin Kenny, who had entered the community in June 1857. In fact Sister M. Teresa, feeling called to a more regular mode of Dominican life, had applied to enter the Second Order nuns, though she was not accepted. Soon after this, the sisters began wearing the full Dominican habit permanently, and to recite the Office of Our Lady in Latin. A small convent, large enough for eight sisters, and with a walled garden, was built for them next to the church on Beeches Green. They received both regular visits from Bishop Clifford and weekly conferences from the friars at Woodchester. Sister M. Austin Kenny's health also gave way and she too was obliged to leave Stroud in June 1860, the Bishop appointing Sister M. Teresa Matthews vicaress. Two years later he confirmed her in office as prioress though it was not until September 1865 that the community numbered six perpetually professed members and she was duly elected to office.

Under Mother M. Teresa Matthews' forty-year tenure of leadership, the Stroud congregation developed on lines not unlike those of Stone. The conventual buildings were erected over a protracted period, in a rather vernacular style, but they were followed in 1887 by the laying of the foundation stone for a chapel, later enriched with finely carved and canopied choir stalls and stained glass, which was decidedly gothic. The Divine Office had been introduced, initially against the will of the bishop, who perhaps thought it too great a burden for women engaged in the active apostolate, on Trinity Sunday 1871. Great pains were taken to ensure that it was rendered with dignity and due attention to both chant and ceremonial. A manuscript constitution adapted from that of the Dominican nuns of the Second Order was followed, but as branch houses were established, these were no longer appropriate for what had become a congregation with central government.[10] Mother M. Teresa worked on drawing up constitutions proper to the congregation and travelled to Rome in 1886 with a view to having them approved. Although the congregation received the initial decree of recognition in 1889, it was not until after considerable revision that the constitutions were finally approved in 1896, or until 1919 that the congregation was officially aggregated to the Dominican Order.

The current archival collections of the English Dominican Congregation hold very little of Mother M. Teresa Matthew's correspondence and almost no personal papers. Apart from a solitary letter asking financial advice, the archives of the Diocese of Clifton retain no trace of the 'vigorous woman' Ullathorne described in a letter to Bishop Butt of Southwark.[11] This makes it difficult to gain much insight into her character. Photographs taken in later life show a serene face beneath the heavily starched coif with a strong hint of both determination and humour. This latter characteristic was clearly passed on to Mother M. Teresa Matthews' community and acknowledged by others. The noviciate and congregational annals note many a practical joke – including sham Christmas hampers – games and elaborate entertainments got up by the sisters. There might have been more starch at Stroud than at Stone but there may well have been more fun!

There was also a close connection with the brethren at Woodchester and for generations of novices the annual croquet games on the feast of St Rose forged bonds which would last, and perhaps give some credence to the oral testimony that the brethren preferred Stroud to Stone. The sisters themselves profited from the formation the friars were able to give them through frequent conferences and retreats. This affection for the Stroud community is emphasized in a letter to Mother M. Teresa Matthews from two friars studying in Louvain:

> We should not be what we are if we could forget, or even seem to forget, the affection and kindness of our Sisters at Stroud. We have need of all our pleasant souvenirs ... and amongst the most pleasant and the most readily recalled are those which have their origin in you, dear Reverend Mother, and your Sisters.[12]

Bishop Burton of Clifton also enjoyed a very familiar relationship with the community at Stroud. The noviciate annals for 1904 begin with an entry in the bishop's own hand, written in a comical manner. On a postcard which he sent from Siena depicting the house of St Catherine he wrote how much he looked forward to spending time on his return with 'your joyful and laughter loving community'.[13] The great Dominican preacher, Vincent McNabb, wrote expressing not only his own feeling for the sisters at Stroud but those of his brethren in religion:

> Not I alone but all the Fathers of our English Province give a very intimate cell of the heart to the Sisters of St Rose. Our affection is the remembrance of kindness that has now become an heirloom and a tradition. In this matter of affection, none outstrips myself; and being unworthy – were I eligible – to be one of your community it is a joy to know that my sister is yours.[14]

Father Vincent may well have been biased given his own sister – also named Vincent – and later his cousin Sister M. Magdalen McNabb, were members of the Stroud congregation. He also refers to another feature of the congregation, the dogged, hard work the sisters have carried out over a half-century of existence.

The first work of the community was education, and the mission school founded by Emily Sandys was maintained, though the numbers continued to be quite small. In 1864 a fee-paying school, St Rose's Convent School, was opened in the brick house purchased by Mrs Sandys before her departure for France. The first teacher was Sister M. Vincent Nevin and although only two pupils arrived on the first day, the numbers soon grew and averaged fifteen to twenty boarders and a similar number of day students by the turn of the century. When the new convent was opened in 1887, St Rose's moved to the top floor, where it remained until a neighbouring property, The Green, was purchased from the Moreton-Ball family in 1921.

The sisters took education seriously, though they clearly did not share Mother Margaret Hallahan's aversion to state funding, as after the 1870 Education Act, the mission school came under government inspection, and sisters began to sit the exams for certification. In 1899 four sisters set out through torrential rain to sit scholarship examinations at Gloucester. A series of vivid cartoons records their sodden arrival at the examination halls where they were refreshed with a cup of tea and changed their shoes, before sitting papers in eleven subjects, including vocal music and freehand drawing. Though the outcome does not seem to be recorded, the final cartoon shows their 'professor' at Stroud who, 'not giving them much hope, left it all in Our Lady's hands'.[15]

At least one parlour boarder was also taken in and, like so many others, Delphine Bunbury, described as 'a little weak in the head', was not an easily managed member of the household. Her pension, paid and frequently augmented by the Carmelites of Darlington, where her sister was a nun, was certainly a boon to the community over a period of thirty years. To finance the new convent, the able-bodied members spent every spare hour making sailor suits and other articles of clothing for an early mail order company, Holloway Brothers. They also took private orders for lace and fancy work. Little surprise that a community photograph of 1871 shows the superior seated at an embroidery frame and Sister M. Agnes Corcoran at a sewing machine whilst others ply needles in various ways. Even the sick played their part, the consumptive Sister M. Imelda Mayo spent several hours a day during the last eight years

Fig. 6 The scholarship examinations at Gloucester; 'She gave them a cup of tea and made them take off their shoes.'

Fig. 7 The scholarship examinations at Gloucester; 'It was freehand copy, they were allowed to measure with the eye.'

of her life propped up in bed penning begging letters to raise money for the new convent. When the money for construction ran short, the non-Catholic foreman, Samuel Cox, would pay the workmen from his own pocket until the cash flow was restored.

Visiting the sick and poor in the town and surrounding district was a prominent part of the sisters' apostolate in the early years. On their visits, the sisters were horrified to see the treatment meted out by childminders to the infants of mothers working in the cloth and stick factories of Stroud. They determined to set up a day nursery, the babies being kept in makeshift cradles made from orange crates which Sisters M. Joseph Barry and M. Clare Whittingham had begged off a local greengrocer. This venture lasted about ten years and was given up only for another urgent work, that of providing shelter and training for homeless girls. Many of these were the daughters of unmarried mothers who worked in service, or were inmates of institutions, and could not keep their children with them. St Mary's School, as it came to be called, numbered up to twenty girls who were educated in the mission school, some becoming pupil teachers, and were also given instruction – and plenty of practical experience – in the household arts that would enable them to earn a living when they left the sisters' care. Many of the girls were received gratis and the archives contain a collection of letters from parents and guardians acknowledging the care and generosity of the sisters.

Though members of the Order of Preachers, the sisters' participation in the essential ministry of the Order had to be carried out in an informal manner. They accepted this role without demur as the annals of the Stroud noviciate demonstrate:

> Sister M. Wilfrid holds a levée of converts on Wednesdays. Tonight, some time after the neophytes had assembled, a girl came to the door to ask when the instruction began, as she had been waiting ever so long for the church to be lit up. She was evidently unaware that St Paul does not permit women to preach in church.[16]

Even giving doctrinal instruction was considered inappropriate by some of the clergy. In 1919, a report from the prioress at Stroud states that the parish priest objected to the sisters instructing converts, which she considered one of their main duties, and forbade them to do it. They still continued their work with the Rosary Guild for older girls, and there was doubtless an element of religious instruction involved in this work.

In 1866[17] the Dominican friars in London called upon Mother M. Teresa to send a community to assist them in the mission of Kentish Town. Sister M. Rose Corbett headed this foundation which was soon established as an autonomous house and would eventually move to Leicester. It was not until 1879 that another branch house was opened, this time at Newcastle-upon-Tyne where the sisters were invited by Bishop Chadwick to undertake the direction of the Wingate Trust Hospital. This charity was financed by an endowment left by a wealthy Dominican tertiary, Elizabeth Wingate, who died in 1871. She endowed the hospital for the maintenance of ten invalids, 'poor females of good character' residing in any of six Newcastle parishes, including St Dominic's. Apart from physical care, they were to be afforded the consolations of religion and Mrs Wingate had expressed her hope that Dominican Sisters would take charge.[18] A small group under Sister Rose Columba Hawkins arrived at Regent Terrace to begin the work and soon established a small private school as well.

After a number of years the community moved to larger premises on Shieldfield Green where there was more room for the work to expand. Sister M. Raphael Smith, who was appointed to Newcastle soon after her profession in 1900, expressed poignantly the contrast many sisters coming from Stroud must have felt confronted with:

> The small house in a back street, with its very prosaic surroundings of rows of small houses and noisy yards and sheds instead of the peace and quiet of the cloisters of St Rose's and the beauty of the surrounding Gloucestershire hills.[19]

In a city such as Newcastle, where so many relied on casual labour at the docks for a living and where difficult working conditions often provoked industrial unrest, the sisters had ample occasion to give practical assistance to the poor. In 1900 the houses on their side of Shieldfield Green were to be acquired by compulsory purchase for the Northern Railway and through the efforts of Father Placid Conway, prior of the Newcastle brethren, three adjoining houses on the opposite side of the Green were acquired as compensation. A fourth house, at the end of the terrace which they were anxious to acquire, was let to a wholesale butcher who took every opportunity when encountering the sisters to make it clear he did not want nuns for neighbours. At Christmas the following year there was great poverty owing to a dockers' strike and the prioress, Sister M. Bernard Dewe, decided to provide fifty small roasting joints for the poorest families to be given out by the sisters involved in parish visiting. In a stroke of brilliance and diplomacy, despite misgivings, she decided to order them from Mr Potts, their grumpy neighbour.

> She, who was of a very timid and retiring disposition, next morning, in company with a Sister, 'bearded the lion in his den' ... asking if he could let us have the meat at wholesale price, adding that she felt sure he would do whatever he could to oblige, etc. She looked so fragile and unassuming and he so fierce and loud that the contrast was ludicrous. His manner was surprising, though he still spoke in a violent tone, 'Madam, I feel greatly honoured by your visit ... but you must allow me to share your good will towards the poor.'[20]

On Christmas Eve, to the dismay of the community, one hundred roasting joints were delivered to the convent at no charge. Mr Potts became both benefactor and protector of St Catherine's Convent and the Christmas bounty of a hundred joints was kept up until his death. That was not all; he also decided to vacate the house in Shieldfield Green so that the sisters could acquire it to expand the school. Perhaps because of this close relationship with the people of the north east it proved a rich source of vocations to the Stroud congregation, providing more than a quarter of the postulants entering before the amalgamation in 1929.

When the exiled French Franciscan friars left the former convent of the Stone Dominicans in Clifton to move to Clevedon in 1884, Bishop Clifford invited Mother M. Teresa Matthews to make a foundation at St Catherine's Convent, Park Place. The sisters established a private school and took on the direction of the mission schools, at that time housed in the crypt of the pro-cathedral. But by December 1898 it had been decided to withdraw from Clifton. The crypt schools were insalubrious and needed replacing, and the steep terrain meant the convent site was the only possible location for new buildings. There was also a shortage of teaching sisters since the opening of new convents at Erdington and Cheadle.

St Agnes' Convent was opened at Erdington, on the outskirts of Birmingham, on 31 July 1890. Sister Agnes Catherine Fairland and six companions took possession of The Limes in Chester Road, accompanied by the Mother General and Sister Agnes Teresa Mayo, who remained until they had settled in. Once again, the usual pattern of teaching in the mission school and establishing a fee-paying school was followed. Within a week of their arrival, the sisters had begun visiting the Workhouse Infirmary, and during the Easter vacation of 1895, they exercised their apostolic zeal in 'visiting almost all the cottages' to ensure the residents had made their Easter duties.[21] The same year, a move was made to The Hollies in Bell (later Orphanage) Lane which, having previously served as a girls' school, was more spacious and better suited to their needs. Numbers in the school grew gradually and a trip to Castle

Bromwich to collect ferns perhaps indicates that botany was on the syllabus,[22] and in 1896 a calisthenics instructor was engaged. The community annals also report that very soon afterwards there was an outbreak of scarlet fever which saw five pupils admitted to the fever hospital.

There were visits for the sisters as well, for the annals note a visit to Lichfield by Sisters M. Wilfrid Hibgame and M. Cecilia Chalk, who visited the cathedral and the small Catholic church which 'conveys such a sad contrast in wealth and beauty'.[23] Until the 1920s, the church at Erdington was served by the refugee German Benedictine monks from Beuron, who had come to Britain as a consequence of Bismark's persecution of the Church. The Dominican Sisters profited from conferences and retreats from the monks, including those of the erudite Englishman, Dom Bede Camm, who later became Abbot of Downside.

The convent at Cheadle in Staffordshire was established in 1898 adjacent to Augustus Pugin's masterpiece, the Church of St Giles. In this small town the sisters became a familiar part of the wider community. On Christmas Eve 1904, while they were busily engaged decorating the church for the festival, they were alerted that the printing works next to the convent had gone up in flames. It seemed certain the convent, sharing a party wall, would take fire, for despite the arrival of fire engines from the town and as far away as Longton, there was insufficient water for the pumps. Father Walter Morris, the mission priest, worked in tandem with the Anglican vicar, Rev. Edward Carlos, emptying the convent of furniture and valuables. In an ecumenical gesture which must have been rare for its day, the vicar offered the sisters the use of his rectory should the need arise. Fortunately the fire changed direction, though the smouldering embers had to be watched all night. Once the danger was over and the furniture restored to its rightful place, the sisters simply returned to their work in the church, much to the surprise of the congregation which arrived for midnight Mass. When Sisters M. Rose Kavanagh and M. Fidelis Overton died at Cheadle within a day of one another in August 1906, as many non-Catholics as Catholics attended the double funeral.[24]

On account of her age – she was in her eighty-sixth year – Mother M. Teresa Matthews resigned as Superior General in 1901 and was succeeded in office by Mother Rose Imelda Harrold. Born at Frome in Somerset in 1842, Mary Harrold was a convert and lived for some time as a lady boarder at St Rose's while teaching music in the Convent School. She was already forty-eight when she entered the noviciate – for the second time, an earlier attempt had ended in a complete breakdown in health. Mother Rose Imelda was a very gifted woman with an excellent command of languages and a fine musician. Sir Edward Elgar sent her all his scripts at his sister, Sister M. Reginald's, behest. Her period of office was dogged by ill health, but despite a heart condition and chronic bronchial problems she kept up a round of constant visitations and business trips consolidating the work of the congregation.

In its first fifty years of existence, the Stroud congregation welcomed over 150 postulants, about half of whom made profession and remained until death. Many of these were gifted and strong-minded women. One who deserves mention is Sister M. Wilfrid Hibgame, who was born in Norwich in 1849, the daughter of a colonel. In her twenties she had been a founding member of the Anglican community of St Laurence which later moved to Belper in Derbyshire. Despite having an excellent grasp of French, German, Italian, Latin and Greek, she set herself to running a refuge for destitute girls and undertaking relief work and begging tours in Walsall and Scarborough and followed a course in nursing at the Liverpool Workhouse Infirmary. Her convert brothers influenced her to enter the Catholic Church and in 1885 she came to Stroud as a postulant. Sister M. Wilfrid was equally at home discussing the Greek text of the prologue of St John's gospel or debating with a free-thinker whose house, filled with a whole library of anti-Catholic literature, she had stumbled across by mistake. She contributed articles to a number of Catholic magazines, held several important offices in the community, including that of novice mistress, but never lost her especial love of winkling out Catholics in the lodging houses and workhouse and giving them instruction.[25]

The sisters lived their Dominican life with enthusiasm despite a heavy workload. At Newcastle in particular, even with twelve choir nuns and six lay sisters in the community, night nursing and illness took its toll. Maintaining the choral office posed difficulties even at the mother house where there were almost twenty choir nuns. It was noted in the jubilee year that:

> For the past half year or so, owing to the fact that there are so few Sisters who are able to sing or take the Offices in choir, our choir has lost much of the reputation for excellence which it formerly held. For the same reason I have frequently been obliged to dispense with reading in the refectory at meal times.[26]

On 21 August 1904 Mother M. Teresa Matthews fell in her room fracturing her thigh and remained more or less bedridden until her death on 2 January the following year. Despite this loss, the community worked on preparing for the golden jubilee of its foundation. A fine stone altar and reredos worked by Walls of Cheltenham was installed and finely carved canopies were added to the choir stalls to mark the occasion. Neither were the poor forgotten in the midst of the celebrations, a dole of fifty loaves being provided for them.

The exertions of the jubilee also took a toll on Mother Rose Imelda who suffered a severe heart attack and resigned from office in February. In common with Stone, the congregation was by now firmly established and benefited from confident leadership. By contrast, it does not seem to have acquired the degree of stiffness and formality increasingly evident at Stone as the new century progressed. Certainly, there were difficulties and hard work, but as Bishop Burton had observed, the sisters knew how to have fun.

The Domincans of Our Lady Help of Christians, Leicester

During the early 1920s, with the assistance of Bishop Thomas Dunn of Nottingham, the Leicester Dominicans were endeavouring to establish themselves as a canonically recognized congregation. As part of the process an account of the origins of the community was prepared to accompany the Latin text of the constitutions being forwarded to Rome for approval.[27] The document states 'The new congregation was presided over by Mother M. Elizabeth Wheeler, who is rightly considered its foundress.'[28] Despite the intended destination of this account, its opening contents could hardly be described as factual. Though a letter exists in the archives of the Diocese of Nottingham stating that Bishop Edward Bagshawe had approved the 'Rule and Constitutions of the Dominican Tertiary Sisters'[29] it is not clear what text is referred to. Neither was there a 'new congregation' but a simple community of the Third Order Regular, probably still following the rule adapted from that of the Second Order nuns in use at the time of their separation from the Stroud Dominicans.

Neither is there any evidence to support the statement that Sister M. Elizabeth Wheeler was the founder of the community. Although she had entered at Stroud in 1858, she had not been part of the first community during its time in London, nor does the brief notice of her life contained in the Leicester necrology make any mention of her being prioress. Sister M. Elizabeth had certainly filled the offices of sub-prioress, novice mistress and local superior of the house at Washington, County Durham.[30] What the account is probably at pains to conceal is that the first superior of the community eventually left the religious life. If the documents of the Second Vatican Council reserve the title of founder to the one who is *pater et legifer* (that is, father and lawgiver, or by association, we would hope, *mater*) then it is clear the Dominicans of Our Lady Help of Christians had no founder at all, and this fundamental lack does much to explain their somewhat troubled and uncertain history.[31]

On 28 February 1866 a group of six sisters left St Rose's Convent Stroud for London, answering the invitation of the friars of the Order who had recently established themselves at Haverstock Hill. The group was led by Emily Sandys' first companion, Mother M. Rose Corbett, and the group settled into a house in Fortress Terrace, Kentish Town. Three years later the London house became an autonomous community, though no documentation of the explicit reasons for its separation from the Stroud congregation can be found in the archives of the Archdiocese of Westminster or the Diocese of Clifton. Nor do the early accounts of the development of the Stroud community shed light on the matter. The account alluded to above simply states that 'it was found convenient' to separate the London filiation. The fact that there were already houses of several religious congregations of women depending on mother houses outside the Archdiocese makes it unlikely that Cardinal Manning would have insisted on such a separation. What is clear is that the new community had to contend with destabilizing factors from the moment it achieved independence.

Sister M. Vincent Nevin had already been ill for some time before the foundation was made, but had been anxious to be part of the group since she was a certificated teacher. Her situation deteriorated rapidly and she returned to Stroud and died there on 27 April 1866. At about the same time Sister M. Columba Lound left the community, reducing the number of choir nuns to two. As a consequence Sister M. Bernard Wathen, who had been received at Stroud as a lay sister, was given the black veil and white scapular of a choir nun. Despite this change of status she was never happy after the separation and begged to be allowed to return to Stroud; already suffering from tuberculosis she died at St Rose's in September 1872.

By this time, the community had moved from Kentish Town to Maitland Park Villas, closer to the new Dominican Priory at Haverstock Hill, and were engaged in teaching in the schools and instructing adults and converts. Here they were joined by Sister Marie-Louis Dubois, a member of the Dominicans of Notre-Dame de Grâce, who had come as a refugee to London at the time of the Paris Commune. The association with their Dominican brethren came to an end in the summer of 1871 when the sisters moved to Kensal New Town to work in the mission staffed by Manning's Oblates of St Charles. Once again, no reason for the move can be found in the sources. At the time this stretch of the Regent's Canal abounded in steam laundries and a crêche was opened to care for the children of the washerwomen. Two postulants with teaching qualifications were received soon after the move and this enabled the sisters to take on the direction of the mission schools which had been placed under the control of the London School Board.

The sojourn at Kensal New Town would also prove transitory. Sister Marie-Louis Dubois died, the teachers did not persevere in the community, work in the schools had to be relinquished. In September 1875 a move was made to Leicester, in the Diocese of Nottingham; one account states that Cardinal Manning had asked the sisters to leave the Archdiocese. Teaching would again form the main part of the apostolate, though this must initially have been in schools which had not been placed under the local education authorities. As well as teaching at Holy Cross, the Dominican friars' mission, and St Patrick's, the sisters also opened a small private school, and conducted night classes in the house on Humberstone Road. The private school soon had an attendance of twenty pupils while between fifty and sixty came to the convent in the evenings. Later, there was a move to Millstone Road and when the convent was housed in larger premises on the London Road, the private school expanded and included small boys as well as girls. The 1891 census also lists several pupil teachers in residence. Just before the turn of the century, lack of space at the convent led the community to rent a house in Fosse Road where the private school continued until 1904, two or three sisters living there with the boarders.

On 4 July 1876 Sister M. Stanislaus McElhatton and three others took up residence in Castle Street, Hinckley, also a mission staffed by the Dominican friars, and began teaching in the school there. Each weekend they returned to Leicester and it is noted on occasions in the school log book that the school register was not taken on a Monday morning, as the sisters had missed the train. From all accounts it was a difficult school. The previous staff had not had the confidence of parents and it took some time for the teachers, Sisters M. Vincent Rosbotham and M. Dominic Johnson, to win them round. The effectiveness of the school was also undermined by the fact that many of the pupils obtained labour certificates to work in the factories and stayed away from school. There were frequent staff changes and mention of the house being a drain on the finances of the community, who eventually gave up the school in 1894.[32]

From the time of their arrival in Leicester the friars, in particular Father Cyril Bunce, provided spiritual support for the community but it is almost certain that things did not progress smoothly. During the first fifteen years in Leicester the community moved at least four times.[33] Stability, both in terms of membership and financial security, dogged the community, as did lack of space to carry out the works which might bring in sufficient income to support it. Lady boarders were taken in as a means of revenue but the income from one of these, the widow of a Russian diplomat who had made her home in the convent, was lost when she was received as a novice in 1880, at almost seventy years of age, under the name Sister M. Magdalen Lientoff. On the other hand, there are instances recorded of what must have seemed quite substantial sums at the time being offered to the community if they would take in parlour boarders until death.[34] It is possible that later on the community attempted to profit from the fashion for cycling as the term 'bicycle tickets' appears as a recurrent item in the account book under receipts![35]

In 1885 Bishop Bagshawe conducted a canonical visitation of the community and removed Mother M. Rose Corbett from the office of prioress, appointing Mother M. Vincent Rosbotham in her stead. This would indicate that there were serious shortcomings in Mother M. Rose's style of government. Although both oral tradition and some documentation retained in the archives give the impression Rose Corbett left the community soon after its arrival in Leicester, this is not the case. Both the Council Book and the annals continue to record her presence until August 1895 and supply ample evidence that she had a disruptive effect on the community, whether she resided in Leicester, or in the north east after the first houses were founded in the Diocese of Middlesbrough in the 1890s.

Although she continued to be a member of the Council, the minutes note several instances when Mother M. Rose refused to attend meetings[36] and others where she raised strong objections to the proposals made. In fact, at almost every meeting of the Council at which we know she was present, a single black ball is recorded for each vote; it is tempting to believe it was cast by Mother M. Rose. It is not surprising that the negative atmosphere and the insubordination displayed unsettled the community and perhaps intimidated some of its members. Annals and council minutes also record a procession of women who were accepted as postulants at Leicester during this time, reporting the unsuitability of many. The attrition rate, for recently professed religious as well as novices, was certainly high and the general malaise in the community cannot have been conducive to the retention of candidates.

There was further discord amongst the Council at Leicester when Bishop Bagshawe tried to make amendments to the constitutions under which the sisters had been living since before their arrival in the Diocese of Nottingham. One of the more contentious issues in the eyes of the councillors was his insistence on introducing a three-year period of temporary vows. This is hardly surprising, given the rate of attrition amongst candidates, already noted. The practice at Stroud, unlike Stone, had been to make temporary vows for three years, so making perpetual profession at the end of the canonical noviciate must have become the practice in London or Leicester. However, this and other changes were vehemently opposed, particularly by Mother M. Rose, who claimed she was unprepared to accept any changes made by the Bishop. Another member of the council, Sister M. Bridget Perkins, who would transfer two years later to the Oakford Dominican Sisters in South Africa, actually stated she had never read the second half of the constitutions! Eventually, despite registering their protests, all agreed to accept the changes.[37]

One way of coping with Mother M. Rose's irascible character was to keep her at a distance. During 1890 she spent a prolonged period on the quest for funds in Ireland and the Council minutes record that she forwarded over £200 that September. An invitation was accepted to teach at Washington, in County Durham, in 1892 and a succession of houses, some of them of short duration, was founded in the north east: Bridlington (1894), Leyburn (1895), and Easingwold (March 1896) from where the commnuity soon moved to Redcar (August 1896). Although the first superior at Washington was Sister M. Elizabeth Wheeler, she was soon brought back to Leicester as novice mistress and Mother M. Rose was dispatched in her place. It seems that she resented her exile in the north where she found the life of inactivity 'injurious to her spiritual and physical welfare'.[38] In August 1895, without the sanction of her superiors, Mother M. Rose and her companion Sister M. Francis King, who had entered the community at Kensal New Town, visited Stroud where they petitioned to be allowed to transfer to the Congregation of St Rose of Lima. A concerned Mother M. Vincent called a meeting at Leyburn to determine how the journey had been financed, and to make certain demands on Mother M. Rose which, if they were not fulfilled, would result in an appeal being made to the ecclesiastical superiors to have her expelled from the community.[39]

The next mention of Mother M. Rose Corbett is found in records relating to the foundation made from Stone, at Crieff in Scotland in 1890, by Mother M. Ignatius Elwes. In a letter to the Bishop of St Andrews written in January 1896, Mother M. Ignatius mentions the imminent arrival of Mother M. Rose and Sister M. Francis.[40] Mother M. Ignatius alludes to letters she has received concerning them from the Prioress of Harrow and from the Dominican Father Bertrand Wilberforce, though she states that the two sisters came with letters of recommendation not from any Dominican authority, but from Mother Mary of the Nativity Owens, superior general of the Poor Sisters of Nazareth. After initial optimism: 'nothing could be nicer than their behaviour in every way'; the tone changes over the next three years to disappointment at Rose Corbett's 'overbearing and disagreeable manner'. [41] The community at Crieff did not survive the death of its founder in December 1899 and very little is known of Mother M. Rose Corbett's life afterwards, though a letter of Mother Rose Columba Hawkins of Stroud makes it clear that she made financial claims on the community there.

At the time of the 1911 census, both Mother M. Rose and Sister M. Francis King are listed as visitors at St Veronica's Retreat in Chiswick. In the 1880s, with the sanction of the Archbishop, Isabelle Smith had founded a community of Sisters of St Veronica who ran a refuge for alcohol-dependent women. This community did not survive long and early in the twentieth century the home had been taken over by the Poor Sisters of Nazareth, with whom we have already seen, Rose Corbett had connections. After her departure from Leicester, perhaps not surprisingly, Rose Corbett seems to have faded from the corporate memory of the community. By the time Sister M. Imelda Smith entered in 1917, although she had heard of Mother M. Rose, never having met her, she assumed that she had died years before. In fact, she did not die until 1923, in St Joseph's Hospice, Hackney under the care of the Irish Sisters of Charity and was buried in St Patrick's Cemetery, Leyton in the plot belonging to Stone's branch house at Bow.

There were also difficulties in the schools at Leicester, particularly at St Patrick's where Father William Hawkins had dismissed Sister M. Paul Doyle from her post as headmistress in June 1895, without notice or salary in lieu.[42] In October the two remaining sisters were withdrawn from the teaching staff of the Infants' School on account of the 'impossible nature of the treatment received' at Father Hawkins' hands. Sister M. Paul, in fact, had hardly been clothed as a novice when she had assumed the headship of St Patrick's. Nora Munro, who arrived as a postulant from Swinford, County Mayo, in December 1898, began teaching at Holy Cross School after Christmas that year, and continued to do so after being received into the noviciate as Sister M. Rose. The census returns also list women who were still novices as teachers in the schools in the north. This certainly adds further legitimacy to the Bishop's concerns about the religious formation of the young sisters. Sister M. Paul left the community within the next two years, while Sister M. Rose Munro had a long career as a gifted infant teacher, particularly in Bridlington.

No sooner had the decision been taken to withdraw from St Patrick's School, than the parish priest at Washington informed Mother M. Vincent Rosbothom that the services of the community there were no longer required. Tenders were being let at the time for the convent at Bridlington – all the bids were much higher than expected – and while it seems the original intention was to conduct a convalescent home, a school was opened instead with about twenty boarders. Difficulties in the schools at Leicester may have prompted the community to look to nursing as an alternative apostolate, though one account states that it was seeing the distress of the chronically ill during their home visiting which persuaded the sisters to undertake this work. Certainly, mention of prospective postulants with nursing rather than teaching qualifications come to the fore in the council minutes and annals from this time on. An approach was also made from the Poor Law Guardians in 1906, asking that the community take Catholic girls from their children's home at Countesthorpe. Although it was decided unanimously to apply for certification of the convent and to accept a dozen girls between the ages of three and twelve at a capitation grant of six shillings per week, nothing seems to have come of the plan.[43]

The financial situation of the community remained precarious. On 30 October 1901 Sister M. Teresa Bowey, who had returned from a decade working as part of the Oakford congregation in South Africa the previous year, together with Sister M. Agatha Phelan, set sail from Liverpool aboard the SS *Oceanic*. They were bound for the United States to solicit alms, armed with letters of recommendation from Bishop Brindle. They met with some success and the following year Sister M. Teresa returned, accompanied this time by Sister M. Antony Keegan. In 1904 a field at Dane Hills was purchased through the agency of Sir Thomas Wright, the community's solicitor. Here there was plenty of space to construct a nursing home and convent, and the foundation stone was laid on 24 August 1905. At the end of September the following year the sisters left London Road and moved into the house at Dane Hills which still lacked doors, windows and stairways! At considerable cost, it was furnished to receive the first patients. A huge debt remained and quests, both in England and abroad, garden fêtes, whist drives and other undertakings continued for many years in an effort to reduce the outstanding sum. At the same time, several sisters were sent for training at the Hospital of St John and St Elizabeth in London. The private school had been closed at the time of the move, though members of the community were now providing staff for Sacred Heart School.

After the departure of Father Cyril Bunce to London in 1885, there is only infrequent mention of the involvement of the Dominican brethren in the affairs of the convent, though they continued to provide chaplains, give conferences and preach retreats. In 1892 Father Sebastian Gates gave a course of drawing lessons to a number of sisters and teachers from the convent school. Five years later the Master of the Order, Father Andreas Frühwirth, visited the convent in Leicester and addressed the community. He promised to send Sister M. Imelda Heweson, a novice in retreat prior to her profession of vows, a biography of her patron.[44]

In the early years of the new century, the community was concentrating its efforts on establishing a viable apostolate at Dane Hills and consolidating the works in the north. However, it was not possible to find amongst its membership women with the qualities to provide effective leadership. Although Bishop Bagshawe had appointed Mother M. Vincent Rosbotham superior, his successor, Bishop Brindle, declared during a visitation in 1907 that neither she nor Sister M. Cecilia Collins should ever hold office or act as councillors in the future.[45] The constant hard work, the rounds of questing, the frequent changing of personnel, created tensions which the community's superiors could not always resolve and such tensions would continue to surface in the 1920s.

The Congregation of the Holy Rosary, Harrow

In terms of personal endowments, education and social connections Catherine Anne Bathurst possessed everything that might have proved useful in her future role as founder of a Dominican congregation. She was born at Wookey, Somerset, on 14 July 1825.[46] She was the youngest of the three daughters and six sons of General Sir James Bathurst KCB and Caroline Stuart, daughter of Earl Castle Stuart. Her father had served as *aide de camp* to the Duke of Wellington and the Wellingtons not only stood as godparents, but also provided their godchild with an income. Catherine's early education was received at home under governesses and she proved to be an intelligent and lively child. She was sent to be 'finished' at a school in York Place, London, where she remained for two years. Minnie Poole, later Mother M. Imelda of Stone was amongst her companions here and one of her music masters was Mendelsohn. Catherine possessed a fine voice and became an accomplished musician, particularly at the keyboard. Being a young woman with connections, she was presented at court at the age of nineteen, after which she set off on the grand tour of Europe.

During her early twenties Catherine Bathurst and her siblings kept abreast of the religious controversies then being debated within the Church of England. A certain interest in Catholicism was clearly not new in the family since an uncle, Henry Bathurst, had been Bishop of Norwich and one of the four parliamentary bishops who voted in favour of Catholic emancipation. On a visit to the reading room at the British Museum, Catherine read the anti-Catholic work *Father Clement: a Roman Catholic story* which had been published shortly before her birth and already run through several editions. Far from being convinced by the book's refutation of Roman dogma and accusations of casuistry and deceit, she was led to question the doctrinal integrity of the Established Church.

Three of Catherine's brothers were clergymen and this questioning was shared in particular by Stuart, who held the living of Kibworth Beauchamp in Leicestershire. He was received into the Catholic Church at Birmingham Oratory early in 1850 and a few months later Catherine followed him, being conditionally baptized at the Jesuit Church in Farm Street, Mayfair, by Father Brownbill. She made her first communion in Paris while staying there with the Duchess of Norfolk and her breakfast companions that day were Père Lacordaire and the Jesuit Gustave de Ravignan. While visiting her brother in Birmingham she was introduced to Newman, who was to remain her guide and friend until his death. More than eighty of Newman's letters to Catherine Bathurst are preserved in the archives at Stone and reveal her gradual development from highly strung, scrupulous young convert, into a confident religious superior. It is unfortunate that Catherine's side of the correspondence has not survived.

Already sure that she wished to be a religious, it would take

Catherine many years, and several false starts, before she determined her particular place in life; for she could not make up her mind as to which community would best suit her. In 1852 she joined a small community of Sisters of Charity of the Precious Blood founded at Greenwich by a fellow convert, Elizabeth Lockhart.[47] But she was also much attracted to the Sisters of Providence – the female branch of Antonio Rosmini's Institute of Charity – and even thought of founding a community on Oratorian lines. Newman surely thought her fanciful plans far outran her ability to bring things to fruition at this stage, for he advised her to keep her sights set on the Sisters of Providence:

> On the whole you cannot do better than keep to the Order of Charity [Rosminians]. You have a drawing to it; it presents great advantages ... as to your castle building about Edgbaston, Harborne, Sisters two by two, bishoprics and the like, my child, I have not your imagination.[48]

In the summer of 1853 she entered the Sisters of Providence at Loughborough but remained there little more than a year, returning to live as a visitor at Greenwich. In 1856 when Elizabeth Lockhart's community was affiliated to the Franciscans and moved to Bayswater, Catherine returned to Birmingham. With several other women, she took charge of the Oratory Poor Schools and orphanage and conducted them successfully for three years.

Through her brother, now mission priest at Stone, Catherine Bathurst learned of Mother Margaret Hallahan's community of Dominican Sisters. She entered as a postulant on 30 May 1861 and was clothed in the habit on 7 November the same year, receiving the name Sister Catherine Philip – Philip for St Philip Neri, founder of the Oratorians. In April 1862 the suicide of Catherine's surviving sister, Caroline, precipitated a complete breakdown and she returned once again to Birmingham. It was Newman who plied Catherine with comfort and reassurance regarding the eternal salvation of her sister and the veracity of her own vocation.

Once more in Birmingham, Catherine devoted her energies to teaching and visiting the poor of the Oratory mission, with several other women who lived in community with her. For a time one of these was Emily Bowles, a former member of the Society of the Holy Child Jesus and another, Lavinia Wilson, who was to be received at Stone as Sister Francis Joseph four years later. Lavinia Wilson had been a student, or perhaps a postulant, at the English Convent in Bruges and it may well have been through her that Catherine Bathurst first made connections with Belgium. Next she went to work with the Dominican friars at Kentish Town and it was here she made her profession as a secular Dominican Tertiary in the hands of Father Augustine Proctor on 30 April 1863. It is possible that Catherine would have been familiar with Mother Rose Corbett and the first sisters who arrived in London from Stroud. If so, this may have influenced her second trial of life in the Dominican Third Order regular, when Catherine and some of her companions went to Stroud in March 1866. Although one of the group, Elizabeth Field, remained at Stroud as Sister M. Veronica, the others did not feel at home.

Soon afterwards, during a visit to Belgium, the Dominican friars in Ghent persuaded Catherine and her friend Maria Dunford, whom she had known since her days at Kentish Town, to begin a foundation of Third Order Sisters in that city. The community was established in 1868 and two years later imposing conventual and school buildings were opened half-way between the villages of Melle and Merelbeke, just outside the city. Newman continued to write and was most helpful in advising Catherine of the practical steps to be taken in raising funds for the new building.[49] In fact, Newman even persuaded his friend James Hope-Scott to become one of the principal benefactors of the new community, and this despite his own conviction that Catherine could be of more help to the mission of the Church in her own country:

> I am sorry you cannot be in England, for England is your place and you are never so useful as when you have a number of young women, girls and boys attached to you, not by vows but by love.[50]

The convent school at Ghent attracted both local and English girls, many of the latter Protestants coming to be 'finished' on the Continent, but there was also a day school for working-class children and an orphanage. Within a few years there were twenty-five orphans being cared for, fifty girls in the boarding school and a similar number in the poor school at Merelbeke.

Arriving at exact numbers for the community at Ghent is not as easy, since the earliest registers of clothing and profession date from some time after the establishment of the convent at Harrow. The petition requesting the aggregation of the community to the Order of Preachers in 1872 is signed by eight women, only four of whom were still members of the community by 1880.[51] Though those who entered the community in Ghent were mainly English and Flemish, one was born in France, another in Australia and there is even mention of a Russian postulant, though the priest recommending her was not sure her Slavic temperament would be best suited for their community.[52] Only three Belgians would remain as members of the congregation after the community was withdrawn from Ghent in 1883, and one of these was subsequently dispensed from her vows. It is likely that others amongst the Flemish sisters may not have wished to move to England.

Relations with Bishop of Ghent, Henri-François Bracq, were not always easy. He seemed undecided as to what sort of community he wanted them to be, sometimes insisting they should be cloistered and at other times a simple association of women living in common. There were difficulties over chaplains and over the relationship of the community to the Order. On one occasion the Bishop even denounced Mother Catherine Philip to Cardinal Manning as 'a disobedient spirit'.[53] Although he had granted permission for the sisters to wear the Dominican habit inside the convent, the bishop constantly stressed that it should not be worn on the rare occasions when the sisters went out. On a more positive note, a visiting Dominican reported to Bishop Bracq that he was struck by the mathematical exactitude with which the community celebrated the liturgy, their spirit of prayer and their earnest endeavours to live a life of holiness. [54] There were also difficulties with the local education authorities, who were reluctant to allow Flemish-speaking English sisters to teach in the poor school. Mother Catherine Philip contrasted the obstructive attitude of the officials in Ghent with the encouragement given to foreigners in England![55]

In 1877 Mother Catherine Bathurst accepted the invitation of Cardinal Manning to open a house at Harrow, where he hoped the presence of the sisters would exercise a discreet Catholic influence on his Alma Mater. Despite the reservations of Bishop Bracq, the mother house was transferred there from Ghent and the Belgian house continued as a branch house. It was closed in 1883 and sold to the Franciscan Sisters of Combreen. Monsignor Arthur Jackman of St Edward's College Ware acted as agent in the purchase of a property at Harrow from a Mr Burns of Hammersmith for the sum of £2500. A few years later a neighbouring property, The Mount, was purchased and this served as the convent. Though the building was subsequently enlarged and a fine chapel was later erected, the convent retained a more domestic scale than most other Dominican mother houses in England. This homely physical environment was reinforced by Mother Catherine Philip having taken to heart Newman's conviction that personal attachment, rather than mere obedience, was at the basis of community life.[56] Before her death the founder welcomed over 100 postulants to Harrow, though almost two-thirds of these did not persevere in religious life. This is a much higher attrition rate than other Dominican communities in England but perhaps, given her own early uncertainty about her vocation, this reflects Catherine Bathurst's patience with the young and her willingness to let candidates who might not have been accepted elsewhere at least make a try.

Catherine Bathurst was a born teacher and her innate sensitivity and understanding of the young were recognized from her early days in Birmingham. She had obtained her teaching certificate at Liverpool in June 1857 and in the estimation of her early examiners she was unusually gifted and adapted for this work. Mother Catherine Philip continued to teach, whether school children or novices, until the week of her death. At Harrow the community established a school for girls and for many years taught in the mission school on the convent grounds. St Dominic's School was small, numbering only twenty-five resident students at the turn of the century, but the curriculum was decidedly academic. The ageing Newman expressed his reservations about this modern trend in one of his last letters:

> I cannot but be anxious about this tiptop education for girls. Of course, as you ever used to say, that high education excludes a number of evils which else abound, but I fear we may find ourselves out of the frying pan into the fire.[57]

In the 1890s Mother Catherine Philip managed to persuade Cardinal Manning of the necessity of allowing girls at St Dominic's to sit for the Oxford and Cambridge local examinations, and was successful in pressing for a specially adapted Scripture paper for Catholic candidates. Her efforts were crowned with success when the first two girls presented passed first and second respectively in England in Modern Languages and Latin.

A branch house was founded from Harrow, and a day High School opened, in 1881 at Quex Road, Kilburn. Some years later the sisters began teaching in the large mission schools connected with Sacred Heart church. This was not an easy task for the new headmistress, Sister M. Dominic Wilkes, as her predecessor, a lay woman who had several times handed in and then withdrawn her notice, was finally taken at her word by the school managers and dismissed. Before departing, this woman had destroyed the larger part of the school records and carefully instructed the older children in the incapacities and ignorance of women religious as teachers! Sister M. Dominic was a talented and imaginative teacher

Fig. 8 Some of the young ladies who enjoyed a 'tiptop' education at St Dominic's, Harrow.

with a playful spirit and was soon able to win over her pupils. The home conditions of many of the Kilburn children were deplorable and every morning before school, Sister M. Dominic would be busy in the tiny school kitchen preparing pea soup and bread to give many of them a nourishing start to their day. When the time for the annual first communion Mass approached, she would pass many late nights with another sister, making up outfits for the 80–100 communicants, some of whom had to be taken in and scrubbed and made presentable the evening before the great event. In fact, shopping in the sales and buying up remnants, whether for making clothing or costumes for plays, was a year-round practice, as was visiting the homes and giving practical relief.[58]

Neither were the poor forgotten at the second branch house, opened at Watford in 1882 to provide for the care of destitute children. Initially the convent was in Queens Road but soon larger premises were needed and a move was made to Percy Road. Here an ongoing programme of building, with designs and drawings made by Sister M. Vincent Dunford who had acquired these skills from her father, a master draftsman, were financed largely by begging quests. At first St Vincent's provided only for girls but later accommodation was provided for boys as well, and by 1907 the small community of sisters had received 518 girls and 245 boys, mainly from London, with about sixty in residence at any one time. The sisters also taught in a small iron school which was replaced by a brick structure adjacent to the mission church in 1888.[59] When the house at Watford was opened, Mother Catherine Philip delighted in driving a pony and cart out as far as Berkhamstead, Hemel Hempstead, Boxmoor, Little Gaddesdon, and King's Langley, instructing children and adults in all these places.

A third branch house was opened in 1886, initially at Southsea in Hampshire but soon afterwards moving to Shoreham in Sussex. A small boarding school for boys was conducted at Buckingham Terrace for four years, until larger premises were required. In 1890 the sisters were invited by the Servite friars in Bognor to take charge of the mission schools there. Since Bognor seemed to offer greater possibilities, the house and staffing of the school at Shoreham were handed over to the Dominican Sisters from West Grinstead. The community and the boys' school were installed in Belvedere House, a sizeable property, including a lodge and stables, on Upper Bognor Road, which was first rented and finally purchased in 1898. About forty to fifty boys attended St Dominic's School and the admissions register lists the schools, mainly the larger Catholic public schools, where the boys continued their education. Strangely enough three girls are also listed! The 1901 census shows boys born in the United Kingdom, India, Sri Lanka, Assam, France, Belgium, Switzerland and Italy, perhaps indicating that their fathers were in colonial, military or diplomatic service. Two sisters walked daily to the mission school down near the station. After some effort, and when a certificated sister could be provided to take charge, this school was placed under the School Board and the sisters continued to teach there and draw a salary until 1918.

Other short-lived branch houses were opened at Sale in Cheshire, where a small High School and mission school were maintained from 1891–7 and at Beccles in Suffolk, a mission administered by the Benedictine monks of Downside Abbey, from 1897–1905. The archives at Stone retain a contract drawn up between the Harrow congregation and the mission priest of Beccles, which outlines the reciprocal obligations and duties of the two parties:

St Michael's Lodge, Grange Road, Beccles, 27 August 1896

I: Conditions on the part of the nuns:
1 An order with some choir duty.

2 Must supply teachers in accordance with the demands of the Code and be able to earn grants sufficient to maintain the efficiency of the school.
3 The engagement of Pupil Teachers, and if necessary of lay head teachers, shall rest with the nuns, subject to the approval of the manager.
4 a) to instruct the women and children.
b) to visit – at the request of the priest.
c) to sweep and dust the sanctuary and dust the altars, keeping them always clean and tidy. To take charge of the vestments, candles, flowers, lamps etc.

II: Conditions on our part:
1 We will take all the receipts of the Elementary School, paying the nuns (and through them the Pupil Teachers) fixed salaries.
The salaries would be from £60–£70 and from £10–£15.
2 We will give the nuns £50 per annum for three years to begin from the time of entering upon the work.
3 The nuns may have the use of St Michael's Lodge which has been purchased for £1400, provided they pay interest upon £900, or repay that £900 (interest at 4%).
4 So far as it concerns us we shall have no objection to their opening a school for day or residential boarders.
Addendum: Any difference of opinion to be solved by the Bishop of the Diocese and the prior of Downside whose decision is to be final.[60]

The sisters took advantage of the leave given them to open a small private school to provide additional income, but there was difficulty in attracting boarders and insufficient day pupils to make the operation viable. Although the foundation was endowed by John Kenyon of Gillingham Hall it did not prosper and the decision was made to close the house.

Increasing age and infirmity caused Mother Catherine Philip to resign as Superior General in 1906. One of her first companions from Ghent, Mother M. Anne Claeys, was elected to succeed her in office and continued as Superior General until 1924. At the same time the offices of Superior General and local prioress of the convent at Harrow were separated and each of the local houses set up its own Council.[61] The transition of authority does not seem to have been entirely smooth. Perhaps the founder had held the reins of authority gently, yet strongly enough to discourage leadership qualities coming to the fore in the younger generation of sisters, or perhaps some confusion of authority developed between the general and local superiors living in a small community and working out new roles. The General Council deliberations for the following year carry admonitions to obedience and changes of local superiors between the houses. Another concern of the General Council at that time was, as everywhere else, that of raising money. Sister M. Hyacinth Dubrullé, one of the small number of Belgian sisters who had come to Harrow, was deputed chief quester for the orphanage at Watford. Although she was assigned to the community at Harrow, she was exhorted to visit Watford on a monthly basis so that she could state truthfully that she came from there![62]

The founder had little time for retirement, for she died just over a year later, on 14 December 1907. Sixteen priests and thirty-six of her sisters assisted at the requiem Mass and interment two days later. Newman's confidence in Catherine Bathurst had not been misplaced; uncertainty gave way over the years to wisdom, and the young woman so unsure of her vocation or her ability to live the religious life, established a congregation that was stable, close-knit and hard-working. The Harrow congregation would learn to live and develop without its beloved founder with increasing confidence and vigour.

The Congregation of St Vincent Ferrer, London

To appreciate the development of the London congregation it is necessary to understand something of the origins of the congregation from which it derived, that of the Dominicans of Notre-Dame de Grâce. In 1832 a nineteen-year-old Bretonne, Victoire-Thérèse Chupin, arrived in Paris and began working in the Patronage de la Sainte-Enfance in the rue du Bac, under the guidance of the Paris Foreign Mission Society. Despite her age, she showed an innate ability to assist and win the confidence of marginalized women living in the tenements and streets of Paris. Within four years her reputation was such that the metropolitan Prefect of Police appointed her superintendent of the women's section at the prison of Saint-Lazare. After the revolution of 1848, management of the prison was transferred to the Sisters of Marie-Joseph, but Victoire-Thérèse Chupin continued her work amongst newly released prisoners until, in 1854, she set up the Refuge Sainte-Anne in the rue de Vaugirard to receive, rehabilitate and protect ex-prisoners, prostitutes and young girls at risk.

With the exception of Mademoiselle Chupin and her first companion, most of the early members of this household who helped her in the work were secular Dominican tertiaries. Gradually, under the influence of the Dominican friars – and despite her own personal disinclination – the establishment transformed itself into a religious community.[63] During a visit to Rome in 1862 Victoire-Thérèse laid the question of the institute's future before Pope Pius IX and Père Jandel, Master of the Order. Both counselled the adoption of the religious life as a means of ensuring the future stability of her work. The Dominican habit was adopted in 1865 and the following year the founder, known in religion as Mère Vincent-Ferrier – though usually referred to as 'Bonne-Mère' – and twelve companions, pronounced their vows.[64] A move was made to Clichy, in the north of Paris and in 1882 to Châtillon-sous-Bagneux, just to the south of the capital. The community was not canonically erected as a congregation, however, until 1892 and Mère Chupin died four years later.

During the tumult of the Franco-Prussian War and Commune, the community abandoned Paris temporarily and several members sought refuge in England. In 1876 Mère Chupin agreed to make a foundation in the Sussex village of West Grinstead where her fellow Breton, Monsignor Jean-Marie Denis was in charge of the mission. Denis had already induced three religious congregations to make a foundation at West Grinstead in less than a decade, but had driven all of them away by his constant interference in their internal affairs. Because the community in Paris was small and lacked resources, it is difficult to guess the real motives for accepting the foundation other than her expressed desire 'to do a little good'. But in one of the early letters Mère Chupin mentions that, should persecution arise in France the community could find at West Grinstead a place of refuge.[65]

As it happened, the community at West Grinstead was cut off from its mother house two years later by Monsignor Denis, who ruled it as his personal fief until his death at the turn of the century. The community there endured many difficulties and eventually was unable to sustain its independent existence. In 1925, after having its petitions for amalgamation with Harrow, Stroud, Stone and Portobello Road rejected, the sisters of the community were received into the Congregation of St Catherine of Siena of Newcastle, Natal, South Africa, whose generalate had been moved to Bushey in Hertfordshire some years before.

But a second foundation of Mère Chupin's community was made in England in 1896 under the leadership of Mother M. Cecilia Marshall, who had spent several months at West Grinstead as a novice twenty years earlier. Elizabeth Lucy Marshall was born at Brighton on 15 February 1851, into a solidly middle-class family. While still an infant, the family moved to Chichester, where her father, an architect, was engaged in restoration work on the cathedral and later worked on the monastery of the Carmelite nuns in Wyke Lane. Before cloister was imposed, the nuns invited John Marshall to bring his daughters to look over the building and although Bessie was something of a tomboy, the nuns made a distinct impression on her. In 1876, during a visit to the newly established Dominican convent at West Grinstead, Bessie met Mère Vincent-Ferrier Chupin and despite considering the nuns 'queer bundles of cloth' she was won over by the magnetism of Bonne-Mère's personality.[66]

In August of that year, despite the reservations of her father, who was still a Protestant at the time, Bessie Marshall left for Paris and on 21 November, she received the habit and the name Marie-Cécile. Although in his biography Père Mortier attests to the fact that Bonne-Mère felt herself incapable of forming young women to the religious life, she made every effort to procure the help of the Dominican friars in this task and soon afterwards obtained the services of a sister from the ancient Third Order monastery of Langres as novice mistress.[67] So it was that Cecilia Marshall was able to absorb the spirit of zeal exemplified in Mère Chupin's commitment to her work for needy women, as well as that of the Order of Preachers. Several other English and Irish women entered the community at Clichy, even after the house at West Grinstead had been cut off from the mother house. Amongst these was one of Cecilia's cousins who found the dual adaptation to the regulated observance of religious life and the customs and diet of a French house too much for her![68]

It was not long until Sœur Marie-Cécile's obvious ability resulted in her being given responsibilities. No sooner had she pronounced her final vows in 1882, than she was given the delicate task of being sent as superior to a house of Dominicans at Mirecourt, in the east of France, which had just been incorporated into the Clichy community. Four years later, she oversaw the transfer of the community and orphans from there to a former Benedictine monastery at Favernay in the Vosges. With the exception of a year as sub-prioress at La Ronce, she remained at Favernay until the Bishop of Besançon made it known that he was not happy having sisters in his diocese who depended on a mother house outside his jurisdiction. In 1895 the house was closed and Sœur Marie-Cécile returned to Châtillon.

At about this time Cardinal Vaughan approached Mère Chupin, asking her to extend her work to London. Mother Cecilia Marshall crossed the Channel on 21 April 1896 with the intention of establishing a refuge, like that at Châtillon, in the East End. On her arrival in London she was the guest of the Princess Cassano, who was connected with the Lockhart family, to which Mother Elizabeth Lockhart, friend of Mother Catherine Philip Bathurst, and founder of the Franciscan Convent in Portobello Road, had been a member.[69] A few years earlier, the Franciscans Sisters had been decimated by an epidemic of influenza, and at the same time the orphans for whom they were caring were transferred to the new institution opened by the Sisters of Mercy at Orpington.[70] The much reduced community was now living in buildings too large and costly for them to maintain and were preparing to move to a property they had already obtained at Bocking, near Braintree in Essex.

It must have been from the Princess that Mother Cecilia learnt that the convent, which would meet her requirements perfectly, had just come into the market. Certainly, it was the Princess who convinced her that the West End location would place the work more in the public eye and attract greater patronage. [71] The Cardinal would not allow the Franciscans to sell for less than £25,000, and so the new foundation began with ten sisters, not a stick of furniture, £8 in hand, and a debt of £23,000 with the Prudential Assurance Company. The balance had come not from Châtillon but from the Princess, and despite the enormity of the sum, the balance was paid off by 1909.[72]

Since the new convent at Bocking was not yet completed, the Dominicans were obliged to confine themselves to one wing of the buildings awaiting the departure of the Franciscans, and did not gain vacant possession until 25 March 1897. To honour the memory of Bonne-Mère, who had died the day Mother M. Cecilia arrived in London, the convent was placed under the patronage of St Vincent Ferrer and the proposed refuge under that of St Anne. In the early days the Dominicans would hardly have survived without the generosity of the Little Sisters of the Poor at St Joseph's Home, on the other side of the road. Although the original debt was paid off swiftly, other loans for building works and improvements followed and life was always frugal at Portobello Road. From the beginning, however, the convent gained a reputation as a happy and welcoming place, remarkable for its hospitality.

An early register for St Anne's Home contains details of 216 women who entered the refuge, beginning on 8 February 1897 and concluding on 30 July 1900.[73] Since several of the women were admitted more than once, the number of individuals cared for during this time was 197. The register lists dates of departure as late as 1903, and in a solitary case 1919; no date of departure is given for a further six women. Though sparse on details, the register does allow some analysis. The youngest received at St Anne's was a girl of only eleven, while the oldest had passed sixty-five. In total, exactly one third of those listed were under the age of twenty-one and about a sixth above the age of forty. From the start the Home operated a 'knock at the door' principle, though many of the women appear to have been recommended or sent from other institutions. Just over a third were sent by what appear to be lady benefactors whose names recur several times; ten per cent were recommended by priests, mainly from the local parishes of Notting Hill and Bayswater and slightly more from other convents, particularly that of the Daughters of Charity at Blandford Square. Five women came from hospitals or the workhouse, two from Holloway Prison and one from the law courts. Family members recommended three other women, including the husband of one of the thirty-three married women who are identified. Almost a third of the women, sixty-five in number, are listed as being homeless or friendless and destitute.

At a time when employment opportunities for women were limited, and much of the work available to them was of a casual nature, as yet lacking any legal protection, it is not surprising that some women were seeking no more than a temporary roof over their heads. It is likely that others would have engaged in petty theft to alleviate their distress and, just as at Clichy, the house would have attracted some who had drifted into a life of crime. In the observations column inebriety is mentioned five times, though it is not clear whether this was the reason for arrival or the cause of departure!

The average stay was not long. A third of the women admitted stayed less than a month and half of them, less than three months. Fewer than forty stayed more than a year. Since the long-term aim of the refuge was to provide the women with the skills and training that would equip them for independent living, such short stays were not deemed beneficial.[74] In later years the average stay lengthened, and in common with similar institutions, some of the women remained all their lives at St Anne's. Although it did not operate on the scale of the much larger Good Shepherd homes – for instance, on New Year's Day 1900 the register indicates thirty-three women would have been resident – St Anne's certainly considered itself to be a place of rehabilitation.[75] The inmates were expected to work and they would probably have observed a regime not unlike that of the sisters, with early rising and frequent exercises of piety while they worked. To begin with, the women were taught needlework and commissions were taken from the large West End stores, though the irregular nature of this work resulted in a switch to uniform-making. In 1900 a laundry was built and this operated, with an interruption during the First World War, when cleaning agents became difficult to procure, until the 1960s.

The register gives little information on the future lives of the women, who were as free to go as they had been to come. Observations are made on forty-four of the women and over half of these record that the woman went to situations in domestic service, sometimes giving the name and address of the employer. Eleven, including five who were readmitted, left for the hospital or infirmary and one died in the home. Five went to relatives and one transferred to St Michael's Convent run by the Sisters of Our Lady of Charity of Refuge at Waterlooville near Portsmouth. Maintaining a balance between discipline and kindness was probably not easy when dealing with a disparate group, most of whom would have had very different social backgrounds from the sisters. The Council minutes record the removal in 1913 of Sister M. Raymond Butler as mistress of the Home on account of her inability to manage it competently and her replacement by Sister M. Bridget Grimley who would subsequently leave the community.[76]

A second work had been also accepted at the request of the Cardinal, the setting up of a government certified school for girls suffering from trachoma. This school, also named St Anne's, welcomed its first pupil, Maggie Callaghan, in July 1897. It received full certification under the government two years later and the installation of costly equipment, including high-pressure water baths, was paid for by the Cardinal.[77] A contemporary, though undated, manuscript in the general archives of the Dominican friars at Santa Sabina in Rome states that at the time there were 114 children in the school.

In 1897 the community also received its first postulant, Catherine Hardy from Dublin, who would be clothed as Sister M. Winefride in February 1899. She was the first of over seventy women who entered at Portobello Road until the separation from Châtillon, the vast majority of them being Irish. Many of these were directed to St Vincent's by the Dominican friars, in particular Father Stephen Glendon, of St Saviour's in Dublin. Maintaining a separate noviciate in a small community, even if it is established in more than one country, is something of a luxury. The Prioress General and Council at Châtillon would have preferred all candidates to be formed in France, but Mother M. Cecilia, who acted as novice mistress as well as prioress until 1909, insisted that they remain in

London. Perhaps Mère Marie-Dominique Lefort, remembering the separation of the West Grinstead house, feared a further secession.

Whatever the apprehensions at Châtillon, Mother M. Cecilia was still revered by many of the French sisters. The possibility that she might be elected Prioress General at the general chapter of 1909 was not lost on Canon Edmund Surmont, the Vicar General for Westminster, or his counterpart the Abbé Pousset in Paris who expressed himself concerned about the state of the French houses since the death of Mère Lefort earlier that year.[78] Canon Surmont advised Mother M. Cecilia not to accept, should she be elected, and encouraged her to place before the chapter a plan for the separation of the London house from the French congregation.[79] Since Canon Surmont had been involved quite recently in arranging a similar separation from their French mother house for the Sisters of the Sacred Hearts of Jesus and Mary at Chigwell, one wonders whether the separation from Châtillon came about as a matter of ecclesiastical polity, rather than through any desire on Mother M. Cecilia's part.[80]

Although the London house had always been financially independent, there was some negotiation over property deeds, the transfer of dowries of those who had entered in France and the rights to donations which, though they had been made to the congregation, had been intended expressly for Portobello Road. The deed of separation resolving these matters was not issued by the Archbishop of Paris until 4 August 1912, although in reality the London house had already asserted its autonomy for almost two years at this stage.[81] No separation is effected without pain and it would not be until fifteen years later that receipt of the obit notice of the Prioress General of Châtillon, Mère Dominique Lambert, prompted the renewal of cordial correspondence.

Mother M. Cecilia Marshall's attentions were now turned to compiling constitutions for the new Congregation of St Vincent Ferrer and the establishment of the first branch house. In September 1909 Sister M. Augustine Browne and four companions took possession of Banksea at Dovercourt near Harwich. The house was paid for by a legacy from a Mrs Windowe and was intended as a convalescent home for the children from St Anne's School. The following year a neighbouring house in Orwell Terrace was purchased and a small independent school was opened.[82]

In writing the constitutions for her new congregation, Mother M. Cecilia received considerable assistance from the Dominican Père Jean Alix whom she had first met as a young religious in Favernay, at which time he was assigned to the priory in Dijon. He was to remain a firm friend and adviser for the remainder of her life. The constitutions were printed in December 1913 and earned the praise of the English Provincial, Father Humbert Everest, who described them as a 'bond of unity and pledge of stability'. He also wrote of the manner in which the sisters shared in the fullness of Dominican life:

> Just as the Friars Preachers have as the background of their lives the observances of monastic life, so that they who are to lead men to God may themselves be unworldly, so too the Sisters of your Congregation through devoted practice of the works of mercy ... make time to gather together to renew their spirit in the choral chant of the Divine Office, and enjoy the constant support of the observances and sacred ceremonies of the ascetical and conventual life. [83]

As soon as the separation from Châtillon had been effected Mother Cecilia applied for the congregation of St Vincent Ferrer to be aggregated to the Order and this was granted on 30 November 1910.[84] At the same time the sisters, who until this time had prayed the Little Office of the Blessed Virgin Mary, were initiated into the intricacies of the Divine Office. To bring the formation of the young sisters into conformity with recently published directives from Rome, which required the separation of novices from the professed sisters, a house was purchased in Oxford Gardens to accommodate the noviciate.

The Portobello Road sisters had also shown themselves ready to assist other Dominican women. In 1904 an appeal was made by the Dominicans of Nancy for the assistance of an English speaking sister in their newly opened schools in Lewiston, Maine in the United States. These sisters had already suffered much as a consequence of the legislation against teaching congregations which had been enforced in France. Sister Mary of the Blessed Sacrament Walsh remained three years in Lewiston helping build up the bilingual schools in a parish which was largely comprised of French Canadian families.[85] Portobello Road also opened its doors to Dominican refugees from persecution in Portugal, some for a short time en route for the United States;[86] others for longer periods as in the case of two English born members of the Portuguese congregation, Sisters M. Lewis and M. Angela Urbani.[87]

By the time the London foundation became independent of Châtillon it had developed into a vigorous, young, observant, congregation of about fifty sisters. Since she would be the congregation's only major superior, Mother M. Cecilia Marshall was able to infuse it with her own vision of what apostolic Dominican life for women could be. This vision would mature and reach out, in time, to many others.

Conclusion

At Stroud, it took some time before Teresa Matthew's vision of Dominican life eclipsed that of the initiator of the community, Emily Sandys. From the beginning, the close association with the Dominican friars, and the excellent relations the community maintained with successive bishops of Clifton, reinforced the stability of the congregation. It took much longer for Catherine Bathurst to decide how and where her vocation ought to be lived out, and the years in Ghent, where she had to contend with the ambivalent attitudes of both the bishop and the friars of the Order, were not easy. It was only when she had established the work in her own country, where Newman knew she would do well, and where Cardinal Manning gave his unquestioned support, that it began to flourish. It is clear that Rose Corbett lacked the necessary qualities to govern a religious community, or to win the confidence of her ecclesiastical superiors. The Leicester community did develop, but all its endeavours were coloured, and to some extent constrained, by her legacy. Mother M. Cecilia Marshall made the London foundation as a member of a congregation in which contrasting visions had also competed during the early years. Her undoubted ability gained the confidence of her superiors in France, who allowed the work in London to develop with a large measure of autonomy. This accorded well with the outlook of Cardinal Bourne and facilitated the separation of the Portobello Road convent from the Châtillon congregation.

The works undertaken by these Dominican communities, whether on their own initiative, or at the bidding of the clergy, answered local needs, and built up the English Catholic community. A considerable degree of adaptation and change shows that those in leadership were alert to new needs and opportunities. If the primary intention was to work for the poor, the provision of fee-paying schools helped to support non-remunerative works. Taking in parlour boarders, though it might jeopardize the conventual atmosphere of the house, provided financial stability, as did the development of cottage industries, fundraising events and the practice – most appropriate to members of a mendicant Order – of questing.

Within the space of fifty years, more than 450 women entered the four communities; the uncertainty of the early years being characterized by a fluidity of membership for most of them. Fewer than half of these women would end their lives as Dominicans, but more important than the numbers staying or leaving, was the quality of the formation they received. Where communities were well established, the life itself was formative and the noviciate annals from Stroud make much of the instruction given and the impression that the life of regular observance, and preparation and celebration of the solemn liturgy, had on those in formation. On the other hand, at Leicester, there is evidence of inadequate training in the religious life and frequent instances of novices, perhaps through financial necessity, being sent out to teach immediately they had received the habit. All these groups of Dominican women turned to the friars of the English Province for spiritual assistance: the preaching of retreats, conferences, help in formulating their constitutions; though there is little evidence of interaction amongst themselves. Their Dominican identity was always sure, even if the dynamics of community life and the want of effective leadership sometimes limited their ability to live the life as happily and successfully as they might have wished.

Notes

1. Stone STR.25TM, Father Vincent McNabb, sermon preached at the burial of Mother M. Teresa Matthews, 5 January 1905.
2. In fact, there were also three others which will only be touched upon in our story. The community of West Grinstead, founded, like Portobello Road later on, by the Dominicans of Notre-Dame de Grâce in 1876 and unilaterally separated from them by the mission priest at West Grinstead. The community at Crieff in Scotland has been mentioned in the previous chapter. A small community founded in Rome by an Ulster convert settled first in Kew and later in Hunstanton early in the twentieth century but was disbanded in the 1920s.
3. Harding, *The Diocese of Clifton*, pp. 179, 222.
4. Benjamin Bucknall's daughter Josephine would be received at Stroud as Sister M. Imelda in 1883 and spent almost all her life at St Rose's where she was chantress and music teacher; she died in 1942.
5. Emma Langston had served in the Crimea with Florence Nightingale and converted to Catholicism in 1856. She had apparently sought admission to five different Catholic communities but been refused, probably on account of her age as she was about sixty. Her subsequent career is not known though it is said she died in London. Williams & Campbell, *The Park Village Sisterhood*, p. 116.
6. Stone, C6, *Council Book, St Catherine's Convent, Clifton*, 11 July 1863.
7. Stone, T865, *Annals of the Congregation*, 22 January 1867.
8. There is an oral tradition that Morewood became enamoured of Rose

Corbett and that their relationship became inappropriately familiar, it is also said that he spent his final years working as a missionary in India to make atonement. Neither of these stories can now be substantiated. If there had been any known impropriety it would seem extraordinary that Rose Corbett, however difficult a person she might later prove to be, would have been given the responsibility of making the foundation in London.

9. Rose Corbett's *Annals* give breakdown in health as the main reason for Emily Sandy's departude from the community whereas the account of Sisters Agnes Teresa Mayo and M. Magdalen Larkin mentions financial complications and the 'unbusinesslike proceedings of those on whose fidelity she relied . . .' It is not impossible that she no longer felt committed to a way of life which was becoming increasingly structured and conventual.
10. Raymond-Barker, *Conventual Third Order*, p. 63.
11. Southwark, West Grinstead Box, Bernard Ullathorne to Peter Butt, 9 October 1887; Bishop Butt was endeavouring to borrow a sister from Stroud or some other Dominican community to act as novice mistress for the Dominican Sisters at West Grinstead.
12. Stone, STR/14D, Fathers Raphael Moss & Humbert Everest to Mother M. Teresa Matthews, 22 December 1889.
13. Stone, STR/G/5N(i), *Noviciate Annals 1884–1908*, entry for 1 January 1904.
14. Stone, STR/14D, Father Vincent McNabb to Mother Rose Imelda Harrold, 29 August 1908.
15. Stone, STR/4, *Recollections of the Scholarship of 1899*, un-numbered item.
16. STR/G/5N(i), *Noviciate Annals 1884–1908*, entry for 8 February 1905.
17. A variant account in the Leicester records, L1.6.(i) gives the foundation year as 1863, the move from Fortress Terrace as 1865 and the separation from Stroud as 1866.
18. Stroud, N.1(i), *Memoirs of St Catherine's Convent, Newcastle-upon-Tyne from 1879 till* 1929, p. 1.
19. STR/18(M), *Memoir of Sister M. Raphael Smith*, p. 26.
20. Stone, N.1(i), *Memoirs of St Catherine's Convent*, p. 5, *N.1(i)*, AGOPS.
21. Stone, ER18(i), *Erdington Annals, 1890–1917* Easter Sunday 1895.
22. Ibid., June 1891.
23. Ibid., 6 February 1895.
24. Stone, CH18(i), *Cheadle Aannals, 1898–1925*.
25. Stone, STR.9N(i), *Sponsa Christi (Sister Mary Wilfrid, O.S.D.)*.
26. Stone, STR/G/9(ii), *Council Book*, p. 68.
27. The text of these constitutions, though the title page indicates it applies to the Congregation of Our Lady Help of Christians, is probably nothing more than the model constitution prepared by the Dominican curia to assist sisters of the Order in revising their constitutions in accordance with the new Code of Canon Law. The constitutions were certainly not approved and the Leicester community had not achieved the status of a religious congregation by the time of the amalgamation in 1929.
28. Stone, L1.6(i), *A short Account of the Congregation of Dominican Sisters under the Title of Our Lady, Help of Christians*.

29. Nottingham, Convent Files: Dane Hill, FC1. Document dated 26 March 1901.
30. Stone, L9N, *Necrology L9(N)*, 25 December 1899. There are extant Council Minutes for the Leicester community only from 1888 and Annals begin in 1892. The 1871 and 1881 census both name Mother M. Rose Corbett as superior of the community, the 1891 census lists Mother M. Vincent Rosbothom as superior.
31. Even in the history of English religious institutes the lack of transparency concerning founders surfaces more than once. The Congregation of Jesus (formerly the Institute of the Blessed Virgin Mary) was not allowed to claim Mary Ward as its founder because she had been condemned by the Holy Office. Likewise it was not until the 1970s that the Sisters of St Joseph of Peace reclaimed Francis Clare Cusack as their founder; her name had been written out of the congregation's history as she not only left religious life but the Catholic Church as well.
32. Harrison, *Hinckley St Peter's*, p. 36 ff.
33. From Cambridge Terrace in Humberstone Road a move was made in December 1877 to a property in Millstone Road, which was later purchased, this was sold in 1890 and for a brief period the community lived in Abbey Park Road before moving in December 1890 to London Road.
34. Stone, L16.A2, *Council Book 1893–1917,* 2 June 1897.
35. Stone, L15, *Ledger, Dominican Convent, Dane Hills, Leicester 1901–1918*, entries for August-October 1907.
36. Stone, L16.A1, *Council Book 1888–1893,* 19 April 1889, records the first of many instances.
37. Stone, L16.A2, *Council Book 1893–1917,* 26 December 1891, 16 and 20 January 1892.
38. Ibid., 10 June 1894, *L16 A2*, AGOPS.
39. Ibid., 25 August 1895.
40. Edinburgh, DD5/90/1, Mother M. Ignatius Elwes to Archbishop Angus McDonald, 24 January 1896.
41. Edinburgh, DD3/90/8, Mother M. Ignatius Elwes to Bishop James Smith, 20 September 1899.
42. Stone, L18.A, *Annals, 1892–1927,* 23 April 1895.
43. Stone, L16.A2, *Council Book 1893–1917,* 9 December 1906.
44. Stone, L18.A, *Annals, 1892–1927,* 3 September 1897.
45. Stone, L16.A2, *Council Book 1893–1917,* 14 June 1907.
46. Stone H/G25.12, *Account of the Life of Mother Catherine Philip Bathurst* and H/G25.13 *The English Congregation of the Holy Rosary* are the major biographical sources relating to Catherine Bathurst.
47. This community was soon afterwards affiliated to the Franciscans and moved to Portobello Road, building the convent which they were to pass on to the Dominicans under Mother M. Cecilia Marshall in 1897. They subsequently moved to Braintree, Essex and in 1968 amalgamated with the Missionary Franciscan Sisters of the Immaculate Conception, founded in the United States by yet another noviciate companion from Greenwich, Mother M. Ignatius Hayes.

48. Stone, H/JHN/4, John Henry Newman to Catherine Bathurst, 15 April 1853.
49. Stone, H/JHN/53, John Henry Newman to Mother Catherine Philip Bathurst, 16 July 1869.
50. Stone, H/JHN/50, John Henry Newman to Mother Catherine Philip Bathurst, 3 January 1869.
51. Stone, HG/10–6, Mother Catherine Philip Bathurst to Bishop Henri-François Bracq, 9 June 1872.
52. Stone, H/G10–16, B. van Emelen OP to Mother Catherine Philip Bathurst, 16 May 1874.
53. Stone, H/G10–34, Bishop Herni-François Bracq to Archbishop Manning, 13 January 1880. This letter, written in Latin, is concerned principally with Mother Catherine Philip's refusal to accept the confessors appointed by the Bishop.
54. Stone, H/G10–30, B. van Emelen OP to Bishop Henri-François Bracq, 3 September 1877.
55. Stone, H/G10–38, Mother Catherine Philip Bathurst to Bishop Henri-François Bracq, 23 August 1879.
56. Cf. Sugg, *Ever yours affly*, p. 195.
57. Stone, H/JHN/77, John Henry Newman to Mother Catherine Philip Bathurst, 1 January 1884.
58. Stone, HWR.2.G, *A Memoir of Revd. Mother M. Dominic Wilkes, O.P., 1862–1939*. Jubilarian. Ex Prioress General. Councillor General.
59. Stone, W14, *St Vincent's Orphanage Appeal*, dated 24 November 1907.
60. Stone, H/G11.P(I), *Copies of Deeds and Agreements* (Beccles).
61. Stone, H/G9(a), *Deliberations of Councils, 1900–1928*.
62. Ibid., 16 January 1907.
63. The situation of a founder initially feeling no personal inclination to religious life is not uncommon. Catherine McAuley who founded the Sisters of Mercy in Dublin in 1831 originally had no such intention. Cf. Degnan, *Mercy unto Thousands*. Margaret Aylward, foundress of the Sisters of the Holy Faith in the same city in 1861 never donned the habit of the congregation. Cf. Jacinta Prunty, *Lady of Charity*, p. 126.
64. Mortier, *Bonne Mère*, p. 146.
65. West Grinstead, Mère Vincent-Ferrier Chupin to Jean-Marie Denis, 25 January 1876.
66. Sisters, *A Treasure of Joy and Gladness*, p. 12.
67. Mortier, *Bonne Mère*, p. 263.
68. In a letter to her cousin the departing novice mentioned her delight at being able to drink proper tea again rather than coffee. It is likely her cousin's experience at Clichy had a bearing on Mother M. Cecilia's insistence on forming novices from the British Isles in London rather than France. Sisters, *A Treasure of Joy and Gladness*, p. 16.
69. The Princess was the niece of Mother Elizabeth Lockhart's half-brother, William, who was a member of Rosmini's Institute of Charity and the restorer of St Etheldreda's church, Ely Place, London.
70. SMA, *A brief Account*, p. 21.

71. Ibid., p. 25.
72. Stone, LON/P/G5R, *Records of the Convent of St Vincent Ferrer, Portobello Road*, 1896.
73. Ealing, 3B, *St Anne's Home: Arrivals and Departures*. Unfortunately no subsequent register for the home or the school seems to be extant.
74. Sisters, *A Treasure of Joy and Gladness*, p. 51.
75. A critical study of the Good Shepherd convents in Ireland, drawing on the archives of the houses with written with the cooperation of the Religious of the Good Shepherd spells out their philosophy and mode of operation: Finnegan, *Do Penance or perish*.
76. Stone, LON/P/G9, *Council Minute Book*, 29 June 1913.
77. Stone, LON/P/G5R, *Records*, July 1897.
78. Stone, LON/P/G10–22, l'Abbé Pousset to Mother M. Cecilia Marshall, 24 April 1909.
79. Stone, LON/P/G10–28, Canon Edmund Surmont to Mother M. Cecilia Marshall, 19 June 1909.
80. Clerkin, *A Heart for Others*, pp. 56–61. There were, at the time, over 100 members in the English Province of the Servantes du Sacré-Cœur.
81. Stone, LON/P/G10–36.
82. Stone, LON/P/G5R, *Records*, 20 September 1909.
83. Stone, LON/P/G10–36, Father Humbert Everest to Mother M. Cecilia Marshall, 1 November 1913.
84. Carpenter, 'Domenicane di San Vincenzo Ferrer' in Pellecia & Rocca (eds), *Dizionario*, vol. 3, column 944.
85. Stone, LON/P/G5R, *Records*, July 1904.
86. [Hampton], *The Lord may be in a Hurry*, pp. 69–71.
87. Stone, LON/P/G5R, *Records*, 20 October 1910.

Chapter Four

Really going it: adapting to a new century

The curate, Father Wall, asked if he could erect a wireless aerial on the convent flagstaff and in all innocence Mother Prioress consented. The youth of Stone thought 'the convent is really going it'.[1]

Introduction

Between the end of the 'Gay Nineties' and the financial crash in 1929 British Society changed dramatically. The years leading up to the First World War were characterized by expansion of both empire and industry, but also by the beginnings of the modern welfare state. Though the class system was still firmly entrenched, it was an era of social mobility, of confidence and of strong patriotic feeling. It is hardly surprising that when the call to arms came in August 1914, 750,000 men signed up in the first month. In hindsight, it is easy to see the First World War as the inevitable consequence of the arms race and the complex system of alliances developed in the previous twenty years. The experience of total war – ten million killed, twice that number wounded and eight million missing – the conditions of existence at the front, the seeming futility of effort against gain as the lines moved back and forth, affected the collective psyche of Europe.

In Britain, as elsewhere, the war was followed by a period of persistent social and industrial unrest as it became clear that the 'land fit for heroes' was not in the gift of governments of any persuasion. For women it was also a period of tremendous change. The war had given many women the experience of financial autonomy as they flocked to the munitions factories or took the place of men in the service industries and on the land. Although in 1918 their efforts were rewarded by the introduction of female suffrage for those over thirty years of age, their aspirations for equality with men in other areas were more slowly realized.

The Church too was changing, though Vatican polity could seem as volatile as that of the secular state. The encyclical *Rerum Novarum* issued by Pope Leo XIII in 1891 had strengthened the developing commitment to social justice and encouraged a rapprochement with the modern world. This new openness would later be counteracted to some degree by the 1907 encyclical *Pascendi* of Pius X, which would constrict Catholic intellectual life for many years. Beginning with *Ubi Arcano* in 1921, Pius XI issued a series of encyclicals addressing the need to Christianize an increasingly secular society, promoting social and economic security and so the era of Catholic Action began.

The apostolic constitution *Condite a Christo*, issued in 1900, gave to women in simple vows universal recognition as true religious; equals to their enclosed sisters professing solemn vows. A series of *Normae* followed, outlining new legislation for congregations of sisters which, together with the promulgation of the new Code of Canon Law in 1917, would require a wholesale revision of their constitutions. Henceforth, the constitutions of religious congregations were to be purely legal documents, without spiritual exhortation, or even quotations from the Scriptures or the Fathers of the Church. Regulations governing the daily lives of religious were also to be removed from the constitutions and contained in a separate Directory. Anticipating the arrival of thousands of rewritten constitutions, the Sacred Congregation for Religious issued model constitutions, from which nothing could be removed, though additional articles appropriate to particular congregations could be added. To assist Dominican Sisters with the process, the Dominican Curia prepared similar model constitutions. As a consequence, the individual character of different congregations was not so easily detected in these new normative texts; the emphasis moved from spirit to letter and, in many cases, what had simply been customs became imbued with the force of law.

As they adapted to these ecclesiastical changes, Dominican Sisters in Britain also felt the impact, despite their ideological separation from 'the world', of the changes in society. It could not be otherwise, as their apostolate was directed in particular towards girls and women, whose condition and aspirations changed so much. They also had to adjust to the advance of government intervention into their traditional spheres of endeavour and the demands for professionalism that ensued. Those in positions of leadership in the five Dominican groups confronted the challenges of this changing world and the sisters endeavoured to respond to new needs and circumstances.

Keeping up the tone: leadership and ethos

In December 1894 the annalist at St Dominic's Convent, Stone, made the following entry:

> This year has brought us to an important crisis in the history of our Congregation. The first founders, the first Provincials (all three in their different way women of remarkable stamp), the first Sisters, have all passed away. Our childhood is over, so to speak. But we enter the second period of our existence without fear or misgiving.[2]

Just over seventy-five years later, the sociologist of the history of religious life, Raymond Hostie, would postulate his theory of a four-stage life cycle for religious orders and congregations. In her own way, the annalist at Stone articulated the first two stages of this cycle: the foundation period characterized by charismatic leadership and the period of consolidation characterized by a formalization of structures.[3] The two women who followed Mother Francis Raphael Drane in office were certainly capable, and may well have been 'women of remarkable stamp'. However, the fact that they have left so little trace – neither memoirs nor personal correspondence – almost suggests that, with structures and procedures well in place, charismatic leadership was less of a necessity than administrative ability.

The Honorable Mary Isabel Lucy Dormer was born in 1842, the daughter of Joseph, 11th Baron Dormer of Wyng and his wife Elizabeth Tichborne. She entered at Stone in 1862 and was professed in September the following year as Sister Agnes Philomena. Described in the necrology as a born leader, she gained her first experience in this role when appointed prioress of Stoke in 1872 and for the next fifty-two years was in office as a superior. She was elected Provincial in 1894 to succeed Mother Francis Raphael and continued in office until 1918, after which she was appointed local prioress at Stone for two successive terms. From the annals, the impression gained of Mother Agnes Philomena is that of a vigorous worker, a kind hearted and affectionate woman whose quiet and unassuming presence was always welcomed by her sisters. Her years of office ended, it is noted how effortlessly she slipped back into the ranks.

The fifth Prioress Provincial was born Beatrice Wilson in Brighton in 1860, the daughter of an Anglican clergyman. She entered at Stone in 1881 and was given the name Catherine de Ricci. For some years she worked as mistress of the boarding school at St Marychurch before being appointed mistress of novices at Stone in 1901. Mother Catherine de Ricci possessed a gift for administration and is the first major superior for whom a business diary survives, in which are recorded with monotonous regularity meetings with ecclesiastical and civic authorities, solicitors, estate agents, medical and business men. These appointments sometimes required deviations from the accepted norms of conventual behaviour at the time, as the following anecdote reveals. The sale of the property at Bow in 1923 required a visit to the Goldsmiths' Hall, and unable to find a companion for the visit, Mother Catherine de Ricci was compelled to go on her own by public transport, a feat described in the book of Records as being 'terrible and a thing not even a secular lady would have done under ordinary circumstances. However, necessity knows no law and our Mother, by bus mostly, reached EC2 and the Goldsmiths' Hall, a big and beautiful place'.[4]

By 1923 most 'women' and certainly a good many 'ladies' would not have found travel alone on London public transport an ordeal. It would not be fair to attribute the attitudes of the congregation's annalists to all its members, but those of Stone and St Marychurch in particular do display a certain social elitism. An event which took place in April 1898 at St Marychurch demonstrates this. A woman obtained a bottle of brandy from the village store under the pretence that Sister Jane Margaret Ryley had sent her for it. The shopkeeper's suspicions were aroused and a message sent to the convent, receiving the response that no one had been sent on such an errand. The woman – along with the half-empty bottle – was taken into custody and a week later Sister Jane Margaret was summoned to give evidence at the Police Court in Torquay. To save her the indignity of appearing in the public eye, the magistrates were persuaded to meet an hour earlier than usual. The annalist recounts:

> The woman was a poor wretched looking creature well known to be given to drinking. Some charitable lady appeared on the scene and begged that she be 'let off' upon promise of entering a home for inebriates. This she agreed to do and everyone being satisfied, the lady walked off with the prize, greatly to the edification of the Sisters, as she seemed to care nothing about passing through the streets in company with such a disreputable looking companion.[5]

One imagines that forty years earlier, it would have been Mother Margaret Hallahan walking the streets with this social outcast and edifying the general populace, perhaps even setting up a home for the 'poor wretched looking creature' and others like her. Even before the great social upheavals of the First World War and economic depression, the annals, in references to lay sisters, servants and workmen, make statements such as: 'the spirit of the present day militates against submission and hard work'[6] and 'The "spirit of work" does not prevail in this century among the working classes.'[7] On the other hand, the sisters could certainly be taken advantage of in their charitable assistance. In 1907 a change was made in the manner of feeding the tramps, never few in numbers, who came to the door and were fed in the porch of St Dominic's at Stone, sometimes disconcerting other visitors. Although most of them appeared genuinely poor and hungry some, after eating at the convent, would go for a second helping to St Mary's Hospital, behaving in a 'rude and bold' manner and demanding food as 'a right'. In September 1907 the decision was made that all such relief would henceforth be given only at the hospital.[8]

It is a relief, though perhaps not a surprise, that these attitudes do not come to the fore in the records of Stoke-on-Trent or Bow, where the sisters worked much more closely with the working classes. This does not mean the annals of these two houses are without social commentary. As part of the Twelfth Night celebrations at Stoke in 1910 the community got up an entertainment for their prioress, Sister M. Reginald Capes, entitled *The Houses of Parliament* in which 'some good fun was made from suffragettes, the coming election and different bills'.[9] But they were also quick to respond to the relief appeals when the 1912 miners' strike caused the closing down of the furnaces in the Potteries, halting production and throwing thousands out of work. The annalist at Stoke records in great detail the introduction of a minimum wage bill with genuine interest and obvious concern for the wellbeing of the workers.[10]

Another amusing anecdote, from 1923, demonstrates the ambiguous embrace the community at Stone extended to modernity:

> The curate, Father Wall, asked if he could erect a wireless aerial on the convent flagstaff and in all innocence Mother Prioress consented. The youth of Stone thought 'the convent is really going it' but great care was taken to let people know it was not for the benefit of the Sisters.[11]

To their great relief, when Father Arthur Wall was transferred soon after, he took his aerial with him!

At Stroud two different 'leadership styles' are evident after the turn of the century. The election of a successor to Mother Rose Imelda Harrold, after her resignation in 1907, was inconclusive after several scrutinies and the matter was referred to Rome. Perhaps, as we have already intimated in the case of Harrow, living so long and until so recently under the revered founder, the sisters were not comfortable with anyone else exercising authority. On 1 June 1907 Mother M. Pius Pretty, who had held the post of novice mistress for some years, was appointed. She is remembered as a brilliant administrator with a particularly thorough grasp of the constitutions, rather than as one concerned with winning hearts. Not withstanding, Mother M. Pius was elected unanimously for a second term of office. In later years, as we shall see, with her grasp of juridical principles, she contributed a great deal to drawing up the constitutions of the amalgamated congregation. Mother M. Pius died at Stroud in 1949.

Her successor was a quite different cast of woman. Helen Agnes Elgar, always called Dot, was born above the family's music shop in High Street, Worcester, on New Year's Day 1864. Dot was always a delicate and retiring child but like her famous brother Edward, she inherited a talent for music. Although as a young woman she had made arrangements to enter a missionary congregation, she remained at home to care for her mother and act as book-keeper for the family business. It was only after her mother's death in September 1902 that she entered St Rose's, receiving the habit and becoming Sister M. Reginald on 3 March 1903, making profession of vows a year later. Sir Edward became a great friend of the community and wrote a brief, twenty-bar piece, *For Dot's Nuns*, as a present for Mother Rose Imelda. Later he gave one of his Steinway pianos to the convent at Brewood, and one of his conducting batons is still on display in the convent at Stone.[12] After a couple of years teaching in Newcastle-upon-Tyne, Sister M. Reginald returned to St Rose's as sacristan and organist, being elected prioress in 1913 and Superior General at the Chapter of 1919.

The business acumen acquired by the young Dot in the shop at Worcester was put to good use when new foundations were made. But Mother M. Reginald was also a kind and prudent woman, always ready to lend her ear and give considered counsel to those in distress. Because her health was not good, there was no question of her serving a second term, but she continued to live at Stroud and to follow the career of Sir Edward, much concerned that he had drifted away from the Church. Though she never heard his oratorios, despite the fact they were performed regularly at Gloucester Cathedral, she was able to visit him during his last illness, greatly

Fig. 9 Mother M. Reginald Elgar.

comforted by his begging her to recite to him the prayers of his childhood. Mother M. Reginald lived an increasingly retired life at Stroud, much distressed by the deterioration of diplomatic relations in Europe and the outbreak of war; she died on 10 December 1939.

The last Mother General of the Stroud congregation was its founder's niece, Rose Lamburn, who was received into the noviciate and given her aunt's name in religion on 30 April 1889. She held several offices, including mistress of lay sisters, novice mistress and prioress at Newcastle. Mother M. Teresa Lamburn was a woman who inspired enormous affection in her sisters, with an ability to formulate just the words required to encourage or reprove. It is clear that she did not relish spending the ever-increasing amount of time required to manage the affairs of the expanding congregation, though she was also an astute business woman.

During these years there would be new foundations and new works undertaken by the Stroud congregation, but it would not lose its joyful spirit. The practical jokes continued and were not confined to members of the community. George Ambrose Burton, Bishop of Clifton from 1902 to 1931, enjoyed an exceptionally close relationship with the community and was not beyond subjecting the sisters at Stroud to his own mischievous humour. On Christmas Day

1913 he sent three of his clergy, one after the other, to ring the convent doorbell, pretending to be visiting French priests and insisting, in heavily accented tones, upon seeing 'la Mère Prieure'. One by one the clerics were seen into the parlour, the doorbell sounding each time before the prioress had been rung for! Exasperated when the doorbell sounded a fourth time the indignant portress opened it to find the bishop at the door, reduced to fits of helpless laughter.[13]

At Harrow Mother M. Anne Claeys continued in office until 1924. Perhaps her greatest legacy to the community was the magnificent chapel built through the munificence of Mrs Claude Watney and opened in 1921. With all the sisters, apart from those at Bognor, within such easy reach of Harrow it was not difficult to maintain the strong family spirit. However, two innovations proposed and agreed to by the General Council at Harrow, which would have brought them in line with Dominican practice elsewhere in England, were resisted and never enacted. The first was the proposal to separate the lay sisters from the choir sisters at recreation.[14] The second was that diligent preparation should be made to adopt the Divine Office, however, the sisters continued to pray the Little Office of Our Lady until the amalgamation.[15]

Mother M. Dominic Wilkes, whose labours in Kilburn have been recorded in the previous chapter, was elected to succeed Mother M. Anne in 1924. Her attentions were turned mainly towards improving standards in the school at Harrow which had fallen off somewhat since Mother Catherine Philip's day. Not standing on ceremony, Mother M. Dominic could often be found in the kitchen giving culinary advice and assistance. Although a memoir records that she was a loyal supporter of the amalgamation and a kindred spirit to Mother M. Teresa Lamburn, other records give the impression that Mother M. Dominic felt less comfortable in this larger, less familiar world. During her time as a member of the General Council she would have the painful task of closing the convent in West Hampstead, which she had worked so hard to build up. Mother M. Dominic remained at Stone after the amalgamation, spending much of her time working in the habit room, until her death in February 1939.[16]

The situation at Leicester was quite different and will be covered in greater detail, whilst at Portobello Road in London, the young and growing community continued to develop under the eye of its founder, Mother M. Cecilia Marshall. Finding a sufficient number of women with leadership qualities, whether at congregational level or for local convents, was not always easy, even for a larger congregation such as Stone. A prioress could be elected for two consecutive terms of three years each, but in February 1917 it was decided to postulate Mother Catherine de Ricci for a third time as prioress of St Dominic's at Stone, as there was no one in the congregation available who was considered 'equal to the heavy task of governing this large community'.[17] By contrast, in the new London congregation, out of necessity, women below the canonically required age of forty, or with fewer than ten years of profession, were appointed to offices in the Portobello Road convent, or as superiors of the new branch houses. But in all these convents, no matter what the ethos, ability or social background of the sisters, old works went on and new ones came into being, almost all of which flourished.

To meet the needs of the day: old works and new

Although the ministry of Dominican women in Britain took on many forms, its major thrust, in complete accord with the mind of the local church, was in education. This apostolate itself was to grow in variety and scope as the twentieth century progressed, and other new works would also be developed. Perhaps the most remarkable thing about these new undertakings is the utter confidence with which the sisters took in hand work for which, in many instances, they had no previous professional training or experience. The grace of state, accorded by their profession, and the virtue of holy obedience were considered ample preparation for any work.

The fight to maintain and extend Catholic education predated the restoration of the hierarchy in England and Wales, with the creation of the Catholic Poor School Committee in 1847.[18] Supporting this work on the earnings of a Catholic population which was largely composed of the poor and working classes was no easy task and the arduous campaign for rate-aided Catholic education finally bore fruit in the 1902 Education Act. The Act still obliged Catholics to build and keep their own school buildings in repair but the maintenance of the schools, including salaries, was now borne by the new Local Education Authorities (LEAs); while responsibility for staffing lay with the School Managers.

A certain amount of reorganization went on, particularly in the metropolitan LEAs. The parish schools at Bow, where there had been separate heads for the Boys', Girls' and Infants' divisions, were to be merged under a single head. The parish priest, convinced that a woman religious would not be considered for the headship of a mixed school, proposed a lay teacher for the headship. Sister M. Bede Clarkson, who had been headmistress of the Girls' School for many years was now given charge of the top infants' class and felt the 'demotion' keenly.[19] On the other hand economic stringencies could decide the fate of individual sisters. In 1922 the Staffordshire LEA decided to cut the number of certificated teachers on the staff of the parish school at Stone on economic grounds, so that it was necessary to replace Sister M. Dominica Sheil, who was qualified and commanded a higher salary, with Sister M. Basil Regan who was not.[20]

In countries such as the United States, Australia and New Zealand, where Catholic schools remained outside the entirely secular state systems, and received no government grant, they relied on religious, working for subsistence salaries, for their economic survival. Though women religious were not essential to maintained Catholic schools in Britain, they nonetheless remained desirable. The new legislation also meant that professional training for both religious and lay teachers was now a matter of necessity. The Provincial Chapter at Stone had already decreed in 1900 that novices and postulants should receive 'systematic instruction on the judicious management of children'.[21] The task was given to Sister Catherine Magdalen Parker, who was teaching at Stoke at the time and possessed a secondary teaching diploma from Cambridge. But this was no longer sufficient, and in all the congregations' annals and council books, reference is made to sisters being sent to train in the Catholic Teachers' Colleges at Selly Park, St Charles Square and elsewhere.

There is also evidence of sisters engaged in continuing personal and professional development after the turn of the twentieth century. For two months in 1914 Sisters M. Paul Chard and M. Cecilia Eagle attended classes in horticulture at the County Primary School in Cheadle every Friday evening, the latter passing on her knowledge to the older boys in the parish school.[22] Five years later Sister M. Paul, accompanied this time by Sister M. Xavier Dixon, attended a series of evening classes for teachers held in Uttoxeter, going to and fro by train.[23]

To provide an avenue towards qualification for prospective lay teachers, the Stone congregation set up a Pupil Teacher Centre at Stoke-on-Trent under Sister M. Antoninus Dodds. On first inspection in April 1904 it was noted that the Centre 'consisted only of one room, had no scientific apparatus and was not taught by a mistress holding a university degree'.[24] Two months later, a second inspector, observing a lesson given by Sister M. Antoninus, could not understand the former unfavourable report, which the community attributed to the Local Authority's desire to have a single, non-denominational centre in Stoke. Purpose-built premises were opened on 11 January 1906, but from the beginning of the following academic year, the centre was incorporated into St Dominic's High School. Within a year, St Dominic's High School became the first Dominican school in Britain to gain official recognition, when it was granted by both the Staffordshire County Council and the Board of Education.[25] By 1911, when Sister Margaret Mary Dale took over as headmistress, a fully qualified staff was in place, including two with BAs and a third who had passed the BA examinations at Oxford with honours in Latin and French but had not been eligible, as a woman, to graduate. The LEA that year voted a maintenance grant of £2 per capita to eighty-five girls over the age of ten whose parents were resident in the borough, though it would be many years before the county was prepared to make similar grants.[26]

In 1912, seven pupils of St Dominic's High School were sent up for the Stoke Exhibition examinations. They did exceedingly well, Hannah Baker heading the list for the borough, and all receiving book and travel expenses as well as having their fees paid.[27] By the following year candidates were being presented successfully for the Oxford and Cambridge examinations. In 1921 a large property named Cliffville adjoining the convent, and formerly the residence of the Mayor, was purchased and adapted to accommodate the growing senior school. Further classrooms and an assembly hall were also built, the entire cost of all these expansions being borne by the Dominican Sisters. St Dominic's was to remain for many years the only secondary school conducted by the Dominican Sisters in receipt of LEA grants. It developed as a local school whose catchment area was almost exclusively the Catholic elementary schools of Stoke and the surrounding area. As such it proved its worth as an avenue for social promotion in a largely working-class area.

The other Dominican schools had mixed fortunes in the early years of the twentieth century. At Stone there was a constant chopping and changing. The numbers in Blessed Imelda's Pension School had dwindled to eight by 1904 and it was decided to open a day school under Sister Catherine Magdalen instead. The numbers soon reached twenty but went no higher, and the decision was made to admit boarders to St Dominic's High School, as it was now known. However, it was thought that the mix of mainly Protestant day scholars and Catholic boarders did not sit well and in 1914 the school reopened once again as Blessed Imelda's, a 'high class' boarding school which it would remain until 1931.[28] An extraordinarily high percentage of the pupils from this school entered the convent, thirty-five at Stone before the amalgamation, and many more at other religious houses. The fact that the prioress of the Carmelite monastery at Notting Hill, Mother Mary of Jesus Dupont, declared that she was always willing to receive candidates from Blessed Imelda's because 'they were just the sort for nuns' may give some indication of the type of education that was provided.[29]

The schools at St Marychurch and Bow maintained a distinction between the High (class) schools for boarders – the Young Ladies' Schools, as they were called – and the Middle Class schools for day scholars. This arrangement did not make the best use of resources. Several communities exiled from France in the early years of the century as a consequence of the laws against teaching congregations, established convent schools in Devon, contributing to a decline in number of boarders at St Marychurch. The decision was made to close the boarding school in 1921, though the day school continued for another thirty years.[30] Although the day and boarding sections had already been merged, the convent school at Bow closed the following year, ten months before the final departure of the community. Despite the incontrovertible success of the High School at Stoke, the annalist at Stone was quite happy to express her opinion on the decline of the 'Young Ladies'' schools. 'The better class of pupils throughout the country protest against the lowering of the tone of High Schools consequent upon the compulsory admittance of scholars from Elementary Schools and many parents decline to send their girls.'[31]

Efforts had been made to prepare sisters at Stone for the university examinations. As early as 1898, Sisters Margaret Mary Dale and M. Alexis Woodward visited Cambridge to see what would be required and engaged a woman to give the necessary instruction. She proved to be 'a decided failure' and saw out the term of her contract helping in the High School at Stoke.[32] During the First World War, Sister M. Anselm Hewitt was sent to train for secondary teaching with the Society of the Holy Child Jesus at Cavendish Square [33] and Sister M. Patricia Kane studied for her degree, first at the East London College, but completing it at Bedford College.[34] The most qualified did not always make the best teachers. The fact that Sister M. Patricia was 'too delicate to stand the strain of teaching', and that there was no one to replace her, was a contributing factor to the closure of the boarding school at St Marychurch.[35]

Although the school at Newcastle-upon-Tyne was closed, the Stroud congregation's schools at the mother house and at Erdington continued to grow. After The Green was purchased in

1921, numbers at St Rose's Convent School continued to increase, rising from thirty-two to fifty by 1925. In 1910 the community at Stroud completed the purchase of Badbrook House on the corner of Beeches Green and Merrywalks, with a view to develop it as a school for what were then termed 'physically defective and crippled' girls.[36] However, it was not until March 1911 that mention is made of a Mr Hunter coming from London to inspect the building, and certain additions and alterations were required before it could be approved as a special school. A loan of £500, provided by the Dominican nuns at Carisbrooke, and a further £100 given by Sister M. Emmanuel Fuller's sister, allowed the necessary works to be undertaken and the formal opening of the school took place on 22 April 1912. Sister M. Stanislaus Cooling, a mere eighteen months professed, was appointed first headmistress, and the following June, made a trip to London to observe the workings of similar schools.

The original admission register and a notebook containing biographical notes of early pupils are extant but give few details of the conditions which brought the children to the school.[37] One manuscript source mentions that two of the first three pupils were mentally as well as physically handicapped, and the third was a blind baby with no one to care for her. For some, being in a 'very weak state' is mentioned, others were tubercular, a number suffered from curvature of the spine and paralysis of the limbs, Down's Syndrome, polio, and one had lost an arm. Many are recorded as being quite backward or even as being in a state of debility and neglect on arrival. It may be imagined that a child with special needs in a large working-class family, in crowded conditions with both parents obliged to work, would be at a disadvantage. Only half of those who arrived at the school before 1925 had received any formal education at all before coming to St Rose's. Some of the children were cured by corrective therapy, others continued to decline, and three died at the school during the early years. Most stayed at St Rose's until they reached the maximum age of sixteen, a few were either too delicate for school or were not considered 'suitable cases', while others came for short periods by arrangement, perhaps to give respite to their families. A few transferred to other schools and one emigrated to Canada after the First World War.

The school concentrated on basic education in numeracy and literacy and the fact that many of the girls acquired talent for composition and drama is noted. In order to allow the girls to become self-sufficient when they left the school, there was also strong emphasis on needlework, dressmaking and related skills, as well as on commercial subjects. Art, music and acting also played a large part in encouraging the children to develop their talents. The girls entered their paintings and craft work in local competitions and frequently won prizes. In 1919 they presented a concert before Bishop Burton and the canons of the cathedral chapter. The annals record that 'it was pathetic to see them acting, yet, at the same time it was a joy to feel that, for the time being at least, they forgot their deformity in their efforts to please the audience'.[38]

Dr Eicholdy and Dr Williams, inspectors from the Department of Education, paid their first visit of inspection in June 1913 and expressed themselves more than satisfied, particularly with the happy, healthy look of the children.[39] That Christmas Sister M. Aloysia Jones prepared a Christmas tree to delight the children and had been 'indefatigable in her efforts to make it look splendid'. The daughters of the convent physician, Dr Henry Hardy, brought their gramophone and played recordings while the children enjoyed high tea. The annals also record that:

> Each child had several presents, some useful for daily needs and others only to bring out the rippling laughter which seems to be the greatest and most successful tonic in use at the Cripples' School. It certainly is administered daily, for it is impossible to visit Badbrook [House] without finding it in some corner of the building.[40]

The following year there was particular anxiety about the inspection, as it was to be carried out by Dr Williams on her own – the annals underline the fact that she was a lady doctor! – but the care provided by the staff and the achievements of the pupils apparently far exceeded her expectations.

Many of the girls continued to achieve after leaving St Rose's, despite their disabilities. Their subsequent careers are carefully recorded, often complete with photographs, in the *Biographical Notes*. Helen Finn, one of the first entrants, left the school in 1916 and two years later had obtained a post in the office of the Surveyor of Income Tax. By 1921, she had passed her Civil Service examinations, and was holding a permanent position with a salary of £3. 15s. 0d per week, as well as having an occupational pension. This was a considerable sum for any working woman at the time. Edith O'Shaughnessy, despite her callipers and crutches, obtained a clerical post in 1920 and later went on to work in a surgical instruments factory where she rose to be head of department with responsibility for training staff for the work. Lizzie McNeil, who had only one arm, struggled with enormous effort to master all types of sewing and handwork: knitting, darning, crochet, raffia and Tenerife work. She had a talent for design and acquired shorthand and typing skills as well. After leaving St Rose's, Lizzie held a position with the Food Controller's Office, before moving to work for a printing company in Liverpool. Mary Sparling later attended and topped her class at the Manchester Technical College and also became a public speaker for the Catholic Evidence Guild; while Alma Sargent became a music teacher, obtaining her Licentiate, and in 1925 a music degree. Others are recorded as going into service, sometimes in Catholic institutions, or making good marriages.[41]

But the work was not always one of brilliant success and the sisters had to cope with the behavioural problems that resulted from the acute frustration felt by some of the children, or from their lack of previous socialization. There were also deaths, that of Annie Bryan from meningitis being recorded in the annals at St Rose's in 1916, which relate that she 'did not mind her hunched back but she did want to walk' and this she managed to achieve with the aid of crutches just before her death.[42] The work was both physically and emotionally demanding and in the early years there were frequent changes, both of head teachers and assistants; but this was certainly an apostolic work which fulfilled a great need.

At Newcastle-upon-Tyne the work of the Stroud congregation also underwent something of a transformation. The Wingate Trust Hospital continued to offer the chance of a rest cure to local working girls, for whom no other provision could be made in time of sickness. Numbers were limited to ten and many deserving cases had to be turned away. In about 1906 Father Laurence Shapcote, Prior of Newcastle at the time, was able to persuade the other Trustees to increase the funding to allow for fourteen girls to be taken and so things continued until the First World War when the numbers had to be reduced on account of food and fuel shortages.[43] Shieldfield Green certainly did not offer the opportunities for expanding either school or hospital work, so just before the war the sisters began looking for larger premises. Several suitable properties were available but they were either beyond the community's means or outside the bounds of the Dominican parish within which they wished to remain. However, a property named The Minories, set in three and a half acres of land, was standing empty in Jesmond at the time. Negotiations commenced and to speed them along:

> Sisters used to walk up after school hours and go round the walls saying the rosary and other prayers. Dozens of holy medals were thrown over the walls, while [a statue of] St Joseph was solemnly interred inside the gate and asked to take possession on our behalf! Yet in spite of our ardour we met with little success at the time. [44]

The stumbling block was that the property was leasehold, with only thirty years left to run; the head lease being in the hands of Trustees who could not promise an extension. During the First World War, when The Minories was requisitioned for use as a communications centre for wireless operations, all possibility of purchase seemed lost.

After the war, since both works could not be expanded in the space available, it was decided to close the school. There was already ample local provision since the arrival some years earlier of the Society of the Sacred Heart at Fenham and the Filles de la Sagesse at Jesmond. The decision was made to open a private nursing home; the classrooms were converted for use as wards, and a few patients were taken in. But Shieldfield Green was no longer a desirable location for such a work, the railway goods yards with their constant noise were hardly conducive to restoration of health and once again the community began house hunting. In 1921 The Minories came into the market, much dilapidated after its war service, but freehold and affordable. At Easter 1922 the deeds were in the hands of Mother M. Reginald Elgar and the work of renovation began.[45]

It was not until a year later that the community was able to move in and the first surgical case was admitted. Not having a trained nurse available to open the home proved no obstacle to the community who hired a Nurse Warren as matron until Sister M. Leonard McEwan qualified and came to take over. Despite being the only Catholic nursing home in the North East at the time, St Catherine's had difficulty attracting patients in the early years, as many local surgeons also ran nursing homes and filled them with their own patients. In March 1929 St Catherine's satisfied the requirements for full registration and began to run on a more even keel.[46] The community continued its work in St Dominic's parish and that of St Lawrence at Byker, and twice a week opened a lending library, which proved very popular with youths and adults alike.

At St Vincent's Convent, Portobello Road, there were also changes. St Anne's School for the visually impaired continued to meet with the highest approbation, form the Ministry of Health and Board of Education inspectors, as well as from the Guardians of the various unions, as far away as Manchester, who sent girls to the school. Under the headship of Sister Lewis Bertrand Colgan there were also successes for children entered for the Oxford Junior Certificate Examinations.[47] But with better preventive health care, the incidence of such diseases as trachoma declined and fewer girls came, so that by 1928 it had become clear that the school was no longer necessary. The school buildings were soon put to a new use as St Mary's Training Hostel for Catholic Women Emigrants, hailed as 'the newest development in the social works of the Church to meet the needs of the day'.[48] The hostel was founded to address the need for training in the domestic sciences for the increasing numbers of young women who were now emigrating alone to the various British dominions. After lengthy negotiations with the various dominion governments, the Ministry of Labour – which paid seventy-five per cent of the training, travel and migration costs – and the Catholic Emigration Society (CES), the hostel welcomed the first five trainees in May 1929.

The course lasted from six to eight weeks and there were places for thirty-six women at a time. The training was not only in the finer details of cooking, baking, needlecraft and laundry work. An attempt was also made to inform the trainees of the different conditions and customs they would find in their new environments, to teach them to be adaptable and to avoid criticism of 'colonial ways'. This extended to the provision of newspapers and magazines from Canada, Australia and New Zealand and encouraging women who had already emigrated under the auspices of the CES to write giving details of their experiences. In the first year 167 women followed the course of instruction. The great majority came from London, Lancashire and Lanarkshire and although mill girls and shop assistants were well represented, there were also professional women and university graduates. The advantage of adding a little polish, if required, was not lost on Sister M. Aquinas Colgan, who was Superintendant, for the report also mentions that:

> It must not be forgotten that two or three months beneath a convent roof cannot fail to have a sobering and elevating effect on young girls and many who were setting out recklessly and casually on the great adventure have acquired a new sense of responsibility.[49]

During the first year 106 young women set sail, of whom seventy-five went to Canada – almost half to Ottawa – twenty-one to Australia and ten to New Zealand. Representatives of the Catholic Emigration Society were on hand to meet the women off the boat at their destinations and to help them find situations. Not all the young women completed the course, twelve dropped out in the first year, mainly for health or family reasons, and not all decided to emigrate. Within a few years a number would find their way to the Dominican noviciate at Stroud.

Making much headway: new foundations

In the forty years following Mother Margaret's death no new foundations had been made from Stone. Each community was consolidated on the model of the mother house, with a variety of works and a community large enough to ensure the solemn celebration of the liturgy and the full panoply of regular observance. By this time (1908) the congregation numbered 150 professed members, five novices and four postulants. More than sixty of these women were resident at Stone, the others almost evenly dispersed amongst the three branch houses at Stoke-on-Trent, St Marychurch and Bow. By the turn of the twentieth century this last foundation, so ardently desired by Mother Margaret, had become something of a liability. At the end of June 1902 the original house facing Bow Road was condemned after the parapet collapsed and three of the external walls were found to be unsafe.[50] The cost of rebuilding was considered prohibitive. Since several other communities 'better adapted to the active work of the locality' had settled nearby, Mother Agnes Philomena requested permission from Cardinal Vaughan to withdraw and asked whether he knew of any exiled French community which would be willing to take on the property. He replied 'most decidedly and kindly in the negative'.

A new street frontage had to be built at a cost of £6000. At the same time the neighbourhood continued to decline, many of the large elegant terraces on the Bow Road and the squares behind were let to multiple households, thereby depriving the Convent School of a local clientele. Sister M. Bede Clarkson was the only member of the community teaching in the parish school and drawing a salary, the local rates rose steeply and there were not the local benefactors upon whose generosity the other houses could rely. Although these circumstances would make it difficult to transfer the convent to another congregation 'as a going concern' it was clear that the community at Bow could not be self-supporting. Yet an enormous amount of good was carried out from the house.

The 1911 census records four sisters as 'district visitors' and various sources reveal that parish visiting and relief of the poor was undertaken not just in Bow but much further afield. In January 1919 one of the most intrepid visitors, Sister Agnes Catherine Christian, was knocked down and killed by an omnibus while crossing the Romford Road in Stratford, engaged in this work.[51] The various guilds for women and girls continued to flourish and as late as the 1960s Sister Rose Aquinas Thatcher, then living in retirement at Kelvedon, continued to receive visits from former members. Sister M. Reginald Capes was transferred from Hawick to Bow in 1915 to continue her literary endeavours – she had published a *Dominican Martyrology*, various other hagiographical writings and *The Life and Letters of Father Bertrand Wilberforce of the Order of Preachers* – with the hope that any income from these works might benefit the convent's finances.[52] Dispersing a community of twenty-five amongst the three other houses of the congregation would not have been possible, so the Provincial and her council began to consider a new foundation.

In 1908 a decision was made for a foundation in Scotland, making use of a considerable sum of money which had been set aside for the purpose by Sister Teresa Margaret Cumine. Mary Jane Cumine was born near Bombay in 1846, the daughter of an Aberdonian captain in the Madras Cavalry. The family returned to Britain, settling first at Charlton Kings in Gloucestershire and then Aberdeen where, as a young woman, Mary Jane entered the Anglican Sisterhood of St Margaret. Here she fulfilled the role of matron of St Martha's Home and was later appointed novice mistress. Towards the end of the century she took temporary leave to nurse her dying father and also made a pilgrimage to Rome, encouraged by the chaplain at St Margaret's. During a procession on the feast of the Purification, she experienced a moment of conversion and was soon after received into the Catholic Church. About a year later she entered at Stone, making her profession at the age of fifty-eight in October 1903.

Hawick, in the Scottish borders, was selected as the location for the new foundation, mainly on account of the 'industrious nature of the inhabitants' and the scope the town provided for work with women and girls.[53] Though all the founding members had good Scots names – Mother M. Josephine Chisholm as Vicaress, Sisters M. Margaret Sutherland and M. Aloysia Wallace – none was born in Scotland! Sister M. Antoninus Dodds arrived soon after to take charge of the parish school, as did Sister Teresa Margaret herself, who came to act as bursar and to set up the various guilds. Here she was to spend the remaining twelve years of her life, out in all weathers five days a week visiting the poor, ill and needy and consecrating one day a week to instruction of converts. At first the community lived in a house, which soon proved much too small, near the church on Buccleuch Street. The impossibility of finding a large enough property for their needs led to the decision to buy land and build. The architect Reginald Fairlie was engaged and the work financed by the legacy of a Miss Gulson.[54] The compact but elegant building in the vernacular style and boasting some fine decorative work, was completed in 1912.

The community did not find a ready welcome in this very Protestant town. *The Scotsman* had announced the imminent opening of the convent on Saturday 18 January 1909 and immediately letters of protest began to pour in to the editor. A public meeting at the Town Hall, to be presided over by Rev. Mr Johnman and addressed by Pastor Jacob Primmer, assisted by Mrs Walter Young, 'a convert from Rome', was called for Monday 1 March.[55] Although the initial antipathy declined, there was a further disturbance in 1913 outside the newly opened convent on Myreslaw Green. A man by the name of MacDonald held several public lectures in the town at which he attempted to rouse the inhabitants against the Catholics and have the nuns turned out. On a September evening he led a large group of what the annals describe as 'the scum of the town' to the convent gates where he began a threatening discourse. Having been forewarned, Sister Teresa Margaret's guild members crowded about, drowning out MacDonald's voice with lusty choruses of *Faith of our Fathers*![56] Although the mob threatened to scale the walls, the police intervened, though this did not stop repeated visits from MacDonald in the ensuing weeks. It is with a certain note of satisfaction that the annals also record MacDonald's 'exposure' by two Protestant ministers and his subsequent conviction at Motherwell for family desertion.

The salaries of the two sisters teaching in the schools were not sufficient to maintain the community, which began to seek other avenues of remuneration. At first a private school was considered, but this was not thought to be viable in such a small, non-Catholic town. The decision was made to care for incurables and St Catherine's Room, opening directly onto the chapel in the style of a medieval Hôtel-Dieu, was set up to receive the first patients. In 1922 Fairlie designed an extension to the convent and St Margaret's Home was opened under the able direction of Sister M. Alphonsus Beedom. Music teaching was also provided and by the time the home was opened prejudice had broken down so effectively that music pupils flocked to the convent where Sister M. Augustine Fry presided at the keyboard for many years.

Although the future of the convent at Bow was still not resolved, a decision was taken in 1918 to make another foundation to the east of London, in the newly established Diocese of Brentwood. In October Mother Catherine de Ricci Wilson and Sister Rose Magdalen Fellowes visited a convent at Kelvedon in Essex, originally built for Carmelite nuns from Caen, but which the Sisters of Mercy from Harewood Avenue convent had run as an orphanage for some years, and from which they wished to withdraw. The negotiations took the better part of a year to complete and the foundation was made under Sister Margaret Mary Dale as vicaress. The house did not get off to a good start. Three sisters coming up from St Marychurch by rail were caught up in a transport strike, not reaching Paddington until after 10:30p.m. Not knowing their way to Bow, and unable to find a taxi, they began walking in an easterly direction until a Catholic police officer encountered them. He directed them to Portobello Road where, despite everyone being in bed, they were welcomed warmly, and Mother M. Cecilia Marshall organized a hot meal and had rooms made up for them. Not a month later, a fire broke out in a storeroom under the stairs at Kelvedon and Sister M. Dorothea Rankin was obliged to rush across the road to The Angel public house to call for the help of the men at the bar![57]

Nursing was also to be the main work of the community at Kelvedon, where they opened a convalescent and guest house. Sister M. Alphonsus Beedom once again saw to setting up the home while Sister Anne Monica Morgan came from Stone to plan and lay out the gardens. There was no Catholic school in Kelvedon but once Sister M. Bede Clarkson arrived from Bow in 1923, provision was made for the religious instruction of the Catholic children of the town and neighbouring villages of Coggeshall and Tiptree.

By February 1922 it was clear the convent at Bow would have to be closed. As with other convents of the Stone congregation, the Church of Our Lady and St Catherine at Bow had been built, and was owned, by the sisters, not the Archdiocese. As in all their convents, the sisters' choir opened off at right angles from the sanctuary. Now the church needed major renovations, which the Dominicans could not afford. The sisters no longer provided staff for the parish school, while the High School, despite a dedicated staff under Sister M. Anselm Hewitt, had dwindled to a dozen students and was running at a loss. After extended correspondence with the ecclesiastical authorities and solicitors, the church was handed over to the Archdiocese as stipulated in the original agreements at the time of the foundation.[58] A good number of the sisters had been at Bow for many years and keeping up the morale of the community must have been an unenviable task, but one for which its last prioress, Mother Catherine Joseph Crawford was well suited. It was she who organized the enormous task of packing and selling furniture and making arrangements for handing over the management of the guilds and sodalities. It was not until 27 April 1923 that Mother Catherine de Ricci 'turned the key in the lock of St Catherine's Convent – a dismantled, desolate building – left in the hands of a care-taker until it passes into other hands'.[59]

The Stroud congregation made three new foundations about this time. The first of these was made at West Kirby on the Wirral, on 15 October 1912 with Sister M. Winefride Edmonds as vicaress. The prioress at Cheadle provided £50 for furniture and several hampers of provisions, and in November the parishioners presented Stations of the Cross, six tall brass candlesticks and statues of the Sacred Heart and St Dominic for the chapel.[60] There was no parish school at West Kirby but it was decided to open a private school, with the intention of making application at some future date for aided status; within a year there were twenty-one pupils. The other familiar activities: guilds, sodalities and parish visiting were also carried on. The community seems to have enjoyed a good working relationship with the pastor, Father James Abram, who became a constant and welcome visitor 'along with his dog, Scamp, who deigns to look quite at home in the convent and submits with great grace and dignity to the terrible ordeal of being petted by the Sisters'.[61] West Kirby also provided a place by the sea where sisters in need of rest or a change of air could be accommodated.

The second foundation, made at Carisbrooke on the Isle of Wight, was to have only a brief span of life. A community of three, led by Sister M. Emmanuel Fuller, took up residence on 12 September 1913 in Carisbrooke House which had been home for ten years to a group of Visitation nuns from Rouen, who let them have the property rent free for the first year. Once again, a small private school was opened, along with flourishing Sunday schools and a women's guild. The Second Order Dominican nuns were just a short walk away and frequently sent small presents to the Stroud sisters, who often went to the extern aisle of the chapel at the Priory to join in singing the Divine Office. The Visitandines had kept livestock and made hay, and the Dominicans kept this up to assist with the war effort. In June 1915, Mother M. Pius Pretty was visiting and joined the sisters and hired hands in mowing the fields and then tossing the hay. The sisters were well pleased with their efforts and quite deflated when Henry Pierce, their handyman, quipped that the French nuns had not only made the hay on their own, but carried it into the barn in large canvas cloths held at the corners.[62] By this time the General Council at Stroud had already decided that the work was too heavy and the sisters available too few to carry on the house. They advised Bishop Cotter of Portsmouth that they wished to withdraw but agreed to remain until another congregation could be found to take their place. They handed the convent over to the Rosminian Sisters of Providence on 29 July 1915.

Stroud's final foundation was its third in the Archdiocese of Birmingham and within twenty miles of Stone, at Brewood. It came about as the result of a chance meeting with a priest who, after observing them intently for some time, approached Sisters M. Ambrose Ladelle and M. Ursula Walshe as they were leaving the Oratory church in Edgbaston on a late August afternoon in 1919. Father Patrick O'Toole was set on acquiring nuns for his parish school, as his very capable headmistress had recently handed in her notice. Any nuns would do in extremis but above all he wanted Dominicans. The startled sisters referred him to the Mother General in Stroud and within a month the offer, which included the gift of a large house and garden, had been accepted.[63] On Friday 2 January 1920 the first group of sisters including Sister M. Ambrose and the prioress of Erdington, Sister M. Scholastica Donnelly, arrived to establish the Convent of the Immaculate Conception. Bargate was indeed a large house but it was in a deplorable state, lacking light, heating and mains water and the gardens had been much neglected. Undaunted, the new community set themselves to cleaning, whitewashing and painting the house, with Sister M. Ambrose making much headway in the garden and setting up hen runs. Within a year the convent had been fitted with gas, connected to mains water and in 1922 a central heating system was installed at a cost of almost £400.[64]

Sister M. Joseph Blenkinsop was appointed headmistress of St Mary's School when it reopened in January and the following September the Convent School opened under Sister M. Ambrose, with six boarders: three Catholics and three Protestants. During the early years the curriculum was limited to the humanities and commercial subjects and amongst the early members of staff was Sister M. Michael Johnson-Brown, who had the distinction of being the first English Dominican sister to acquire a university degree, having taken a first in philosophy as an external student through the University of London. The school developed slowly, still having no more than thirty pupils, from infants to eighteen-year-olds, in

1929. It was not until the 1930s that science subjects were provided, or that the girls were presented as a matter of course for public examinations. However, what it might have lacked in academic achievement in its early years was compensated for by a strong esprit de corps, tolerance and flexibility.[65]

Although sisters of the Harrow congregation resided at times at Felpham in Sussex from 1911, it does not seem that it was ever canonically erected as a religious house, but served as a holiday and convalescent home for sisters and those in their care until the property was sold in 1931. An opening was offered at Baldock in Hertfordshire during the war but was refused for lack of sisters.[66] The work in the convent school at Kilburn had developed considerably and although sisters continued to teach in the parish schools there, the community moved to larger premises in Chislett Road, West Hampstead, in 1919. By this time there were thirty weekly boarders and 110 day students in the Convent School there. The Leicester community, fully occupied with setting up the nursing home and developing the schools at Bridlington, made no new foundations during this period.

Two foundations were made by the Portobello Road congregation, the first at Haverstock Hill. The Provincial, Father Bede Jarrett, had asked for a foundation there in April 1915, as a house was offered rent free near the Priory. He was certain secular tertiaries would be glad to live there and that their pension would provide sufficient income to allow sisters to engage in parish visiting and the instruction of converts.[67] What he did not tell Mother M. Cecilia Marshall was that he had made the same offer to the Stroud congregation![68] Father Bede did mention the possibility of sisters coming from the United States but made it clear that he would prefer English sisters. A letter to Mother M. Pius Pretty of Stroud, from Miss Baker, who was perhaps the donor of the house, encourages her to make the foundation and warns that 'if you don't go there, he will invite the Stone Sisters or Portobello Road and your chances will be lost forever'.[69] Already struggling with the foundation at Carisbrooke, Stroud did lose its chance and five sisters under Sister M. Lewis Urbani came from Portobello Road on 26 October that year. The house was closed eleven months later. There were already three convents in the parish: one with a children's home, another with a school and the third community engaged in home nursing, and this must have limited the scope for work which would support the Dominican community.

Early in 1919, after he was demobilized from his post as a military chaplain, Father Bernard Longstaff was appointed first resident priest at Harpenden in Hertfordshire. A lineal descendant of St Thomas More, he was certainly imbued with his ancestor's zeal. His first concern was to find a community of religious sisters to assist him in building up the Catholic life of the town. The Vicar General, Canon Edmond Surmont, put him in touch with Mother M. Cecilia Marshall, who was then engaged in negotiations to purchase Woodfield House in Hendon as a children's home. The house was too expensive and too small to serve the required purpose but the offer of Bowers Cottage in Harpenden was accepted. On 30 May 1920, Sister M. Monica Carroll and two companions took up residence.[70]

In September the small school which had been established at Dovercourt was transferred to Harpenden where it grew rapidly. Within three years the numbers had risen to eighty, but there was no hope of expansion on the site and no other suitable property available. For a while Father Longstaff feared Mother M. Cecilia would withdraw the community but quite unexpectedly Harpenden Hall, a Jacobean mansion on the Common, came into the market and was purchased in October 1923. Considerable renovations were required before the community and pupils could move into their new home in January 1924. Apart from the apostolate in the school the sisters also had frequent visits from the gypsies camping on the Common. Sister M. Clare Daly was well acquainted with travelling people in her native Ireland and always interpreted their requests for a billy of boiling water as a declaration of hunger and provided them not only with tea but substantial portions of bread and butter.[71]

There were, however, never enough sisters to fulfil all the requests for new foundations. Once the community at Hawick was well settled, the Stone congregation was asked to make a foundation at Troon in Ayrshire.[72] In June 1920 the annals record the possibility of a foundation in the West Indies, where the friars of the English Province had missions in Trinidad and Grenada. In fact, the Portobello Road sisters had already been invited to Port-of-Spain by the Dominican Bishop Flood as early as 1906, while they were still affiliated to the Châtillon congregation.[73] Requests were made to Stroud for an enormous number of foundations and an impressive list can be drawn up: a house was offered at Hartley in Kent for a special school (1916), sisters were requested for the parish schools in Uttoxeter (1918), at Warwick, Luton and Kings Heath in Birmingham (1919), Gillingham in Kent, Heaton, Ledbury and Waltham Cross (1920), Creswell in Staffordshire (1922), Redditch (1924), Malvern (1925) and even a college for girls as far away as Oslo (1923).[74] These requests certainly show that the work of the sisters was valued and seen as an integral means of furthering the mission and invigorating the life of the Church.

'A certain latitude be conceded . . .': the First World War

The First World War was to cut through this period of development and to affect the lives of the sisters as much as those of the general population. Though the annals at Stroud fail to make any mention of the war until the end of January 1915, the effects at Stone were more immediate. In August 1914 it is noted that 'Our German Sisters have had to present themselves at the police stations and be registered as "enemy aliens".'[75] Each had to carry identification papers, including a photograph, and travel was restricted to a five-mile radius of their notified residence.

There were five German nationals in the Stone congregation when war was declared. Sister M. Benedicta Mathieu was born in Saarbrücken, the daughter of a customs official. We do not know when or why she came to England but she was one of the first postulants to enter the congregation after the noviciate was established at Stone in 1857. Almost her entire religious life was spent at Stoke-on-Trent, the greater part of it in nursing in St Margaret's Hospital there. Sister M. Gertrude Kompel, a native of Heidelberg, had been employed as *Fraulein* at the boarding school in Bow before entering the convent in 1891. The necrology describes her as affectionate, given to scrupulosity and feeling keenly the disasters which befell her native country. These tensions brought on a period of depression and soon after the war, Sister M. Gertrude was admitted, first to the Bon Sauveur Hospital at Carriglea in Ireland, and later to St George's Retreat at Burgess Hill, returning to community life only in 1924.[76] Sister M. Hildegarde Lederer was a Barvarian who had come to England as a young woman and worked as governess to the Somers Cocks family – one of whose daughters would follow her to Stone as Sister M. Christina – before entering at Stone in 1881, at the age of thirty-six. She is described as being 'German with an English heart' and spent many years teaching in the boarding school at St Marychurch. The two other German sisters came from extremely well-connected families and both had entered at Stone with the intention of forming the nucleus of a proposed German congregation which never eventuated. Both were members of the St Marychurch community when the war broke out and their adaptation to life as 'enemy aliens' makes for an interesting contrast.

Ida Augusta von Wangenheim and her twin sister Elise were born on 3 November 1839 in the principality of Hechingen-Hohenzollern, which was absorbed into the Prussian state in 1850. Their father, Karl Hermann, belonged to a north German family of civil servants and rose to the rank of Privy Councillor to the Imperial Court after 1870. Although a Lutheran, he married a Swabian Catholic, Marie Aickner-Heppenstein and according to prevailing custom the daughters were raised in their mother's faith. Marie was a woman of enormous personal charm, cultivated and hospitable. She kept open house for the political, clerical and literary élite of mid-century Berlin where the family made their home. In the 1850s the girls acquired as their tutor the German literary giant Theodor Fontane who, despite his Huguenot origins, became a close personal friend of the family. In one of his autobiographical works, *Von Zwanzig bis Dreißig*, he consecrates a chapter to the Wangenheim family and makes much of their mother's repartee, revelling in his role of 'heretic' and earning the riposte that he would surely end up a Catholic![77] This friendship brought Fontane into contact with the kind of people – priests and Catholic Centre Party politicians – he might otherwise never have encountered, and a value system quite opposed to the strident nationalism which manifested itself in the *Kulturkampf* and the Falk Laws. The empathy and wit, mixed with a measure of critical distance, with which he portrays Catholics in his work surely has its origin in his relationship with the Wangenheims.[78]

With such a background it is hardly surprising that the necrology acclaims Ida as 'one of the most valuable subjects ever granted to our congregation'. Already a Dominican tertiary, she came to Stone in August 1871 and was received as a novice under the name Ida Baptista the following January. While Ida's grasp of philosophy, logic, literature, languages and art gave evidence of her broad intellect, this was matched by a largeness of heart evident to all. Only six years after her profession of vows, Sister Ida Baptista was appointed mistress of novices. Between 1883 and 1915 she moved back and forth between Bow and St Marychurch as prioress, a role she fulfilled with great skill. Her interest in individuals, her powers of persuasion and her maternal nature won affection both inside and outside the community and even resulted in her father undertaking the translation of several of Mother Francis Raphael Drane's works. At the outbreak of war, there was no question of a return to Germany but when the authorities in Devon called for her removal as prioress at St Marychurch, the local populace, Catholic and Protestant alike, petitioned for her to remain. A letter from Bishop John Keily of Plymouth, however, made it plain that he would appreciate the replacement of Mother Ida Baptista by an English prioress.[79] It was thought wiser to bring her to Stone where she remained until her death in 1921.

The Baroness Luise von Loë was born 1863 at Schloss Wissen in Westphalia, the daughter of Count Maximilian von Loë and Countess Therese von und zu Arco-Zinneberg, a direct descendent of the Hapsburg empress Maria Theresia of Austria. She entered at Stone just before her twenty-third birthday and was professed in March 1888 as Sister M. Elisabeth. The family not only provided a dowry and a generous annuity but also made several benefactions to the various houses of the Stone congregation. Sister M. Elisabeth, like her compatriots, taught in the young ladies' schools at Stone and St Marychurch and was also an amateur photographer. The archives at Stone preserve a photograph showing her before a mounted camera, a second black veil concealing her head and shoulders, caught in the act of photographing the children about to take part in a procession honouring the coronation of Edward VII in June 1902.

The nineteenth century had been a period of intense cultural interchange between Britain and Germany and this, together with a similarity of temperament and the dynastic alliances of the royal houses, encouraged amongst many Germans a climate of anglophilia in which Sister M. Elisabeth doubtless shared. For such people the First World War was an intellectual and affective catastrophe. On the other hand, some forty members of the extended von Loë family were officers of the Imperial army and the annals note that Sister M. Elisabeth was 'a great patriot and devoted to the Kaiser'. Her position as a German member of an English congregation became increasingly difficult, though it is interesting to note that Bishop Keily declared in a curt manner that he would have nothing to do with assisting her return to Germany.[80] Nonetheless, a year after the war broke out Sister M. Elisabeth petitioned to be released from her obedience to Stone and travelled to the Netherlands where a countess cousin received her until her transfer to a German Dominican congregation could be arranged. She died at Arenberg in the same year as Sister Ida Baptista.

The traffic was not entirely one-way. In 1916 a member of the Lubbeck Dominican congregation in Belgium was recommended to Mother M. Pius Pretty at Stroud by the provincial, Father Humbert Everest. Kathleen McCaffry had been at school at St Dominic's at

Fig. 10 Sister Ida Baptista von Wangenheim, seated fifth from left, with her community at St Marychurch, 1896.

Harrow and completed her education in Lubbeck, where she entered the noviciate in 1898 and was given the name Marie-Benoît. After the German occupation and the court martial of her prioress, the strain of living in a community with several German members became too much for this Yorkshire woman. She came to England and taught for some time with the Sisters of the Holy Child Jesus at Harrogate and then with the Stroud Dominicans at Cheadle. Accepted by the vote of the chapter at St Rose's, she made a second noviciate and was professed as Sister M. Raphael in August 1918, teaching for the next thirty years at Stroud and Brewood before retiring to Stone where she died in 1959.

On a day-to-day level the annalist at Stone records the first casualties from the town: two brothers by the name of Gaitley killed in action in November 1914, and the arrival at Stoke of seventy-seven wounded soldiers. Red Cross hospitals were set up close to the convents at both Stone and Stroud. At the end of October 1915, as many of the wounded soldiers as were able, were invited to a 'fairy party' staged in their honour by the girls of St Rose's Special School in Stroud. They responded magnificently to the singing and acting of the disabled children and could hardly be persuaded to leave, maimed soldiers and crippled children singing and dancing together until late. It is noted that a similar entertainment organized by the ladies of the Convent School in Stroud did not manage to elicit the same level of empathy amongst the convalescents.[81] At Stoke too, the High School pupils put on a concert for the wounded soldiers from the North Staffordshire Infirmary and provided each one with a packet of sweets, cherries and cigarettes.[82]

The director of nursing at the Red Cross Hospital at Stone, Miss Meekin, approached the prioress at St Dominic's to request the services of Sister M. Christopher Hughes, who had qualified as a therapeutic masseuse before entering the congregation in 1910. Despite a prohibition against such work having been issued by Vatican officials in 1908 as being 'not altogether becoming to virgins dedicated to God',[83] the prioress was only too happy to 'contribute to the patriotic work'.[84] The necrology states that Sister M. Christopher was possessed of a clever and original mind, able to 'rise to heroic acts then whimper like a child over trifles'. Certainly she rose to the challenge of working for the wounded soldiers and her mornings were spent entirely in this work, which was carried out so effectively that the Hospital Committee offered a salary. This was declined in order to assist the war effort, though her skill was recognized as exemplary and her services retained until the last convalescents left the hospital in 1920. At Carisbrooke the Stroud

Sisters provided meals for the soldiers guarding the waterworks and also made flannelette suits for the wounded survivors of the Anzac offensive at Gallipoli who were convalescing in Egypt. The director of the hospital in Ghezirah was Lieutenant General John Brady Nash whose daughter, Sister M. Hyacinth, was a Dominican nun at Maitland, New South Wales.[85]

The war brought refugees, mainly Belgians, to England and a party was held for them at the convent in Bow in January 1915. The annalist at Stroud records, two months later, that more than a hundred Belgian refugees who were living in Stroud and its vicinity came to breakfast at the Special School after Sunday Mass. The following September sixteen children from this group were prepared by the sisters for their First Communion. Other religious also came as refugees and were accommodated on a temporary basis in several English Dominican houses: the Irish Benedictines of Ypres and the Ursulines from Lier amongst them.[86] As early as October 1914, Portobello Road community gave refuge to Dominican sisters from Knocke-sur-Mer in Belgium, the first of several groups they received during the war. German prisoners of war were also held in a camp at Stone and two of them, 'quiet, Catholic men' were put to work painting walls in the convent, though they were unable to attend public Masses in the Church for fear of the hostile feelings their presence might arouse.[87]

As the war progressed the sisters often recorded the shortage of basic foodstuffs, the impossibility of procuring fish or eggs for abstinence days, and the rapidly mounting prices. By 1917 pure wheaten flour was unobtainable and the adulterated substitute was not canonically acceptable for the production of altar breads – quite a large scale operation at Stone. It was only with great difficulty and at great cost that the required flour was obtained by special licence. A certain latitude in matters of dress was also necessary on account of wartime conditions. At Stone, petty as it may seem in view of the general carnage at the front, the decision was made rather reluctantly, on account of the difficulty procuring them and their great cost, to give up the white house shoes which had been part of the habit since Clifton days. The annals are at pains to state that the decision was made 'not from a desire to give up the white shoes, which we shall much regret, but from holy poverty and the desire to agree with superiors'.[88]

This is not to say that the sisters, particularly in the larger cities, did not share in the real hardships of war. The chronicler of St Catherine's Convent, Newcastle-upon-Tyne, mentions the endless queuing for food rations and coal in the bitter winter weather.

There was also the difficulty of undertaking parish visiting and other work through the unlit streets in heavy fog. In fact their lot was now perhaps worse than many of the people they had formally aided as:

> The usual poverty of the poor was, for the time, entirely banished, since most of the women and girls were working at the munitions sheds and earned high wages. Others replaced the men in the schools, shops and offices while the wives and mothers who stayed received the regular army pensions due to their men at the front. Yet sorrow and deep distress of mind abounded, proving beyond doubt that money alone cannot bestow happiness. The atmosphere of woe was so universal that it seemed a species of heartlessness to even think a cheerful thought.[89]

The urban communities also witnessed the novelty of aerial warfare; zeppelins passed over the convent at Shieldfield Green before dropping their bombs on Wallsend.[90] In September 1915 several bombs fell in the vicinity of the convent at Bow, destroying the Black Swan public house across the road. On this occasion a zeppelin was brought down and 'To those who saw the burning Zeppelin fall at a distance, this magnificent but terrible sight made a deep impression and left on some an alarming sense of insecurity.'[91] Apparently the locals felt secure at the convent, as the annals later record the presence of seventy to eighty people taking shelter in the cloisters during the frequent air raids of June and July 1917, Mother Margaret Mary Dale, the prioress, keeping up their spirits by praying aloud for them for hours on end. At Portobello Road the sisters and residents became used to taking refuge in the chapel at night during the increasingly frequent raids, always warned by their watch dog, a red and white collie, whose keen sense of hearing detected the noise of the approaching airships.[92]

The register of the boys' preparatory school at Bognor, run by the Harrow Dominicans, lists those of the ex-pupils known to have been killed in action: a quarter of those who entered the school between 1899 and 1906.[93] This indicates that the sisters kept up with their former pupils and there is certainly evidence of correspondence with them and their families. Although seldom mentioned in the annals, many sisters lost family members and note is made of special permission being given to visit brothers on leave. A letter from Dom Placid Pritchard, a monk of Erdington Abbey serving as an ambulance driver with the Red Cross, was written to Sister M. Hilda McLean of St Agnes' Convent from 'somewhere in France' in 1915. He had been very much moved to find in the pocket of a wounded soldier, a comforting letter many months old, from his cousin, Sister M. Hilda. In a letter full of allusions to the horrors of war and of blood being the price of societal sin, Dom Placid recounts the lad's last days and burial:

> I saw the spot where they laid him, beneath the shadow of a single large wooden cross, the only peaceful spot amidst an ocean of blood and hate and sin ... he remained faithful to his God through all the temptations of army life and the ties of human frailty.[94]

With so many men at the front, the Dominican Sisters, like so many other women, took on much of the heavier work in their houses which they would formerly have paid men to do. A delightful Easter greeting from Mother M. Raymond Goldrick of St Agnes' Convent Erdington, sent to the mother house at Stroud in 1918, shows how they acquitted themselves. The card states proudly that the prioress 'hath a care for the property, & moweth her own lawn in war time' and is shown in action, ably assisted by Sisters M. Hyacinth Scott and M. Ursula Walshe. The card is decorated with a suffragette ribbon, and seems to indicate the reward the sisters deemed worthy of their efforts – 'vote[s] for women' is inscribed at the base!

The annals of St Agnes' Convent Erdington also record Armistice Day with a red letter entry. At Portobello Road the sisters assembled in the choir to chant the *Te Deum* and the house was hung with Chinese lanterns, and the trees outside with coloured lights. 'Here the children and girls disported themselves, dancing and singing to the music of a gramophone and playing all sorts of games.'[95] Elsewhere there seems to have been more concern with the influenza epidemic.

Despite the cessation of hostilities and the end of shortages, the white shoes did not reappear at Stone, though almost every other aspect of the lives of the Dominican Sisters in England returned to the familiar patterns of the pre-war period. The communities were not by any means immune to change and certainly noticed the transformation of society around them. Since the new canonical legislation for women religious was introduced at the beginning of the century, reinforced by the promulgation of the new Code of Canon Law during the war, a more legalistic mindset was descending on religious communities. This emphasis on detail did much to sacralize traditions and customs, some of them quite peripheral, and attributed to them the force of immutable law. As society changed, the sisters' lives did not, and many aspects of everyday conventual life became further removed from the lived experience of the women who entered religion after 1918, and less comprehensible to them. In all five Dominican groups the attrition rate at all stages of formation, and even after perpetual profession increased. This may well reflect a certain dislocation between the religious communities and those they sought to serve. A lack of internal cohesion, however, could be much more problematic as we shall now see.

'They have always clashed . . .': crisis at Leicester

In December 1919, Father Leo Moore, OP was deputed by Bishop Dunne of Nottingham to undertake a canonical visitation of the Dominican Sisters at Leicester. While the general state of the house is considered to be 'fairly satisfactory' the relationship between the chaplain and the Sisters had given rise to tensions. It was also noted that the lay sisters seemed to have insufficient understanding, or at least a lack of instruction, in their religious duties and life. The net result, in Father Leo's estimation, was an almost total breakdown in the maintenance of silence, and a neglect of chapter meetings at which the prioress might have taken the opportunity, by instruction and exhortation, to improve matters. Instead, superiors were inclined to take any criticism of the state of affairs personally and the visitation interviews had revealed a conspicuous breakdown of charity and increase in petty behaviour and vindictiveness.[96]

Father Leo's description of the chaplain's behaviour shows how the dynamics of the community could be upset by undue intrusion:

> The chaplain looked on the convent as a home in which he could do as he liked. So he was there at all times, went continually to the community room when the Sisters were there and during the day time, as the Prioress used this room as her business room, sat with her and prevented the Sisters by his presence, from being able to speak in privacy, smoked going about the house and so on. This was resented and when it was represented to the Prioress that it had become somewhat of a scandal, nothing was done and the complaining Sisters were reproved etc.[97]

The situation improved markedly with a change in chaplain and prioress but despite valiant efforts, the community was unable to forestall further difficulties. Reports had certainly reached the Dominican Provincial, Father Bede Jarrett, that the Yorkshire houses founded from Leicester were far from satisfactory.[98] The parish priest of Redcar, Canon Albert Gryspeert, had written to Bishop Dunne in 1921 critical of the sisters teaching in his schools, claiming that, quite apart from their shortcomings in the classroom, 'discipline seems to be very weak and they do not seem to have had much religious training'.[99] The community had a heavy work load, was burdened with debt from the ambitious building programme on which they had recently embarked, and had also experienced both a high recruitment and defection rate after the First World War. Any one of these circumstances would have been sufficient on its own to place strains on community life.

When Bishop Dunne himself carried out the next canonical visitation in March 1927, the general situation was much better. The Leicester annals state that the Bishop spoke encouraging words to the community and suggested that the time was ripe for applying to Rome for confirmation of their constitutions. He also looked forward to returning before too long to lay the foundation stone of the new chapel which he had recently given the Sisters permission to build.[100] From the text of Bishop Dunne's address to the community, preserved in the Diocesan Archives at Nottingham, it is clear he had approached the visitation with apprehension. The Bishop praised the religious spirit of the house and particularly that of the junior sisters – 'the happiest possible augury for the future of the convent' as he put it. But it is also evident that he found the attitudes and behaviour of several of the more senior sisters far from acceptable In fact he took the unusual step of shaming two of them – Sisters M. Benedict Murphy and M. Cyril Graham – publicly, before the whole community. Two other sisters were also named in the report as being particularly vulnerable to the influence of the troublemakers who were, in Bishop Dunne's opinion, suffering from 'swelled head'.

Sisters M. Benedict and M. Cyril had both qualified as teachers at St Charles' Training School in London and at the time were teaching in Sacred Heart School in Leicester. It is apparent that the other two sisters named in the report were also employed in the schools, since it was noted that 'they have been and are daily exposed [to the influence of Sisters M. Benedict and M. Cyril] by their association outside the convent …' The public proclamation had been intended to act as a decisive antidote to the pride of the two culprits, who not only considered themselves 'valuable assets to the convent' but would, according to the bishop, like to rule the community as well. The reaction of the two sisters was perhaps a little more extreme than had been anticipated.

Sister M. Cyril Graham's immediate reaction was to give in to feelings of desperation and walk out of the convent there and then. However, she thought better of this and returned, in order, as she put it, 'to leave decently'. A week after the conclusion of the visitation she wrote to the bishop admitting that she was 'not great enough to rise above the public reprimand' and gave her own estimation of her 'crimes':

> 1) I have objected to Father Ambrose (the chaplain)
> 2) I have not been too regular but I have been doing my best
> 3) I do not think as my superiors do
> 4) I was out late doing apostolic work.[101]

A less heated letter followed three days later, in which one may detect hints of a tension not mentioned in the bishop's visitation report. Sister M. Cyril wrote:

> The community's interests are alien to those of the school and they have always clashed and always will. Dane Hills has no interest in the school as a school, only in the income ... only the school has kept me here ... I am not saying I did not deserve a reprimand, very likely I did, but not a public one like that.[102]

Even in communities where a single apostolic endeavour was shared by all there could be tensions. At Leicester the sisters had always been involved in school work, both in the parish schools and, for a short time, in running a private school. But with the move to Dane Hills in 1906, hospital work came to the fore. The expense involved in building the new nursing home and saving money for the proposed new convent and chapel, was met by increasingly stringent economies. The community also lived at close quarters, mainly in the attic of the nursing home. With the permission of Bishop Brindle, Sisters M. Winifrede Keane and M. Martha Scally had set sail on the SS *Baltic* on 14 November 1907 bound for the United States where they spent several months on yet another begging campaign to service the community debt of £6,000.[103] By the year of the visitation it had even been decided to forego holidays at the branch houses as a means of economy.[104]

The annals give further evidence of the changing apostolic priorities of the community. There is much more frequent mention of candidates being received with nursing qualifications, or of newly professed sisters being sent to acquire them. Likewise, when the majority of the community is involved in a single work within the house, the timetable will be geared towards this. It is perhaps understandable that the teaching sisters, having to travel across the city, and being away from the house for the greater part of the day, began to feel alienated and this might account, to some extent, for their laxity in following the regular observance.

Following the visitation, both Sisters M. Cyril and M. Benedict ceased attending choir altogether and went out to the parish church for Mass on Sundays. The prioress, Mother M. Winefride Keane, mentioned their bitter feelings to the Bishop and opined that 'the sooner they get their dispensations the better, as where there are novices and postulants it is serious for them to see things like this'.[105] She also mentioned Sister M. Benedict's long-standing dissatisfaction and the fact that six years previously she had asked for a dispensation from her vows, but had almost immediately withdrawn the application. This time dispensations were despatched and duly signed, the two sisters leaving the convent on the evening of 3 April 1927, without letting even the prioress know where they were going. In what must have been an almost unique situation for ex-religious of that era, the two returned to teach at Sacred Heart School the next day in new apparel and under their secular names. A commemorative publication produced by Sacred Heart School in the 1970s reports that Miss Graham and Miss Murphy were strong disciplinarians, the latter being nick-named 'Juicy Lemons as she wasn't half bitter'.[106] Both women continued to serve at the school until they retired in the 1950s.

The difficulties at Leicester did not end with the departure of Sisters M. Cyril and M. Benedict, though it was perhaps a catalyst for the great organizational change that was to come. The inability of the community to master the difficulties in which it found itself, or to provide strong and effective leadership from its own resources, would lead the Bishop to seek a remedy outside.

Conclusion

In a society in rapid transition, the English Dominican Sisters did all they could to meet new needs and actively embraced professional training to better equip themselves to do so. But as we have seen, certain elements of their lives did not change at all and a measure of dislocation developed, not only between their lifestyle and that of the people they served, but between the private and public spheres of their own lives. A sister could read literature at university, but was not allowed to read the newspapers at home. After 1918, a lay sister over thirty years of age could vote for her Member of Parliament, but she could not vote for delegates to the

General Chapter of her congregation or give her views on any matter concerning the life and work of her community. Another thirty years would pass before this dislocation was addressed and resolutions sought.

On the other hand, this period, particularly the 1920s, saw the different Dominican groups begin to move out of their relative isolation. This was caused in part by the requirement for them all to rewrite their constitutions, though this was not the only reason for increasing contacts and cooperation. So we find mention of Mother M. Cecilia Marshall and Sister M. Catherine McHale arriving at Stone to learn how the officers of that congregation managed business and financial arrangements.[107] The arrival is also recorded of Mother M. Ambrose Kilbride, Prioress of Leicester and another sister, coming to Stone to be instructed in the recitation of the Divine Office, which the Leicester sisters were adopting.[108] Two years later, Mother M. Pius Pretty came from Stroud to assist the General Council at Stone in drawing up their new constitutions.[109] In October the following year, the General Council at Stone was clearly in a position to welcome Mother M. Winefride Keane and Sister M. Augustine Murphy from Leicester, to give these sisters advice on drawing up their constitutions.[110]

Neither were the visits all for business. As early as 1912 Mother M. Pius Pretty and a young sister from Cheadle stopped at the convent in Stoke-on-Trent and took tea with the community there. The following Thursday, Mother Catherine Magdalen Parker and Sister M. Anthony Tregoning accepted the Cheadle sisters' pressing invitation for a return visit.[111] Similar visits would be exchanged between Stoke and Stone and the Stroud sisters at Brewood once the convent was established there. These visits, particularly the more formal ones, must have given the major superiors and senior members some idea of the strengths and weaknesses of the other Dominican communities.

It is not altogether a surprise, then, to read in the annals of St Agnes' Convent Erdington that when Mother M. Teresa Lamburn arrived on a visit in February 1929 and asked the sisters to pray for a 'very special intention', some were so convinced of what it must be that they committed their guesses to paper and two months later, when the plan of amalgamation was revealed, they were proved right.

Notes

1. Stone, G20, *Annals of St Dominic's Convent, Stone, 1922–1929*, March 1923.
2. Stone, G18, *Annals of the Convent of St Dominic, 1892–1913*, p. 80.
3. Hostie, *Vie et Mort*, p. 289ff; the remaining stages are decline and extinction.
4. Stone, G28, *Records, July 1920–December 1924*, 4 July 1923.
5. Stone, St.M/18(E), *Annals of St Mary's Priory, 1888–1948*, April 1898.
6. Stone, G18, *Annals, 1892–1913*, p. 326.
7. Stone, G19, *Annals of St Dominic's Convent, Stone, August 1913–April 1922*, 13 September 1913.
8. Stone, G18, *Annals, 1892–1913*, p. 229.
9. Stone, STK18(ii), *Annals: Convent of Our Lady of the Angels, Stoke-on-Trent, 1910–1926*, p. 270.
10. Ibid., p. 312.
11. Stone, G20, *Annals, 1922–1929*, March 1923.
12. Richard Smith, *Elgar, Dot and the Stroud connection*.
13. Stroud, STR18(i), *Annals of the Congregation of St Rose of Lima, Vol. 1. 1901–1925*, 25 December 1913.
14. Stone, H/G9(a), *Deliberations of Council, 1900-1929*, 14 August 1918.
15. *Ibid.*, 13 March 1920.
16. Stone, HWR.2.G, *A Memoir of Revd Mother M. Dominic Wilkes, OP, 1862–1939*.
17. Stone, G19, *Annals 1913–1922*, February 1917.
18. Whitehead, 'A View from the Bridge' in *From without the Flaminian Gate*, p. 218.
19. Stone, G18, *Annals, 1892–1913*, p. 214.
20. Stone, G19, *Annals 1913–1922*, April 1922.
21. Stone, G1-b, *Register of St Dominic's Priory, Stone, in the County of Stafford*, p. 99.
22. Stone, CH18(1), *St Joseph's Convent, Cheadle. Annals, 1898–1925*, 9 October 1914.
23. Ibid., 22 September 1919.
24. Stone, G18, *Annals, 1892–1913*, p. 193.
25. Stone, STK3/1a, Christina Cyples, *Aspects of Roman Catholic Education: a study of St Dominic's High School, Stoke-on-Trent*, 4th Year B.Ed. Paper, Coventry College of Education, 1977.
26. Stone, STK18(ii), *Stoke Annals, 1910–1926*, p. 288.
27. Ibid., p. 229.
28. Stone, G1-b, *Register of St Dominic's Priory*, p. 328.
29. Stone, G29, *Records, January 1925–September 1929*, 26 June 1926.
30. Stone, St.M/18(E), *Annals of St Mary's Priory, 1888–1948*, April 1921.
31. Stone, G18, *Annals, 1892–1913*, p. 342.
32. Ibid., p. 122.
33. Stone, G19, *Annals 1913–1922*, October 1914.
34. Ibid., 29 September 1918.
35. Ibid., June 1921.

36. Stone, STR3(ii), *Compilation of Manuscript Sources in the Convent Archives*, p. 17.
37. Stroud, PH/STR3-2, *Admissions Register*.
38. Stroud, STR18(i), Stroud *Annals, 1901–1925*, 11 May 1913.
39. Ibid., 9 June 1913.
40. Ibid., 29 December 1913.
41. Stroud, PH/STR3-5, *Biographical Notes on Pupils, 1912–1927*.
42. Stroud, STR18(i), Stroud *Annals, 1901–1925*, 20 January 1916.
43. Stone, N1(i), *Memoirs of St Catherine's Convent, Newcastle-upon-Tyne from 1878–1929,* p. 8.
44. Ibid., p. 11.
45. Stroud, STR18(i), Stroud *Annals, 1901–1925*, Easter 1922.
46. Stone, N1(i), *Memoirs of St Ctaherine's Convent,* p. 15.
47. Sisters, *A Treasure of Joy and Gladness*, p. 48.
48. Stone, LON/P/Box 2, *First Annual Report: St Mary's Training Hostel for Catholic Women Emigrants*, 1930.
49. Ibid.
50. Stone, G18, *Annals, 1892–1913*, p. 174.
51. Stone, G19, *Annals 1913–1922*, 22 January 1919.
52. Stone, G28, *Records, June 1914–August 1921*, 17 June 1915.
53. Stone, G15, *Register of the Branch Houses*, p. 197.
54. Ibid., p. 203.
55. *A house with a past – St Margaret's Nursing Home*, BBC Radio Scotland website, http://www.bbc.co.uk/radioscotland/gallery/stmargarets/ accessed 14 September 2009.
56. Stone, G19, *Annals 1913–1922*, September 1913.
57. Ibid., 2 and 22 October.
58. Stone, G15, *Register of the Branch Houses*, p. 167.
59. Stone, G20, *Stone Annals, 1922–1929*, April 1923.
60. Stroud, STR18(i), Stroud *Annals, 1901–1925*, 16 November 1912.
61. Ibid., 2 May 1913.
62. Ibid., 15 June 1915.
63. Stone, ER18(ii), *St Agnes' Convent Erdington Annals, 1918–1947*, August 1919.
64. Walters, *St Dominic's School Brewood*, p. 6. It is interesting to note that the first sisters were driven to Brewood by Alfred Haden whose sister, Mildred would enter the Dominicans in 1935 and teach at Brewood as Sister M. Denis.
65. Ibid., p. 14.
66. Stone, H/G9(a), *Deliberations of the Council, 1900–1929*, 25 August 1916.
67. Stone, LON/P/G9, *Council Minute Book*, 7 April 1915.
68. Stone, STR14, Fr Bede Jarrett to Mother M. Pius Pretty, undated (1915).
69. Stone, STR14, Miss Baker to Mother M. Pius Pretty, 30 September 1915.
70. Stone, LON/P/G5R, *Records of the Convent of St Vincent Ferrer*, 1920.
71. Sisters, *A Treasure of Joy and Gladness*, p. 62.
72. Stone, G19, *Annals 1913–1922*, November 1913.
73. Stone, LON/P/G9R, *Records of the Convent of St Vincent Ferrer*, 1906.

74. Stone, STR14, *Miscellaneous correspondence*.
75. Stone, G19, *Annals 1913–1922*, August 1914.
76. Stone, G28, *Records, July 1920–December 1924*, 24 February 1924.
77. Fontane, *Von Zwanzig bis Dreißig*, pp. 414–26.
78. Sagarra, 'Theodor Fontane' in *German Life and Letters*, vol. 58, no 2, pp. 124–5.
79. Stone, G19, *Annals 1913–1922*, 17 June 1915.
80. Ibid., 1 June 1915.
81. Stroud, STR18(i), Stroud *Annals, 1901–1925*, 30 October and 21 December 1915.
82. Stone, STK18(ii), *Stoke Annals, 1910–1926*, July 1917.
83. Wall, *Unlikely Entrepreneurs*, p. 182.
84. Stone, G19, *Annals 1913–1922*, July 1917.
85. Stroud, STR18(i), Stroud *Annals, 1901–1925*, 1 July 1915.
86. Stone, G19, *Annals 1913–1922*, January 1915.
87. Ibid., 26 February 1918.
88. Stone, G26, *Records, June 1914–August 1921*, 24 May 1915.
89. Stone, N1(i), *Memoirs of St Catherine's Convent*, p. 13.
90. Ibid., p. 12.
91. Stone, G19, *Annals 1913–1922*, 23 September 1915.
92. Stone, LON/P/G5R, *Records of the Convent of St Vincent Ferrer*, 7 July 1917.
93. Stone, BGN(iii), *Admissions Register*.
94. Stone, STR2/14/E2, Dom Placid Pritchard to Sister M. Hilda McLean, 1915.
95. Sisters, *A Treasure of Joy and Gladness*, p. 66.
96. Nottingham, Convent Files: Dane Hills, *Report of canonical visitation at Leicester*, 3 December 1919.
97. Ibid.
98. Nottingham, Convent Files: Dane Hills, Fr Bede Jarrett to Bishop Thomas Dunne, 17 September 1923.
99. Nottingham, Convent Files: Dane Hills, Rev. Canon Albert Gryspeert to Bishop Thomas Dunne, 13 September 1921.
100. Stone, L18A, *Leicester Annals*, 5 March 1927.
101. Nottingham, Convent Files: Dane Hills, Sister M. Cyril Graham to Bishop Thomas Dunne, 12 March 1927.
102. Ibid., 15 March 1927.
103. Stone, L18A, *Leicester Annals*, 30 October and 15 November 1907.
104. Stone, L16A2, *Leicester Council Book 1893–1929*, 21 July 1927.
105. Nottingham, Convent Files: Dane Hills, Sister M. Winefride Keane to Bishop Thomas Dunne, 31 March 1927.
106. *Sacred Heart Mere Street,* p. 11.
107. Stone, G20, *Stone Annals, 1922–1929*, 22 October 1922.
108. Stone, G28, *Records, July 1920–December 1924*, 30 November 1924.
109. Stone, G29, *Records, January 1925–September 1929*, 3 March 1926.
110. Ibid., 27 October 1927.
111. Stone, STK18(ii), *Stoke Annals, 1910–1926*, 21 September 1912.

Chapter Five

What others must reap: the amalgamation

Although the final accomplishment of the grand work may never be in your lifetime, yet you must bear in mind that you are only now sowing what others must reap, like those who saw the Promised Land only in vision and never in reality. Fr Bede Jarrett, OP[1]

Introduction

At the end of the 1920s it might have seemed to the various communities of Dominican women in England that life would continue much as it always had. There may have been internal tensions, such as those at Leicester, or a slight decline in recruitment as at Stone, and for all there was the challenge of adapting their constitutions to meet the requirements of the new Code of Canon Law. However, the round of liturgical and private prayer, and their investment in developing the various apostolic works to which they were committed, probably heightened the sisters' sense of stability. But in 1929 they would be struck with the full force of a seismic shock: within a few short months the five distinct groups would cease to exist and would be amalgamated into a single English congregation. A familiar landscape would emerge but beneath the surface the tectonic plates had shifted, leaving fissures that would make their effects felt for many years to come.

Of amalgamations in general

From the time religious orders as we currently understand them began to emerge out of the purely generic forms of consecrated life, the phenomenon of amalgamation of institutes has been known. From the time of the second Lateran Council at the beginning of the thirteenth century, when the establishment of new orders was forbidden, there were moves to unite small groups of male religious following the rule of St Augustine.[2] By the end of the nineteenth century, by which time there was a distinct Congregation for Religious established in the Vatican Curia, Leo XIII had succeeded in amalgamating several branches of the Franciscan Order.[3]

The foundation period of many of the hundreds of congregations of women religious founded in the nineteenth century was characterized by isolation and instability. For some of these, amalgamating with a community which had already weathered such difficulties could ensure continuation of the works begun. There are two such examples in Britain. The Sisters of the Infant Jesus, from Nivelles in Belgium, were invited by the Vicar Apostolic for the Eastern District, William Wareing, to make a foundation at Northampton in 1845, on the understanding that it would be an independent congregation. However, an epidemic of typhoid fever decimated the community ranks and in 1852 the remnant of the community was accepted into the congregation of the Sisters of Notre Dame de Namur.[4] Some years later, a group of women working with the Oblates of Mary Immaculate in Leeds were formed into a religious congregation of the same name, adopting constitutions used by two similar communities of women associated with the Oblate Fathers in southern France. In 1868 the English houses were absorbed into Sisters of the Immaculate Conception, a branch of the Association of the Holy Family of Bordeaux, whose founder, Pierre-Bienvenu de Noailles, was a close friend of the Oblate founder, Eugène de Mazenod.[5] Even so, the amalgamation of several congregations with a sustained period of independent development behind them, remained almost unknown.[6]

At the same time, there was a move towards centralization of government in those religious institutes – such as the Ursulines, the Company of Mary, the Presentation Sisters and the Sisters of Mercy – who had a monastic structure of government, whereby each community was autonomous. Moves towards union were stimulated by the desire of many of these communities to have a single set of constitutions revised in accordance with the new canonical legislation. Most of these amalgamations were characterized by lengthy consultation and, unlike the English Dominican amalgamation, arose from the initiative of the sisters themselves. There was often quite strong feeling for and against such unions on the part of individual houses, but at least for the Ursulines of the Roman Union, there was the prospect of withdrawing from the union subsequently.[7] It does well to keep these trends in mind while considering the English Dominican amalgamation of 1929.

Surprisingly, the 1917 Code of Canon Law made no specific provision for the merging of institutes, though it outlined the requirements for their suppression in canons 110–112.[8] The legal basis for the amalgamation of religious institutes was found in the legislation for the merging of benefices, laid down in canons 1409–1499 of the Code. Here two types of union are specified. In the first, a simple fusion, one entity is absorbed by another; the former becomes extinct, while the latter retains its moral personality. The union of the West Grinstead Dominicans with those of Newcastle, Natal, mentioned in Chapter Three, was this type of amalgamation. In the second type of union, an extinctive union, all the participants lose their moral personality and a completely new entity results as in the case of the creation of the English Dominican Congregation by the amalgamation of the Stone, Stroud, Leicester, Harrow and Portobello Road Dominicans.

An unwitting agent: the role of Bishop Thomas Dunn

The key movers in initiating the English Dominican amalgamation were Thomas Dunn, Bishop of Nottingham, the Dominican Provincial Father Bede Jarrett and Father Louis Nolan, an Irish Dominican working as a Consultor to the Congregation for Religious. Bishop Dunn was something of an unwitting agent in the process. In his dealings with women religious he was an ideal bishop who expressed a genuine concern for the welfare and progress of the houses in his diocese.

The Leicester Dominicans had not been the only religious community to seek refuge in the Diocese of Nottingham during the nineteenth century. During the episcopacy of Edward Bagshawe (1874–1901), the diocese had become something of a haven for communities experiencing difficulties elsewhere. Mary Potter had founded the Little Company of Mary there in 1877 when opposition had made it impossible for her to do so in her home diocese of Southwark.[9] The famous Nun of Kenmare, Mother Clare Francis Cusack, brought her Sisters of Peace to Nottingham in 1884.[10] The Franciscan Minoresses, whose first members had seceded from the Poor Servants of the Mother of God in London in 1888, found themselves unable to establish the close rapport which they had enjoyed with Cardinal Manning, with his successor Herbert Vaughan, and left London for Nottingham in 1897.[11] There was also, at Woodhall Spa in Lincolnshire, a community of Franciscan Sisters of the Holy Ghost, established there after the suppression, in

1913, of their houses at Ashton-under-Lyne and Nelson in the Diocese of Salford.[12]

Soon after his appointment in 1916, Bishop Dunn undertook a survey of the houses of women religious in his diocese and began a systematic round of canonical visitations. While the general tone of religious life was good, some houses, particularly the small, autonomous communities, gave him cause for concern. It was in December 1919 that the Dominican Father Leo Moore was deputed to carry out the visitation of the Dominican Sisters at Leicester. The internal difficulties which the community was experiencing have been discussed in the previous chapter. The situation prompted the Bishop to approach the Dominican Provincial, Father Bede Jarrett, to ask his advice about the possibility of amalgamating the Leicester community with a larger, more vigorous Dominican congregation. The Provincial replied:

> Certainly I am all for amalgamation of these small congregations with larger ones, particularly from the point of view of their religious life. A novice mistress is impossible to be found in every little convent, a real novice mistress, so that only indifferent ones are provided, to the loss of discipline and training.
>
> Moreover, in that particular Congregation, the Yorkshire houses are, from what I hear, unsatisfactory. I have already written to the Master General on the matter but he has told me that, since these Tertiary Sisters are under the local Ordinary, he can do nothing. You may be sure I would do all in my power to help your Lordship in any way I could in this matter.[13]

There the matter seemed to rest for a number of years. Although the situation in the Leicester community was somewhat improved by the time the Bishop himself undertook the next visitation in March 1927, he decided to take up the matter of amalgamation again. This time he addressed himself to Father Louis Nolan who had just seen through the amalgamation of the Dominican Sisters in Ireland.[14] Father Nolan sent a somewhat cautious reply early in August 1928:

> The remedy can be applied only by the Holy See. Hence we favour an examination of their case by the S[acred] Congregation of Religious. There is, however, a certain repugnance on the part of the Holy See to use the obvious remedy – amalgamation – owing to its knowledge of the unhappiness resulting in many cases from such alliances. Very often, indeed, the unhappiness is occasioned by the manner in which the amalgamation is effected rather than from the principle.[15]

He also suggested that Bishop Dunn prepare a candid assessment of the Leicester community for the Sacred Congregation, along with an expression of his views as to the inconvenience of there being so many small Dominican congregations in England. Although careful not to deprecate the Sisters in any way – the Bishop considered them just as estimable as other regular tertiaries in his diocese – he expressed himself as being 'not particularly impressed' by what he considered a 'very average sort of tertiary establishment'. Perhaps his most pungent argument was an appeal to prestige:

> I deprecate very much indeed the useless multiplication of small and independent bands of female tertiaries of all Religious Orders. Whatever degree of 'home rule' they may enjoy, they ought all to be linked up under some central control in the hands of some member of the 1st or 2nd branch of the Order whose name they bear. Otherwise, so it seems to me, the prestige of such 1st and 2nd Orders is exposed to danger.[16]

Rome had already dealt with this matter in the nineteenth century, when it had insisted that congregations of Dominican Sisters in simple vows could no longer remain under the jurisdiction of the friars. Although there had been cases of sisters of the Third Order being under the jurisdiction of nuns of the Second Order, as at Speyer in Germany, neither was this arrangement approved by Rome any longer.[17] Bishop Dunn's role as a catalyst was more or less complete. Despite the caution advised by Father Louis Nolan, the project of amalgamation was about to be launched on all five English Dominican groups and would become an established fact in a remarkably short period of time.

Selling the idea to the sisters

On the last day of 1928 the English Dominican Provincial, Father Bede Jarrett, wrote to Mother Catherine de Ricci Wilson, major superior of the Stone Congregation.

> I would like to talk over with you the subject of some sort of amalgamation between the Congregations of Dominican Sisters who say the Divine Office. Partly the arguments in favour of this are the fact that several English Bishops in whose dioceses there are convents are urging it on the Sacred Congregation of Religious and that the Roman and Dominican authorities favour it and partly because I

> think only so will you have in England the influence you should have and which is, or may be, much desired by you.
>
> I say some sort of amalgamation because I think your separate identities and histories ought, if it comes at all, to come slowly. I would suggest a beginning with a separate noviciate, a single house of studies, a training school for teachers, and a Mother General advised by a Council on which sit the Mothers General of each Congregation and an assistant from each and that some such system should be given trial for a fixed period of years.[18]

It would be interesting to know which other bishops had been proposing such a union, for none of the diocesan archives apart from Nottingham has any record of episcopal interest before this date. Another point to note is the inclusion in the plan of only those congregations which recited the Divine Office. The Leicester community and the London congregation had adopted the Divine Office fairly recently, but the Harrow sisters, although they had considered taking the same step, were still reciting the Little Office of the Blessed Virgin Mary. Most important of all was the Provincial's understanding of the distinctive identities of the five English groups. This was an appreciation which the other key player in the amalgamation, Father Louis Nolan, seems to have lacked.

At this stage Nolan's experience both of Dominican women and the dynamics of amalgamation was confined largely to his own Irish province of the Order and to congregations stemming from Irish houses. The five Irish communities and their filial houses united by the decree of 14 February 1928 were all descended from the monastery of Second Order nuns at Galway. They shared a common heritage and cultural background and yet even for them the prospect of union had not been greeted with immediate or universal enthusiasm. They had also had a considerable time to get used to the notion of amalgamation. As early as January 1919 Louis Nolan had been promoting an amalgamation of all Dominican communities stemming from the Dublin house of Cabra. This included communities in Portugal, Australia, New Zealand, South Africa and the United States as well as Ireland.[19] He had also acted as consultor for a proposed amalgamation of several Dominican congregations in southern Africa.[20]

As for the Sisters in England, despite their common affiliation to the Order of Preachers, in their everyday lives they had little more to do with one another than they had to do with the Daughters of Charity or the Society of the Sacred Heart.[21] But the epistolary campaign continued. In January, Father Bede wrote to Mother M.

Cecilia Marshall, assuring her that both the English hierarchy and the Dominican authorities in Rome were in favour. At this point he still saw the eventual union as a 'long way off'.[22] By the beginning of February 1929 he had received encouraging responses from the superiors at Stroud and Leicester, and copies of the different congregations' Constitutions were exchanged.[23] The Provincial wrote again to Mother Catherine de Ricci:

> I found yesterday Mother General of Portobello Road favourable to the scheme as outlined. I shall now go to Harrow to tell them what is afoot, lest afterwards they should complain that they weren't asked, tho' I think the Divine Office will be a difficulty for them. I think after I have been to Harrow the next move will be for me to tell Father Nolan that there is every reason to hope for an amalgamation on the conditions I have outlined ... and to ask him if these conditions are likely to be accepted by Rome.[24]

A meeting of the five Prioresses General and their assistants, to be held at the Portobello Road convent in London, was proposed for Passion or Easter Week. They were asked to consider the following scheme:

1) A single noviciate.
2) A single House of Studies.
3) One Mother General.
4) An interim Council of the 5 Mothers General and one assistant each
5) The following conditions:
   a) No professed Sister to be moved from the houses of her original Congregation unless immediately after the amalgamation she informs the new Mother General of such a desire.
   b) The staff of all existing schools and hospitals to be kept up to their present effective strength for the length of years of the interim Council.[25]

In the event the meeting took place at Stone on 9 April 1929. The advantages of the amalgamation were outlined by Father Bede: strengthening the organization of Dominican life in England; ensuring better training through a larger noviciate; ensuring the better education of young sisters at a high standard in a regular House of Studies; the importance of the intellectual life and a solid preparation for apostolic work were underlined as essential elements of authentic Dominican life. It was proposed that, in time, the sisters ought to establish their own training centres for teaching and nursing. The Provincial also laid emphasis upon the influence for good the sisters could exercise by a joint effort, pooling their considerable gifts and resources.[26]

Before considering the particulars of the scheme, the meeting determined that when the plan was put before the membership of the five groups, it should be made clear that a favourable vote meant accepting the amalgamation with all its stated conditions. It was also agreed that all perpetually professed religious, choir and lay sisters, would vote. By a vote of six to four Stroud was chosen as the common noviciate and the choice of Portobello Road as the House of Studies for junior professed religious was unanimous. It was only on a second vote, after a tie with Stroud, that the residence of the Prioress General was fixed at Stone, again by six votes to four. The other conditions were all accepted unanimously.

Several important considerations were also gone into. The assembly to elect the new Prioress General was to consist of the members of the current meeting, plus one delegate from each of the groups elected by their respective membership. It was also decided, by nine votes to one, that the new congregation should be named the English Congregation of St Catherine of Siena. No immediate changes were to be made to financial arrangements, with the exception of the proposal of a general levy being made on all houses for the support of the central noviciate and House of Studies.

Letters written to two of the major superiors shortly after the meeting hint that there were different levels of comfort with the proposed order of things. One senses there was a keen disappointment amongst some sisters at Stone that they would no longer have a noviciate. They would surely have felt even more marginalized had the vote for the residence of the Prioress General and Council gone against Stone, as it so nearly did. There is a note of anxious reassurance in the Provincial's letter to Mother Catherine de Ricci later in the month:

> Please do not speak about trouble to me over this work. I think Mother Margaret would have wished it in her big generous way and I know that if the Holy Ghost brings it about it will be because of the greater good it will add to our lives and their effect. I should hate to think really that the project should be imperilled amongst your Sisters by the shifting of the noviciate to Stroud. After all, it is the Dominican thing to accept.[27]

Meanwhile, there is resounding praise for the manner in which Mother M. Cecilia Marshall participated in the meeting:

> I must just add this line to say how wonderfully they caught that spirit of generosity from you, which you showed so magnanimously at Stone ... not only a Mother General, but a Mother foundress and for you to have thrown in your lot with the others required a measure of generosity beyond theirs.[28]

We shall find this difference appearing again, and there is further oral testimony that the Stroud and London congregations were the most wholeheartedly in favour of amalgamation, while Stone was the least. Why should this have been so?

It is difficult to imagine the prestige the Stone congregation enjoyed. Its founder, Mother Margaret Hallahan, was revered as a saint; its third superior, Mother Francis Raphael Drane, had been a scholar of international renown; its constitutions had been offered as a model to Third Order Dominicans around the globe – it was the acme of Dominican perfection. Stone was also a very English community with only eight per cent of its recruitment being from Ireland. For a community enjoying such stability and good order, the prospect of amalgamation might seem to have little to offer. Perhaps there was also a certain elitism, a resting on the laurels of the past. But in fact, the community was past its first flush of youth and recruitment had begun to decline. It had a larger proportion of older sisters than the other congregations and a considerably smaller percentage of young sisters.[29]

At Portobello Road in London, Mother M. Cecilia governed a young, vigorous community which demonstrated both apostolic adaptability and a keen interest in liturgical and theological developments. It could just as well be said of her community that it did not need the amalgamation. What she could see, and convey to the members of the congregation of which she was founder as well as major superior, were the overall benefits the amalgamation could bring to Dominican life in Britain as a whole. This extended to the condition regarding the right of religious to remain within the houses of their congregation of profession, proposed in the scheme. The young sisters at Portobello Road walked in the garden discussing the matter and wholeheartedly embraced the principle of voluntary mobility.[30] It is easier for a younger community to have a sense of adventure.

The attitude at Stone was certainly neither as enthusiastic nor as open as at Portobello Road. At Easter, Mother Catherine de Ricci Wilson sent a circular to the houses of her congregation in which she stated that the proposed amalgamation should not be discussed either by word or letter, even amongst the sisters themselves.[31] After the meeting at Stone, a further letter went out, in which she sought to elucidate some of the 'points which might otherwise cause you undue perplexity and perturbation'.[32] This letter emphasized the place which the community at Stone would play in the formation of junior sisters who would be 'drafted to Stone' where they would be trained in the same manner as they themselves had been trained. Admittedly, Mother Catherine de Ricci referred to the best characteristics of the other congregations 'with whom we shall be associated' but the emphasis is on retaining and propagating the spirit and teaching of Mother Margaret and the early members of the congregation. Considering the decision of the assembly to fix the house of studies in London the tenor of the letter is surprising. The tone of the letter is defensive, and the sisters are encouraged to pray for light, so that their votes may be cast from purely supernatural motives, with a mind directed towards the common good.

Finding explicit evidence of Stroud support for the amalgamation is more difficult. Mother M. Teresa Lamburn's election as first Prioress General of the amalgamated congregation may, in itself, have been an indication of this.[33] Mère Saint-Julien Aubrey, who was the driving force behind the formation of the Roman Union of Ursulines, was elected its first Prioress General, and Mother M. Carmelita Hartman, whose campaign of correspondence had led to the formation of the Sisters of Mercy of the Union in the United States, was also elected Superior General at the inaugural General Chapter.

Several technicalities arose as the time for voting drew near. How should a sister who objected to particular points of the proposal vote? What would be the position of religious who voted against the amalgamation, but who might soon find themselves members of a congregation of which they had never wished to be part?[34] When the vote was taken at Kelvedon, a house belonging to the Stone congregation, Father Bede was asked to introduce a further conditional clause into the scheme. Though the correspondence does not state what the clause was, it makes it clear that it was introduced as a *quid pro quo* for Stone's losing the noviciate.[35] In view of the eventual model of amalgamation approved by Rome, it is important to stress that the Provincial made it quite clear to the sisters voting that acceptance meant acceptance of the scheme exactly as proposed, not of just some vague notion of amalgamation. In regard to the situation at Kelvedon, he stated twice in his letter to Mother Catherine de Ricci that, if the condition were not fulfilled, the votes of that community would have, in conscience, to be taken again.

When the votes were in, there was an overwhelming majority in favour of accepting the scheme as proposed. Amongst the Stroud, Leicester and London sisters the votes were unanimous. At Harrow there was a solitary vote against amalgamation, whereas nearly ten per cent of the members of the Stone congregation voted against the scheme.[36] The results were forwarded to Rome.

England proposes, Rome disposes

Now that the positive reaction of the membership had been ascertained, the next step was to draw up a petition to be forwarded to the Sacred Congregation for Religious. A meeting was held at Stroud on 17 May, chaired by Father Louis Nolan in his capacity as Consultor to the Sacred Congregation. Father Louis now made it clear to the Mothers and their assistants that it was most unlikely that Rome would sanction certain aspects of the scheme, particularly the interim Council and the conditional clause regarding the rights of individuals to remain within the houses of their congregation of profession. In his opinion the former would blur the lines of executive authority, and the latter was contrary to the spirit of obedience. More than thirty years later one of the Stroud Sisters would recall:

> Father Nolan told me personally that it was Pope Pius XI who said there was to be no five year trial, as all the congregations concerned were sufficiently mature, having each been in existence some years; but I have no written evidence of this.[37]

There was an air of anxiety, and a general feeling that members who had voted for a distinct scheme and a gradual transition to the new order of things, would resent changes to the plan. In reply Father Louis Nolan confirmed his opinion that the omission of these clauses constituted 'no substantial change' and he insisted that, since the majority had voted in favour, they had voted in favour of amalgamation itself.

Father Louis' insistence did not reassure all the delegates. On account of the continued anxiety of some, particularly Mother M. Dominic Wilkes, Prioress General of the Harrow congregation, a second meeting had to be held the following day. In his response to this anxiety, we see an obvious difference between Father Nolan's understanding of what the sisters had voted for, and that of the English Provincial: 'Rome will make the conditions and for the rest nothing further must be said to those who voted. Their obedience will be the answer.' [38] In Nolan's defence, it is probably true to say that he was better informed as to what would be acceptable to Rome. But why had he not expressed his views more candidly at the preparatory meetings before the votes were cast?

On one point he was certainly mistaken; that regarding the movement of personnel. Little more than two months earlier, the decree establishing the Sisters of Mercy of the Union in the United States had specifically stated that individuals who had not consented to the formation of the new institute, while still obliged to observe its constitutions, could not be moved outside the houses of their profession without their expressed consent.[39] As for the proposed interim Council, it was a novelty, and having not long completed the codification of Canon Law, such a novelty was not likely to be sanctioned by Rome. The proposal as it had been voted upon was more akin to the federations that would be encouraged for monastic communities of women following the 1950 constitution *Sponsa Christi*. Only later would this structure be applied to congregations of apostolic religious. One possible solution that does not seem to have been discussed was the adoption, at least in the first instance, of a provincial structure with each of the former congregations comprising a separate non-territorial province. This solution would be adopted subsequently in two Australian amalgamations, one of them involving Dominicans.[40]

What must the women gathered at Stone have been thinking? The official documentation of all the meetings during the amalgamation process provides no more than a simple record of the proceedings, excluding any account of the discussions which led to the decisions taken. The general archives of the Dominican friars in Rome, the archives of the English Province and those of the Congregation for Religious shed no further light on the unseemly haste of proceedings, nor do they give any substantive reasons for Father Bede Jarrett's plan for a gradual process of amalgamation being put aside. Mother Catherine de Ricci Wilson's prohibition of discussion might seem draconian to contemporary readers, but it was no more than an extension of the principles which applied to official deliberations at any level within religious congregations. From the rank and file, who must have awaited eagerly every scrap of news, almost no written evidence seems to survive. Schooled in religious obedience, personal feelings were subordinated to the acceptance which the Provincial had praised as being the Dominican way.

On 5 August, Archbishop Thomas Williams of Birmingham notified Stone that the decree of union, dated 27 July 1929, had arrived from Rome. It was forwarded to the various communities and the first elective chapter was convoked for 28 August. Just how trying the process had been for Father Bede Jarrett is revealed in a letter written from Stone to his friend and benefactor, Charlotte Tytus, two weeks before the chapter. 'The Nuns here are all strung up and excited: the 5 Congregations meet on August 27th and then become amalgamated. The sooner I leave England after that, the better for my general health!'[41] The English Provincial had his own Order's General Chapter to attend in Rome.

There is also evidence that Father Louis Nolan did not come through the English amalgamation with the satisfaction or acclaim which followed the Irish union. The Dominican archbishop of Adeliade, South Australia, Robert Spence, wrote to the Prioress General of the New South Wales Dominican Sisters on the question of amalgamation several months later: 'It is a dangerous thing to push this matter in any way. I understand that Father Nolan has got into trouble with more than one Bishop over this matter of amalgamation.'[42] During the 1930s, when Nolan was working to establish the Conference of Dominican Prioresses in the United States, there was an underlying suspicion on the part of some Dominican major superiors there that this was an attempt at amalgamation through the back door.[43]

Forty-nine delegates, ex-officio and elected, attended the General Chapter which elected Mother M. Teresa Lamburn of Stroud as first Prioress General. Oral tradition suggests that this result was quite a shock to the Stone community, and that there was a general feeling amongst the other capitulars that the amalgamation should

Fig. 11 The first General Chapter of the amalgamated English Congregation, Stone, 1929.

not become a 'Stone take over'.[44] The other former major superiors: Mothers Catherine de Ricci Wilson (Stone), M. Ambrose Kilbride (Leicester), M. Dominic Wilkes (Harrow) and M. Cecilia Marshall (London) were elected to the General Council. The chapter was then prorogued until 28 April 1930, to allow time for work to begin on the new constitutions. Drafts worked on by Mothers M. Pius Pretty of Stroud and M. Bonaventure Burke of London were circulated to all the houses, blank pages being interspersed for the comments of the sisters. This work was completed with despatch and the approbation of the constitutions was granted on 30 November 1930.

One of those who sent congratulations was the Bishop of Nottingham. Thomas Dunn expressed his delight that the amalgamation was an established fact not only because he was sure it would prove for the best, 'but partly because I think it was I who set the ball rolling in the first instance'.[45]

The excellent spirit shown everywhere: growing together

In the first instance the ball rolled on at a moderate pace, as Mother M. Cecilia Marshall wrote later in the year to her spiritual guide, the Dominican Père Jean Alix:

> So far nothing has changed in our ordinary, everyday life ... one of our qualified teachers has been sent to help in one of the large schools of the Congregation – I offered this Sister knowing their great need and that it would help the superiors through a difficulty. In the many convents of the Congregation there are doubtless some troubled souls, but I am not amongst the number.[46]

By December there had been further calls on the generosity of the Portobello Road Convent:

> Two of our young professed choir Sisters, trained teachers, have been taken to teach in schools. I do not complain, on the contrary, I am rather proud that amongst us we have found capable and useful subjects to render service to our large Congregation.[47]

In the latter part of 1930, Mother M. Cecilia would be writing that life was full of change, and that the meetings of the General Council were often an occasion of great suffering for her, as she saw certain Dominican customs to which she was attached disappear.[48] But none of these things, she was quick to add, touched the foundation of Dominican life.

Certainly, difficulties were sometimes experienced by junior sisters leaving the central noviciate at Stroud for other communities. Mother M. Cecelia Marshall was aware of these incidents for she mentions them in another letter to Père Alix:

> I could not give all the details, but I will simply tell you that certain amongst the elderly religious at Stone, rather opposed to the Amalgamation, consider as being disloyal to Stone all the young professed Sisters with the spirit of the Amalgamation. Just now the young Sisters are suffering acutely.[49]

Perhaps the greatest responsibility for inculcating the spirit of union lay with the director of the common noviciate at Stroud. This was inaugurated on 24 October 1929, under the direction of Mother M. Bonaventure Burke, who approached the task with the seriousness and enthusiasm which had characterized the noviciate in London. The looms disappeared from St Rose's, and lessons in weaving and spinning gave way to classes in theology and external examinations in doctrine. Three novices and four postulants arrived from the former mother houses, but none of the former was able to cope with the strain of a change of residence and all three left. Of sixteen postulants who entered before the end of 1931, only nine received the habit and only four of these would persevere in their vocation until death. The reasons for the high attrition rate, which would continue throughout Mother M. Teresa Lamburn's tenure, are difficult to ascertain. Although the annals speak of the candidates in a very positive tone, the minutes of the General Council are more qualified regarding the initial period: 'A spirit has evolved which would be impossible as a basis for the future of the amalgamated congregation, a spirit which has shown itself chiefly in criticism and discontent.'[50]

Perhaps the first novices arrived already having acquired a partisan spirit for one or other of the former congregations. Is it possible that candidates were conscious of the malaise that followed the amalgamation? Since, according to the prescriptions of Canon Law, the novices were kept separated from the rest of the community, this would have been unlikely, though possible. Those who already knew the sisters, having been taught by them or nursed with them, would have been in a better position to sense this. Even twenty years later, Sister M. Henry Yeaman, who had spent all her school life at Stoke, can remember being advised by Sister M. Barbara Pearce that it was 'too soon' after the amalgamation to think of entering.[51] Throughout the 1930s the minutes of the General Council also record votes in favour of applications from many women who, for one reason or another, decided not to enter the congregation.

Mother M. Bonaventure did not foresee the difficulties of which Mother M. Cecilia spoke of, but 'years later they told me of their experiences, difficult to say the least, but assured me it was from individuals, not from communities'.[52] Sisters who entered in the years immediately before the outbreak of the Second World War certainly noticed a different flavour at Stone, where they generally spent at least a year after their first profession of vows. Their comments are certainly not all negative. At that time the junior sisters were under the direction of Sister M. Patricia Kane who, it is reported, informed them that they would now be turned into good Stone nuns!

An amalgamation concerns not only persons, but goods as well. The amalgamation of 1929 required the introduction of uniform accounting procedures, merging funds and investments, transferring title deeds and other legal documents into the name of the new congregation. Here it was a member of the former Stone congregation who made a magnificent contribution to the process of amalgamation. Sister M. Vincent Morrison had been Bursar General at Stone, and continued in the same post in the new congregation. To her fell the onerous task of rationalizing finances and solving puzzling problems, requiring a round of correspondence, visits, meetings and diplomacy which lasted several years. She carried out this task with efficiency, tact and charity, continuing to assist her successor after her term of office ended in 1941.[53]

By May 1930, the new Prioress General felt able to write to the sisters on a note of optimism:

> One of my chief duties after the conclusion of the first part of our General Chapter was to pay a short visit to our many convents. I have been to each one; and though the experience has made me feel the sense of responsibility even more keenly than before, still, the excellent spirit shown everywhere, is a most valuable human consolation to me, in the onerous work that God has laid upon me.[54]

Union or uniformity?

The five women who sat around the council table at Stone in August 1929 had only a brief acquaintance with one another, and each had a different level of comfort with the notion of amalgamation. Apart from the General Councillors, for almost two years the community at Stone would continue to be composed exclusively of sisters who had been professed there. It cannot have been easy for Mother M. Teresa to feel at home, a situation which must have been exacerbated once Mother M. Cecilia Marshall, the councillor with whom she seems to have been most in sympathy, returned to live at Portobello Road on account of continuing poor health. The report of a canonical visitation of the community at Stone made by Archbishop Williams in May 1930 does not give the impression of a universally happy community. The lay sisters, and several of the younger choir sisters, are described as 'splendid' and having the spirit of the amalgamation. On the other hand, some sisters felt excluded by a tendency to cliquishness on the part of others, and it was noted that recreations were not very merry as a consequence. The Archbishop was also concerned that some of the senior sisters displayed an excessive dependence on the local prioress.[55]

Whatever the atmosphere might be at Stone, Mother M. Teresa Lamburn was determined that the new congregation should be built up, in every detail, on purely Dominican lines. She also wished this to be done in a manner that would lessen the strain on individuals in every possible way.[56] The arbiter of what was 'purely Dominican' would, in most instances, be the practice of the friars. The circular letters sent out to the congregation by Mother M. Teresa would give detailed instructions on matters of ceremonial for choir, customs in the refectory, concerning dress and every other conceivable facet of the sisters' lives.

For the time being, as the General Chapter had decreed, local customs and practices would obtain. In such a highly formalized life, once sisters began moving between houses of the former congregations, these differences must have been thrown into relief. A different interpretation in rendering the chant during sung Mass or Office, or the length of the pause in the verses of the psalmody, can make an ordeal of choral prayer. From the early days, the sisters at Stroud had followed closely the practice of the friars, but at Stone, where the influence of the Benedictine Ullathorne had also been considerable, there was a certain sense of alarm at how much their own hallowed practices required change to fit in with standard Dominican practice. It was only in 1931 that the community began to sing Vespers and Compline daily, rather than reciting them *recto tono*. The annals also record the first occasion on which the community at Stone made the solemn Dominican prostration, the *venia*,[57] before communion at the conventual Mass.

> Some of the altar servers were heard in school that day asking one another if they had 'seen the nuns diving in church'. As for the sisters, it very soon became difficult for them to realize that they had not carried it [the *venia*] out all their lives.[58]

It was not only the ritual element of community prayer that underwent change. On a more fundamental level, and in line with liturgical trends in the Church at large, the Divine Office was seen as the major, indeed the essential public vocal prayer of the congregation. It was not until June and November 1931 that the last of the houses of the former Harrow congregation, Watford and Bognor, began the recitation of the Divine Office in place of that of the Little Office of Our Lady.[59] The inaugural General Chapter had also ordained that all prayers of devotion formerly said in common, with the exception of the rosary, should cease and in future be a matter of personal choice.[60] Stone, in particular, had added a whole series of devotional prayers in Mother Margaret's day and many of those professed in her congregation regretted the culling of these accretions.

It was two years before the most obvious sign of uniformity, the new head dress, was introduced; though sisters changing community had adopted that being worn in the house to which they were assigned. Detailed instructions on the width of hems, the necessity of tucking in the strings that secured the guimpe at the back of the neck, the positioning of pins in the veil, along with helpful hints on the use of Borax for laundering the linen underveil, were sent out early in May 1931.[61] The following year the sisters were advised to adopt the device JMDC (Jesus, Mary, Dominic, Catherine) as a heading on their correspondence, uniform crockery was to be used on refectory tables which were, in future, to be of polished rather than stained wood.[62] The process continued apace: sheets and bedding, aprons, even the undergarments to be used when laying out a deceased sister would be regulated. On 15 June 1931 the Master of the Order, Father Martin Gillet, visited Stone and praised the sisters for their willingness to accept the amalgamation 'because this showed that details dear to individuals had been sacrificed for the greater principle of unity and efficiency'.[63]

As Mother M. Teresa began her frequent round of visitations, the *Register* of the Prioress General shows a punishing schedule of journeys, taking her from St Marychurch to Hawick, from London to Stoke. It is perhaps no surprise to read that by the end of May 1931, while visiting Portobello Road, Mother M. Teresa's health had broken down completely. By July the secretary general, Sister Rose Imelda Raymond-Barker, was writing a circular letter describing the slow but consistent improvement in the Prioress General's condition as her course of treatment continued. With two other members of the General Council, Mothers M. Dominic Wilkes and M. Cecilia Marshall, almost complete invalids, more and more of the business of the congregation would fall to Sister Rose Imelda. Mother M. Cecilia was to resign from the Council on grounds of health in 1934 and was replaced by Sister M. Aquinas Colgan, one of the earliest members of the Portobello Road community.

To make the Prioress General's journeys less of an ordeal it was decided to accept the offer made by Mr Wengelin, a long standing benefactor of the Harrow convent, of a *Sunbeam* limousine. The friars at Haverstock Hill recommended a chauffeur, and so Aubrey Miller was engaged for what would be a lengthy service, first as driver and later as general factotum for the sisters. In their light-hearted, upbeat tone, the annals note that the very name had about it something of a cheerful symbolism, and tells how the communities looked forward to a visit from 'Mother General in the *Sunbeam*'.[64] But the new means of transport did not suit all, for the annalist later reports that two sisters were so sick on the journey from Stone to Newcastle that they had to be put on the train at Derby![65] A worse mishap occurred in October 1934, despite the due diligence of Mr Miller, who was obliged to brake suddenly. Mother M. Teresa, dozing in the back seat, was thrown forward and was left semi-conscious with a gash in the left temple and had to be taken to Stafford Infirmary, where she remained for some days.[66]

It was not only the Prioress General who fostered unity by her visits. The sisters of the different communities were encouraged to visit one another, whether for celebrations such as jubilees or when enjoying R & C (rest and change) breaks in the summer. Perhaps the best gauge of acceptance of the amalgamation by the membership was the willingness of sisters to be assigned to houses outside the group in which they had been professed. By 1933 seventeen per cent of sisters who had entered at Portobello Road were already assigned to houses which had not formed part of their congregation of profession; the figures were twelve and a half per cent for former members of the Stroud congregation, twelve per cent for Leicester, six per cent for Harrow and only three per cent for Stone. By 1948 the percentages had increased significantly, being forty-four per cent for former Harrow sisters, thirty-seven per cent for Stroud, thirty-six per cent for Portobello Road, thirty per cent for Leicester, but only seventeen per cent for Stone. It should be kept in mind that all the houses of the former Stone congregation remained open, meaning that communities did not have to be dispersed amongst other houses, whereas half of the Harrow and Leicester houses had been closed. Even so, if Mother M. Teresa kept to her conviction of not asking the sacrifice of those not prepared to make it, the raw data is probably a good indication of the level of acceptance of the amalgamation by the membership of the former groups.

Sister Rose Imelda, sending a progress report to Archbishop Williams on Mother Teresa's state of health in May 1931, wrote with typical enthusiasm and exuberance:

> May I venture to slip in here a personal note to your Grace, to say that the Holy Spirit is working wonderful things among us? I venture to add this word, for I know it will be a consolation to your Grace to hear that throughout the congregation and even at Stone, the spirit of 'amalgamation' is growing stronger.[67]

It might, indeed, have been growing stronger, but time would show that there remained uneasy minds and restless religious not altogether reconciled to the amalgamation or the manner in which it had been brought about.

Conclusion

The aftermath of the amalgamation was a period of difficulties and change, with no certainty as to what the end product would be. Doubtless, there were some who thought it had been unnecessary, but at least in the opinion of Bishop Dunn, amalgamation had been the only realistic means of assuring the future of the Leicester community. The process of acceptance would be best achieved through the integration of new members formed in the spirit of the new congregation. But an increase in recruitment was one fruit of the amalgamation that was not to be realized; in fact there was a quite dramatic drop. In the fifteen years that followed the amalgamation sixty-two novices would make profession whereas in the fifteen years before the total number of professions across the five congregations had been 194. It would not be until the end of the 1960s that the number of post amalgamation sisters exceeded the numbers professed before 1930. Numbers are not the sole criteria for success but one wonders whether the malaise of the immediate post amalgamation period was in part to blame for the decline in recruitment.

The fact that the amalgamation followed so closely on the revision of canon law may also have coloured the general perception. As we have already seen, the universal effect of this revision for women religious was a highlighting of the juridical elements of their lives. It was not just in the noviciate that life became more formalized. The Harrow sisters had been used to sea bathing when on holiday at their house in Bognor, albeit at an hour when few other humans would be about; such recreation was not permitted after 1929.[68] This is only one of several examples of how the daily lives of the sisters changed, enhancing their estimation that life became somewhat 'stricter' after the amalgamation.

Although the cultural and social milieu at Leicester may have been a far cry from that of Stone, the shared values and dynamism of the Dominican tradition united the communities at a more fundamental level. While it is true to say that many sisters professed before 1929 clung quite tenaciously to their pre-amalgamation identity, and the occasional whisper, 'is she one of ours?' was not entirely unknown, this did not necessarily deflect their loyalty from the new, larger group. Uniformity of observance, equated to some degree at the time with fidelity to charism, was embraced. Despite the fall in numbers, the greater mobility of personnel after the amalgamation, and the sharing of resources amongst the houses allowed a greater degree of adaptation and flexibility. In these terms the amalgamation was undoubtedly a success. True, the new congregation might not realize its potential to the full, but neither do many successful organisms. It is well to judge the amalgamation in terms of its own time when principles of discernment and subsidiarity, which govern contemporary moves towards unity, had not become part of the culture of religious life. In the aftermath of the amalgamations the sisters involved continued to do a prodigious amount of good, and in doing good one cannot fail.

Notes

1. From a sermon preached by Fr Bede Jarrett at Portobello Road Convent, cited in Sisters, *A Treasure*, p. 73.
2. Lawrence, *Medieval Monasticism*, p. 268.
3. Aubert, *The Church in a secularised Society*, p. 115.
4. Hanoteau, *Une grande Nivelloise*, p. 89–91.
5. Darricau and Peyrous, *Father Noailles*, p. 234.
6. Although I can find numerous examples of infant congregations being absorbed by established groups I can find none for congregations with more than fifty years' existence. Such unions have become increasingly common, however, since the Second Vatican Council.

7. Jégou and Kogoj, *L'Union romaine des Ursulines*, p. 234–75. These tables show that fourteen houses left the Roman Union mainly under pressure from their bishops.
8. Geser, *Canon Law*, p. 45.
9. West, *One Woman's Journey*, p. 61.
10. Eagar, *The Nun of Kenmare*, p. 175.
11. McDonnell, *Growing unto Christ*, p. 14.
12. Salford, Box 060 Franciscan Sisters of the Holy Ghost, *Relatio*.
13. Nottingham, Convent files, Dane Hills, Fr Bede Jarrett to Bishop Thomas Dunn, 17 September 1923.
14. Horgan, *Weavings*, pp. 19–21.
15. Nottingham, Convent files, Dane Hills, Fr Louis Nolan to Bishop Thomas Dunn, 6 August 1928. Emphasis Nolan's.
16. Ibid., Bishop Thomas Dunne to Fr Louis Nolan, 11 August 1928.
17. The congregation became independent of the Monastery of St Mary Magdalen in 1910. *150 Jahre Institut St Dominikus*, p. 8.
18. Stone, G2000/Am1, Fr Bede Jarrett to Mother Catherine de Ricci Wilson, 31 December 1928. Emphasis Jarrett's.
19. Northey, *Living the Truth*, p. 267. The South African and Lisbon houses subsequently joined the Irish congregation.
20. This debacle is recounted in Boner, *Dominican Women*, p. 218, and Cleary, *Being driven Forward*, p. 115.
21. Nor was this phenomenon peculiar to Britain, there was an almost complete lack of interaction between the two Dominican communities in Adelaide, one of which had been founded from Ireland and the other from Stone, Northey, *Living the Truth*, p. 134.
22. Stone, LON/G10–43, Fr Bede Jarrett to Mother M. Cecilia Marshall, 9 January 1929.
23. Stone, LON/G10–48, Fr Bede Jarrett to Mother M. Cecilia Marshall, 18 March 1929.
24. Stone, G2000/Am1, Fr Bede Jarrett to Mother Catherine de Ricci Wilson, 4 February 1929.
25. Stone, G2000/Am1, Fr Bede Jarrett to 'Dear Mother Prioress General' (almost certainly Mother Catherine de Ricci Wilson), 1 March 1929.
26. Stone, G2000/Am1, *Summary of notes of meeting at Stone*, 9 April 1929.
27. Stone, G2000/Am1, Fr Bede Jarrett to Mother Catherine de Ricci Wilson, 2 April 1929.
28. Stone, LON/G10–48, Fr Bede Jarrett to Mother M. Cecilia Marshall, 25 April 1929.
29. The comparative age structure of the five congregations on 1 May 1929 highlights this:

	% aged 65+	% aged -35	total professed
Stone	23	13	141
Stroud	14	22	92
Leicester	11	36	46
Harrow	21	25	53
London	7	24	74

30. Stone, G2000/Am1, *Memoir of Mother M. Bonaventure Burke*, 1976.
31. Stone, K1–30, *Circular Letters*, Mother Catherine de Ricci Wilson, Easter 1929.
32. Stone, K1–34, *Circular Letters*, Mother Catherine de Ricci Wilson, Easter 1929.
33. Stone, G2000/Am1, Several anonymous recollections of pre-amalgamation Sisters collected in the 1980s state that one major superior in particular, never named, was particularly in favour of the union.
34. Stone, G2000/Am1, Fr Bede Jarrett to Mother Catherine de Ricci Wilson, 21 April 1929.
35. Ibid., 27 April 1929. This may have been a request for temporary professed sisters to continue their formation at Stone after completing their noviciate.
36. Stone, G2000/Am1, The votes in the local communities of the Stone congregation are recorded as follows: Stone 34 in favour, 7 against; Stoke-on-Trent 27 in favour 2 against; St Marychurch 30 in favour; Kelvedon 9 in favour; Hawick 12 in favour, 2 against.
37. EdinburghOP, Sisters' File, Sister M. Laurence Kelly to Fr Bede Bailey, 24 September 1961.
38. Stone, G2000/Am1, *Notes of meeting at Stroud*, 18 May 1929.
39. Darcy, *Institute of the Sisters of Mercy of the Americas*, p. 63.
40. O'Sullivan, *Dominican Sisters of North Adelaide*, p. 25. The overall number of Sisters involved was 492, the four congregations ranging in size from 54 members to 220.
41. Jarrett, *Letters*, p. 150.
42. Archbishop Robert Spence to Mother M. Philippa Byrne, 21 November 1929, quoted in Northey, *Living the Truth*, p. 275.
43. Mullay, *Place of Springs*, pp. 162, 189.
44. The former tradition is supported in a letter of Sister M. Hugh Shayler, to Sister Melanie Blair OSF, 17 June 1987, Stone, G2000/Am2.
45. Stone, G2000/Am1, Bishop Thomas Dunn to Mother Rose Imelda Raymond-Barker, 4 September 1929.
46. Stone, LON/P/G25–65, Mother M. Cecilia Marshall to Père Jean Alix, 29 October 1929.
47. Ibid., 30 December 1929.
48. Ibid., 2 September and 22 December 1930.
49. Ibid., 12 March 1931.
50. Stone, G(x), *General Council Book, August 1929 to October 1934*, 26 November 1929.
51. Sister M. Henry Yeaman, conversation with the author, May 2009.
52. Stone, G2000/Am1, *Memoir of Mother Bonaventure Burke*, 1976.
53. Stone, G99a, *Necrology, 1953–1959*.
54. Stone, G100(a), Mother M. Teresa Lamburn to 'My dear Mothers and Sisters', May 1930.
55. Birmingham, CC-S-6, *Visitation of St Dominic's Priory, Stone*, 23 May 1930.
56. Stone, G100(a), Mother M. Teresa Lamburn, Circular letter, 18 December 1929.
57. The venia was made when commanded to do something 'in virtue of holy

obedience', such as when a friar or sister was assigned to a new house or post, or in reparation for a fault. The sister lifted the front half of her scapular, knelt and extended herself prostrate on the ground, turning the body on its right side. The head remained facing the ground, the lifted scapular under the face. For more agile religious the *venia* could be made in a matter of seconds in a single harmonious movement. Some religious took pride in how well it could be made!

58. Stone, G(xv), *Annals of the English Congregation of St Catherine of Siena, July 1932–December 1934*, p. 15.
59. Stone, G21, *Annals of the English Congregation of St Catherine of Siena, 1929–1932*, p. 70.
60. Stone, G98, *Acts of the General Chapter*.
61. G100(a), Mother M. Teresa Lamburn, Circular letter, May 1931.
62. Stone, G(xv), *Annals 1932–1934*, p. 14.
63. Stone, G21, *Annals 1929–1932*, p. 128.
64. Stone, G(xv), *Annals 1932–1934*, p. 1.
65. Ibid., p. 22.
66. Ibid., p. 149.
67. Birmingham, CC-S-6, Sister M. Rose Imelda Raymond-Barker to Archbishop Williams, 26 May 1931.
68. Interview with Sister M. Paul Goebel, October 1999.

Chapter Six

Resolve yourselves into one: 1929–53

You must realise that you are no longer Stone, Stroud, or anything else ... if you don't resolve yourselves into one congregation, the fewer of you I see in the Diocese the better, for you will not be of any use to the Church.
Archbishop Thomas William

Introduction

Three months after the decree of amalgamation had been promulgated, the Wall Street Crash ushered in the Great Depression. Although the economic crisis does not feature large in the annals of the English Dominican Congregation, the sisters were certainly aware of the grinding poverty that blighted the lives of so many of those for whom they worked. By contrast, those lucky enough to remain in full-time employment enjoyed reasonably stable salaries during the 1930s, and their purchasing power increased as prices decreased. No sooner had the economic situation begun to ease, than the trauma of global war, for the second time in a generation, brought civilian casualties on an unprecedented scale, the spectre of genocide and the fear of nuclear conflagration. Post-war austerities and the anxiety of the Cold War were offset, to some extent, by the growth of the Welfare State, which provided a greater measure of security from the cradle to the grave.

During this time, particularly in the post-war period, there was a marked decline in religious practice in Britain. The Roman Catholic Church, however, seemed impervious to this decline.[1] The social interaction of the tight-knit urban Catholic communities was centred largely on church, school, social club and a plethora of sodalities and societies. Numerically, the Catholic community was reinforced by a new wave of immigration from Ireland which began during the war and would peak in the 1960s. By the time they celebrated the centenary of the restoration of the hierarchy in 1950,

Catholics in England were no longer a self-conscious community, keenly aware of their disadvantages. This was the era of confident demonstrations of faith: rosary rallies, the Marian Year, vocations exhibitions. Tens of thousands of Young Catholics Students and Young Catholic Workers were learning to 'see, judge, act' and, particularly in Scotland, began participating actively in the liturgy at dialogue Masses. But by the mid 1950s, the Catholic community was also enjoying greater social mobility and educational advantages that would lead to a closer identification with the middle-class and academic aspirations of their non-Catholic peers, weakening the sense of 'otherness' which had kept them such a cohesive community.

During these years two major preoccupations confronted the English Dominican Sisters: their own internal cohesion and managing their apostolic commitments in the face of declining numbers and the increasing demands of the society they served.

Free and open discussion: the General Chapter of 1935

The second General Chapter of the English Dominican Congregation was, perhaps, more important than the first. The forty-one delegates assembled at Stone during the second weekend of June 1935, proceedings opening on Monday 10 June with Mother M. Teresa Lamburn presenting the report of her administration. The questions which came from the delegates in response to the report focused concern upon the numbers leaving the noviciate, the selection of candidates and means of recruitment. Some of the delegates asked for further clarification concerning the decisions made to close specific houses, and regarding the withdrawal from and acceptance of schools. Mother M. Teresa may have been impressed by the 'excellent spirit shown everywhere' and Sister Rose Columba may have perceived 'the Holy Spirit ... working wonderful things among us' but perhaps neither was prepared for the declarations of discontent that would be made the following day.

On the Tuesday Archbishop Williams addressed the chapter. He began by stressing the fact that the amalgamation was there to stay and that, however regrettable the manner of its formation, it could not be broken up. The way to resolve remaining misgivings, the Archbishop insisted, was through frank and open discussion and by proposing any changes to the Constitutions which the delegates might consider necessary to ease the way towards greater unity. As he continued, his tone changed to one of almost undisguised exasperation:

> You must realise that you are no longer Stone, Stroud, or anything else. You are a congregation. There has not been enough free and open discussion, I consider. If you don't resolve yourselves into one congregation, the fewer of you I see in the Diocese the better, for you will not be of any use to the Church.[2]

Mother M. Teresa must have felt increasingly uncomfortable as it became clear that the Archbishop had received a number of letters from individual sisters which gave evidence of a sense of disunion within the congregation. She would surely have felt further undermined had she known that amongst these was a letter from one of the General Councillors expressing her own anxiety. Accusations that Mother M. Teresa spent too much time away from Stone must have been particularly wounding, for her absences were either directed towards the good of the congregation as a whole, by visiting the local communities, or caused by illness. The revelations were obviously sufficiently surprising to the Prioress General that she had to ask the Archbishop, in front of the assembly, whether he thought there was disunion in the congregation. Although he replied emphatically in the affirmative, Archbishop Williams stressed once again his support and admiration for Mother M. Teresa in the difficult task she had had to undertake, congratulating her on her administration and expressing confidence that she could defend her actions and decisions.[3]

It is perhaps not surprising that the letters received by Archbishop Williams all came from members of the former Stone and Harrow congregations, the only two groups which had registered any opposition to the original, transitional model of amalgamation. The major concern, entirely understandable, was not only that the sisters had voted for one plan and had a different one imposed upon them, but that these changes had not been communicated openly; in fact, many sisters had remained under the impression that the amalgamation could still be reviewed. As a former Harrow sister expressed it:

> A few were dead against Amalgamation but the vast majority were for giving it a trial. Do you think, Your Grace, that if we had been told that our votes would settle the affair for good and all and that there would be no going back, that the votes would have been almost unanimous?[4]

The writer also reasoned that if obedience required the immediate formation of the new congregation, why had the sisters' opinion been solicited in the first place? At the General Chapter itself a similar opinion was recorded from Sister M. Columba McQuillan, who was local prioress at Harpenden and would subsequently be elected to the General Council. She too had known nothing about the change from the proposed five year trial, and although she had no wish to undo the amalgamation, Sister M. Columba was distressed by the lack of straightforwardness involved, something she saw as being completely un-Dominican.[5]

Though some may have feared the amalgamation would be a 'Stone takeover', one of the letters preserved in the archives of the Archdiocese of Birmingham gives the opinion that it was nothing short of 'a reform on the Stroud pattern' with the other four groups being 'annexed'. Each of the five groups, the writer stressed, had admirable qualities, 'something to teach and something to learn' and admits there was splendid material to work on. The exercise of authority was judged to be arbitrary, the craze for efficiency leading to a loss of family spirit and the development of an ethos more akin to that of a limited company.

Another correspondent, writing from Stone, was concerned that the General Fund of the new congregation, almost all of which (in her opinion) derived from the dowries of sisters professed at Stone, was underwriting the capital debts of houses which had belonged to other congregations. Attention was drawn to the fact that there was no hired domestic help at St Rose's in Stroud, whereas twenty seculars had to be employed at Stone. Anxiety was also voiced regarding the noviciate, not only in terms of the paucity of vocations but also regarding the level of instruction given and the accommodation provided. The fact that the sisters in temporary vows remained in the noviciate house and were unknown at the mother house, where the General Councillors who would vote on their acceptance for perpetual profession resided, was also seen as a disadvantage.[6]

For the most part, specific accusations made in these letters can be contradicted by evidence from the minutes of the General Council. The complaints came from a tiny fraction of the membership, though it is highly likely that the writers were articulating the views of a number of their sisters. Despite the Archbishop's insistence that the amalgamation could not be broken up, this remained a persistent obsession for some. Feelings against it would still be running sufficiently high at the time of the 1941 General Chapter for two petitions to be presented from individual sisters, one requesting the dismemberment of the English Congregation into its five previous entities, and the other its division into two separate congregations centred on Stone and Stroud.[7]

Retrenchment, consolidation and new works

Undoubtedly, the greatest source of anguish for many religious in the new English Congregation – one which was voiced at the 1935 General Chapter – was the handing over to others of works their former communities had laboured to establish and maintain; or worse, to see them close altogether. This sense of loss was compounded by the fact that several new works were undertaken and some existing works expanded during the same period. For some the ultimate conclusion was that 'their' works had been sacrificed to sustain those of 'others'. Such decisions lay within the remit of the General Council and the culture of religious life at the time vested their deliberations in secrecy. Although there was definitely some consultation with local prioresses, the general membership of the congregation was not considered in the decision-making process. In deciding whether to close a particular convent there were sometimes circumstances beyond the congregation's control which might require a change of plan. The Code of Canon Law in force at the time required the permission of the local bishop for the closure of a religious house, or for a congregation to give up a particular work, whether the institute concerned was of diocesan or pontifical rite.[8] Whatever the reason, decisions were not made hastily or without considerable deliberation.

On 26 November 1929 the General Council had met around the sickbed of Mother M. Cecilia Marshall at the convent in Portobello Road, London. One of the major topics for deliberation was the advisability of closing some of the smaller houses of the congregation. The main reason for considering this course of action, one which would become increasingly acute, was the decreasing number of sisters available to undertake all the works to which the English Dominicans were committed. The desire for a thoroughly Dominican form of community life, with sufficient choir sisters in each convent to assure the solemn celebration of the Divine Office and the full array of regular observance, was not considered possible in the smaller houses.

The first house to close was that at West Kirby which had belonged to the former Stroud congregation. Although the community was much appreciated by the clergy and parishioners, the small private school enrolled very few Catholic children. The other need this house had served, as a seaside rest home for the former Stroud congregation, could now be met by several other houses of the amalgamated congregation. The sisters left West Kirby at Christmas 1929 and by February the house had been let.[9]

The following June Mother M. Teresa visited Bishop Thomas Shine of Middlesbrough seeking his approval for the closure of two more convents at Redcar and Leyburn, both of which had small communities of fewer than six sisters. Despite the unsatisfactory reports given a decade previously, the new parish priest at Redcar expressed his reluctance to part with the Dominicans who, he claimed, had built up the school and won the confidence of the parishioners.[10] Although other religious could not be found to replace them, the Dominicans left Redcar at the end of 1930. Similarly, a decision was made to withdraw the community in the tiny rural parish of Leyburn, which numbered only three sisters. At Easter 1932 this house was also closed, leaving Bridlington the sole Dominican convent in the diocese.

By 1931 the convent at Dovercourt was experiencing severe financial difficulties. Since the removal of the boarders to Harpenden in 1920, the numbers in the school at Dovercourt, which had never been more than forty, had dwindled to ten. Neither was the convalescent home paying its way. Consideration was given to undertaking work with juvenile offenders under the auspices of the Home Office, but there was not sufficient scope for developing the property at Dovercourt for this purpose. Reluctantly, Mother M. Teresa approached Bishop Doubleday of Brentwood for permission to close the house and communicated his approval to the parish priest.[11] Mother M. Augustine Browne, who had been vicaress at Dovercourt, was appointed prioress of Kelvedon and half the community, as well as the convalescents, moved with her. In this way the works of two houses which had belonged to different congregations before the amalgamation, were merged and consolidated.

Perhaps the most difficult closure of this period was that of the convent at Chislett Road,[12] West Hampstead, as one of the General Councillors, Mother M. Dominic Wilkes, had been so much involved in its development. The principal of the school, Sister M. Bertrand Bingham, who suffered from chronic asthma, was unable to continue teaching and there was no one available to take her place. Making provision for the full range of subjects at senior level was also proving a considerable challenge and while the school was well attended, there was ample provision for senior girls in other Catholic schools within easy reach. Although the house was large, it was in a residential street and was not easily adapted to the perceived conventual requirements of the time. Development would depend on neighbouring properties coming into the market and planning permission being obtained for the expansion of the school buildings. The local prioress, Sister M. Albert Egan, was convinced that the obstacles could not be overcome and this opinion carried weight with the Council.[13]

Cardinal Bourne, however, was not prepared to allow the school to close and insisted that the Dominicans find another community to replace them. Eventually the Daughters of Charity of St Vincent de Paul agreed to carry on the school for junior children and to continue visiting the poor, sick and needy, which had been such an important part of the Dominican community's work since their first days at Mutrix Road. On the last day of 1931 the Dominicans handed over the keys to the Daughters of Charity who moved in on New Year's Day. The school continued for another thirty years and the Daughters of Charity remained on for some time after its closure.

There were also increasing tensions at another foundation of the former Harrow congregation, St Vincent's at Watford. The convent and children's home was adjacent to the parish church and school, the latter undergoing a period of rapid expansion as the town developed into a dormitory suburb of London. The parish priest, Monsignor Arthur Jackman, made repeated requests for a room in the convent to be converted for school use, but the sisters had resisted. Eventually the two isolation cottages in the grounds were offered for conversion as classrooms but these did not meet with the approval of the local Education Council.[14] By the end of the year there seemed no resolution to the impasse and consideration was given to moving the children, then numbering almost sixty, to Bognor or some other place where there might be opportunity for training in agricultural and farm work. The sisters were anxious to keep the home mixed, so that brothers and sisters could remain together, though this provided further difficulties in terms of relocation.[15] A plan to move the home to Kelvedon was thwarted by Bishop Doubleday's insistence that no boys above the age of seven be admitted.

It was not until a year after Mother M. Teresa Lamburn's term of office ended that an offer of £4,000 for the property made by Monsignor Jackman was accepted by the congregation and the convent was closed on 24 April 1937. By this time numbers had been reduced considerably as no new children had been accepted for over a year and others had already been found places elsewhere. Once again, the opportunity was taken of uniting works and personnel from houses which had previously belonged to two different congregations. Sisters M. Gabriel Sutherland and M. Vincent van Kerkevoorde arrived at St Marychurch early in 1937 bringing eleven of the former Watford girls with them. A similar number of boys, mostly brothers of the girls newly arrived at St Marychurch, took up residence at St Vincent's Home in Torquay.[16]

There were also some significant changes in the schools in which the sisters worked during the years immediately after the amalgamation. At this time, the appointment of a lay head in a parish school was considered by many major superiors to present a conflict of interest in terms of obedience. When a headmaster was appointed to St Anselm's School in Harrow in 1932 the decision was made to withdraw the remaining sister from the staff. There were two urgent requests from Newcastle-upon-Tyne at this time for sisters to take charge of the schools in St Lawrence's parish Byker and St Vincent's in neighbouring Walker, and two sisters were provided for each school.

The first two headmistresses, Sisters M. Peter Tohill (head at St Vincent's 1932–60) and M. Angela Stone (head of St Lawrence's 1939–64) both became something of a legend in Newcastle. Both were well aware that many of the children in this area of the city came from families experiencing real poverty. They and their companions would walk from the convent in Jesmond, stopping at the market en route, using their tram fares to purchase vegetables from which they made nourishing soup to supplement the diet of their young pupils. A further educational endeavour was begun at Newcastle, also in 1932, when the parish library and rooms in the grounds of The Minories were converted and extended to house a boys' preparatory school. It is interesting to read that Sister M. Colette Quigley, who was appointed as principal, was considered too delicate to continue teaching in the parish elementary schools![17]

Requests continued to be made for teachers for both parish and private schools, though for want of personnel these had to be declined. The opportunity of working with university students, a quintessentially Dominican work, was offered by the Catholic Women's League. They proposed a hostel for female students at either Oxford or Cambridge providing classes in philosophy and social science, but in the end the terms of the agreement were considered too restrictive by the General Council.[18] The idea of an apostolate amongst students in Cambridge was also encouraged by Edward Bullough, who lectured in psychology and philosophy of art at the university and was appointed Serena Professor of Italian in 1933. Both the Bullough children, Halley and Leonora, had entered the Dominicans in 1931 to become Father Sebastian and Sister M. Mark, and both would die at Stone having made a valuable contribution to the work of the Order and the congregation.

There was also some rationalization of works between the houses at Stone and Stoke-on-Trent during Mother M. Teresa Lamburn's term of office. Blessed Imelda's School at Stone, which had been reopened at the beginning of the First World War, had never managed to run at a profit and in 1930 was staffed by three sisters, though it numbered only twelve girls. Sister M. Rose Gray, who was headmistress at the time, voiced her concerns to Archbishop Williams during the canonical visitation of the community at Stone in May of that year.[19] The continuing uncertainty over the school's future and the constant changes of staff were, she felt, unfair to the girls. The General Council's feeling was that the spirit and tone of St Dominic's at Stoke were considerably above those of other schools of its kind and the decision was made to transfer the boarders from Stone to Stoke the following year.[20] To accommodate them, it was also decided to close St Margaret's Home and transfer the women to either St Mary's Home in Stone or St Catherine's in Leicester.

The deserted school buildings at Stone would become something of a bone of contention over the next few years. Certainly a number of the sisters at Stone were convinced they would provide much better accommodation for the noviciate than the convent at Stroud could offer.[21] The possibility of converting the school wing into a retreat house was also considered, but in 1934 it was opened as a school of Domestic Science with ten students enrolled on opening day. At Leicester and Hawick plans for expansion were in hand; Sister M. Ambrose Ladelle drew up the initial plans for the new convent at Leicester which would enable the community to move from cramped quarters in the attic of the Home. On the 24 September 1934 the new extension to the convent at Hawick increased the accommodation in St Margaret's Home to forty-five.[22] Although there was retrenchment, rationalization and consolidation in the work of the English Dominican Sisters during the first six years of the new congregation's existence, there was, as yet, no sense of alarm about the future.

Cautious leadership in difficult times

In his final address to the General Chapter of 1935, Archbishop Williams had urged the delegates to vote for a Prioress General, not out of loyalty to their former groups, but for one who would continue the task of building a united congregation. To assist them in their task by the enjoyment of a good breakfast, he had dispensed them from their Wednesday fast. On the first ballot, Mother Rose Imelda Raymond-Barker was elected Prioress General with the required two thirds of the votes. Although, under the circumstances, she was probably relieved not to be re-elected, the fact that all but three of the remaining votes were cast for Mother M. Teresa Lamburn, is an indication that she still had the confidence of the sisters. The outgoing Prioress General was elected first councillor almost unanimously. After the 1941 Chapter, Mother M. Teresa served a term as prioress at Newcastle before moving to Brewood, where she died in August 1951. The new General Council was completed by Sisters M. Ambrose Kilbride and M. Dominic Wilkes from the previous administration and Sister M. Columba McQuillan who, having been professed at Portobello Road, ensured an even representation from the former groups.

The new Prioress General, the daughter of Edward Raymond-Barker and Rose Crawford, had been born in Madeira on 22 March 1885, and christened Mary Rose. Her father was an electrical engineer and the family moved back to England when Mary Rose was still a young child, settling in Wimbledon. A maternal aunt, Sister Catherine Joseph Crawford, was a Dominican at Stone and three younger sisters became Carmelite nuns. Sister Rose Imelda made her profession at Stone in 1910 and was soon afterwards appointed head of Blessed Imelda's Pension School. She also spent four years as novice mistress, before serving two terms as prioress at Stoke. Mother Rose Imelda was a gifted writer, having published several brief works related to the history of the Dominican Sisters in Britain. Vitality, exuberance, gracious manners and a certain elitism were all part and parcel of her makeup; she was much loved by the former Stone sisters but was committed heart and soul to the amalgamation and capable of instilling this enthusiasm in others.

Mother Rose Imelda doubtless recognized the need for a breathing space, though there continued to be developments and changes in the life and work of the congregation during the first half of her administration. Since uniformity in most aspects of the daily lives of the sisters had been achieved, there were few circulars from the Prioress General heralding further changes, apart from those

1a. Mother Margaret Hallahan.

1b. Mother M. Imelda Poole.

1c. St Dominic's Convent, Stone, sketched by Mother Francis Raphael Drane, *c.*1870.

2a. Sisters during recreation at Stone, 1860 including a self-portrait of Mother Francis Raphael Drane at right.

2b. Archbishop Ullathorne's tomb in the church at Stone.

3a. Detail from a Collectarium illuminated at Stone showing the antiphon and prayer for the feast of St Dominic.

3b. Detail from the hood of a cope embroidered by Sister M. Gonzaga Ullathorne, 1901.

4a. The community at Stroud in 1871. Mother M. Teresa Matthews is seated second from left with the embroidery frame.

4b. A view of St Rose's Convent, Stroud, *c*.1900. Photographs courtesy of Stone Archives.

5. Easter greeting sent by Mother M. Raymond Goldrick, Prioress of Erdington, to the community at Stroud, Easter 1918.

6a. The community about to leave Stroud for London in 1866. Mother M. Rose Corbett seated front left.

6b. St Catherine's Nursing Home at Dane Hills in Leicester, opened in 1906. Until the adjoining convent was opened thirty years later the sisters lived in the attic.

7a. The chapel at St Dominic's, Harrow.

7b. Mother Catherine Philip Bathurst *c.*1900.

7c. St Dominic's Convent, Harrow, *c.*1960.

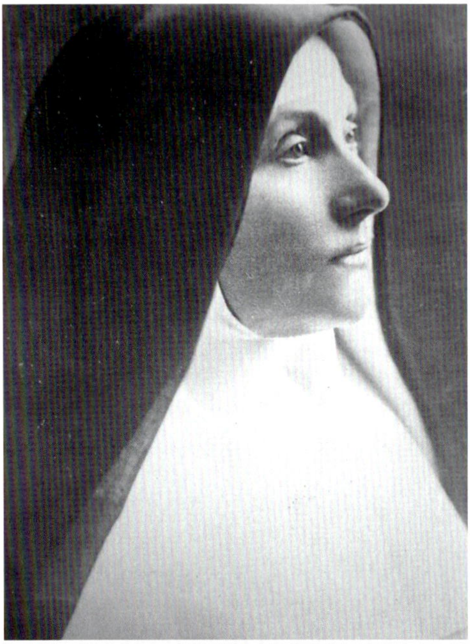

8a. Mother M. Cecilia Marshall, *c*.1882.

8b.Chapel at Portobello Road *c*.1920.

8c. Recreation in the cloister garth at Portobello Road convent, *c*.1914.

9a. The somewhat anxious faces of the first General Council of the amalgamated Congregation. Seated: Mothers M. Catherine de Ricci Wilson, M. Teresa Lamburn, M. Cecilia Marshall. Standing: Mothers M. Ambrose Kilbride and M. Dominic Wilkes.

9b. Hope for the future: Mother M. Bonaventure Burke, seated in the centre, with novices and junior professed sisters at St Rose's Convent, Stroud, 1934.

10a. The community at Hawick praying the Divine Office, *c.*1958.

10b. Sisters M. Leonie O'Driscoll and M. Quentin Colclough with children at St Rose's Special School, Stroud, *c.*1963.

11a. The original convent, presbytery and church at Bodø, *c.*1980.

11b. Sister M. Alberta Barry with some of 'the dearest little Vikings'.

11c. Sister M. Ruth Earley with a ballet class, *c.*1965.

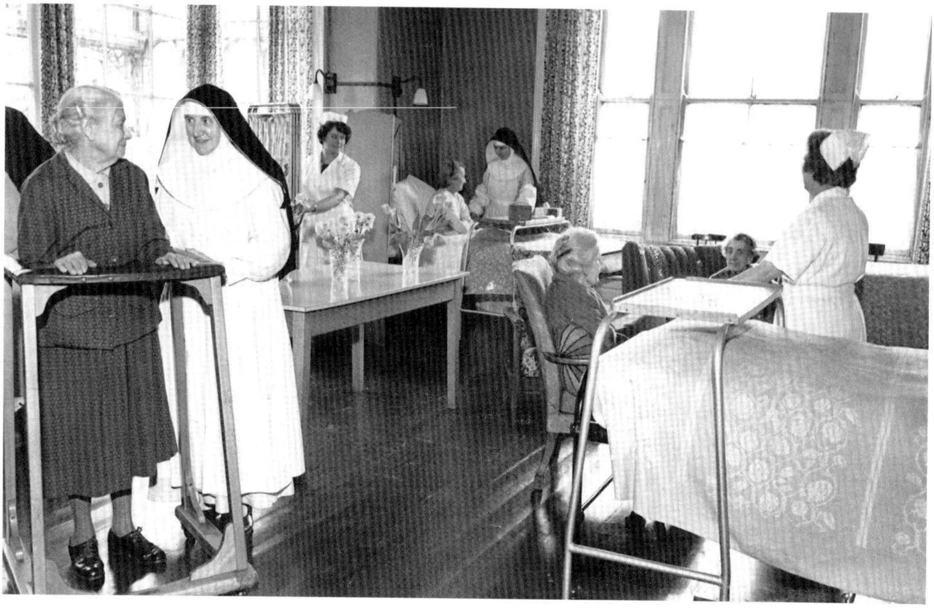

12a. St Catherine's Nursing Home, Newcastle-upon-Tyne, 1962: Sisters M. Fidelis Curran and M. Antony McLoughlin.

12b. Sister M. Aemilia Daly teaching at St Agnes' Convent School, Erdington, *c*.1962.

13a. Sister M. Amata Smith peeling the vegetables.

13b. Procession at Harrow, 1967.

13c. Temporary professed sisters who attended St Catherine's Centre enjoying themselves together at Harrow, 1967.

14a. Sister M. Lucy Moran with a group of parents at the new school at St David's, Belle Vue in Grenada, 1969.

14b. The lower ground floor of the Convent at Leicester housed a play group during the mid 1980s.

15a. Sister Bertranda Mulryan, Father Richard Finn and Sister M. Edward (Anna Mary) House with other members of Dominican Peace Action at Aldermaston, *c.*1986.

15b. Sister M. Cecily Boulding is greeted by Pope John Paul II during the ARCIC2 meetings at Palazzola, 1987.

16a. Sister M. Conleth Lawless and a resident of St Mary's Home, Stone.

16b. Sister Tamsin Mary Geach, teaching.

16c. A meeting between sisters and brethren.

16d. Sisters in the choir at Stone, 2008.

necessitated by wartime conditions. At the General Chapter of 1935, before the elections took place, Mother Rose Imelda had proposed that some sort of statement should be issued from the chapter explaining the changes that were made to the original plan of amalgamation, admitting the errors that had been made.[23] Although Archbishop Williams had agreed with this, no mention is made in the official Acts of the Chapter, nor is the matter mentioned in any of the Prioress General's letters to the Congregation. It was reported that important matters were discussed with 'complete liberty and mutual consideration' but the overwhelming emphasis was laid upon the need to 'foster by means of outward uniformity, the spirit of union'.[24]

During the Second World War, Mother Rose Imelda penned a constant stream of circular letters. In her dramatic language she saw the war, not so much as a conflict between democracy and totalitarianism, but as an apocalyptic struggle in which the Church was confronting the onslaught of the forces of evil arraigned against her. At the General Chapter of 1941 Mother Rose Imelda was elected to the General Council, and subsequently served terms as prioress or sub-prioress at Stoke-on-Trent, St Leonards, St Marychurch and Kelvedon. The last ten years of her life were spent at Stoke where, while still retaining a certain air of grandeur, she was a much loved member of the community. She died some weeks after a fall, aged ninety-two, on 8 November 1975.

The third General Chapter of the congregation was held at St Rose's Convent Stroud from 31 May to 11 June 1941. It was only on the fourth scrutiny, and on a simple majority of a single vote, that Mother M. Emmanuel Fuller was elected Prioress General, the remaining votes having been for Mother Rose Imelda. Minna Fuller, the daughter of a military engineer, George Fuller and his wife Antoinette Cumming, was born in Belfast though she spent most of her youth in London. She was brought up with military austerity (it is said that she began each day with a cold bath[25]) and though she would win the lasting affection of many of her sisters in religion, to others she seemed aloof and reserved. Like her predecessor she was something of a *grande dame*, small in stature yet commanding and capable. Like Mother Rose Imelda she also had a sibling who was a nun, Sister Joseph Emmanuel of the Poor Sisters of Nazareth. Minna entered St Rose's Convent Stroud at the end of October 1908 and made her profession of vows in March 1910. Like so many of the Prioresses General, Mother M. Emmanuel was appointed to positions of authority early in her religious life and continued to hold office for many years.

A more practically minded person than her predecessor, Mother M. Emmanuel's circular letters were less dramatic, more calming. She was very much convinced that the future of the congregation required difficult decisions but the wartime conditions that obtained during the greater part of her term of office made any major change virtually impossible. Her approach was innovative for the times; well in advance, but clearly seen as a preparation for the General Chapter due in 1947, Mother M. Emmanuel prepared and circulated an extensive questionnaire. Although intended for the local superiors, she made it clear that something more than their own personal opinions was required:

> Please discuss the matter with your Council and note down the substance of their arguments and the conclusions you draw. You are free to ask the opinion of any choir sister who is assigned to the house and whom you deem to have a considered judgment and experience of life.[26]

The Prioress General saw several policy options available to ease the strain of having no one available to stand in when illness or age prevented sisters from carrying out their work. Should certain works be concentrated in particular houses or be given up entirely? Should houses be closed and if so, which ones? Should private schools be preferred to parish schools? Where should the apostolic priorities of the congregation lie? This type of consultation would not be familiar to most religious congregations until twenty years later.

From the number of replies, it seems that few superiors were prepared at the time for devolved decision-making. The opinions expressed were too few and inconclusive, except on two points: there was unanimity that the number of works had to be reduced but in stark contradiction to this, an insistence that no house should be closed! It was felt that any closure would be an admission of failure and deter candidates from entering the congregation. Only in the area of educational work is it possible to detect anything like a consensus, with a slight preference being shown for work in parish schools, particularly if the apostolic needs of the neighbourhood would benefit from the presence of the sisters. On the other hand distinct disapproval was voiced of sisters teaching in schools at a distance from the convent, necessitating their absence for most of the day.[27]

After her term as Prioress General ended, Mother M. Emmanuel was appointed prioress at Harrow for two terms. Following a similar period at Brewood, she was assigned in 1959 to Harpenden until her declining state of health made a move to St Mary's Home at Stone necessary. To all these houses she brought a peaceful presence and a profound spirit of prayer. Despite suffering from appendicitis and cataracts in her old age Mother M. Emmanuel showed remarkable powers of resilience, dying at the age of ninety-seven on 22 August 1977.

What might have happened if Mother M. Emmanuel had obtained a second term as Prioress General? Once again, at the 1947 General Chapter, the voting went to a fourth scrutiny before Mother M. Aquinas Colgan was elected on a simple majority of a single vote. Mary Josephine Colgan was a Dubliner, born on 17 April 1880 to Bernard Colgan and Anne Corbally. She made her profession at St Vincent's Convent, Portobello Road in 1903 and Mother M. Cecilia Marshall was quick to recognize her ability. She was to serve as novice mistress and local superior before taking on the task of establishing St Mary's Training Centre. Not as forceful a personality as her three predecessors, Mother M. Aquinas was certainly approachable, remembered for her sense of justice as well as a sense of humour, and her ability to take advice as well as to command.

The austerities of the post-war period and the adaptations necessary to bring the works of the congregation into line with new government legislation affecting education and health care were major preoccupations of Mother M. Aquinas' administration. She was certainly committed to a reorganization of the houses and works of the congregation. In a letter to Father Aelwin Tindal-Atkinson, a member of the General Curia of the Order at Santa Sabina, written in April 1951, Mother M. Aquinas hinted at some of the reasons why she was unable to bring this about. The main reason was that her health was deteriorating and she felt the delicate task would be carried out more effectively by a younger woman with greater energy. Another difficulty was that the vicaress, who was far from well herself, was now incapable of working harmoniously with the other members of the General Council. In fact, Mother M. Aquinas asked Father Aelwin's advice on convoking the General Chapter early for, although she could resign her office, this would leave the government of the congregation in the hands of her vicaress which, for obvious reasons, she wished to avoid.[28] The response is not extant but it must have been, 'hold on!' for the chapter opened only on New Year's Eve the following year, by which time Mother M. Aquinas was too ill to attend. After successful surgery for the removal of cataracts, she returned to Portobello Road Convent where she gradually deteriorated until her death on 6 May 1960.

War and rumours of war

Amidst all these difficulties came the Great Depression and the Second World War. Though financial concerns form a major part of the official records of the English Dominican Congregation during the 1930s it is surprising that no mention seems to be made of the economic depression and its effects. On the other hand, from 1938 the annals make frequent mention of the deteriorating diplomatic situation in Europe and the expectation of war. In September of that year the prioress of the Dominican Sisters at Gleisdorf, near Vienna, wrote to Mother Rose Imelda asking whether she would be willing to take thirty or more sisters who had been expelled from their convents by the Nazis since the *Anschluss*. The required permits were obtained from the Home Office and the Austrian sisters began arriving in small contingents by the end of the year, and were dispersed, two or three together, amongst the houses of the congregation.[29]

This act of charity turned out to be a major commitment which went well beyond the provision of board and lodging. One of the sisters developed tuberculosis and eventually died at the sanatorium run by the Daughters of Charity at Warley in Essex. Another, unable to adapt to the stress of wartime conditions in an alien environment, became mentally unstable and had to be institutionalized; while yet another died suddenly from thrombosis only a month before she was due to return to Austria after the war. The English Dominicans provided their Austrian sisters with every care, even intervening at the War Office to arrange visits to her nephew, who was a prisoner of war, for one of the Austrian sisters.[30] It is perhaps not surprising that several of them asked to be received into the English Congregation, though only Sister M. Vinzentia Benischka was eventually accepted. She continued to teach German and music at Stone and Stoke and to delight sisters and pupils with her inventiveness, turning a few matches and a piece of cloth into a glove puppet in a trice. A devoted and prayerful woman she continued as organist at Stoke until shortly before her death in 1965.

Almost a year before the declaration of war, the War Office had advised the evacuation of the elderly and infirm sisters and residents from Portobello Road. A photograph was sent from London showing the windows crisscrossed with tape in a very artistic fashion to prevent the shattering of glass in the event of bombing. Mother Rose Imelda travelled south and noted the obvious feeling of tension in the capital; a trench was dug in the garden for an air raid shelter and even at Stone three 'gas proof' areas were set up in the convent. Several of the sisters were evacuated to Hawick, but on 29 September came the news of 'peace in our time' and for twelve months things returned more or less to normal.[31]

Dramatic changes would follow the declaration of war on 3 September 1939. At once, Cardinal Hinsley ordered all women religious in the Archdiocese of Westminster to adopt soft headdresses, devoid of pins which might damage gas masks. Detailed and inventive instructions requiring a yard of tape, much stitching and dispensing with the starched linen 'stiffner' which lined the black veils, were despatched from Stone a week later. Despite the calamity of war, Sister M. Constance Sleigh, running the laundry at Stone at the time, still remembers her relief at not having to launder and starch fifty stiffners each week and her near despair when the good Mothers of the General Council reintroduced them on the cessation of hostilities in 1945![32]

The annals record the enormous number of evacuees moving in

Fig. 12 Sisters at St Marychurch wearing the pin-free war-time veil, 1940.

all directions to and from the different convents during the period of the 'phoney war'. What an enormous strain this must have placed on resources and nerves. Two sisters teaching in Newcastle accompanied 1400 pupils from Catholic primary schools in the city to Morpeth. Bridlington arranged for the reception of 100 evacuees from Middlesbrough and Hull, while at Cheadle the sisters were appointed billeting officers for 110 young Mancunians and their teachers. St Rose's Special School at Stroud took in children from a similar school at Pinner, near London. Children from Edmonton and Wood Green were billeted at Kelvedon and once the Battle of Britain began a second exodus from London headed towards St Marychurch. Numbers in the schools were swelled by the arrival of forty-four children and two Sisters of St Joseph of Peace from Hanwell and the convent also gave refuge to several Franciscan Missionaries of Mary who had been bombed out of their convent in Canning Town in the East End of London.[33]

Not all the evacuees settled in well despite the best of intentions. The prioress at St Leonards, Sister M. Augustine Browne, agreed to take evacuees into the boys' preparatory school provided they were 'well behaved and gentlemanly'. The children who arrived were five young brothers from the East End who refused to sit down to meals, preferring to run about leaving a trail of half-eaten buns, wailing, 'Miss, we wants to go 'ome!' They were clearly not prep. school material and like so many evacuees were hopelessly out of place and did not stay.[34] The young gentlemen did not remain long at St Leonards themselves, as the house was requisitioned for military purposes and they too were evacuated, some to a school in Banbury run by Mother Rose Imelda's sister-in-law, others to Bitham Hall at Avon Dassett in Warwickshire, put at their disposal by the Worralls, whose son was a Dominican. Another group of East Enders arrived at St Marychurch during the war, most of them from utterly deprived backgrounds; some of these girls stayed until well after the war and at times proved quite beyond the control of the sisters who were caring for them.

Despite the confusion and dislocation, and the strain of almost continuous air raids over London, valiant attempts were made to maintain a semblance of normality. On the other hand, a sister who was a pupil in the school at the time remembers Sister M. Genevieve d'Otrante allowing the junior girls, worn out by sleepless nights during the incessant bombing raids over the city, to put their heads on their desks and rest during Religious Education class.[35] There was also great rejoicing at Stoke, despite the war, when two pupils of St Dominic's High School, Mary Stanney and Elfrida

Johnson, won scholarships to Oxford. Although the onset of hostilities had stalled the informative process for the beatification of Mother Margaret Hallahan, which had been opened in May 1937, this did not prevent a restrained celebration of the centenary of her arrival at Coventry in 1942 or that of the first profession three years later.

An unexpected communication arrived in January 1942 from Mother M. Philomena Moloney, Prioress of the North Adelaide Dominicans, expressing a desire for amalgamation and seeking the views of the General Council at Stone. Mother M. Emmanuel prepared a comprehensive reply on the state of the English Congregation and despatched this, along with a copy of the constitutions. The North Adelaide community was willing to accept the English constitutions but despite several further exchanges of correspondence the plan for amalgamation was deemed impracticable during wartime. In 1958 the North Adelaide Sisters would become part of the Australian amalgamation.[36]

Support for the war effort became a feature of life as the sisters acted as ARP (Air Raid Precautions) wardens, set up First Aid posts, and organized Girls' Training Corps in the senior schools, in which their pupils were instructed in First Aid, military drill, despatch carrying, carpentry and home maintenance. At Stoke a club room was made available to the Free French sailors who were encamped at Trentham, while the prioress, Mother M. Monica Brook-Milne, adopted a whole regiment whom the community kept supplied with a constant stream of knitted comforters. At Brewood the girls adopted the HMS *Whitehall* and were delighted to receive a large tub of sweets sent from the crew while they were docked in New York.[37] Everywhere, sisters and pupils were 'digging for victory' and at Stoke, as well as raising a variety of poultry, Sister M. Wereburg Wilcox supplemented the meat rations by rearing rabbits for the table.

In 1940 several bombs had fallen twenty yards from the convent at Harrow leaving a huge crater, and another fell in the garden of St Agnes' Convent at Erdington. In January 1944 the laundry at Portobello Road was destroyed by an incendiary bomb and a month later the terrace of houses opposite the convent was bombed, killing seventeen residents. The force of the explosion blew out the chapel windows and rendered the hostel and ancillary buildings uninhabitable.[38] The fact that none of the sisters or their charges was injured was seen as a mark of God's special mercy and the intercession of His blessed Mother.[39]

Formation and intellectual life

Both before and after the war, recruitment to the noviciate continued to be a major concern. During Mother Rose Imelda's term of office sixty-three postulants entered, but only forty received the habit and only thirty-three completed the noviciate. Wartime conditions resulted in a decline in entries for almost all religious orders and congregations and during Mother M. Emmanuel's term as Prioress General the figures were two-thirds those of the previous six years. Under Mother M. Aquinas, entries again averaged ten per year, a record number of sixteen entering in 1951.

The quinquennial report, prepared for the Congregation for Religious in Rome, for this period also shows that dispensations had to be obtained for receiving almost a third of the postulants, as they were above the age limit of thirty years laid down in the constitutions. Most of these older women, despite a great desire to be Dominicans, could not adapt themselves after many years of independence, to the type of discipline required of women religious at the time. Even amongst the younger postulants the attrition rate was high and one, referred to as the 'B&B postulant', could hardly be persuaded to stay overnight before departing. In total forty-six novices professed their vows while Mother M. Aquinas was in office. Overall, during these eighteen years under review, there were 123 deaths in the congregation, while thirteen perpetually professed sisters and six in temporary vows either sought dispensations or returned to secular life when their temporary vows expired.

It is not surprising that both the 1941 and 1947 General Chapters expressed reservations over the method of recruitment and suggestions were made for promoting religious vocations more vigorously in the schools. It was also proposed that areas rich in vocations, such as Lancashire and Lanarkshire, where the congregation had no houses, and even Canada, should be targeted. One factor singled out as a deterrent to applicants was the lack of foreign missionary work.[40] There was also an admission at the earlier chapter of the difficulty inherent in having a mistress of novices and a mistress of temporary professed sisters with different traditions, training and outlook, having charge of the young religious in turn. The necessity of providing special training and careful instruction during the last six months before final vows was also stressed. Not every local superior had the necessary qualities for training young sisters, but to take them out of the schools or other works for this period would have been a great inconvenience.

Sister M. Teresa Wilmot, who had succeeded Mother M.

Bonaventure Burke as novice mistress in 1944, remained in office until 1951. Sister M. Teresa was not a born teacher but her example and her 'cosy chats' left a deep impression on her novices. The General Council then appointed Sister M. Edward Stocker to replace her, but this gifted young sister's health broke down and she was to die four years later at the early age of forty-seven. Sister M. Damian McGimpsey, who was appointed in her stead, had nursed in the East End before entering the congregation, and the experience had given her a good insight into the varieties of human nature. Noviciate training concentrated on instruction in the obligations of the religious life, the nature of the vows and the constitutions; it was not intended to be an academic exercise, in fact, some novices did not find it sufficiently challenging on this score. However, Sister M. Damian, who was well read and had an enquiring mind, was able to encourage and develop her charges, though she could not bear pretention or conceit. Her approach was positive; no matter what their age or background, she tried to treat her novices as individuals and aimed at building up, rather than knocking down.

In an era when there was a stigma attached to leaving religious life, many institutes offered those leaving only the bare minimum in financial support which the demands of charity required. There is plenty of evidence in the General Council minutes and elsewhere that Mother M. Emmanuel had a much more understanding and compassionate approach. This is demonstrated in the case of Sister M. Regina Nixon, who had been appointed headmistress at Harrow in 1937. Although she had seen through a major building project to a successful conclusion, Sister M. Regina's own lack of confidence, and the stresses of wartime, led to a complete physical breakdown. In June 1942 she was taken to the seaside convent at Bridlington for rest. Mother M. Emmanuel took the time to visit her at the end of the month and, in her diary, describes their long walk on the seafront, festooned with barbed wire defences, and cheering the flagging spirits of the younger sister with an ice-cream tea, before they made their way home to the convent along the country roads. When Regina Nixon was dispensed from her vows early in 1945, Mother M. Emmanuel ensured generous financial support over a number of years. The following year the Prioress General covered the cost of returning to the former sister, now earning her living as a music teacher, a piano given to the convent at Stone by her mother.

Two other sisters simply walked out of the convent during this time, and although Mother M. Emmanuel might write in highly formal style to the Archbishop of Birmingham that she 'had the honour to inform your Grace of a sad event' the approaches made to the women concerned, in order to regularize their situation so that they could 'leave decently', show her genuine concern and diplomacy.[41] In the eight years after the war only one sister left the congregation, not having received the necessary votes to make her perpetual profession. It is possible that this abrupt decline in departures shows that the stresses of the immediate post-amalgamation years and the difficulties of war may have been contributing factors in the decision-making process of those who left.

The setting up of a central house of studies in conformity with the plan for amalgamation had long been deferred for lack of personnel. Sisters initially spent their period of temporary profession at Stroud where they followed the syllabus and sat exams for the Higher Certificate in Religious Studies. After 1935 the practice of sending the newly professed sisters to Stone for at least a year after making profession was introduced, though no plan of studies has survived. Soon after the amalgamation a determined effort was made to send the most gifted younger sisters for higher education. Three sisters began studies at Bedford College in the University of London in 1931: Sister M. Cecilia Oddie reading chemistry, Sisters M. Imdela Geary and M. Laurence Mitchener reading history. The first two, despite doing brilliant work, had to be withdrawn after a year, as balancing the demands of academic and religious life threatened complete physical breakdown.[42] Sister M. Cecilia returned to Bedford, eventually taking a Master's degree and publishing a series of general science textbooks. Sister M. Imelda went on to Edinburgh where Sister M. Barbara Pearce was reading English and Sister M. Antony Waterhouse, geography. The latter was given special permission to wear a black, waterproof habit when going on field trips.[43]

During the Second World War Mother M. Emmanuel had been quick to take advantage of the opportunity which presented itself when an Anglican Teachers' College, St Katherine's, was evacuated to Torquay. Other Catholic religious were already training there and the Prioress General was sufficiently ecumenically minded to enrol Sisters M. Oliver O'Connor and M. Mark Bullough. No sooner had the war ended than arrangements were made for Sisters M. Gilbert [later Patricia Mary] England and M. Joan Isaac to attend Queen Mary College in Mile End. The former, who graduated with first-class honours in English, still remembers the daily trek from Portobello Road, walking to the College from Stepney Green underground station past terraces of bombed-out and boarded-up shops.[44] She found her years of study stimulating, her only regret was that, because of the strictures of religious life at the time, she was unable to immerse herself more fully in student life and extra-curricular activities. Most sisters destined for teaching attended the various Catholic Teachers' Colleges and for those who attended university, this was considered not only sufficient preparation for the classroom, but for assuming the role of headmistress as well!

It was not only those preparing for the apostolate whose intellectual development was considered. Even before the first General Chapter was concluded, Mother M. Teresa Lamburn announced that Father Adrian English had agreed to give a three-year course of weekly lectures at Portobello Road convent. The ambitious programme including cosmology, philosophy, logic, metaphysics and natural theology, was attended by over forty sisters from the convents in the London area. A second series of lectures on scripture was offered on Saturdays by Father Vincent McNabb and proved just as popular. The prior of Hawkesyard, Father Rupert Hooper-Dixon, offered a similar course at Stone to sisters from the Staffordshire convents while the friars from Woodchester made provision at Stroud. No other nuns in England or even Europe, the annals claimed, were given such opportunities for intellectual development.[45]

Individual sisters sometimes fostered their own intellectual and spiritual development. Sister M. Veronica Madden, who had been professed at Harrow in 1923, was later given charge of religious education at St Dominic's School there, and also instructed a large number of converts. In order to deepen her own understanding of the scriptures, and make them better understood by her students, she undertook the study of Latin, Greek and Hebrew. There is no indication that Sister M. Veronica's expertise was ever brought into play for the direct benefit of her sisters in religion. Intellectual virtuosity, carried with it the danger of pride and also had to be balanced against any appearance of singularity.

Being of use to the Church: the active ministry

Three commissions were established during the 1935 General Chapter as a means of coordinating the various works of the congregation: one for schools, one for hospitals and homes and another to oversee building schemes. These groups, which held regular meetings, also fostered a sense of common purpose and helpful exchange between the sisters. The first meeting for teaching sisters was held at Stone at the end of May 1936 with Sister M. Winifred Lambe, Directress General of Studies for the congregation and headmistress of St Dominic's High School at Stoke-on-Trent, chairing the sessions. A series of topical papers was delivered and the ensuing discussion focused on infant and nursery teaching, the secondary school curriculum, and also laid great importance on encouraging as many pupils as possible to stay at school until Leaving Certificate.[46] The commission for nursing sisters was headed by Sister M. Leonard McEwan and after its first meeting in July 1937, several sisters attended the Catholic Nursing Congress which opened at University College London, following an inaugural Mass at Westminster Cathedral.[47]

The works of the congregation continued to develop despite the smaller number of sisters. In the summer of 1936 yet another attempt was made to re-establish a private school at Stone with St Joseph's opening in the converted bookbinding room. Within a year the numbers had risen to fourteen and the decision was made to combine this school with the Domestic Science school, with Sister M. Edmund Lewis in charge, under the name St Dominic's Priory School. The purchase of Beech House at the end of the convent garden gave ample scope for expansion. When three Spanish girls, refugees from the Civil War – rather surprisingly, the daughters of a Republican – applied to the new school, accommodation was found and other boarders soon joined them.[48]

An extension comprising classrooms, domestic science room, dining room and art room was opened at St Dominic's High School in Stoke by Oliver Stanley, Minister of Education, at the end of June 1936.[49] At Harrow it was Bishop Edward Myers who officiated at the opening of the new tennis courts, hockey field and a classroom block which would allow the school to expand numbers to 450 – a figure which would never be reached. Sister M. Catherine Anderson was appointed headmistress of St Catherine's at St Marychurch in 1936 and began to reverse the school's decline. Art and domestic science rooms were opened the following year and numbers soon rose to ninety with several boarders residing in the guest house; particular strengths in teaching German and English were noted.[50]

In July 1935, the Bognor Town Council issued a compulsory purchase order on the convent in connection with a proposed road-widening scheme. After several false starts an offer was made on Hill House in St Leonards and the boys' preparatory school moved there for the beginning of the new school year in 1936.[51] In

November the following year the General Council decided to close St Joseph's Convent at Cheadle. Although there were twelve sisters in the community, considered an ideal number for full Dominican life, since the retirement of Sister M. Joseph Blenkinsop as headmistress in the summer, only one sister was teaching in the parish school and drawing a salary. As a consequence, the house had to be subsidized from the General Fund. Attempts were made to find another community to replace the Dominicans, but difficulties with the Staffordshire Education Committee regarding staffing of the school made Cheadle an unattractive proposition. The community won a reprieve and the Dominicans remained until 1948 when the Sisters of Charity of St Paul from Selly Park replaced them.[52]

Despite the fact there had been no one available to replace Sister M. Joseph at Cheadle, the congregation agreed to provide staff for three new primary schools in the years running up to the Second World War. The first of these was St Teresa's at Trent Vale, where two sisters from Stoke had been giving religious instruction to the children of the new parish since its foundation in 1926. Sisters M. Xavier Doran and M. Norbert Brown opened the school in September 1938 and pioneered the work until the end of the 1943 school year.[53] Rev. Edward Armitage, first pastor of the new parish at Wheathampstead in Hertfordshire, not far from Harpenden, applied for sisters to staff his school the same year. Two sisters began teaching a dozen children in a bungalow next to the church. They were collected from Harpenden daily, assisted at Mass at Wheathampstead and then breakfasted before school began. Within three years the numbers had risen to thirty-eight and a third sister was requested. Instead, the General Chapter of 1941 decided to withdraw from the school as the daily routine kept the sisters from their community meals and choir.[54] Just before the outbreak of war in 1939, a preparatory school for girls was opened at Portobello Road though it was unable to survive the ensuing trauma.[55]

Developments were not confined to the schools. At Newcastle the hospital had acquired new X-ray equipment and a dark room had been set up for developing plates. Additions to the convent, providing more bedrooms, a library and a new refectory, allowed for a slight increase of the number of hospital beds.[56] At Leicester the new convent with its fine chapel was blessed and opened on 30 April 1938 and soon the local branch of the Catholic Nurses' Guild was holding its regular meetings there.

A new Nurses' Registration Act come into force in 1944 and made further demands on the small group of fifteen sisters who were SRNs.[57] After the war, times were even more difficult for the nursing and convalescent homes than for the schools, for they faced an uncertain future as the National Health Service came into existence. As a consequence there was very little development in the health care apostolate of the congregation recorded during the immediate post-war years. Nursing sisters were on call day and night to cover in emergencies and did not benefit from term holidays as the teaching sisters did. Allowing them time for rest and change in other convents, and ensuring that they made their annual retreat away from their own convents became a priority. Despite the pressure of work, communities at both Leicester and Kelvedon continued to expand their work of religious instruction for children not able to attend Catholic schools, while those at Hawick began to provide weekend retreats for groups from the Border parishes.

At Stone the workrooms, which employed several local women as well as the sisters, were seldom short of orders for liturgical vestments and altar linen and the work continued to be of a very high standard. However, the shortage of luxury materials during the war brought an end to the work and the last orders were received in 1941. Baking and sending out altar breads was also a considerable business, with seven sisters being employed at least part-time in the work at the time of the canonical visitation in 1930. This work would continue into the 1960s.

Before the war ended, R. A. Butler's new Education Act had been passed, raising the school leaving age and opening the way to an enormous expansion in post-primary education. Mother M. Emmanuel was quick to note that under the provisions of the Act private schools would require adequate premises and qualified staff in order to gain recognition. In 1946 the English Dominican Congregation was running ten private schools with only twenty-six qualified sister-teachers between them; a further fourteen qualified sisters were employed in Voluntary Aided Catholic primary schools. The small number of sisters available to teach in their own schools meant increasing dependence on lay teachers, whose salaries were now set by the Burnham Scale. Increased salaries could be covered only by raising fees which, in turn, put the schools out of reach of many working and lower middle class Catholic families. As it was, just over fifty per cent of the pupils in the congregation's own schools were non-Catholics.

The preoccupation in the schools in the immediate post-war years was to gain recognition from the Ministry of Education. The provision of better amenities, particularly science laboratories, was essential and for the smaller schools, such as St Marychurch and

Harpenden, it was eventually judged better to concentrate on primary classes. To make space for the new facilities and to lighten the burden on community members, almost all the schools closed their boarding sections, beginning with Harrow in 1945. Funding the renovations was beyond the budgets of most of the houses but to assist them the General Council sold investments in excess of £30,000.[58]

In June 1945, St Dominic's Priory School at Stone was recognized as efficient and St Dominic's High School at Stoke had its Direct Grant status confirmed under the Act. Stroud, Harrow and Erdington obtained recognition the following year though at Brewood, where there were only thirty-five in the secondary forms in 1950, bringing the small school up to the required standard took longer. Perhaps to boost numbers, Brewood retained its boarding house until 1964, by which time the roll had doubled and there was pressure on space.[59] At Stroud, Erdington and Harrow arrangements were made to accept scholarship students funded by the Local Education Authorities. When the small Catholic Secondary Modern School at Wealdstone was closed in 1950 the LEA asked whether St Dominic's at Harrow would take in sixty-five of its students. Though there was certainly sufficient accommodation, the General Council was anxious that such a move might change the character of the school and affect its prospects for development, so the proposal did not go ahead.[60] However, acquiring full Direct Grant Grammar School status was certainly an aspiration for all these schools, though only in the case of St Agnes' at Erdington would this eventually be achieved.

During the war the Home Office had asked to inspect the children's home at St Marychurch, since the Londoners evacuated there were publicly funded. The inspectors had made a number of negative observations concerning the accommodation and staffing levels, and after the war the building was totally renovated, though it had not been found possible to arrange self-contained group accommodation which was becoming the norm in children's homes at the time. Sister M. Alberta Barry, who arrived at St Marychurch at this time, initially found working with the children something of an ordeal. Some of them refused to use cutlery to eat and there were problems with bullying. It was only when she came to understand the harrowing backgrounds of these children that Sister M. Alberta's own approach to the children changed, and she was able to win their confidence and consequently see their patterns of behaviour transformed.[61]

After the war, St Mary's Training Centre at Portobello Road was not reopened, but the buildings were converted into Rosary House, a hostel where working girls, students and an increasing number of religious sisters from Britain and abroad who were studying in London, could find accommodation.[62] It was many years since penitents had been received into St Ann's Home, and the remaining residents, mainly women who, for one reason or another, required a sheltered environment, were now housed in Oxford Gardens. The 'girls' helped with the work in the laundry and developed close bonds with the sisters. Though the home was registered by the Home Office under the 1948 Children's Act in 1950 and London County Council inspectors expressed themselves well satisfied, the work continued on a quite informal basis.[63]

Although the chapter in 1947 had been opposed to the closure of any houses, the acute shortage of sisters continued, despite the withdrawal from Cheadle. In May 1951 the General Council voted to close the convent at St Marychurch. The guest house, which counted seven more or less permanent residents and had accommodation for twice that number of visitors, paid its way and was always full, though some had reservations as to whether or not this was a truly Dominican apostolate. Despite the recent improvements, bringing the children's home up to standard would be costly and sisters would still have to qualify in child care. Where the school was concerned, the Filles de la Croix at Torquay had expanded their boarding school and opened a day department, which had already affected numbers at St Catherine's.[64]

Mother M. Aquinas had arranged an interview with Bishop Francis Grimshaw of Plymouth for the end of May to discuss the closure. She must have met with opposition, for the General Council met again within a week to vote on an alternative plan. All votes were in favour of closing St Margaret's Convent at Hawick. The annals had noted the arrival of a headmaster, Mr Love, in the parish school after Sister M. Aloysius Watson retired in 1949, but stressed the amicable working relations which existed between the lay head and the two sisters who remained on the staff.[65] Working under a lay head was now cited as a reason for withdrawing the sisters, while the future of the home was deemed precarious under the new National Health legislation. Approaches were made to the Little Company of Mary and the Edinburgh Sisters of Mercy to take on the home, but neither congregation was able to accept the proposal. No further action was taken on closing either house and both would remain centres of Dominican work and prayer for another thirty years.

Fig. 13 Procession at the centenary celebrations of St Dominic's Convent, Stone, 1953.

Conclusion

During the twenty or so years after the amalgamation, the English Dominican Sisters gradually resolved themselves into a single, united congregation. The process would doubtless have been eased somewhat had a Prioress General or General Chapter provided a public statement, as was considered at such length on more than one occasion, of the reasons why the original plan for gradual amalgamation had been put aside. Without public acknowledgement, the anxieties and discontent simply festered beneath the surface. An inexorable decline in membership exacerbated these underlying tensions. By 1953 the number of professed sisters had declined from 403 to 326 – a drop much steeper than that of most other religious congregations in Britain at this time. By contrast, the Sisters of Charity of St Paul increased from 639 to 678 in the same period and continued to hold their numbers until the beginning of the 1960s.[66]

At enormous personal sacrifice, and perhaps more through a fear of failure than through prudence, the English Dominican Sisters managed to maintain an enormous number of apostolic works and to take on new ones. Mother M. Emmanuel had urged the sisters to 'undertake a little extra work, to supply for the helpers who are not forthcoming'[67] while the General Chapter of 1947 insisted that whatever free time sisters had should be spent, not on hobbies which might afford them relaxation, but on work that would benefit the community.[68] Perhaps because those who compiled them were so hard pressed, the congregational annals for this period lose their narrative flavour, the lack of colour enhancing the sense of gloom during the years of economic depression, war and austerity.

By the time the General Chapter convened in January 1953 the sobriety of the post-war years was giving way to the exuberance of the 'new look', the Festival of Britain, and the coronation of a young queen. Before long the British populace would be told, with good reason, that they had 'never had it so good'. A new enthusiasm would also be evident in the English Dominican Congregation. The difficulties of war, dreadful as they might have been, must also have strengthened the sense of common purpose amongst the members of the congregation. On the last day of 1952 the General Chapter convened and on the following day elected Mother M. Ansgar Sheldon Prioress General. Although she had been educated by the Stroud Dominicans at Erdington, she was the first member professed since the amalgamation to be elected to this office. The amalgamation had, as it were, come of age. At Stroud there were fourteen novices and five postulants at the beginning of Mother M. Ansgar's term of office, a good augury for the future.

The Church itself was beginning a gradual process of change and Pius XII was making his first appeals for women religious to divest themselves of customs and practices that were at odds with modern life. The congregation, despite the difficulties it was experiencing in maintaining its current works, was also about to make its first foundation. The fact that this house was to be 'on the missions' and that every member, no matter where she had made her profession, could help support and take pride in its development, would make it a potent focus of unity. This new foundation, requiring sisters to adapt themselves to a new cultural and ecclesiastical context, would result in a new type of apostolic involvement for the English Dominicans and provide a prototype for the times of change to come.

The pace of change accelerated, particularly after the Second Vatican Council, and would permeate every aspect of the congregation's life and mission. But despite these changes, constant elements would remain. Though they would be re-evaluated, the four pillars of Dominican life: community, prayer, study and mission would continue to underpin the lives of the sisters. The other great development which would occur in the coming decades was the growing cooperation with other branches of the Dominican Order and also with the laity. For this reason the period after 1953 lends itself more to a thematic rather than a chronological treatment.

Notes

1. McKibben, *Classes and Cultures*, p. 285.
2. Stone, G98, *Account of the General Chapter, 1935.*
3. Ibid.
4. Birmingham, CC-S-6, Sister M. Jerome Hasler to Archbishop Thomas Williams, 8 May 1935. Sister M. Jerome was professed at Harrow in 1922 and was a member of the Erdington community when the letter was written. She sought a dispensation from her vows and left the congregation in 1942.
5. Stone, G98, *Account of the General Chapter, 1935.*
6. Birmingham, CC-S-6, Sister M. Agatha O'Grady to Archbishop Thomas Williams, 18 May 1935.
7. Stone, G98, *Proceedings of the General Chapter, 1941.*
8. Canon 498, cf. Geser, *Canon Law*, p. 51.
9. Stone, G(x), *Council Book, August 1929–October 1934*, 27 February 1930,.
10. Stone, L14, Rev Charles Calvert to Mother M. Teresa Lamburn, 15 December 1930.
11. Stone, Dv/B23(a), Mother M. Teresa Lamburn to Rev. Bernard Clay, 20 October 1931.
12. Chislett Road was incorporated into Compayne Gardens in the 1940s.
13. Stone, G(x), *Council Book, August 1929–October 1934*, 19 May 1931.
14. Ibid., 17 November 1932.
15. Stone, G(xvi), *Annals of the English Congregation of St Catherine of Siena, January 1935–December 1938*, p. 46.
16. Ibid., p. 108.
17. Stone, G(x), *Council Book, August 1929–October 1934*, 6 May 1932.
18. Ibid., 19 May 1931.
19. Birmingham, CC-S-6, *Visitation of St Dominic's Priory, Stone, 23 May 1930.*
20. Stone, G(x), *Council Book, August 1929–October 1934*, 19 May 1931.
21. Birmingham, CC-S-6, Sister M. Agatha O'Grady to Archbishop Williams, 18 May 1935.
22. Stone, G(xvi), *Annals 1935–38*, cit., p. 140.
23. Stone, G98, *Account of the General Chapter, 1935.*
24. Stone, G98a(ii), *Acts of the General Chapter 1935*, p. 5.

25. The author heard the story of the cold bath in a conversation with Sister M. Constance Sleigh, November 2008.
26. Stone, G100(c), Mother M. Emmanuel Fuller, Circular letters, 1 February 1946.
27. Stone, G98, *Proceedings of the General Chapter, 25 May-2 June 1947.*
28. Rome, Stone XII.4.1456.10, Mother M. Aquinas Colgan to Fr Aelwin Tindal-Atkinson, 17 April 1951.
29. Stone, G2000/60, *Register of the Prioress General, June 1935–June 1941*, 25 September 1938. The exact number of Austrian sisters who came to Britain is not stated in any extant records, but it was certainly more than 20.
30. Ibid., 19 May 1945.
31. Stone, G100(b), Mother Rose Imelda Raymond-Barker, Circular letter, 29 September 1938.
32. Conversation with Sister M Constance Sleigh, November 2008.
33. Stone, G(xvii), *Annals of the English Congregation of St Catherine of Siena, January 1939–December* 1946, pp. 14–25, 56.
34. Ibid., p. 17.
35. Conversation with Sister M. Henry Yeaman, 23 May 2010.
36. Stone, G(xii), *General Council Book, February 1942–August 1948*, 26 February 1943.
37. Stone, G(xvii), *Annals 1939–1946*, pp. 20, 55, 101, 126.
38. Ibid., p. 156.
39. Stone, G100(b), Mother Rose Imelda Raymond-Barker, Circular letter, Holy Week 1941.
40. Stone, G98, *Proceedings of the General Chapter, 25 May–June 1947.*
41. Birmingham, CC-S-6, Mother M. Emmanuel Fuller to Archbishop Williams, 18 August 1944.
42. Stone, G(xv), *Annals 1932–34*, p. 16.
43. Stone, G(x), *Council Book 1929–34*, 1 February 1934.
44. Interview with Sister Patricia Mary England, 2007; Sister is featured in a virtual exhibition of *Women at Queen Mary* accessible on the Queen Mary website http://www.women.qmul.ac.uk/virtual/women/atoz/england.htm (accessed 15 September 2010).
45. Stone, G(xiv), *Annals 1929–32*, p. 38.
46. Stone, G100(b), *Notes of Meetings of School Sisters, 30 May–1 June 1936.*
47. Stone, G2000/60, *Register of the Prioress General, June 1935–June 1941*, 14 July 1937.
48. Stone, G(xvi), *Annals, 1935–38*, p. 117.
49. Ibid., p. 74.
50. Ibid., p. 133.
51. Stone, G(xi), *General Council Book, October 1934–December 1937*, 4 March 1936.
52. Stone, G(xii), *General Council Book, November 1937–January 1942*, 18 November 1937.
53. Stone, G(xvi), *Annals, 1935–38*, p. 147.
54. Stone, G98, *Proceedings of the General Chapter, 1941.*
55. The General Council also agreed to provide sisters for the school the

Pallotine Fathers were building in their new parish of Our Lady of the Visitation at Greenford. Although the Annals state that three sisters from Harrow began teaching there in 1940 both the Victoria County History and the school's website state that building restrictions meant the school was not completed or opened until 1946.

56. Stone, G(xvi), *Annals, 1935–38*, p. 79.
57. Stone, G100(c), Mother M. Emmanuel Fuller, Circular letter, 1 February 1946.
58. Stone, G(xiii), *General Council Book, August 1948–March 1953*, December 1951.
59. Walters, *St Dominic's School Brewood*, p. 89.
60. Stone, G(xiii), *General Council Book, August 1948–March 1953*, 19 June 1950.
61. Interview with Sister M. Alberta Barry, 2008.
62. Stone, G(xviii), *Annals of the English Congregation of St Catherine of Siena, January 1947–December 1955*, p. 43.
63. Ibid., p. 57.
64. Stone, G(xiii), *General Council Book, August 1948–March 1953*, 15 May 1951.
65. Stone, G(xviii), *Annals 1947–55*, p. 47.
66. Scarisbrick, *Selly Park and Beyond*, p. 88.
67. Stone, G100(d), Mother M. Emmanuel Fuller, Circular letter, 30 August 1930.
68. Stone, G98, *Proceedings of the General Chapter, 1947*.

Chapter Seven

Givers and sharers: re-making community

If we are 'total givers' and sharers, and not demanders, community life is always on a sure foundation.[1]

Mother M. Silvester Brennan, OP

Introduction

Community provides the context for Dominican life. For the English Dominican Sisters, every aspect of community life would undergo radical change during the second half of the twentieth century. At both general and local levels the manner of governance and decision-making was transformed. A greater emphasis was placed on democratic processes, and perhaps nowhere was this more obvious than in the final integration of the two classes of religious: choir and lay sisters. Amongst the sisters themselves the natural reserve and formality of a highly structured lifestyle gave way to more natural personal interaction.

These changes were in tune with the times. As the 1950s gave way to the 1960s, authenticity became the watchword. The civil rights movement encouraged people to believe that a just society was attainable, medical advances allowed organ transplants to prolong life and technological advances could put man on the moon. The Second Vatican Council certainly caught the spirit of the age in its call for an engagement with all that is good in society. For women religious, who took the call to renewal so seriously, there was great hope for the future. By the end of the following decade much of this enthusiasm had given way to cynicism. As the 1980s progressed there was an increasing emphasis in the western world on individualism rather than collectivism, less confidence that legislation could cure ills. There had been a sharp decline in religious practice, a revolution in sexual mores, and increased consumerism fuelled by built-in obsolescence.

The English Dominican Congregation felt the full impact of this societal swing. Hope for the future seemed to be under constant assault from anxiety: why are our sisters leaving us? Why are so few joining us? Where are we going? How are we getting there?

Authority and governance transformed

Even in the early years after the Second Vatican Council, major superiors still 'governed'; their Council gave advice and the General Chapter of elected delegates, which had always been acknowledged as the highest authority within the congregation while it was in session, legislated. Although there was increasing consultation and preparation at all levels during the 1960s and 1970s, the management style of the congregation would certainly still have been analyzed as hierarchical.

Mother M. Ansgar Sheldon, who began her six-year term of office in 1953, although she possessed such an artistic temperament, set great store on conformity. Certainly, her decision to undertake the mission in Norway broadened the congregation's vision, but she could be quite unyielding when it came to considering other courageous innovations. During her later years in Norway, however, she is remembered as a wise and sympathetic prioress. Mother M. Bonaventure Burke, who was elected to succeed Mother M. Ansgar at the General Chapter of 1959, had been in positions of authority from almost immediately after her perpetual profession of vows at Portobello Road in 1922. Although she exhorted the sisters on more than one occasion to use their own judgement,[2] she was also a woman imbued with a keen sense of the authority of her office. Although she had a legalistic approach and preferred to deal in certainties, the exhortation she gave to the General Chapter at the end of her term of office in 1965 shows her commitment to the renewal of the congregation.

Mother M. Silvester Brennan, who guided the congregation through the difficult years of renewal, from 1965 until 1977, brought a completely different style. She succeeded in maintaining a balance which kept together the many strong personalities within the congregation, some of whom were inclined to look only to the future, others too much to the past. Quite clearly, she did not wish all her sisters to think alike, but stressed constantly the need for mutual trust which would heal divisions and build harmony. Mother M. Silvester certainly gave her trust, though she was astute enough not to allow others to take advantage of her kindness, nor was she afraid to make demands on the sisters. Her approach was one of simplicity, anxious to see the good in all, a woman with a natural gift for friendship, even with those quite different in outlook from herself. She was a woman who made herself available to all.

There was little surprise when the General Chapter of August 1971 expressed its confidence in Mother M. Silvester's leadership by re-electing her, the first Prioress General of the amalgamated congregation to serve a second term of office. The obvious delight of the sisters was expressed by a standing ovation from the capitulars and the community sisters who had been summoned to the chapter room. The proceedings of the chapter were interrupted by a brief celebration over sherry and biscuits, yet another novelty.[3] Mother M. Silvester's second term was even more demanding than the first, as the initial euphoria in the wake of the Council gave place to a certain measure of despondency. But in her report to the General Chapter of 1977 she could point out that though strains in community life were still obvious, they were no longer crippling and that there was a greater willingness to accept and appreciate different ideas.

Mother M. Rupert Fitzpatrick, who succeeded Mother M. Silvester in office from 1977 until 1983, was an able administrator and an understanding and supportive superior with a keen sense of social justice, in so far as it concerned the congregation and the world at large. She was, perhaps, more impetuous than her predecessor and less inclined to alter her own views; not all her decisions met with universal acclaim. Following someone as revered as Mother M. Silvester cannot have been easy.

The Prioresses General who have followed Mother M. Rupert: Sisters M. Edward [Anna Mary] House (1983–95), Angela Mary Leydon (1995–2007) and M. Pauline Bürling (elected in 2007), entered the congregation either just before, or during the Council, and its language and principles were absorbed at an early stage in their religious life. It is not surprising that their approach has been more collegial or that the role of the General Council has become more clearly that of a leadership team, each member making her own unique contribution to decision making and planning. In some ways their task has been made easier by the smaller numbers in the congregation. A real possibility emerged for engaging with each one on more than a superficial level, becoming aware of individual gifts, aspirations, anxieties and needs.

The composition and function of the General Chapter also underwent dramatic change. Traditionally, more than half the capitulars were ex-officio members of the chapter, including the members of the General Council, former Prioresses General and the prioresses of the local convents; each house also elected a delegate. Beginning with the 1971 General Chapter, instead of delegates being elected from each individual house, they were chosen from the membership of the congregation at large. This was something of a watershed which led gradually, as will be seen, to full participation of all perpetually professed members in the General Chapter. Since the amalgamation, following the election of the Prioress General and other officers, the chapter moved on to consider propositions which had been submitted by communities – which took precedence – and only then from individual sisters. Specific time was not allotted to these propositions so if there were a great number of them, discussion was limited.

A Special General Chapter, to implement the renewal called for by the Council, was mandated for every religious institute in the document *Perfectae Caritatis*. For the English Dominican Sisters, this took place in two sessions, the first in August 1967, the second in April 1968. A group of consultors was appointed, an extensive reading list prepared, questionnaires were circulated and frequent meetings were held in preparation for both sessions. One such meeting between the five consultors and the General Council in January 1968 was described as 'a very lively one. Arguments were carried on in great frankness, but because all were objectively seeking the good of the congregation – even in the heat – not a hair was lost'.[4]

As 1968 drew on, the media was flooded with news of student and youth protest at home and abroad. Neither were the junior professed sisters of the English Dominican Congregation reticent in putting forward their views. There was a real sense of excitement and propositions went to both sessions of the Special General Chapter from this group requesting a more active participation in its affairs. They saw an incongruity in being able to vote in a general election from the age of eighteen, yet not being considered to have reached the maturity required to vote in the affairs of the community which concerned them most until many years later. 'We feel that being given active voice would help us to achieve that greater responsibility and commitment which the [Second Vatican] Council has encouraged, and which should be particularly the mark of Dominicans.'[5]

The idealism of youth can be extremely demanding and the junior sisters certainly put their finger on many of the pressure points. The decline in numbers and the burden that would obviously fall upon them in future years were a matter for concern to them. If there was any criticism of the younger sisters, Mother M. Silvester, in her report to the 1971 General Chapter, noted that: 'The young are expected to be the best behaved, while additional years in religious life seem to bestow a strange kind of autonomy.'[6] Before the 1971 Chapter commissions were set up to canvass opinions and prepare papers on various topics, such as community life, liturgy and formation. One of these commissions was appointed to rewrite the Constitutions, bringing them into conformity with the proposed new code of canon law. It completed its work and presented a draft to the Sacred Congregation for Religious in January 1981. Some revisions were required and it was some time before the constitutions were granted definitive approval on 29 April 1983. New norms governing the life of the congregation might be in place, but the process of renewal and of change would not cease.

In contrast with the past, the General Chapter was now seen as the concern of the whole family and even members of the extended family. Though the Provincial of the friars had usually presided at the elective session of the sisters' General Chapter, he did not remain for the entire proceedings. However, in 1970 Mother M. Silvester had been invited to address the friars' Provincial Chapter, and along with the Prioress General of the Bushey Dominicans, she assisted as an observer for the duration of their 1974 chapter. In the 1980s mutual attendance at one another's chapters became the norm for these three groups and enhanced the sense of belonging to the Dominican family.

The move towards more representative participation developed further at the 1983 General Chapter at which Sister M. Edward House was elected Prioress General. For the first time members of the congregation who were not elected delegates were invited as non-voting observers. This practice was continued at the following chapter in 1989 when the principle of an 'open chapter', in which all perpetually professed members of the congregation would have voting rights, was adopted. This change required an indult from the Holy See as well as modifications to the Constitutions, but these were granted without difficulty. The use of outside facilitators was a further innovation at the 1989 General Chapter when an Irish Dominican from Cabra, Sister Sylvia Diamond, assisted with the group discussions and plenary sessions. The experience was seen as a very positive one and Sister Sylvia and other facilitators, continued to work with the congregation at subsequent chapters. There was also a call for sisters of the English Congregation to be trained as facilitators.[7]

The 'open chapter' was considered an invigorating experience for the congregation. Accommodating the number who wished to attend meant that a move was made from holding the chapter in a convent of the congregation, to meeting at a conference centre. The first session of the 1989 chapter took place at the University of Keele, the second session at Newman College Birmingham. Subsequent chapters have been held at All Saints' Pastoral Centre, London Colney and Hinsely Hall in Leeds. Joining together as a family, not just to deliberate but to celebrate the Eucharist and Divine Office together and to enjoy social events, is greatly valued. Whatever the anxieties and doubts they bring with them, those who attend seem to leave with a positive attitude for the future, a sense of hope.[8] From 1983 until 2001 the General Chapters were held in two sessions, an elective session around Easter and a business session in the summer. This enabled those who were elected to office, an increasing number of whom were employed outside institutions owned by the congregation, to give adequate notice and made possible a proper handover period. Smaller numbers, and the expense involved in the double session resulted in a return to a single session chapter.

The custom of a biennial congregational meeting was also introduced at the 1989 General Chapter. These meeting are an opportunity for the Prioress General to present a progress report as to how the decisions of the previous chapter have been implemented. There is also a financial report, an opportunity for updating the sisters on various undertakings and to invite speakers on relevant topics. Just as at the General Chapters there is the opportunity of celebrating the liturgy together with greater solemnity and to enjoy each other's company. The first of these meetings was held at London Colney in 1991, followed by an even more successful meeting at Loyola Hall near Liverpool two years later. The latter meeting focused on the viability of local communities and the input from the congregational membership empowered the General Council to make the difficult decision to close the convents at Newcastle and Kelvedon.[9]

Documentation produced by all these General Chapters insisted that renewal is a matter of the heart, a process of conversion rather than of external changes. It went to the core of religious life with a re-evaluation of the evangelical counsels by which the sisters vowed to live: poverty, chastity and obedience. As in most other congregations, the English Dominicans could make use of things or money, or be exempted from various obligations of community life, with the sanction of the superior. The sisters had the security of knowing that their needs would be supplied and the assurance that permission conferred legitimacy. Now they were to be poor in spirit and in fact, and for some, developing a sense of responsibility in using money and material goods did not come easily. There was also an increasing emphasis on the obligation of hospitality, and upon not being demanding in ones requirements. Unlike many other congregations, there was initial resistance to the introduction of personal allowances or budgeting. While not wanting the sisters to suffer inconvenience in respect of necessities, and to be reasonably provided for, dependence of the individual on the group was seen as an expression of poverty.

Many sisters felt the need for a more positive understanding of the vow of chastity. Rather than a renunciation, it was seen as providing the freedom to engage in the apostolate and was also embraced as a sign of the Kingdom of Heaven. As Sister Joyce Mary [M. Ebba] Webb reminded those gathered for the Easter Meeting in 1974, the Dominican Order was founded to combat the recurring tendency to create a dichotomy between body and spirit.[10] A greater understanding of the importance of the affective life for religious began to develop, and more danger was seen in a lack of love than in expression of feelings.

Obedience was no longer to be understood as a passive acceptance of commands, but as a listening process which included consultation. The reciprocal nature of the obligations between superiors – who were to exercise their authority in a spirit of service – and sisters was stressed. In a broader perspective the sisters also had an obligation to use their mental and spiritual gifts in carrying out the tasks assigned them. The new understanding of the vow of obedience was also linked with the redemptive work of Christ who, in submitting himself in obedience to the will of his Father, earned salvation for all. Notions of personal responsibility and self-fulfilment developed at the same time as this new understanding of obedience and the exercise of authority became a more delicate task. It was observed that superiors were 'supposed to guide without being able to enforce, to lead but not able to push'.[11]

At various times during the 1980s, in order to hear the views of local communities more readily and to evaluate their particular needs, the General Council met in turn at the various convents. There were also joint meetings with the local prioresses to exchange ideas and give support. In September 1990 the General Council gathered at St Beuno's, the Jesuit spirituality centre in North Wales, to participate in a workshop on Christian governance. This was followed by a 'graced history retreat' during which time they prayed and reflected on the history of the Order and the congregation. This exercise of examining God's dealings with the 'family' and with themselves enabled the Prioress General and councillors to evaluate the current situation of the congregation and gain hope for the future.[12]

A story is told of Mother M. Silvester Brennan enjoying a visit to the community at Stoke-on-Trent on a major feast day, but hastening away, insisting that she must be back at Stone in time for Vespers. Of course, Vespers was also sung at Stoke and the incident shows how closely a Prioress General, even one of Mother M. Silvester's breadth of vision, could come to identify her office as much with St Dominic's Convent Stone, as with the congregation as a whole. It was partly to prevent the concerns of the local community at Stone – where almost half the members of the congregation, particularly the older members, then resided – from drawing attention away from the needs of other communities that the 1989 General Chapter decided that the residence of the Prioress General and her council should be moved away from Stone. It was thought that an independent generalate community would be able to focus its concerns more clearly on the congregation as a whole. It would also seem like a new beginning and show that major changes, led from the top, were possible. Given the location of the various houses the most accessible locations were deemed to be London or Birmingham, and the latter was decided upon.

As a result, a six-bedroom house was purchased on Pershore Road, on the boundary line between what Sister M. Edward described as 'the decaying gentility of Edgbaston and the "red light" district of Balsall Heath'.[13] The house was across the road from the Anglican Church of St Ambrose and, quite appropriately, within the Catholic parish of St Catherine of Siena. There was also a large local Muslim population and the members of the generalate community were soon making contacts on an ecumenical and interfaith basis through the local Neighbourhood Forum. Unfortunately three of the members of the General Council were not able to live with the generalate community on account of their apostolic obligations, but several other sisters, some of them students, were assigned to the community at various times. One of these was Sister M. Jude Davies who served as local prioress and bursar until her unexpected death in January 1992. A natural homemaker, she enjoyed the more informal setting of a small community, and brought a sense of constancy to a house where the Prioress General and her vicaress were constantly coming and going. When at home, all took their share in maintaining the large garden, seeing to the housekeeping and welcoming the frequent guests.

Four or five times a year Dominican Days were held at Pershore Road, for as well as the many new contacts the community had made, there were still strong loyalties to the congregation amongst those who had known the sisters during their many years in Erdington. Although the house provided a pleasant and welcoming environment and was a good centre from which to work, there was the disadvantage of being separated from the Bursar General and the archives, both still at Stone.[14] At the 1995 General Chapter the decision was made to close the Birmingham generalate, not because it was deemed an unsuccessful venture, but because there were insufficient sisters available to sustain a local community. The options were to return to Stone or adapt the accommodation at Ealing, and after long deliberation and a professional survey the decision was made in favour of returning to Stone. The house in Birmingham was put on the market in January 1996 and temporary quarters set up at Stone until the refurbishment of the top floor of the west wing of the convent was completed the following July.

Another significant change was the election of local prioresses by the communities, rather than their appointment by the General Council. This was a move in line with the democratic tradition which the friars had always enjoyed and was also the practice amongst Mother Margaret's sisters during her life time. The first change came in 1967 when the Special General Chapter allowed local communities to forward a slate of three names from which the General Council chose. The interim Constitutions of 1971 legislated for the direct election of prioresses, though a house could choose to have a superior appointed; if an election was inconclusive, the Council also retained the right to appoint. There were attendant difficulties in this arrangement, as sisters who could not easily be replaced in their apostolic work might be elected superior of another house. It must be said, particularly as the lifestyle of the sisters became less structured, and an increasing number of sisters were involved in individual apostolates, the role of superior became more complex than in the past. Though many local prioresses are remembered for their administrative ability and personal warmth, some who held office at the time would admit that it was not an experience they relished.

At local level the structures of authority also underwent change. Before the 1970s, one of the rare occasions on which the conventual chapter – composed of the perpetually professed members of the community – met was to vote on candidates for profession of vows. Decisions regarding the business of the convent, routine or extraordinary, were made by the prioress and her council. Once the move was made from the General Council appointing prioresses, to the local community electing them, the locus of decision-making also moved, from the prioress and her council, to the conventual chapter, or as it effectively became, the community meeting. As communities became smaller, distinctions between local council and chapter disappeared and there was considerable discussion about the role of superiors, even whether it was necessary to have them at all.

A community of equals

All the developments in the area of governance created a more participative and democratic atmosphere within the English Dominican Congregation. But until the General Chapter of 1965 there was an inherent lack of equality within the congregation as a consequence of having two classes of religious: choir and lay. As early as July 1948 the General Council had discussed the possibility of integrating the lay and choir sisters, but had decided to refer the matter to the General Chapter because of the changes this would require to the constitutions.[15] As a consequence, although the decision was made not to integrate the two groups, from July 1953 the lay sisters began to wear the black veil when they went out, and joined the choir sisters for the evening recreation.[16]

Mother M. Ansgar Sheldon held a strong conviction that lay sisters were a necessity for a congregation bound to the choral recitation of the Divine Office, an obligation which could not be fulfilled without their support. She recognized two distinct vocations within the congregation and was eager to give the type of training that would best support their special role. To provide them with a formation specifically geared to their particular vocation, she received permission from Rome to move the lay sisters' noviciate to Harrow. To members of the congregation who justified their argument for integration by appealing to Mother Margaret's original intention of not having lay sisters, Mother M. Ansgar pointed, with more conviction than historical accuracy or analysis, to the first printed constitutions of 1853 which, as noted earlier, did make mention of them. She had also taken advice from Dominican authorities in Rome and would not be easily swayed from supporting their opinions. One thing upon which she insisted absolutely, was the dignity of the vocation, one which she would not see belittled.[17]

Fig. 14 A lay sister novice in the garden at Harrow, *c.*1960.

The work of the lay sisters was often extremely heavy, with such tasks as cleaning chimney flues requiring both enormous time and dedication. It is undoubtedly true that many choir sisters did not understand just how difficult and tiring such work could be. By Mother M. Ansgar's time as Prioress General, the introduction of labour-saving devices and an increase in the number of lay helpers employed in the convents had certainly alleviated the work. There is also plenty of evidence that the sisters enjoyed their work; Sister M. Stephen Scott, for instance, was known to take immense pride in finishing delicate laundry work to a state of perfection and many others excelled in the kitchen. At Stroud, generations of novices remember the kindness of Sister M. Margaret McCleane, who was always ready to spoil them with left over treats during the annual 'big sweep', as spring cleaning was known, or at other times when there was heavy domestic work to be done. Portobello Road, where the laundry and other works required a number of lay sisters, is remembered as a particularly happy house because of the homely atmosphere the lay sisters created.

For some, domestic work offered an environment conducive to prayer. Sister M. Placid Delaney, who had tried her vocation with a contemplative community before entering the Dominican Sisters, claimed she got much more time for contemplation and peace at St Rose's in Stroud than in the contemplative monastery. Others thrived on the social contacts the work could bring with their opportunities for apostolic engagement; Sister M. Martha Forrester was never happier than when dealing with trades people and postmen of Leicester who frequently turned to her for help and advice.[18] These encounters at the back door of the convent included seeing to the needs of the poor men, some of them veritable tramps, who came seeking food and other help. No one had a softer spot for these men than Sister M. Fintan Boland who collected socks and other warm clothing for them as Christmas treats. The young lay sisters at Portobello Road were initiated into the art of questing when, armed with a notebook of addresses, they would set off, each pair taking a district and calling upon known benefactors. Although the work was not to everyone's taste it did provide a change from the more routine tasks.[19]

In the minds of some, the Latin liturgy presented an obstacle to the integration of the two groups, though as fewer choir sisters had the benefit of a firm grounding in the classics, this surely posed as much of a problem for them. The solemnity of the Latin Office and Mass are cited by very many sisters as a contributing factor in the initial attraction towards the Dominicans. But though the beauty of this liturgy could lift the mind and heart to God, this did not always come hand in hand with complete understanding. The question that was not addressed by those in authority was why sisters who made such a necessary contribution should not have a voice in the affairs of the congregation. Could they not have been exempt from choir yet accorded active voice in chapter? There is no questioning Mother M. Ansgar's sincerity, or to believe there was a significant level of discontent with the status quo amongst the lay sisters themselves. Times were changing and this very specific vocation seemed less attractive to young women of the late 1950s whose education and aspirations led them elsewhere. The Harrow noviciate was not to welcome many recruits, and few of those who entered persevered.

During Mother M. Bonaventure Burke's tenure a significant change occurred for the lay sisters. On 1 July 1960 they discarded the black scapular and white veil, and adopted the same habit as the choir sisters. The following day the last lay sister to make her profession in the congregation did so at Harrow wearing the white scapular and receiving the black veil.[20] Seven more women would enter as lay candidates at the Harrow noviciate, but none persevered, the last departing of her own accord at the end of August

1963. The deliberations of the Second Vatican Council had made it clear that there should be only one class of religious in non-clerical institutes and that all should enjoy the same rights. Though the documents of the Vatican Council had still not been published, the General Chapter of 1965 voted in favour of integrating the two groups.

The indult confirming the decision was received from Rome on 11 May 1966 and Mother M. Silvester wrote to the members of the congregation; 'From now on, each Sister in the congregation must unify in herself the highest ideals of both these former states.'[21] In October the former lay sisters were asked what their preferences were for community prayer. Ten wished to retain the traditional office of *Paters* and *Aves*, forty wished to wait until the office was recited in English to join in choral prayer, but twelve were quite prepared to join in the Latin office at once.[22]

This new equality brought great changes to many who had been lay sisters. Though some continued happily in their domestic employments, others adapted themselves readily to new apostolates as parish workers or in chaplaincy work. Sister M. Aloysius Somers, who had been professed at Harrow in 1927 and assigned to Stone in 1950, spent much of her life as a cook, even instructing several Dominican lay brothers in this work. However, she later began nursing at St Mary's Home and was appointed Matron in 1980. In this role Sister M. Aloysius developed a natural empathy with the dying and was called upon to present papers on the subject to the Stafford Postgraduate Medical Education Centre and elsewhere. Sister M. Constance Sleigh qualified as a nursery teacher, and began a new career at Newcastle-upon-Tyne until she reached retirement age.

From 1981, when Sister M. Columcille Browne was elected prioress of Kelvedon, several of those who had previously had no voice in the affairs of the congregation, were called upon to exercise the service of leadership.[23] They are remembered for their practical approach, wise counsel and understanding. After almost a century, the unity of the community as envisaged by Mother Margaret Hallahan was restored.

Welcoming new members

It seems incredible nowadays that on a single day in May 1953, 11,000 people should crowd into National Vocations Exhibition at Olympia to view the stalls of the different religious orders and congregations. For those who staffed the stalls this was exhausting work. Numbers entering the congregation remained steady during the next fifteen years with about half those remaining to make perpetual profession. There was some concern that good vocations were being lost because many Catholic girls who showed an interest in religious life were unable to continue at school beyond the age of sixteen and subsequently lost the contact that could foster their vocation. The General Council decided to begin an apostolic school, which would allow such girls to continue their secondary education at one of the congregation's schools. Begun at Stroud in 1955 and later moved to Stoke, the scheme was not a success and was discontinued in 1961.

In the summer of 1961 the first 'Holiday with a Difference' was held at Stroud and although this was not primarily an effort at recruitment, it gave young women the opportunity to join the community for part of the Divine Office and to meet the novices. Some of those who attended did go on to enter, for others the week was a time of reflexion which led some, in their own words, to 'sort themselves out'.[24] Two years later Sister M. Crispin Mitchell was called upon to produce a short documentary film, *The Dominican Way*, showing the life of the English Dominican Sisters in formation and in the apostolate. This film had its debut at the National Vocations Exhibition held that year at Newcastle. In September 1962, a recruiting tour in Ireland lasting two months was undertaken, two sisters visiting schools and hospitals in Dublin and the west.[25] The numbers entering the noviciate during Mother M. Bonaventure's term may have been small, only thirty, of whom just fourteen made profession, but the noviciate annals give a picture of enormous enthusiasm. The Cotswolds provided an idyllic setting for initiation into religious life and there were weekly walks with picnics in the summer which might conclude with sung Vespers, looking down from vantage points such as Uley Barrow.

The fun which marked Stroud from the beginning continued in the noviciate and the dramatic talent of some of the novices came to the fore. On Holy Innocents' Day on 28 December each year the junior novice would be elected 'abbess' and exercise misrule for the day. At Epiphany, the novices entertained the community with singing, recitals and plays. In January 1960 *Sherlock Holmes and the Case of the False Dichotomy* was presented, featuring an agent of the Bank of England, a lord and lady in coronets, a duke disguised as a jockey and a race horse constructed from brown paper and blankets – one half of which later became a distinguished seminary professor.[26] The legendary short Dominican, Blessed Fred of Wigan, makes repeated appearances over the years, reaching his apogee in

Off-White and the Seven Dwarfs. The annals also record a visit to a scripture exhibition at the British Museum in 1963 and a recreation in June the same year when the novice master from Woodchester, Father Nicholas Wollard, played the sisters a new release by a Belgian Dominican novice nicknamed *Sœur Sourire*. It is noted that they particularly enjoyed her song *Dominique*!

Towards the end of the 1950s there seems to have been a greater effort in providing more solid theological instruction. It was reported to the General Chapter in 1965 that Father Wilfrid Ardagh considered the written work of the novices equalled and even surpassed that of his students attending the university extension lectures.[27] In 1962 Sister M. Damian McGimpsey was appointed prioress at Hawick and her place as novice mistress at Stroud was taken by Sister M. Nicolas [later Nicola] Loeb. She was the first novice mistress to receive any specific preparation for her new role, though this consisted of just two weeks at Stone undertaking a crash course in canon law under Mother M. Bonaventure, before following a week's intensive course in psychology at the Convent of Our Lady of Sion at Acton Burnell. In 1965 Sister M. Nicolas followed a course of study, specifically designed for those responsible for religious formation, at Regina Mundi College in Rome.

The years immediately following the Council were difficult ones for the friars of the English Province and this had a certain impact on the sisters. Early in 1965 the novice master at Woodchester left the Order, all but one of his novices following suit, and the noviciate for the friars was subsequently moved to Hawkesyard. Since the community at Woodchester was reduced to two and the priory buildings subsequently demolished, the sisters' noviciate could no longer expect the same level of support the friars had so generously supplied in the past. Since St Catherine's Centre was opening at Harrow, it was decided to move the noviciate there. At the same time there were a number of changes of novice mistress. When Sister M. Nicolas Loeb had left for Rome her place was taken first by Sister M. Humbert van Eyken and then Sister M. Benedict Cole. But the noviciate did not remain long at Harrow. Once the centre and the junior sisters moved to Portobello Road, the Harrow community moved into Mount Lodge which was too small to house the novices as well. It was decided the noviciate should move once again to Stone.

By this time the Special General Chapter had made a thorough revision of the programme of studies for the noviciate which included theology, scripture and Dominican history as well as the

Constitutions. It was also decided to double the period of the noviciate to two years, extend the period of temporary profession to six, and to arrange psychological assessments for sisters before they pronounced perpetual vows. Whereas prospective postulants twenty years before were provided with a long list of requirements including such things as a sampler and sewing box, one of the four enthusiastic young women who entered towards the end of 1968 remembers being told to 'bring a tennis racquet, and a skirt considerably longer than one you are wearing'.[28] These four spent their time as postulants with local communities and began their noviciate together at Stone on 4 August 1969 with Sister M. Rupert Fitzpatrick as their novice mistress.

The noviciate annals record with enormous excitement the changes and debates that were going on in the congregation at this time. If there were misgivings in some quarters, for the novices and younger sisters it was certainly a time of tremendous optimism in which they themselves felt caught up. But despite this enthusiasm, the number entering continued to decline sharply during the 1970s. By the time Mother M. Rupert Fitzpatrick was elected Prioress General there was a single second-year novice who completed her noviciate at Erdington under Sister M. Stephen Wilson. The process of renewal, which had been entered into with

Fig. 15 The noviciate returns to Stone, August 1969.

such hope, had encouraged a high level of introspection as religious examined every aspect of their lives and mission. There was a tendency to think that it was the fault of the congregation that vocations were so few, that somehow it was a reflection on their failure to modernize and renew. Only gradually was there an acceptance that the enormous societal changes of the times were a much more significant factor in the decline of religious vocations.

For a number of religious congregations of women in Britain, it seemed during the first half of the 1980s that there would be a revival of interest in religious life. The recruitment trends for some certainly appeared much brighter than in the previous decade. Perhaps this was in part a consequence of the enthusiasm generated by the preparations for the National Pastoral Congress held at Liverpool in 1980 and the papal visit of 1982. It is also possible that declining economic conditions encouraged younger women to think more carefully about life options than they would otherwise have done. After a gap of two years, two novices received the habit in September 1978, when Sister Joan Agnes Horn was appointed novice mistress. The fact that she was a widow who had brought up four stepchildren – one of whom became a nun – and was an experienced teacher before she entered the Dominicans proved an excellent foundation for her new role.

A small but steady stream of candidates continued to arrive for several years. But whatever the causes, the trend proved ephemeral and the attrition rate, particularly during the period of temporary profession, was extremely high.[29] By March 1985 the noviciate was empty and the following year Sister M. Edward wrote; 'We are not at present "celebrating a noviciate" and we have no firm applicants who are at the moment asking to enter the congregation.'[30] It was to be ten years before the English Dominican Sisters welcomed a new candidate, but by this time initial formation would be undertaken in a new cooperative venture.

The decline in numbers was compounded by departures from the religious life, something experienced by all congregations at this time. Between the General Chapters of 1965 and 1983 thirteen sisters in perpetual vows and four in temporary vows left the congregation. What contrasts with most other congregations is that the number of departures was actually fewer than during the previous fifteen years, when a total of twenty-five professed sisters had left the congregation; neither were all those who left young, one was just short of her golden jubilee. Though these departures were perhaps not always a surprise, they were still a shock, and the reasons why women chose to leave the religious life cannot be generalized. As early as 1939 a young sister who had been professed at Portobello Road sought a dispensation from her vows in order to take up work to counter the influence of the Soviet backed Anti-God Campaign, which had held its international conference in London the previous year.[31] At the time such a work, so evidently in accord with the Dominican mission of preaching the truth, was not seen as appropriate for a Dominican sister. By contrast, the Second Vatican Council emphasized the universal call to holiness, and some members of the congregation realized that being a religious was not the only means of exercising a valid apostolate in the Church.

In the past, the departure of sisters from the congregation had hardly been adverted to, but the tone changed by the time Mother M. Rupert wrote to announce the departure of two sisters in 1978: 'Saddened as we are by the loss of these two much loved members of our congregation, let us not give way to recrimination, criticism or bitterness in any form.'[32] While once it would never have been considered that the congregation shared any responsibility for their departure, later it became yet another occasion upon which to evaluate the depth of renewal within the congregation. There is some evidence that as community life amongst the English Dominicans became less structured, apostolic activity more diverse and communities grew older, newly professed sisters sometimes felt isolated when assigned to local convents for the first time. Whether or not this was the case, contacts with those who left are often maintained. Former sisters continue to visit and kept in touch with members of the congregation and some have been welcomed as residents in St Mary's Home at Stone in their old age.

Although professed religious left the congregation, some to try their vocation in other congregations or secular institutes, four sisters who made profession elsewhere transferred to the English Dominicans between 1976 and 1990. Two of these sisters had been professed in monasteries of contemplative Dominicans at Carisbrooke and Glasgow, both of which communities had been closed and their members dispersed. This could not have been an easy move as neither was young, nor in good health, but both expressed deep gratitude for the welcome they received. The sisters also had the great and genuine joy, perhaps unique amongst religious women in Britain, of welcoming back a sister who had left the congregation in 1964 and who, after a period of probation, made her vows once more in 1986.

Preaching to one another

Within the formal structures of the religious life which held sway before the Second Vatican Council it was possible for sisters to live in the same community, even for years at a time, and know one another only on a superficial level. Much of the day was spent in silence, and recreations, seated round a table doing mending, conversing on general topics could resemble, in the opinion of one sister 'something too much like a Jane Austen drawing room'.[33] This is not to say that true and deep friendships did not flourish, they certainly did, and there is little evidence of the fear of 'particular friendships' which were such an obsession in some other religious congregations. In most cases, these friendships developed during the shared experience of the noviciate or grew out of working together.

There was a long-felt desire for an internal publication to share news and views within the congregation and a need to develop communication skills if the aim of involving the entire membership in the process of renewal was to be successful. In April 1968 the first number of *Each for All*, came off the roneo machine under the editorial direction of Sister M. Jude Davies. It began, perhaps significantly, with an excellent article on *The Conditions for fruitful Discussion* written by the Dominican friar Aelred Squire, but also contained news from the various houses. The publication soon became the venue for debate on a range of topics such as the changes in the liturgy, the structure of community life, the care of elderly sisters or the retention of the title 'Mother' for superiors. While there were regular contributions from a small number of sisters, an effort was made to get copy from as many as possible.

The debates could be surprisingly frank. When one sister wrote what could only be described as a scathing response to another's defence of the congregation's involvement in private education, the text was interrupted by a recipe for a fruit cordial. Sister M. Jude, excusing the editorial error, informed readers; 'I have left it as it was, as I thought a drink might not be a bad idea at this stage!'[34] Another, who felt very keenly the loss of the Latin liturgy, called for less self-consciousness in the English office, abhorring the impression sometimes given that meaningful prayer arrived with the vernacular. 'One sometimes wonders how God managed until we came along to give Him His due worship!'[35]

Reports of meetings, conferences and book reviews helped to fill out each issue. There were also lighter touches, including poetry – sometimes satire on the serious matters being debated – handy hints, an occasional 'market place' where books and furniture might be offered or pleas put in for 'borrowed' items to be returned! Perhaps most interesting of all are the personal accounts of their everyday lives sent in by the sisters. An early issue contained a series of articles from sisters undertaking professional training, including a vivid narrative from Sister M. Theodore [later Theodora] Crook who was working in the Casualty Department at St Charles' Hospital in 1969. She describes in graphic detail the arrival of a big, burly butcher who had almost cut off three fingers but balked at having to endure an anti-tetanus injection; a labourer coming with his hand wrapped in a towel who, when asked what had happened, fell backwards in a faint putting his head through the glass partition.[36]

As any editor knows, animals make good copy and Brack, the community pet at Erdington, who is not remembered with particular affection by many of the sisters, was featured in a report at Christmas the same year. He was taken for a daily walk in the park where he was adored by the local children who all wanted to pet him and be chased up and down. Many of the children were Catholics attending a local county school because there were two busy roads to cross between their homes and the Abbey School. Interaction with Brack became a starting point for interaction with the children and sometimes, later on, with their parents. This, in turn, could lead to providing religious instruction and sacramental preparation for the children. 'Brack may look like a small wolf, but he is a true "hound of the Lord" and his business is pastoral care!'[37]

The spring 1973 issue of *Each for All* announced a change of orientation. Following the recent meeting in London of superiors of the different branches of the Dominican family, it had been decided, with the encouragement of Mother M. Silvester, to expand the publication to take articles from all the congregations of Dominican women and communities of nuns working in the British Isles. Although there were still some excellent articles and reports, a certain edge was lost. A wider audience, however, demands greater discretion and the editor, by this time Sister Patricia Mary England had, on occasion, to slip in an addendum 'for the English Congregation only'. One sister, for instance, wanted to voice her opinion that the novices, who had spent a week working at the City of the Poor in Lourdes, might have been better employed in the congregation's own nursing homes, where the residents would have been delighted to see them and the regular staff might have been given some relief from their hard labour! Not all contributors wanted to express their views in the new, wider forum.

The need to revive an exclusively internal newsletter led to the appearance in December 1978 of *News Chronicle* edited by Sister M. Nicola Loeb and later *Our News*. By this time much of the intensity had gone out of the earlier debates and, on the whole, the new bulletin was more news than views. These publications played an integral part in allowing the sisters of the congregation to air their views, to communicate and to get to know one another better. It also did much to develop an appreciation of the very different works sisters undertook, from the more traditional to the more innovative. Above all, they provide an extremely vivid picture of the English Dominican Congregation engulfed in the tide of change.

Community discussions had become part and parcel of the regular life of all the communities during the late 1960s and early 1970s. Not all found it easy to express themselves, even on subjects about which they felt quite passionately. More articulate speakers and those with more forceful personalities might allow their views to dominate discussion even if they did not reflect the majority opinion. For some, such meetings became a positive ordeal. Mother M. Silvester was well aware of the tensions that could develop and wrote to the sisters in November 1973 providing a thoughtful analysis of the benefits and hazards of such exchanges.

> Now that community discussions are leaving the superficial, some storms are inevitable. Reconciliation will never mean that we all think the same way, but it will mean that personally, each one of us is convinced that every other Sister has the right to express her thoughts and feelings in her way. We must trust each other and we must be worthy of trust. We should never have a thought of condemnation when zeal or even irritation or bad temper have caused a Sister to over-step the bounds of discretion. We all have depths to which we can descend – but 'out of the depths . . .' Community meetings, courteous but honest, will show us betimes just how frail we are, and just how good and loveable also. Good community meetings are a sure antidote to crippling self-righteousness – which can be a professional hazard – but God forbid![38]

Another venue for exchange of views was the series of Easter meetings which began in 1974 and were held at Spode House, the conference centre which adjoined Hawkesyard Priory. The Prioress General prepared herself for the first meeting by signing up for a five-day course at Hawkstone Hall on 'The contemporary theology and future of religious life'. Initially these 'Easter Risings', as they soon came to be called, were attended by the General Council and a group of twenty sisters, half elected from those above and below the age of fifty. The second and later meetings were open to all and the numbers increased, though everyone attending was expected to make some contribution. At the first meeting papers covered such topics as chastity, study, silence, regular observance, the constitutions, the relationship between Gospel and faith, and prospects for the future. Mother M. Silvester reported that: 'Discussions were frank and wholly uninhibited. The ability to listen to each other and to argue without rancour was surely a proof of valuable lessons learned at community level.'[39]

One of the most striking things about the Easter Risings was the enthusiasm with which sisters participated as the years went by. Not all of them were used to speaking in public, still less to writing papers on theological topics, but they rose to the challenge. For instance, one who had entered as a lay sister and had spent most of her religious life quite happily in the kitchen, could deliver a most thoughtful exposition on obedience quoting St Benedict, Karl Rahner and Anthony Bloom amongst others.[40] The wide range of topics covered and the broad range of opinions expressed show that, however much anxiety there may have been about the future, about the difficulties inherent in religious life, or about the failures of the past, there was also mutual acceptance and appreciation.

The need for expert help in forging a constructive plan for the future of the congregation and determining the best use of its resources, both human and material, had been put before the Easter Meeting in 1976 by Sister M. Cecilia Oddie. At the venerable age of seventy-five, Sister M. Cecilia stressed the importance of involving the younger sisters in the decision making, and of gaining the adherence of the older sisters in view of the personal sacrifices the plan might entail.[41] In April 1981 Mother M. Rupert Fitzpatrick, after much hesitation, proposed first to the General Council, then to the prioresses, and finally to the congregation at large, that a team from the Tavistock Institute of Human Relationships be engaged to carry out just such a study in preparation for the following General Chapter.[42] Although such projects had been carried out in North America, they were something of a novelty in Britain.

The Institute has its origins in the Tavistock Clinic, founded during the First World War to investigate and treat the effects of psychological trauma on shell-shocked soldiers. In 1946 several key members of the Clinic, which was incorporated into the NHS at that time, formed the Institute to carry out educational, research and consultancy work in the area of the social sciences and applied psychology. Their clients ranged from private companies to government departments and public institutions; they had experience of working with Indian textile makers, British coalminers and university administrators and were well known for their work in promoting the management of change.[43]

In October a steering group including Mother M. Rupert and Sisters M. Nicola Loeb, M. Jadwiga Świątecka and M. Gonsalvo Sutcliffe was set up to assist the consultants, led by Gordon Lawrence and Olya Khaleelee. Mother M. Rupert asked for the earnest prayers of the congregation for the successful outcome of the project in improving mutual understanding and communication and bringing about a renewal and revitalization of the apostolate. The consultants began a round of visits to the different convents, conducting group meetings and interviewing individual sisters. Although she had encouraged all to cooperate with the project, Mother M. Rupert had made it quite clear that no one was obliged to do so, the decision lying with the individual.

The project did meet with opposition from both individuals and even communities as a whole. Some sisters questioned the value of employing consultants who knew nothing about the principles of the religious life and could not understand the faith dimension.[44] Others were critical or suspicious of the psycho-analytical methods employed. There was also a laudable desire on the part of many to be loyal to the congregation and to avoid baring its wounds to the outside world. Sisters who were happy expressing their views at the Easter Meetings sometimes sat by silently during the Tavistock meetings. Others who were not known for their active participation in discussion showed no hesitation in voicing their objections to the project. The negative reactions, however, were balanced by the constructive working relations that developed elsewhere.

It is quite clear that Mother M. Rupert found it difficult to understand the resistance that surfaced and there is an obvious impatience in her communications on the subject. A year into the project there was question of abandoning it, but the General Council decided to go ahead, judging that it would be more damaging to stop when little positive result had been achieved. Where individuals and communities had cooperated actively, it was noted, the general opinion was that meetings and discussions had been positive.[45] In hindsight, making her report to the General Chapter in 1983, Mother M. Rupert admitted that a more thorough preparation might have enabled the project to run more smoothly. Where there had been lack of cooperation, she conceded, this was not due to ill-will and overall, communities seemed to be saying that communication had improved.[46]

Although they may not have led to any orchestrated or collegial action, the effects of the Tavistock project were far reaching. On the individual level, people were altered by the experience. The traditional culture of religious life, reinforcing the monastic ideal of *fuga mundi* – flight from 'the world' – discouraged any talk of oneself or one's family or background. Suddenly, during the group sessions, sisters realized how little they knew about some of the women with whom they had been associated, sometimes for many years. In the course of one such meeting, which brought together members of three houses, a group was asked to talk about how they had become Dominicans. What a surprise it was when each of the six in turn revealed that during the process of decision making she had first considered, or even applied to enter, the Cistercian nuns at Stapehill! For the first time the sisters were encouraged to talk about their lives, and for many it was a defining experience and one which encouraged much deeper mutual acceptance. Since, in the Thomisitic understanding of the theological virtues, love proceeds from knowledge, this was an appropriately Dominican conclusion.

The project was certainly a challenge, as some of the group sessions delved deep into the life of individual houses. It required the sisters to justify to others, who did not share the same belief system, who they were, what was their mission and what they believed. No one found the process easy, even those who could see its advantages, but it introduced a new openness. Sisters began to discuss things with greater ease and this completely changed community meetings from then on. As one sister put it; 'The ice could never totally reform again once it had been broken and the depths stirred up.'[47]

The Institute produced three working notes by way of report. Far from depicting a totally dysfunctional community, the report provided an insightful picture of a group of women struggling to come to terms with change and attempting to forge a contemporary and collective identity that all its members could share. It did not deny the tensions that existed, none of which was unique to the English Dominican Congregation, but could apply to any religious institute or even any workplace. The greatest problem to be overcome, according to the report, was that the congregation was not experienced by its members as a cohesive totality. This resulted in houses enacting different visions for the future and a sense of competition developing as to which type of future would prevail. In the past, anxieties could be projected into the structures which had helped to give meaning to the religious life, but since these had been swept away, anxieties could only be introjected and forced back on the individual. The state of uncertainty also impeded the exercise of leadership, few sisters feeling they had the qualities to fulfil the role of local prioress.

In a meeting with one of the local communities in which the members were displaying a certain reticence, Gordon Lawrence challenged them; 'If you belong to the Order of Preachers, preach to me!' Though he may not have 'had the faith' it is clear that he developed a keen sensitivity to the culture of religious life and that the interaction with the congregation affected him as well. The second part of the report concluded with a consideration of the Paschal mystery which gives evidence of just how well the sisters must have fulfilled their vocation as preachers.

> The symbolism of the resurrection is rich. Among its many features, one is worth holding to. When Christ rose from the dead He still had His wounds from the crucifixion, and also the experience of His life. Any renewal, change, social resurrection of the congregation will mean that it will occur with the full experience of the wounds (which in this context symbolise loss, guilt, deprivation etc.) of the past, but also knowledge of what has been good in it.[48]

Olya Khaleelee addressed the sisters assembled for the General Chapter in 1983. In speaking to them of the need to resolve the perceived lack of cohesion within the congregation she warned them that they might well be the last generation. For many this was a moment of realization that the survival of the congregation might not be a certainty.

Building Dominican communities

Amongst the reports from the Easter Rising in 1975 was an impassioned plea for the congregation to consider a new model of community life.

> Can it be accepted as a fact that there are some Sisters in the congregation who really and honestly think that a valid religious Dominican life could be worked out by a small group with a fluid time-table and a minimum of structure, adhering to the heritage in present day circumstances which may mean not always wearing the habit, not always reciting every hour of the Divine Office, replacing liturgical prayer sometimes with a discussion of the Gospel theme, studying together, groping after some new forms? Can this be seen as valid and tolerable?[49]

For many members of the congregation, this proposition would have met with an anathema. Some sisters clearly felt threatened at the prospect of losing the traditional structures which in their experience had added both beauty and value to their Dominican life. For some years there would be an uncertainty about which way to move, whether it was possible to have differing models of community life within the one congregation. As the Tavistock report later emphasized, there were differing and competing visions of the future. Yet already by this time the community at Erdington consisted of only five members living in a suburban house where limited numbers, varied apostolic work and the house itself made some traditional observances impossible. This would become increasingly common.

Making her report to the congregation at the General Chapter of 1983, Mother M. Rupert Fitzpatrick conceded that the concept of pluriformity had been accepted in principle within the congregation, but that its practice was in danger from those who could appreciate no other form of religious life than that which they had personally chosen.[50] Despite fears that positions would polarize, during the term of office of her two successors, the way in which the sisters lived their community life continued to change. A great deal of effort was put into establishing exactly what size of community, and what level of structure, would best serve the needs of the apostolate and the personal needs of the sisters. Two types of community seemed to have developed. There were larger communities, where the full Divine Office was maintained, the habit was always worn, sisters were appointed to various offices such as chantress, infirmarian and librarian, and other structures were adhered to. On the other hand there were smaller communities where such a degree of structure and organization was impossible, either because of fewness of members or the variety of works carried out. A small number of sisters continued to live on their own because of the individual apostolates in which they were involved, though they were always assigned to a particular community.

If some felt there was a suggestion that the smaller houses were considered 'less authentic', the responses to a survey on community life preceding the 1993 biennial meeting show an almost universal consensus that both forms were considered valid and needed to be supported. The freedom for those in smaller communities to work out their own lifestyle, compatible with their particular mission was highlighted in the responses of large communities as well as small. Some noted that in the structured life of the past there had always

Fig. 16 Musings on changes in community life; 'We don't like rigid structures.'

Fig. 17 Musings on changes in community life; 'How many do we need in our community, Sister?'

been a need for dispensations from the regular observance, and the flexible life of the smaller communities was an extension of this very Dominican principle; that the mission of preaching, in whatever form, takes precedence.

In smaller communities there was an admission that 'kindred spirits' worked best together and that, ideally, most would like six or seven in community rather than three or four. It was felt that small communities, not having full-time bursars, required modifications in financial arrangements and the need for personal allowances for those sisters who felt they required them was acknowledged. There was also a consensus, as already stated, on which houses ought to be closed. However, given the age profile of the congregation, the number of both larger and smaller houses most respondents considered it feasible to maintain was simply not sustainable in the medium term. [51]

Attempts were also made to build communities around sisters engaged in individual apostolates. At various times one or two other sisters were able to join Sister M. Ninian Averill in George's Square, Edinburgh, and for a time she shared community with a Bushey Dominican, or built her community with students who were committed to a similar lifestyle. In 1987 a community was formally erected with Sisters M. Felix Riley and M. Joanna Currie joining Sister M. Ninian. The previous year a house had been purchased in Havelock Street, Canterbury and a small community was established comprising Sister M. Jadwiga Świątecka, who was teaching at Christ Church College, and Sister M. Sunniva Cummins who was following a course at the Franciscan Study Centre in Canterbury. They were later joined by Sister Máire Colette Ludden. After Sister M. Sunniva's return to Norway, when there was a room available, the community at Havelock Road even took in lodgers, including students from Christ Church and a young teacher in the local Catholic primary school.

At St Rose's in Stroud the building known as the Annex was deemed unsuitable to the needs of the increasingly disabled students. Since the cost of converting the building to the required standard was prohibitive, it was decided to build a bungalow for the students and convert the Annex for the use of the sisters. On New Year's Day 2000, the community moved into its new home, complete with its own chapel, providing a greater measure of privacy and the possibility of offering hospitality.

When Sister Angela Mary Leydon submitted the report of her administration to the 2007 General Chapter, St Dominic's at Stone was the only house to which more than five sisters were assigned.

Not even the most ardent enthusiast for Dominican regular observance would have doubted by this time that it was possible to live a genuinely Dominican life in a community of two, even if it might not be possible one hundred per cent of the time. Even at Stone, the style of life adapted as the community profile changed. Although some of the oldest members of the community are the last to retire and the earliest to rise, the timetable for community prayer is geared towards the needs of the majority in order to enable the greater number to participate. No matter what the size of the community, or the age of the members, there is, perhaps, a greater acknowledgement that the best means for making community life a happy and enriching experience is through providing spiritual, intellectual, physical and emotional support, both from one another and from outside. In any community, there are tensions and difficulties, but outsiders certainly notice the warmth of relations and genuine care the sisters have for one another.[52]

Conclusion

In the last half century the structures of Dominican community life have relaxed from an almost rigid formalism to a more natural informality. In the past the sisters lived at close quarters, but were expected to maintain a respectful reserve with one another. Nevertheless, for most sisters the experience of life in community was a happy and positive one, and deep friendships certainly flourished. But for most there was little scope for discussing matters in great depth, except if one was lucky, with one's confessor.

The gradual openness to the world at large initiated by Pius XII and brought to fruition in the teachings of the Second Vatican Council brought about a revolution in these structures. The style of government within the congregation moved from hierarchical to collegial through the often difficult process of dialogue, listening and trust. No longer could superiors be 'very dear Mother' or subjects 'my dear child', for all now constituted a community of equals with the common goal of discerning God's will. Though structures have become less rigid, there has been no loss of respect for authority, in fact the indications are that as the exercise of authority within the congregation has become more collegial and personal, it is better appreciated.

Community life will never be perfect, though the changes of recent years, the smaller size of the congregation, and the chance this has given to get to know one another on a deeper level, have contributed to a greater ease with one another. Even the accounts of the deceased sisters, circulated with the Acts of each General Chapter, have adopted a more familiar style. What is remembered and celebrated in the last thirty years or so is not what particular devotions and virtues a sister exhibited in her life, but who and what she was, in all her glorious humanity, foibles and imperfections included. The impression is both more interesting and more edifying.

What inspires and challenges the sisters in their endeavour to live community life more genuinely is nothing new. The Rule of St Augustine which generations of English Dominican Sisters heard read in the refectory until it was engraved on their memories, begins with the words 'Before all things, my dearest sisters, let God be loved and after Him, your neighbour.'[53] The rule then reminds the sisters that they are called together to dwell in unity, to have one soul and one heart. Sixteen hundred years after these words were written, the Constitutions of the English Dominican Sisters challenge them in the same way. 'The love that unites us should be directed towards a total giving of self, not in work alone, but in a whole-hearted acceptance and service of one another; in fellowship and support, compassion and gentleness, respect and courtesy.'[54]

Notes

1. Stone, G98a(iii), *Proceedings of the General Chapter, 11–20 August 1977, Prioress General's Report.*
2. Stone, G100(f), Mother M. Bonaventure Burke, Circular letter, 22 March 1960.
3. *Each for All*, no. 12, October 1971, p. 15.
4. Stone, G100(g), Mother M. Silvester Brennan, Circular letter, 11 January 1968.
5. Stone, G98b, *Proceedings of the Special General Chapter, August 1967.*
6. Stone, G98a(iii), *Proceedings of the General Chapter, 5–16 August 1971, Report of the Administration of Mother M. Silvester Brennan.*
7. Stone, G98a(iii), *Proceedings of the General Chapter*, Second Session, 1–11 August 1989.
8. Stone, G98a(iii), *Proceedings of the General Chapter*, 3–15 August 2001.
9. Stone, G98a(iii), *General Chapter 1995, Report of the Prioress General.*
10. *Each for All*, Special number, Easter Week 1974.
11. Stone, G98a(iii), *General Chapter 1971, Responses to Questionnaires sent out in 1970.*
12. Stone, G100(i), Sister M. Edward House, Circular Letter, 5 September 1990.

13. Stone, G98a(iii), *General Chapter 1995, Report of the Prioress General.*
14. Ibid.
15. Stone, G(xii), *General Council Book, February 1942–August 1948*, 12 July 1942.
16. Stone, G100(e), Mother M. Ansgar Sheldon, Circular letter, 21 July 1953.
17. Ibid., 7 March 1956.
18. Cf. *Necrology, 1977–1983*
19. Conversation with Sister M. Camilla Flynn, February 2010.
20. Stone, G100(f),Mother M. Bonaventure Burke, Circular letter, 24 June 1960.
21. Stone, G100(g), Mother M Silvester Brennan, Circular letter, 9 June 1966.
22. Ibid., 29 October 1966.
23. Sister M. Columcille's gifts had also been recognized in October 1973 when she was appointed to assist the novice mistress, Sister M. Rupert Fitzpatrick, in the formation of new members.
24. Stone, G(xix), *Annals, 1956–1965*, p. 92.
25. Stone, G2000/64, *Register of the Prioress General, 1959–1965*, p. 75.
26. Stone, *Noviciate Annals*, 6 January 1960.
27. Stone, G98a(ii), *Proceedings of the General Chapter, 5–18 June 1965.*
28. Discussion with General Council, 22 May 2010.
29. From oral evidence this was certainly the case with the Poor Servants of the Mother of God, the Congregation of Jesus (at that time known as the Institute of the Blessed Virgin Mary) and the Faithful Companions of Jesus.
30. Stone, G100(i), Sister M. Edward House, Circular letter, 13 November 1986.
31. Birmingham, CC-S-6, Sister M. Xavier McLaren to Monsignor Joseph Healey, 20 May 1939.
32. Stone, G100(f), Mother M. Rupert Fitzpatrick, Circular letter, 20 May 1978.
33. *Each for All*, vol. 1, no. 3, October 1968.
34. Ibid., vol. 1, no. 4, January 1969.
35. Ibid., no. 13, Trinity 1972.
36. Ibid., vol. 1, no. 4, January 1969.
37. Ibid., no. 7, Christmas 1969.
38. Stone, G100(i), Mother M. Silvester Brennan, Circular letter, 27 November 1973.
39. Ibid., 27 April 1974.
40. *Each for All*, Special number, Easter Week 1975, AGOPS.
41. Ibid., Special number, Easter Week 1976.
42. Stone, G100(h), Mother M. Rupert Fitzpatrick, Circular Letter, 27 April 1981.
43. Cf. http://www.tavinstitute.org/ accessed 29 April 2010.
44. In fact, one of the Tavistock team was a Catholic, though his contribution is not remembered as being as helpful as that of the other members. Meeting with General Council, 22 May 2010.
45. Stone, G100(h), Mother M. Rupert Fitzpatrick, Circular Letter, 20 August 1981.

46. Stone, G98a(iii), *Proceedings of the General Chapter, 1–10 August 1983, Report of the Prioress General.*
47. Meeting with General Council, 22 May 2010.
48. Stone, G2000/8, *Tavistock Institute, Working Note 2.*
49. Stone, un-numbered, Sister M. Nicola Loeb, *Report of the Easter Meeting 1975*, p. 49.
50. Stone, G98a(iii), *Proceedings of the General Chapter, 1–10 August 1983, Report of the Prioress General.*
51. Stone, G100(i), *Recommendations arising from the Third Preparatory Meeting*, March 1993.
52. Stone, G98a(iii), *General Chapter 2007, Report of the Administration of the Prioress General, 2001–2007*, p. 2.
53. Dominican Sisters, *Rule and Constitutions*, 2009, p. 6
54. Ibid., Article 28, p. 24.

Chapter Eight

A harmonious preparation: prayer, study, and regular observance

All these practices contribute not only to the glory of God and our sanctification, but serve directly the salvation of mankind, since they prepare harmoniously for preaching, furnish its incentive, form its character, and in turn are influenced by it.

Fundamental Constitution of the Order of Preachers, §6

Introduction

Just as community provides the context for Dominican life; prayer, study and the traditional observances of the Order nourish this life and sustain its mission. Until the twentieth century, any movement of reform or revival within the Order of Preachers was based upon a return to primitive observance. The essentials of Dominican life were protected and enhanced by centuries-old observances imbued with ritual meaning; and as a consequence the life developed a formative quality of its own. As true daughters of St Dominic, the founders of the various groups of English Dominican Sisters adopted these observances uncritically.

The renewal of religious institutes which gathered pace from the 1950s called upon religious to focus on the essential elements of their lives, and to discard those practices and customs which were at odds with modern society. In obedience to this call, and keeping in mind the sound traditions of the Order, the English Dominican Sisters evaluated their manner of prayer, their commitment to the intellectual life, and the regulation of their daily lives.

Prayer: the centre of our religious life

Following a pattern which had varied very little in more than a hundred years, the life of an English Dominican Sister was permeated with private and communal prayer. Until the mid 1960s the first words heard each morning at 5:30 were the greeting of the caller as she knocked on the cell door, '*Benedicamus Domino!*' ('Let us bless the Lord!') The first words uttered, whether she was grateful or not for such an awakening, were '*Deo Gratias!*' Within half an hour the community would have gathered, each in her stall in choir, for half an hour's meditation. There was considerable liberty left to the individual for this meditative prayer, with no imposed form or method such as those popularized by the Jesuits.

The English Dominicans were one of the few congregations of active sisters who were bound to the full recitation of the Divine Office in choir. This prayer, which with the Mass constitutes the official liturgy of the Church, has its origins in the Jewish practice of prescribed hours for praying the Psalms. By the early Middle Ages, its format as laid down by monastic legislators such as John Cassian and St Benedict, had become accepted throughout the Roman Church. Its purpose was to sanctify the day by punctuating it with regular prayer: Matins before dawn, Lauds at dawn, the hours of Prime, Terce, Sext and None at the first, third, sixth and ninth hours respectively, Vespers at sunset and Compline before retiring. The major components of each hour were the Psalms with their antiphons, hymns, readings with their responsaries and concluding prayers. Matins was by far the longest hour and included nine psalms, and readings from the Fathers of the Church. Lauds and Vespers were about half the length of Matins, while the hours from Prime to None, known as the 'Little Hours', were considerably shorter.

From the earliest days of the Order, the office of Compline was considered a particularly significant hour for Dominicans. It concluded with the singing of the *Salve Regina* as the sisters processed to Our Lady's altar, and this was followed by the singing of the anthem to St Dominic, the *O Lumen Ecclesiae* as they processed back to choir. Once they returned to their stalls, the necrology would be read, naming those sisters whose anniversary of death would occur the following day; finally the psalm *De Profundis* was prayed on their behalf as the convent bell was tolled.

For most religious communities, particularly those who carried out apostolic works such as teaching and nursing, the accent was on the obligation of recitation, rather than appropriate timing. The various hours of the Office were fitted into the working day at what seemed the most convenient time. So for most, the English Dominicans amongst them, the period of meditation was followed by the recitation of all four Little Hours, with the reading of the Martyrology, commemorating the saints who had died for the faith that day, coming after Prime. Mass followed the Little Hours, and where there was a Dominican friar serving as chaplain, this would be celebrated according to the Dominican Rite, which differed from the Roman Rite. In the evening there was a second, briefer period of meditation followed by the recitation of the rosary, and the singing of Vespers and Compline. At 8p.m. Matins and Lauds of the following day would be anticipated, taking the better part of an hour on ordinary days.

In most houses, Vespers and Compline were sung each day, the rest of the Office being recited *recto tono*, that is, on a sustained note. On greater feasts more of the Office and the proper chants for the Mass would also be sung. During the most solemn seasons such as Christmastide and during Holy Week and Easter Week these proper chants – some of them unique to the Dominican Order – if rendered well, were of incredible beauty. Singing them well gave not only a sense of satisfaction to many sisters, but a sense of prayerfulness, awe and joy. Because of the intricacy, particularly of the Mass chants, a great deal of preparation was required, though even if they were sung only once a year, a surprising familiarity could develop. The body was also used in prayer with ritual movements, such as the profound bow at the *Gloria Patri* which ended each psalm, and sitting and standing alternately on opposite sides of the choir during the psalmody to symbolize the active and contemplative aspects of the Dominican vocation.

Until the use of the vernacular was permitted by the Second Vatican Council, Latin was the liturgical language of the western Church. Although many of those who entered as choir sisters had a basic grounding in Latin, and some were gifted classicists, as time passed this became less common. The psalms of the Divine Office followed a weekly cycle and with sound instruction many sisters were able to recite the psalms in Latin with reasonable understanding. The patristic readings at Matins, however, must have been quite a different matter as the style differed, from classical writers such as St Leo the Great to medieval writers such as St Bernard of Clairvaux. For those not linguistically gifted, the Latin Office could become a chore which inhibited prayer, or at the best something which carried them along with its rhythm or beauty.

Praying for the souls of its deceased members and benefactors was also a Dominican tradition. Once a week there was a procession called the *Libera*, during which intercessory prayers were sung on their behalf, and if the convent had its own cemetery, as at Stone, Stroud or Harrow, the procession would make its way there. Each Sunday there was also a procession with its own particular chant and prayers, alternately in honour of Our Lady of the Rosary, the Holy Name of Jesus, the Blessed Sacrament or St Dominic. Normally there was Benediction of the Blessed Sacrament once a week, during which the reserved sacrament was solemnly exposed for a brief period and a blessing given.

Every year the sisters made a retreat of eight days during the summer and another of three days during the Christmas period. The former did not have to be made in the community where one was assigned, but it was always made together. Apart from providing extra time for personal prayer there were generally three conferences a day, normally following a particular theme, given by the retreat master who was usually a Dominican friar. The retreat master also made himself available to give spiritual counsel to those who required it, though this was normally done in the context of the confessional. Having Dominicans who understood their traditions, and some of whom knew the congregation very well, was much appreciated, as was the more relaxed pace of life during the retreat.

During the inter-war period a vigorous liturgical movement had

Fig. 18 *Libera* procession in the cemetery at Stone, *c.*1962.

developed in the Church, particularly in France, Germany and North America, fostering greater understanding of, and more fruitful participation in the liturgy, particularly amongst the laity. But for the English Dominicans at this time, the Divine Office was still thought of primarily as a community prayer rather than a public liturgical act. In 1956 Pope Pius XII introduced a revision of the ceremonies for Holy Week and Easter, including the restoration of the East Vigil. Mother M. Ansgar Sheldon sent out a circular letter explaining the changes to the congregation, together with a timetable for Holy Week. Both the timetable and the annotation added by Sister M. Patricia Kane show how ingrained was the distinction between the Divine Office and other liturgical functions. For although Sister M. Patricia explains that 'The leading idea of the new Ordo is to have every liturgical ceremony at the correct time', on Good Friday, when the Commemoration of the Lord's Passion begins at 3p.m., all the Little Hours and Vespers as well are 'fitted in' during the morning![1]

Enhancing the celebration of the liturgy was a priority of Mother M. Bonaventure Burke, and early in her term of office the Dominican liturgist from Santa Sabina, Father Ansgar Dirks, spent some time at Portobello Road convent, introducing the sisters to the theory of interpreting the chant of Dom André Mocquereau, a Benedictine of the famous abbey of Solesmes. He also promoted Justine Ward's method for teaching liturgical music in the schools. The following year Sister M. Gilbert [Patricia Mary] England, who taught chant to the novices at Stroud, spent a weekend with her sister, an Ursuline who was following a course in chant at the Catholic Faculty in Lyon, to study organ accompaniment and the directives of the Sacred Congregation for Rites concerning sacred music.[2]

The first document published by the Second Vatican Council was that dealing with the liturgy, and though it reinforced the primacy of Gregorian chant, it also opened the way to a vernacular liturgy. By degrees English would supersede Latin in the liturgical prayer of the English Dominican Sisters. Change in the liturgy was something experienced by the whole Church as the move from Latin to the vernacular in the Mass progressed. This change also affected the Divine Office, not only in terms of language but in its format, and a renewed understanding of its purpose in sanctifying the day. The Vatican Council reduced the length of the Office considerably making Lauds and Vespers, as morning and evening prayer, the two hinges of the liturgical day. It was no longer appropriate to anticipate hours or to run them together in order to 'fit them in' as in the past.

It was not until February 1968 that the English edition of the Dominican rite Divine Office was available; by this time a rescript had been issued from Rome allowing the recitation of only three of the nine psalms of Matins. Unfortunately, the rescript made specific mention only of priests, not women religious, so for some time the sisters were obliged to recite all nine psalms while their brethren prayed only three![3] Just a few months after the new breviaries arrived, the General Chapter of the friars convened at River Forest near Chicago decided upon the adoption of the Roman Rite and in 1974 the sisters adopted first the new interim breviary and three years later the finally approved version.

Although the change to English in the liturgy is mentioned by many sisters as the greatest benefit to accrue from the Second Vatican Council, there were many who, nonetheless, felt a profound sense of loss as the Latin liturgy disappeared. To one sister, who had entered in the mid 1920s, it was something 'most beautiful, most "civilising" and, for those alive to it, a perfect means of contemplation', while for another – almost the same age – it carried no particular mystique.[4] No one seemed to advert to the fact that the same document which had brought in the vernacular liturgy had also argued for the preservation of Gregorian chant. Sister M. Barbara Pearce, though happy to bow to the majority voice, pleaded for 'the minority privileges which are conceded in all true democracies' with occasional Latin Mass and Office accorded even 'as an act of charity' and suggested a Latin Society to preserve the best of the Dominican chant.[5]

Neither was love for the chant always the sign of rigid conservatism. Although she found the English Office an impoverishment, Sister M. Justin Lane was quick to put her mind and pen to the work of translating some of the Latin hymns, and at a date when inclusive language had hardly become a major concern even on the other side of the Atlantic, she bemoaned the lack of any recognition of women in the English translations. Sometimes, she admitted, she would sing 'sisters' or 'daughter' *sotto voce*, since anything else went too much against the grain![6]

Though festive Vespers and parts of the Mass continued to be sung in Latin at Stone well into the 1970s, English was the established norm by the time of the 1971 General Chapter. Providing new music for the English Office was a difficult task. It soon became plain to chantresses that the rhythms and cadences of the English language did not suit adaptations of plainchant. Sister M. Chrysostom Naylor composed settings for several offices and psalm tones produced by the Benedictine nuns at Stanbrook and

Kylemore were also tried, though perhaps the most popular tones were those of the Benedictine Dom Lawrence Bevenot.

The constant experimentation added a certain self-consciousness to the Divine Office, and the Prioress General's report to the General Chapter in 1971 noted a lack of enthusiasm in its study and preparation. Sister Patricia Mary England assisted the local communities by giving workshops and even drawing up guidelines for 'praying the Divine Office in a community of four where none has a good voice'![7] In 1977 she undertook a diploma course in liturgy at the Pastoral Liturgy Centre at Portarlington in County Laois, Ireland and began to work full time as a liturgist. By the time of the next General Chapter, Mother M. Silvester could already point out how the strains had subsided and how much the music had improved. Gradually, communities began to welcome guests and visitors into choir to celebrate the liturgy with them, increasingly aware that it was not just their prayer, but that of the Church.

More recently the smaller communities and ageing membership of the congregation have posed their own challenges for liturgical prayer. An increasing number of communities no longer have the possibility of daily Mass in the house, and for them the celebration of the Eucharist is normally in the context of the wider parish community. Considerable effort is put into praying the Liturgy of the Hours together, though in the smaller houses, finding a convenient time can be problematic. While in a larger community, Compline might be at a set hour; in a smaller house it might depend upon what time one member returns from a meeting, another from a choir practice, or even how long it takes Inspector Barnaby to clear up a murder or two. In a larger community, as was always the case, there can be tensions in maintaining unison and tempo in choral prayer and adequate time for preparation and practice is still necessary. There is greater variety in the way the Divine Office is prayed and in recent years there have been efforts to make language more inclusive, with a series of guidelines being circulated after the 2001 General Chapter.[8]

After the Special Chapter in 1967 daily meditation no longer had to be made in common, and although some missed the mutual witness of silent prayer together; the emphasis moved to one of personal responsibility. A growing interest in prayer in the Dominican tradition and of *lectio divina*, the meditative reading of scripture and other texts, characterized the years after the Second Vatican Council. Some sisters also found that sharing in charismatic prayer groups, which became popular in the 1970s, added to the intimacy of their personal prayer and there was also increasing openness to new forms of meditative and centring prayer.

From the 1970s there was also greater liberty allowed in making annual retreats. These sometimes differed greatly from the traditional community retreats. Two sisters attended a retreat in Birmingham in 1978, directed by two members of the Indian province of the Society of the Sacred Heart, in which Sanskrit chants, traditional hymns, charismatic songs, clapping, cymbals and bells featured in the liturgy. There was also a 'kind of chapter of faults' where 'false gods' were burned.[9] Even the Jesuit thirty-day retreat following the *Spiritual Exercises* of St Ignatius of Loyola began to enjoy popularity with some Dominican Sisters. Others made private directed retreats, especially those in smaller communities where the variety of works make it difficult to organize a retreat together. Retreats are recognized as a means of allowing the sisters to deepen their spirit of prayer and apart from the annual retreat of at least six days, communities are recommended to have a monthly day of recollection as well. The Constitutions also state that, wherever possible, these retreats ought to be led by a Dominican.

Although the liturgy may have been simplified, and a greater emphasis is placed on personal responsibility, prayer is still deemed the centre of Dominican religious life. In the best Dominican tradition, the current constitutions acknowledge the mutual relationship between public liturgical prayer and personal prayer, each being able to feed and add meaning to the other.[10] Fidelity to the choral recitation of the Divine Office continues to be a distinctive mark of the congregation and although many of the traditional observances of Dominican life have disappeared, emphasis is still placed on creating and maintaining an atmosphere in which prayer can flourish.

Regular observance: 'remaining faithful to our calling'

Traditionally, the atmosphere of prayer and recollection was preserved through the observance of a panoply of ritual observances, which sacralized the lives of the English Dominican Sisters from their beginnings until the early 1960s. A mentality carried over from the nineteenth century, and expressed in the Book of Customs used by the first sisters at Portobello Road, emphasized the importance attached to these observances. 'Although some points may seem, at first glance, superficial and of little importance, it is necessary to set store by every little observance, for fear that in despising little things we fall little by little.'[11]

Until the 1960s, these rituals began in the early morning, as the sisters rose after the caller's greeting. As a sister donned the white tunic of her habit she prayed; 'Clothe my soul, O Lord, with the nuptial robe of chastity, and grant that pure and undefiled, I may carry it before the judgment seat of God.' There was a prayer recited when fastening the cincture and rosary, when she pulled the scapular over her head, and another when she fastened the veil, after having tied the ends of the wimple at the top of her head and secured the bandeau across her forehead. The scapular, which tradition held was added to St Dominic's Augustinian habit by the Blessed Virgin herself, was considered the most sacred part of the religious habit. It lay across the foot of each sister's bed during the night, and out of respect, the back half was drawn aside when sitting down.

The greater part of the day was passed in silence. The 'great silence' lasted from after the Divine Office in the evening until after breakfast the following morning; though conversation was kept to a minimum at all times except during the afternoon and evening periods of recreation. The refectory was sacrosanct, talking was not allowed at all. Breakfast was taken in silence after Mass and the other meals were governed by ceremonial as solemn as that of the choir. Before dinner the community gathered in the cloister according to seniority and recited the *De Profundis* for the souls of their deceased benefactors. They then processed, juniors first, and lay sisters before choir sisters, and took their places at the inside of the tables that lined the room, seniors at the top. There was a sung grace and then the reader took her place at the lectern. First a passage from the Scriptures or the Rule of St Augustine was read, followed by the reading of an 'improving' book, often a religious biography. In accord with the earliest Dominican tradition, the juniors were served first, the servers, cooks and others who were prevented from attending, took their meal at second table. While the formal meal might last forty-five minutes, those at second table would have considerably less time to eat if they had to be back in the classroom or on the wards.

On greater feasts, jubilees and other celebrations there would be a high tea in the community room, where the sisters were able to talk, and various types of entertainment such as songs, recitations and plays might be produced. These are remembered as being great fun, the tables decorated and groaning with sandwiches, cakes and sweets. Eating sweet things became almost synonymous with celebration, and at one time led a sister with more savoury tastes to ask why they couldn't celebrate with cheese and beer!

It was not all feasting; as 'Sisters of Penance' the English

Fig. 19 The refectory at Harrow, 1967.

Dominicans were committed to the penitential life. Though dispensation was given as a matter of course to those engaged in teaching and other demanding occupations, the English Dominicans followed the traditional regime of fast and abstinence observed throughout the Order. Although the general law of the Church has been greatly relaxed in the last fifty years, the sisters are still required to fast on Fridays, on the vigil of some of the greater feasts, and to abstain from meat at least twice a week.

Either weekly or once a fortnight, the Chapter of Faults was held in the chapter room. Beginning with the junior, each sister in turn proclaimed her infractions of the rule, after which other members of the community might proclaim her 'in all charity' for further faults they had observed. A penance was then imposed by the prioress, who might also make a brief exhortation. Though it could become a mere routine, or an ordeal for those inclined to scrupulosity or shyness, at its best the Chapter of Faults could be extremely edifying. For the younger members of a community, seeing a senior sister acknowledging and asking pardon for her faults could be quite a moving experience.

In many religious congregations influenced by the spirituality of

St Ignatius and the Jesuits, public penances were seen as a means of combating pride and were often performed as a matter of course at specified times, sometimes penances were even picked out of a hat! In the Dominican tradition such practices were always directly related to infractions of the rule or ceremonial. The choir, refectory and chapter room were the amphitheatre for performing these penances. They were either imposed at the Chapter of Faults or were prescribed and undertaken as a matter of course at the volition of the individual sister. Kissing the scapular for minor errors during the recitation of the Divine Office, making the *venia* prostration for more serious faults, or kissing the feet of the sisters in the refectory were typical penances. In the Dominican tradition, the penitential life was aimed at union with God and was part of a much wider monastic observance.[12]

Although the English Dominican Sisters were not enclosed, the major part of each convent was reserved for their exclusive use and outsiders were not admitted. Obvious exceptions were made for priests bringing communion to the sick, medical visits, workmen and bishops and, according to canon law, heads of state, should they be inclined to visit. Visitors were received, but lodged in a distinct part of the convent, and dined in the parlour, not the refectory. The sisters never dined with visitors, even if they were close relatives. This separation from 'the world' followed the sisters when they left the building. Sisters needing to go out always had a companion, they retained a reserved demeanour and if they should meet people they knew, acknowledged, rather than greeted them and kept 'custody of the eyes'. In normal circumstances, eating in public was not permitted and visits to one's family were made only in the case of critical illness of a parent; sisters never spending the night with the family unless this was unavoidable. There were no holidays though there was the possibility of short breaks at other convents for 'rest and change'.

The consistency with which Prioresses General mentioned in their circular letters the need for greater care in observing religious decorum when going out, perhaps shows that it was not observed uniformly. Mother M. Ansgar Sheldon reminded the sisters in 1953 that they must not accept lifts in cars alone with lay people, nor travel alone on coach journeys. Attention was drawn to the proscription against eating sweets or taking meals in public without express permission, and the sisters were even forbidden to borrow works of fiction from public libraries![13] But change was soon to come as every feature of regular observance was evaluated and reassessed in the years following the Vatican Council.

The first external change the general public noticed in the English Dominican Sisters after the Council was the modification of the religious habit. Such changes, for all congregations, affected their public image and perception and for this reason often assumed an exaggerated importance. Judging by the documentation in the archives at Stone, although there were obvious tensions over the question of religious dress, it does not seem to have taken up more time for discussion than obviously more important matters. Reporting on the proceedings of the 1971 General Chapter, an article in *Each for All* noted that the writers had 'dreaded the length of time expected to be required to deal with the habit, but having decided it was too cold, we polished the subject off quickly'.[14] There was a clearly expressed desire to retain a habit which was Dominican in form and this desire governed the changes that were made.[15] The first, at Easter 1966 was to an unstarched wimple, cap and forehead band; a year later the sisters began wearing the wimple under the scapular so that it appeared as a roll collar.

The Special General Chapter allowed for this habit, with narrower sleeves, or for a combination of pinafore and blouse with a scapular worn over the top. Although this may not have been the most elegant arrangement it was practical and allowed for more frequent changing without having to launder the whole habit. Utility was a key issue; this was the era of new, synthetic drip-dry fabrics and a letter from the Bursar General, Sister M. Hugh Shayler, advertized the availability of the new habit material, at 27 shillings a yard from the convent at Kelvedon. Since cutting out the pattern was no more trouble to an expert seamstress such as Sister M. Gonsalvo Sutcliffe, than cutting the length from the bolt of cloth, the habits could be provided ready-made.[16]

Gradually hemlines went up and the cap and veil were worn further back on the forehead, showing the hair. There was still some emphasis on uniformity in terms of the cut and manner of wearing the veil but it was pointed out that even the traditional habit had left scope for individual difference and, as one sister expressed it, 'We can either be comfortable, or all the same, but not both.'[17] The wearing of secular dress on appropriate occasions was conceded and from the mid 1970s sisters were granted permission to wear it for a number of reasons, particularly when on holiday or when, as became increasingly common, sisters were working in individual apostolates outside the Catholic sector. Though the sight of a sister in secular dress could, until quite recent years, send a frisson up the spine of another, there was often more tolerance than expected. The General Chapter of 1995, while wishing to leave the article relating to the religious habit in the Constitutions unchanged, accepted a recommendation that secular clothing be permitted. The need for sensitivity to others is acknowledged, both in respecting the choices individuals make, and in deciding appropriate occasions when the habit ought to be worn by all.[18]

At the beginning of the 1970s, while most houses continued to have one formal meal with reading or silence each day, ten years later communities had grown smaller and timetables more varied. Greater emphasis was placed on hospitality and guests were welcomed at table in the refectory, rather than the parlour. Self-service was introduced and the old refectory tables gave way to smaller dining tables, with conversation at meals becoming the norm. For the smaller communities, living in ordinary houses, the evening meal often became the only genuine recreation time the sisters could enjoy together and for this reason has acquired the quality of a family meal rather than a religious observance.

Since the Church was calling religious to engage more fully with the world, maintaining a strict separation from it was no longer an option. Simple and unaffected interaction with colleagues and others outside the convent were now required and there was a recognition that mature women did not need all the props and safeguards that had formerly been imposed. A companion was no longer required when going out, nor a blessing from the superior before setting off. When postulants had 'left the world' in the past, they were resigned to minimal contact with their families, especially if they lived at a distance. Often the sacrifice was felt more keenly by the family than the candidate and in the years since the Second Vatican Council there has been a renewed emphasis on family obligations. Parents and relatives had often been accepted into the nursing homes run by the congregation in the past, but by the 1970s it was also realized that it was often easier for the congregation to make a sister available to care for a sick or aged parent than it was for a sibling, with a secure job and family responsibilities, to do so. Several sisters have been able to assist parents and relatives in this way, sometimes for prolonged periods.

Sisters who remember the annual community retreats of the 1950s highlight two advantages which these occasions brought to their busy lives: the slower pace of life and the luxury of sleeping in as late as 6a.m.! Providing the sisters with the opportunity for rest and refreshment; physical, emotional and spiritual, became increasingly necessary as numbers declined and workloads increased. At the 1965 General Chapter each sister was accorded two weeks' annual holiday, excluding travel time. Two years later delegates at the Special General Chapter first proposed allowing sisters to return to their families, or to take holidays away from their own convents. Groups of sisters enjoyed holidays together, many of which are remembered as having been extremely enjoyable.

In more recent years sisters have arranged their own holidays, whether at another convent, or with their families or friends, and each has a budget for the purpose. St Mary's Home at Stone purchased a holiday house in Llandudno in North Wales in 2001, suitable for those residents who still have reasonable mobility. The house is also made available to the congregation, and relaxed – or sometimes quite eventful – seaside holidays have been greatly enjoyed by senior sisters. The advantages of hobbies, particularly those of a creative nature, far from being discouraged as in the past, were also allowed to flourish and sisters developed their artistic and other skills or joined local historical and other societies.

Other aspects of regular observance were also evaluated. Adapting the traditional chapter of faults proved difficult, as neither the penitential services, nor the more introspective review of community life given a trial by some communities, seemed to fit. The current constitutions require the local communities to assess their community lives, in meetings structured on simple lines. Public penances also disappeared, being judged out of step with the modern mindset. Though the obligation for personal asceticism continued to be stressed, it was realized that such rituals could be more of a distraction to prayer in choir than a benefit. Perhaps of all the elements of regular observance that which was most valued, and has proved most difficult to preserve in the sisters' current living situations is silence. Nevertheless, a prayerful atmosphere is often noticed by visitors, as Sister Angela Mary Leydon reminded those gathered at the 2007 General Chapter, 'It is sometimes surprising to us that others feel in our houses a peace of which we ourselves are not conscious.'[19]

Study: essential to the work of the Order

All Dominicans share the obligation to engage in the assiduous study of sacred truth. Until the years immediately preceding the Second Vatican Council, this was generally interpreted by the leadership of the English Congregation as providing adequate professional training to equip its members for the apostolic tasks to which they would be assigned. Mother M. Ansgar Sheldon was keen that there should be scope for increasing professional awareness and sisters attended courses on human psychology at the Cenacle Convent in Hampstead, the annual conferences of the Convent School Association, seminars on contemporary difficulties in the teaching of religion, and even the Catholic Press Exhibition.

At the General Chapter of 1965, study was reaffirmed for its own sake as a constitutive element of Dominican life. The sisters were exhorted to study the documents of the Second Vatican Council, particularly those concerned with the renewal of religious life, and encouragement was given to wider theological reading. Sisters began undertaking courses of all kinds, many of which were geared towards their own intellectual and theological development. From the start there was a sense of excitement and innovation in the choices made. In 1965, at the same time that Sister M. Nicolas Loeb set off for Regina Mundi in Rome, Sister M. Ebba [later Joyce Mary] Webb enrolled at the newly opened Corpus Christi College in Bayswater to specialize in catechetics.[20] The college had been set up by Cardinal Heenan the previous year as a means of propagating the teachings of the Second Vatican Council by offering priests, religious and lay people the opportunity to study scripture, theology and catechetics. Hubert Richards, a priest of the Westminster Archdiocese – who as a boy had delivered meat to the Dominican convent from his father's butcher shop further up Portobello Road – was appointed principal, and the students benefited from visiting lecturers who were luminaries of the time such as Gregory Baum, Donald Nicholl and the Dominicans Herbert McCabe, and Edward Schillebeeckx.[21]

When, some years later, it was decided to send a sister for formal theological education, Sister M. Cecily Boulding enrolled at Heythrop College which had just moved up from Oxfordshire and been incorporated as a college of the University of London. After obtaining her BD in 1974 she went on to receive a doctorate from the University of Durham and enjoyed a distinguished career as an academic theologian. By the time Mother M. Rupert Fitzpatrick submitted the report of her administration to the General Chapter of 1983, she could rejoice that three sisters had been awarded Ph.D.s, three Master's degrees, one qualified as a State Registered Nurse, three attended one-year courses in theology and nineteen followed three-month courses at Hawkstone Hall during the preceding six years. It was not only the younger members of the congregation who undertook formal study; Sister M. Matthew Morgan defended her doctoral thesis on the nineteenth-century German author Annette von Droste-Hülshoff in October 1978 at the age of sixty-six. Reflective holidays with a light study programme specially tailored to their needs were also offered to more senior sisters.[22]

Although a Study Commission had been set up in the 1970s and met on an ad hoc basis, the 1983 General Chapter called for the establishment of a more formal group, to which three sisters were appointed. In late October that year sisters from seven of the convents, as well as several Dominican Sisters of the Bushey congregation, met at Spode House to participate in a *Learn to Study* course; the first of a series of study weeks organized by the Commission. A travelling 'circus' also began the rounds of the houses with Sisters Patricia Mary England and Catherine Marie [M. Robert] Keighley leading an in-depth study of the week's liturgy which included meditation and study of the scripture readings.

The Commission decided against a set programme of studies as the needs of the local houses differed considerably, but encouraged communities to take up topics of their own. Reporting to the General Council a year after the Commission's establishment, Sister M. Ninian Averill noted the efforts that had been made at local level, the only real obstacle being the uncertainty on the part of some sisters of the value of their personal contributions.[23] Generating ideas to maintain momentum, quite apart from finding the time to do so, is always a challenge. At the 1995 General Chapter the Study Commission gave way to a Congregational Promoter of Studies. In more recent years the General Council has assumed this role and study days have been organized on a broad range of topics: vocation, ethics, justice and peace, Dominican history, understanding Islam, enculturation, ecclesiology and understanding dementia.[24] At a local level there is a greater willingness for sisters to share their knowledge and insights with others on a one-to-one basis, and at Stone small groups have met to read and discuss documents from the Master of the Order or the latest papal encyclical.

A generous study fund has long been maintained by the congregation and a considerable number of sisters have benefited from it, undertaking courses in religious renewal or diplomas in theology. One of the most appreciated courses was that provided by the *Casa di Studi* which had been established in Rome by the Oakford Dominicans from South Africa. Dominican Sisters, mainly from the English-speaking world, came for a year's study of Dominican history and spirituality. Here they benefited not only from the chance to deepen their knowledge of the writings of St Catherine of Siena or the German mystics, but also to visit places associated with the history of the Order and to make friendships, many of which have endured, with other Dominican Sisters from across the globe. Sisters who lived in the community at Ealing were very appreciative of the courses offered at the Benedictine Study and Arts Centre at the neighbouring St Benedict's Abbey, and missed its facilities when they moved to other houses. A number of sisters have also attended conferences organized regularly by such groups as the Dominican Sisters of northern France, ESPACES (the European Dominican Institute for Spirituality) and by Dominican Sisters International (DSI).

In the area of study, one member of the congregation made history by becoming the first Dominican Sister to gain the Licentiate in Sacred Theology, the traditional qualification for teaching in a Dominican house of studies. It all started off innocently enough when Sister M. Justin Lane was asked to assist Father Simon Tugwell with some Latin translation work. Feeling in need of a refresher course to better prepare herself for the task she was granted a year at Blackfriars, Oxford, and began studying for a diploma in theology. But she enjoyed the first year so much that she asked for an extension, then another and was soon following the STL programme.[25] The experience of studying for six years in the male Dominican environment at Blackfriars was not only a great joy for her, but something of a revelation. Sister M. Justin was taken somewhat by surprise to realize for the first time in her religious life, she was being listened to, as a woman. In August 2010, Sister Ann Catherine Swailes became the second English Dominican Sister to obtain the Licentiate, graduating *summa cum laude*.

Of all the elements of regular observance, study is perhaps the one which has undergone the most profound change. Its value is not judged in terms of mere utility, but in its ability to develop the individual and enhance the mission of the congregation; it has been integrated successfully into the sisters' Dominican life. On an informal level, many of the sisters are prodigious readers, willing to discuss their reading matter and to encourage others to do so. The fact that several sisters who were already well qualified for their particular apostolate have been prepared to study for further academic qualifications, in areas as diverse as medical ethics and spirituality, is another indication of the seriousness with which the call to study has been heeded.

Conclusion

Until the early 1960s a small book of regulations for the noviciate was in use. Its quaint phraseology reminded the novices that they must put up with the devotional pictures hung on the wall as 'the piety supplied shall not be changed'. The young women entering the congregation in the years before the Second Vatican Council found such directives amusing and had difficulty internalizing many of the minor customs and observances then in vogue. Since they were not internalized, many of these practices lost their meaning and, having been discarded, were not missed. On the other hand some elements of religious observance were appreciated. One that is mentioned frequently is the practice of reading at table in the refectory; the mind as well as the body being fed during the course of the meal. Some elements of regular observance were not rejected, but became increasingly difficult or impossible to carry out as communities grew smaller.

Writing to the sisters early in 2010, the Prioress General, Sister M. Pauline Bürling, observed: 'It hasn't been popular to talk about regular observance in recent years, but it is essential for any form of religious life. It seems that today's enquirers are looking for these aspects of our life which make us different.'[26] There has certainly been a revival of interest in the traditional observances of the Order amongst the younger brethren of the English Province, just as there was amongst those sisters who entered the joint Dominican noviciate at Oxford and Boxmoor, which will be mentioned later. The genius of St Dominic was that he was able to adapt the traditional patterns of religious life as they were understood in his time, and create something new that would make the apostolate of preaching more effective.

Though many of the formal structures of regular observance have disappeared from the life of the English Congregation, the essential pillars of Dominican life remain. Fifty years after the process of renewal began, the sisters of the English Dominican Congregation are still zealous in their celebration of the liturgy, more assiduous in study than perhaps they have ever been, and still committed to the wholesome traditions of the Order.

Notes

1. Stone, G100(e), Mother M. Ansgar Sheldon, Circular letter, 26 March 1956.
2. Stone, G2000/64, *Register of the Prioress General, 1959–1965*, p. 88.
3. Stone, G100(g), Mother M. Silvester Brennan, Newsletter, 12 November 1967.
4 *Each for All*, vol. 1, no. 6, July 1969.
5. Ibid., no. 7, Christmas 1969.
6. Ibid., no. 16, Summer 1973.
7. Stone, G100(h), Mother M. Rupert Fitzpatrick, Circular Letter, 2 July 1980.
8. Stone, G98a(iii), *General Chapter 2001, Report of the Administration of the Prioress General, 1995–2001*, p. 5.
9. *Each for All*, no. 29, January 1978, p. 10.
10. *Rule and Constitutions*, 2009, article 41, p. 27.
11. *Coutumier des Dominicaines du Tiers-Ordre régulier*, 1890. Prologue, p. 3.'Bien que plusieurs points paraissent, au premier aspect, léger et de peu d'importance, il faut faire cas de toutes les petites observances, de peur que, si nous venions ... à mépriser les petites choses, nous ne tombions peu à peu.'
12. Curran, *Grace before Meals*, provides an excellent comparative analysis of the Dominican and Ignatian approaches to penances.
13. Stone, G100(e), Mother M Ansgar Sheldon, Circular letter, 3 August 1953.
14. Report by Sisters M. Ephrem Bottomley and M. Edward House on the General Chapter, in *Each for all*, no. 12, October 1971, p. 15.
15. Stone, G98a(iii), *Proceedings of the General Chapter, 5–16 August 1971.*
16. G100(g), Sister M. Hugh Shayler, Circular Letter, 24 April 1969.
17. G98a(iii), *Proceedings of the General Chapter, 11–20 August 1977, Minutes.*
18. G98a(iii), *Proceedings of the General Chapter, 2–8 August 1995.*
19. Stone, G98a(iii), *General Chapter 2007, Report of the administration of the Prioress General, 2001–2007*, p. 4.
20. Stone, G100(g), Sister M. Silvester Brennan, Circular letter, August 1965.
21. Cf. obituary notice for Hubert Richards, *Catholic Herald*, 16 April 2010, p. 12. Despite its popularity, Corpus Christi was considered a controversial establishment by many and it was closed in 1972. Hubert Richards, and a number of the other clerics on the staff leaving the priesthood at the time.
22. Stone, G98a(iii), *Proceedings of the General Chapter, 1–10 August 1983, Report of the Prioress General.*
23. Stone, G100(i), *Report from the Study Commission*, August 1984.
24. Stone, G98a(iii), *General Chapter 2007, Report of the administration of the Prioress General, 2001–2007*, p. 2.
25. Stone, G100(i), Sister M. Edward House, Circular letter, 11 January 1984.
26. Stone, Generalate current files, Sister M. Pauline Bürling, Circular letter, 24 February 2010.

Chapter Nine

The work of one is the work of all: a changing mission

The work of the one, or of the small group, is a shared work; there must be from the house of assignation support of prayer and of interest ... it needs to be reaffirmed until we all believe it in our hearts: 'The work of one is the work of all.

Sister M. Edward [Anna Mary] House, OP[1]

Introduction

Until the mid 1960s an English Dominican Sister could expect to spend her active life working in institutions owned and operated by the congregation, or in Catholic primary schools within reasonable distance of her convent. Along with the living of the religious life, these works were seen as part of the raison d'être of the congregation. Every effort was made to maintain the congregation's works and increasing care was taken in preparing sisters to take their place working in them. Provided labourers came to help with the harvest, there was no reason to expect this would change.

There was nothing particularly revolutionary about making a missionary foundation. However, when the sisters went to Norway in 1953, it was not to staff an institution or undertake a particular work, they went quite simply 'on mission'. This was indeed a completely new departure for the congregation and eased the way towards a new understanding of apostolic involvement. Although there would still be homes and schools owned by the congregation, they would no longer be 'our works' but constitute part of something much larger, 'our mission'.

A new kind of mission: Norway

It was a truth universally acknowledged by British Catholics in the 1950s that 'going on the missions' meant heading for Africa or Asia where countless millions of 'pagans' awaited the light of the Gospel and the saving waters of baptism. Not for the English Dominican Sisters; they headed instead for the Arctic Circle, to a land which already boasted a Christian tradition stretching back a thousand years. Perhaps the first faint glimmer of this new venture came at Easter 1946, when Mother M. Emmanuel Fuller mentioned in a circular letter that she had been asked whether the congregation would join an association of prayer for obtaining Norwegian vocations to help evangelize the country. In those days before ecumenism the fact that Norway was, and remains, a predominantly Lutheran country did not lessen the sense of urgency. The salient fact was that Catholics constituted considerably less than one per cent of the population at the time, and the Prioress General reminded the sisters of the missionary zeal the Dominican St Hyacinth had shown for northern Europe. In her polished style Mother M. Emmanuel informed the sisters 'it becomes us to assent'.[2]

Soon after her election to office it was Mother M. Ansgar Sheldon who received an invitation from the Prefect Apostolic of Northern Norway to make a foundation at Bodø. Bishop Johannes Wember was a member of the Missionaries of the Holy Family who had been entrusted with the Prefecture, and although he was German he had won the admiration of the Norwegians during the war on account of his opposition to the Nazi occupation. He was quite determined to have English sisters, convinced of the affinity of the national temperaments, and because so many Norwegians spoke English. On 21 April 1953, the Prioress General, accompanied by Sister M. Aelred Quinn, set out on a tour of investigation. She was impressed by the possibilities the town offered and by the resident priest, Father Theodor Rusche. Mother M. Ansgar was utterly captivated by the beauty of the landscape which, in her words, 'cried out for sanctification and Angelus bells'![3] On her return to England, she applied to the Sacred Congregation of Propaganda for permission to make the foundation and this was received on 11 August. A call went out for volunteers and was answered by eighty-six sisters.

How receptive would the citizens of Bodø be to Angelus bells? Despite its nominally Lutheran status, Norway was a much more secular state than Britain at the time. Although Norwegians were presented with positive images of their Catholic past in the historical novels of the Nobel Prize winner Sigrid Undset, a deep-rooted suspicion of Catholicism still lingered in the national consciousness. Perhaps because seafarers with a long history of distant contacts are more outward looking, there was greater openness amongst the people of the far north. Religious sisters were not unknown, for since the 1860s the German Sisters of St Elizabeth and the French Sisters of St Joseph of Chambéry had set up a network of highly regarded hospitals, and also a number of schools, in the major centres of population.[4]

Although British troops had constructed an airfield in Bodø at the beginning of the Second World War, the town was almost completely destroyed in a German Luftwaffe attack in May 1940. The process of reconstruction was well underway when the sisters arrived, so it might be said they 'grew up' with the town. Although the airport opened for civilian flights the year the sisters arrived, the railway was not extended to Bodø until December 1962. Traditionally a fishing port, the town also developed as a major Norwegian military base and seat of the Joint Operational Command of the Norwegian armed forces. As the Cold War intensified, and the fear of an attack over the northern flank grew, the town's strategic position resulted in the establishment of a NATO base which soon became the major employer in Bodø.

Selecting the members of the new community was a delicate task since they would be few in number, far from home and thrown entirely on their own resources. It was important that the group should be cohesive, with no individual member dominating too much. Time would prove what a wise choice was made when the names were announced: Sisters M. Magdalen Curley, M. Adrian Vincent, M. Alberta Barry and M. Carmel Daly. Travelling in two groups, one accompanied by Mother M. Ansgar and the other by Mother M. Emmanuel, the sisters sailed from Newcastle-upon-Tyne to Bergen and then took the costal steamer north. They arrived in Bodø at the end of May, to the blaze of press photographers' lights. A sizeable wooden building, which had served as a tuberculosis sanatorium before the war, was divided up into three units: the chapel dedicated to St Eystein, the presbytery and the convent. The Jensen and Siversten families, counting fourteen souls in all, were the only parishioners. On 8 September the formal blessing of the new convent, the St Sunnivahhjemmet, took place.

Staggering as it may seem, the pioneers arrived without a word of Norwegian between them and although they began informal lessons with Father Rusche it was some time before they acquired any degree of fluency. Sister M. Magdalen remembered the horrified look of the greengrocer when instead of asking for leeks she asked for a corpse! It was during these shopping expeditions and the daily visit to the dairy – there were no milk deliveries, except to the hospital – that the sisters made their first contacts with the locals. There were a number of cultural differences to which the sisters had to accustom themselves. A small hostel was opened, intended for students from outlying towns attending the secondary school, though in the first three years the residents were mainly older women working in the town. Not realizing that young women kept much later hours in Norway, Sister M. Magdalen spent many an anxious hour waiting up until she was convinced that their own mothers would not be so disapproving.[5]

The Norwegian venture was a new type of community for the English Dominicans and the members themselves were responsible for its development. Their situation might, necessarily, be much less formal than that of the houses in Britain, yet nobody questioned that they were living the true Dominican life, even if there were only four of them. Sitting at the ends of the benches in the small chapel, they prayed the Divine Office, with sung Compline each evening. In summer they learned to cycle, in winter they travelled across the snow by *spark*, a kind of kickboard. Wherever they went in the early days, they were conscious of being observed. From the day of their arrival, tiny pairs of eyes could be seen gazing through the letter box, and soon a constant stream of small children had plucked up the courage to ring the doorbell and introduce themselves to their strange new neighbours.

These casual encounters were the origins of another work, the *Barnevennen*, literally translated, 'the children's friend'. For the children kept on coming every day, and in such numbers that it was difficult for the sisters to maintain their routine. It was soon decided that Wednesday afternoons would be the children's visiting time and every scrap of imagination and ingenuity was brought into play to entertain them. The entertainment and help were mutual, as the sisters were also able to acquire basic conversational skills from the children quite different, but perhaps more useful, from that of formal lessons.[6] But as winter drew in and the children arrived with multiple layers of clothing it became impossible, in the cramped quarters, to find space for both the children and their discarded garments. To mutual regret the experiment ended, but not without a promise that a nursery school, which was sorely needed since there was only one in the town, would be built.

The early years in Norway were not always easy with both Sisters M. Adrian and M. Alberta having to undergo surgery in the late

1950s. But the sisters adapted well to the midnight sun of June and the permanent dark of December, never losing their fascination at the sight of the Northern Lights 'which danced about like fine, filmy curtains of many colours'.[7] They also helped build up the tiny local Catholic community – two more Catholic families, the Nicolaysens and the Lillehaugs arrived towards the end of the 1950s – and in turn they received marvellous assistance from the friars of the French Province (the Prior of Oslo was a Norwegian convert) and the sisters of the Châtillon congregation who also had a convent in Oslo. The simple insertion of the English sisters into the local community was a prototype of the lifestyle they, and many other congregations, would adopt in later years. The sisters did not engage in proselytism nor did they enter into debate, but their simple, everyday lives of committed service preached eloquently.

Meanwhile at home in Britain, fundraising events, with Norwegian singing and dancing a marked feature, were held regularly in London and Newcastle. At the end of 1958, when sufficient funds were available, the foundations of a building which would house the *Barnevennen* and a youth club were laid. The work took some time and it was not until 29 February 1960 that forty of the 'dearest little Vikings you ever saw' arrived in the new building, which had been equipped with a generous grant from the Town Council.[8] A little more than two years later Sister M. Priska Affolter, who was Swiss and very quickly acquired fluency in Norwegian, was assigned to Bodø. After several months she left for Oslo where she lived with the Châtillon Dominicans while following a course at the College for Nursery Teachers. After graduating with state recognition in March 1965 Sister M. Priska returned to take up duties as director of the *Barnevennen* until her departure in 1972. The *Barnevennen* continued to operate until 1980, by which time there was better provision for pre-school children in Bodø. Subsequently it was leased by the Audiology Department of the local hospital and used as a kindergarten for children with hearing and speech impairments, eventually serving the entire province of Nordland.

Sister M. Carmel was instrumental in detecting another need of the local community, a youth club. This opened in the autumn of 1960 and became so popular that three distinct age groups had to be formed. Children as young as seven and youths up to twenty years of age attended the sessions which included dancing, acting in Norwegian and English, musical groups – including a dance orchestra and a 'pop' band for the older members – carpentry, singing and even classes in Latin, which was not taught at the local

Fig. 20 Blessing of the *Barnevennen* at Bodø, 1960.

High School but was still required for admission to medical faculties. As Sister M. Magdalen's English-language students continued to increase, afternoon socials were organized for them on a regular basis. By 1967 when the Catholic pictorial *Word* contained a feature on the community at Bodø, the activities included judo – with Sister M. Carmel pictured stretched out on the mat, in a pose not unlike that of the Venus de Milo, judging a bout – and ballet lessons. These ballet lessons were taught by Sister M. Ruth Earley, who had been a ballerina before her entry into the congregation, from the time she arrived in Bodø, until her return to England in 1977.[9]

The sisters had integrated themselves thoroughly into the life of the local community and had shown a willingness to respond to local needs. When the town hospital was destroyed by fire in 1968, the community offered the Youth Centre above the *Barnevennen* and within hours it was set up as the maternity ward with its own doorbell and telephone. Mothers and babies stayed in the makeshift accommodation for seven months. The ballet classes begun by Sister M. Ruth expanded beyond all expectation and twice a year ambitious productions, with up to two hundred participants, were staged in the town hall; the elaborate wardrobe being prepared by Sister M. Magdalen. It was not altogether surprising that in 1971 the Town Council awarded the community the annual Cultural Prize of 4000 kroner in recognition of the enormous contribution they had made to the town. It was clear that the sisters were considered an integral part of the local community.

Maintaining 'our' works

At home, with the exception of the parish schools, the work of the congregation developed almost exclusively within the context of its own institutions. As the rapid pace of change in education accelerated, the preoccupation of the School Council of the congregation was how to make best use of the small number of teaching sisters to ensure a truly Dominican education in its schools. As the number of sisters decreased there was constant movement between the schools which probably worked against this aim; on one occasion St Rose's Convent School at Stroud had three headmistresses in less than three years.[10]

Certainly there were some who felt ill-prepared for the roles they were expected to fill. One sister, who was a former pupil of St Dominic's at Harrow, had completed her degree in English and Philosophy at Keele, where she was one of the first intake of students, before entering the noviciate at Stroud. After profession of vows, she taught at St Rose's for two years before being transferred to Erdington for a year, and then back to Stroud, where she taught a whole range of subjects from General Science to Latin as needs required. When asked by Mother M. Bonaventure Burke to take over as head at Stroud, at the age of twenty-eight, with no teaching qualification and barely three years' experience she could not help expressing her opinion: 'But that's ridiculous!' But not impossible! She made her *venia* and, by virtue of holy obedience, took up the post.[11] The experience was not atypical.

By contrast there were some sisters who remained for many years in particular schools and became very much identified with them. At Stoke-on-Trent, Sister M. Winifred Lambe was headmistress from 1928 until 1953 and led St Dominic's High School through a period of enormous development. She continued for many years as a governor of the school and was held in high esteem by the Local Education Authority. Sister M. Laurence Mitchener, who had already had charge of the junior school at St Dominic's for many years, was headmistress from 1957 until her death in 1970. Sister M. Aemilia Daly was another dedicated and gifted educator, always calm and elegant, who spent fifteen years as head of St Agnes' School at Erdington and almost as long at St Dominic's, Harrow, where she kept up morale and academic standards during the final years before the Sixth Form College was established. The longest tenure as headmistress was that of Sister M. Mark Bullough at St Dominic's Priory School at Stone. She was appointed head of what was a tiny school in 1939 and presided over its expansion for forty-seven years, by which time there were over 500 pupils and it was difficult to believe she would ever retire! During twenty-five of those years, Sister M. David Burton was in charge of the junior department at the school and continued there for a further five years after Sister M. Mark retired. In the parish schools, Sister M. Anselm Howard's name was almost synonymous with the Priory School at St Marychurch, while Sister M. Oliver O'Connor spent almost twenty years in charge of St Dominic's at Stone, overseeing the planning and building of the new school.

During the 1950s the schools at Bridlington and Harpenden both attained Voluntary Aided status as primary schools, though in 1962 the Dominicans withdrew from Bridlington and handed the convent over to the Sisters of Mercy from Hull. There was a reorganization of the schools in the Torquay area and for a time the vacated buildings of St Catherine's High School housed the newly established St Cuthbert Mayne Secondary Modern School until their new buildings were ready, after which the parish school moved in. New parish primary school buildings were in prospect at Hawick, Stroud and Byker, and elsewhere a litany of building works, curriculum development and experimental ventures went on apace. Innovative work was done at St Thomas' School in Stone-on-Trent in the 1960s and a film company from the USA produced a documentary on the teaching of phonics in the infant department there. But as the older sisters retired, fewer and fewer parish schools could count a Dominican Sister on their staff.

St Agnes' School in Erdington was granted Voluntary Aided Grammar School status, to take effect in 1965. In order to build the new school for a projected role of 580 pupils the original convent, Norwood House, had to be vacated and demolished. Two adjacent houses in Silver Birch Road, with gardens backing onto the school site, were purchased and adapted as a convent. A chapel was built on, conservatory style, at the rear and one of the garages was converted into a laundry; when completed there was accommodation for up to fifteen sisters. At the same time, following a precedent already set at Harrow, the primary division of the school was closed.[12] In changing times, when there was a move towards more open application, the appointment of religious sisters to local authority schools was no longer a foregone conclusion. It was reported at the School Council in May 1965 that the appointment of a sister as first head of the new St Agnes' Grammar School had been made 'in the face of great opposition' by the representatives of several of the surrounding parishes.[13] At both primary and secondary levels sisters began to take posts in schools where Dominicans had not taught before, even in non-Catholic schools, and to teach on supply.

In 1957 the centenary of the convent at Stroud was celebrated by the opening of the new St Rose's Special School, which provided state of the art therapy rooms and extra classroom accommodation for the increasing numbers. The following year there was a further move into special education at Portobello Road where, after many proposals and various difficulties, St Ann's School was opened for twenty maladjusted girls. Despite the fact that many of the girls were severely disturbed, they responded well to the secure environment and soon the school was achieving excellent results, particularly in speech and music.[14] Both St Ann's and the special school at Stroud benefited from generous government funding provided through the Ministry of Education and at both places the work was extremely demanding. The decision to close St Ann's in 1972 was precipitated by the illness of Sister M. Aquin Bools who had managed the school since its foundation. Many of the children were greatly distressed by the prospect of moving elsewhere and the final months were anything but calm. Sister Joan Mary [formerly M. Olav] English, a first-class teacher with a particular interest in special needs, saw the school through its difficult final year.[15]

During Mother M. Ansgar's term of office there was a particular concern for the nursing apostolate, where it was felt developments had not kept up with those in education. Links with the Catholic Nurses' Guild, of which Sister M. Jordan Barbier had been a founding member before her entry into the congregation, were encouraged and she played a leading part in the annual conferences. It was still customary for priests, not usually as well informed on the specific issues but always ready to express decided opinions, to chair such meetings. In 1954 Sister M. Jordan took issue with the clerical chairmen over the question of membership, insisting on the importance of affiliation to other professional and international groups, which would be jeopardized if membership was open to unqualified nurses as he proposed. The fact that two bishops were also present at the meeting, and commented on the public disagreement to Mother M. Ansgar, shows once again how delicate the balance remained between the desire for modernity and traditional values such as docility.[16]

Fig. 21 Sister M. Aquin Bools with children at St Ann's School, Portobello Road, London, *c*.1960.

Another long-established work would be given up after almost a century with the closure of St Mary's Children's Home at St Marychurch in July 1963. Financial difficulties had been a significant factor as late as the mid 1950s as many of the children were privately funded. Although weekly payments were assessed and agreed, parents or others responsible often fell behind and arrears could easily mount to £100s per child. Gradually, the percentage funded by local authorities or the Plymouth Rescue Society increased. A brochure from this time states that the sisters 'endeavour to provide an atmosphere of security amid homely and cheerful surroundings'.[17] In her report to the Prioress General in 1962, when there were twenty-six children resident, Sister M. Bernadette Burnett made it clear that the Home Office inspectors were not so positive in their assessment. Although the devotion of the sisters was not called into question, the inspectors' report considered the alterations made to the children's accommodation fell far short of the Home Office norms. There was little likelihood that Local Authorities would be prepared to send children to the Home.

Sister M. Paula Torley, who was on the staff of the Home and loved the work, wrote to Mother M. Bonaventure in July. A Good Shepherd Sister had been staying in the guest house while undertaking a practice session in another local children's home as part of the Home Office Certificate in Child Care. Since the visitor had been so enthusiastic and considered the course well worthwhile, Sister M. Paula asked if she might be considered for professional training. Perhaps by this time a final decision on the future of the work had already been made by the General Council, for it is clear from sister's next letter that the request was denied. In August she wrote again making plain the difficulties under which she was working: fourteen sheets and nightdresses to launder every day without a wringer or drying cupboard; the difficulty of maintaining a spirit of prayer when on the go with the children from 6:30a.m. until 11p.m. and often up in the night. She begged for one willing sister who would be a tremendous help and ease the worry and strain.

> As I watch the rain falling into pail after pail on the verandah of the Home, I feel it is time to let you know how we are placed, so that perhaps you will be able to make a decision as to the future of the home, for we really cannot manage as we are doing much longer.[18]

The decision soon came; the impossibility of providing the staffing and other arrangements required by the Home Office made it inevitable that the home must close.

None of the congregation's apostolic works could have continued without the support of a large number of sisters who were neither teachers nor nurses. The contribution of those who had been lay sisters before the distinction was suppressed in 1965 has already been mentioned. Not only did their unstinting work transform the convents into real homes, but almost all of them are remembered as warm, affectionate and caring women, so often alert to their sisters' needs. Everyone was expected to take some share in the work of the house and this in itself fostered a sense of belonging. Perhaps nowhere is this more evident than in memories of sisters who were assigned to Portobello Road during the 1960s and 70s but studying elsewhere during term time. On returning to the convent at the weekend or for holidays they would gravitate towards the kitchen where Sister M. Camilla Flynn would find a job for them, sometimes directing half a dozen or more young sisters simultaneously in different tasks.

Many of those who had entered as choir sisters were also engaged in support and administrative roles, and there was ample scope for them to exercise their talents in a number of ways. Until the 1960s each convent had a vestarian responsible for the 'habit room', another in charge of the refectory, a sacristan and an infirmarian. There were sisters who excelled at all these tasks: Sister M. Josephine Birtles was amongst the many sisters who were expert seamstresses and ruled the habit room at Stone for many years; Sister M. Desmond Barrett was a most meticulous refectorian at Leicester for over twenty years; Sister M. Imelda Smith a diligent sacristan at Stoke-on-Trent who taught generations of altar boys to serve Mass; while Sister M. Oswald Williams carried out the duties of infirmarian not just with professional expertise, but with sound judgement and sensitivity. Other tasks which required specialist skills or aptitude, but which might well be carried out as 'extras', were those of chantress, librarian, archivist and guest mistress.

Administering a large household in the days when communities might number more than twenty-five sisters was no sinecure. Sister M. Eugene Beer is remembered as an efficient and dedicated bursar who, even during the London Blitz, would not let air raids interrupt her routine. When the bombs fell on Portobello Road and the sisters were forbidden to enter the convent buildings, she slipped in through the back and rescued all the account books! As communities became smaller, the task sometimes became more complex and standards of accountability more stringent. In a quiet and efficient manner Sister M. Bertrand Buckley was willing to undertake this work, for which not everyone feels a natural affinity, in several houses as the need arose. At Stone, where a considerable number of people are employed in the convent and infirmary, Sister M. Joanna Currie combines the task of bursar, purchasing officer and wages clerk.

'To be young was very heaven': St Catherine's Centre

The long deferred plans for establishing a house of studies had been revisited during the 1959 General Chapter. Three years later, perhaps recalling Father Bede Jarrett's original intentions for the amalgamated congregation, the conventual chapter at Harrow voted to propose the closure of St Dominic's School and its replacement by a Teachers' Training College. When the Prioress General, Mother M. Bonaventure Burke, approached the Catholic Education Council, she was advised that the required expansion of places was already underway at existing colleges. However, an alternative use for the site was suggested; a centre for the theological education of religious sisters in temporary vows. The suggestion was received favourably by the General Council and an approach was made to the women's section of the Council of Major Superiors, of which Mother M. Ansgar had been the first president, to promote the venture.

The Conference gave its support and during the summer of 1963 Mount Lodge at Harrow was completely refurbished for the purpose. A programme of studies embracing church history, doctrinal theology, liturgy, scripture and catechetics was drawn up with the assistance of Dominican Father Bonaventure Perquin, who would become first Director of Studies and carry the major teaching load in theology. Approaches were made to experts in these fields and over the next few years renowned scholars taught at the centre and shared their insights: Fathers Peter Simpson and Pierre Fédérlé of the White Fathers taught scripture, the Jesuits William Lawson and Frederick Copleston taught church history and philosophy respectively, and Sister Romain [Anne] De Sousberghe of the Society of Helpers of the Holy Souls, who was an acknowledged leader in the renewal of catechetics at the time, was also on the staff.[19] Father Gerard Meath, English provincial of the friars at the time, gave wholehearted support, and several of the brethren, including Fathers Aelred Squire, Paulinus Milner and Piers Linley, taught at the centre. Classes began on 11 October 1963, bringing together sixty-nine young sisters representing twenty-three religious congregations, English Dominicans amongst them.

Within a few years the St Catherine's Centre had outgrown Mount Lodge and the decision was made to adapt the Rosary Hostel building at Portobello Road. Classes began there in September 1966, with a second-year programme being introduced for more advanced students, which expanded the course into philosophy, religious sociology and critical analysis of current theological literature. Saturday refresher courses and programmes designed specifically for those involved in religious formation were also provided at the centre. By this time there were 285 sisters from over sixty congregations, including several contemplative communities, following the courses at St Catherine's and Portobello Road seethed with energy. Since some of the young sisters came from a considerable distance, a new building, named Siena House, was built in the grounds and offered residential accommodation as well as additional lecture space.

The experience of mixing with sisters from other congregations was considered mutually enriching and undoubtedly encouraged greater cooperation in the future. Though most of the sisters were from Britain and Ireland, there was an increasing number from Asia and Africa, as well as several from Latin America. In 1968 the chapel at Portobello Road, so accustomed to the Gregorian tones, would echo with the visceral strains of the Congolese *Missa Luba* sung perhaps for the first time in England by a choir of White Father students and sisters. The colourful nature of the Notting Hill area at the time, with its markets, large numbers of immigrants and 'alternative' people, as well as its share of social problems, must have added to the vitality of the experience for the student sisters.

The Dominican Sisters are remembered as making the student sisters 'feel cared for, loved and welcomed'.[20] Nobody contributed more to this sense of wellbeing, perhaps, than Sister M. Conleth Lawless who acted as a kind of administrator, catering and estates manager rolled into one. It is true to say that all the sisters in the Portobello Road community thrived on the presence of the young students. There was also enormous generosity extended by the Dominicans to missionary congregations by offering reduced fees for sisters from developing countries, even though the centre did not always cover its costs.[21] A sister of another congregation who was on the staff of the centre remembers not only the generosity of the Dominicans, but the sense of freedom they exuded – something they were perhaps not so aware of themselves.[22] Father Bonaventure Perquin continued his close involvement with the centre until his sudden death in 1970. By this time Sister M. Nicola Loeb had already taken over as director of the centre and was followed in this role by Sister Patricia Mary England from 1972 until 1975. During the 1970s numbers at St Catherine's declined and before the convent in Portobello Road closed in 1976, the centre moved to St Wilfrid's Convent in Chelsea and Dominican involvement ended.

For over 1,000 young women, the centre offered not only a first-class grounding in theology, but a sense of being part of the movement towards renewal in the Church. Although, to suit students of mixed ability and different backgrounds, emphasis was more on the learning experience than academic achievement, the young sisters were encouraged to develop their critical and speculative faculties. Many of these women would not remain in religious life, but the spiritual and human development so many experienced at St Catherine's Centre was excellent preparation for the future. Through the agency of the centre, the English Dominican Congregation, though now much reduced numerically, did fulfil

Father Bede Jarrett's aspiration that the amalgamated congregation should exert a greater influence for good.

More pioneering work

Towards the end of Mother M. Bonaventure Burke's term of office a new work was being planned at Shannon in County Clare, which like that in Norway, would involve the sisters in developing their own way of living and working. The congregation undertook the Irish foundation with the avowed intention of fostering vocations, but it was also in response to the request of the Shannon Development Committee, who wanted the sisters to manage a hostel for working women. The new international airport at Shannon had tax-free status and this attracted a large number of foreign businesses which set up factories in order to export without paying duties. The new town which grew up around the airport attracted workers, most of whom were returning after several years in England. The majority had grown up in rural areas of Ireland, not necessarily in the west, and were returning to a country quite different from the one they had left. There was a high degree of instability in the employment market as the modern purpose-built factories frequently changed hands. Although the town benefited from the most recent theories in urban planning, this in itself did not create the desired social cohesion amongst its new residents.

It was on 11 May 1965 that three sisters, with Sister M. Andrea Kuss as superior, moved into two adjoining terraced houses. Negotiations with the Development Committee regarding the proposed hostel were protracted and plans changed from a home for 240 workers to one for psychiatric patients in transition to working life. Eventually a group of ten to twelve residents shared a building next to the sisters' house, with a sister as warden. The women remained in the hostel until they were sufficiently restored in health to find employment in the factories, though the sisters often found themselves acting in a supportive role for some time after they had moved to independent living situations. From the start, proximity to the international airport made the community a house of hospitality in the tradition of Portobello Road.[23] There was a great deal of parish visiting, encouraging and befriending people, and helping those experiencing difficulty settling back into Irish life. The community worked out its own rhythm of life and lived on a slender budget. Although there were excellent educational facilities in Shannon, basic medical services were under resourced, and in 1970 Sister M. Sunniva Cummins, who had recently qualified, joined the community and undertook district nursing.[24]

Shannon was another example of pioneering work as the English Dominican Sisters took up work that well established Irish religious communities were not prepared to undertake. It became increasingly clear as time passed that the works needed to be sustained on a more professional basis, and there was also pressure from the Bishop of Killaloe for sisters to teach in the schools. With pressure on the works of the congregation elsewhere, there was no possibility of the Dominicans fulfilling either need. Since by this time other congregations in Ireland were beginning to diversify their works and were seeking new openings, the decision was taken to withdraw from Shannon. In September 1974 the house and works were handed over to the Sisters of Mercy from Ennis.[25]

In June 1970, Father Bruno Quail, a Dominican working in the West Indies, met with the General Council seeking their collaboration in establishing a Catholic secondary school at St David's, Belle-Vue, on the island of Grenada. He hoped to find four Dominican Sisters, not necessarily from the same congregation, but stressed he must have qualified teachers or the Grenadian authorities would not allow them into the country. After several years of negotiation, plans for developing St Rose's Convent School in Stroud into a comprehensive school were rejected by the Department of Education and Science, and the school was closed in July 1970. Sister M. Lucy Moran, who had been on the staff, was extremely keen to assist with the venture in Grenada and decided to forego the offer of a place to read English at the University of Hull in order to volunteer.[26]

Mother M. Silvester Brennan made it clear that the Grenadian venture would not be a foundation, but a mission undertaken for as long as it took to get the school up and running smoothly. Since no other teacher could be found to accompany Sister M. Lucy the call went out for volunteers and Sister Francis Margaret Connolly agreed to offer her financial acumen to school and parish, and to make herself useful in whatever way she could. In preparation for their departure the two prospective missionaries spent a week at the Overseas Services College at Farnham where most of the group were Anglican missionaries also en route to the island. Thanks to a chance visit made by Sister M. Nicola Loeb to the Caribbean Office, the sisters acquired an unexpected travelling companion who turned up in his carry cot at Heathrow! Russell was a five-month-old baby on his way to live with his grandmother in St David's and, as may well be imagined, he and his unlikely chaperones received a great deal of attention from the stewardesses.[27]

On their arrival the sisters were met not only by the Dominican friars but by the deputy Governor, Leo de Gale, who was the nephew of the late Sister M. Rose Belmar. Classes had already begun and as an experiment, the first-year intake had included many older children who had missed earlier opportunities for secondary education but gave proof of ability. Sister M. Lucy thought that the Grenadian education system had retained too many of the worst aspects of the English system: it was too academically focused, almost to the exclusion of art, craft or music, and placed too much emphasis on examinations. There were two volunteer teachers in the school, one a Canadian and the other a Peace Corps worker from the United States. Classes began early and ended, much to everyone's relief, at 12:45p.m. as sustained work in the excessive heat was impossible.

Living conditions were Spartan and supplies of water and electricity unpredictable but Sister M. Lucy fell in love with the people. Apart from teaching she gave sessions to primary school teachers, many of whom were unqualified and had to cope with large classes, undertook parish visiting, helped with the youth group and gave night classes to older folk. She was impressed at the obvious love the locals showed for the Dominican liturgy, Gilda St Pierre, the housekeeper at the presbytery, seemed to know the Mass chants of the *Graduale* from cover to cover.[28]

Sister Francis Margaret did not adapt so well. The rainy season was probably the worst time to arrive in a tropical climate and it proved not to suit her at all. Since the Dominicans were handing St David's over to the Kiltegan Fathers, who had recently been expelled from Nigeria as a consequence of the Biafran war, she struggled valiantly to put the parish accounts in order. Once this was accomplished it was clear Sister Francis Margaret would be unable to remain and she returned to England in November.

Sister M. Lucy remained alone in Grenada for another eighteen months, by which time the fast-expanding school had already gained government recognition. This was due in great measure to Sister M. Lucy's adaptability and the leadership she provided to her multicultural staff. Father Zedislaus Umlauf wrote to Mother M. Silvester saying how proud the brethren were of her magnificent achievement and what wonderful witness she had given.[29] On her return to England Sister M. Lucy spent a sabbatical year in Ireland before being elected prioress of Hawick and began studying for an Open University degree. Four years later she was assigned to Erdington and took up another teaching post at the Paget Comprehensive School in Pype Hayes, a school with a high level of low achievers. Here too Sister M. Lucy soon gained the admiration of staff and pupils alike though she was not to remain there long. On the morning of 29 October 1978, Sister M. Lucy was found dead in her bed, having suffered a coronary during the night; she was just forty-eight years old.

Interest in the mission at Belle-Vue, and hopes that a link with Grenada could be maintained, continued even after Sister M. Lucy's death. Following the political upheavals and the US invasion of Grenada in 1983, this desire had an unexpected fulfilment. The former presbytery housekeeper, Gilda St Pierre, who had so impressed Sister M. Lucy, wished to come to London to work with Caribbean families. Since the English Dominican Sisters could not go to Grenada, the General Council reckoned, Grenada could come to them. For more than twenty years the congregation has provided the financial support allowing this mission to the West Indian Catholic community in South London to be maintained.

'Our works' become 'our mission'

After the 1965 General Chapter there was a constant reassessment, not only of the institutional works carried out by the congregation, but how it should best employ its membership for the good of the Church and to make best use of the sisters' individual talents. That year also ushered in the first in a series of closures, none of them easy. For some time it had been felt that the boys in the preparatory school at St Leonards could be easily accommodated in other schools and it closed its doors in July.[30] In 1982 the congregation would withdraw from St Marychurch, and two years later from Erdington.

Although long-established works might cease, the congregation opened itself to a broader understanding of apostolic involvement. Many works were considered, though not all of them – such as participating in a mission to travelling people – were taken up. The deciding factor was how easily the work accorded with the perceived Dominican mission. This move away from corporate to individual apostolates was not viewed favourably by all and sometimes sisters were faced with such questions as; 'When are you coming back to teach for us?' But whether new works were taken up by individual sisters or small groups, sisters were still assigned to a particular community, to which they returned on a regular basis. The community also has an obligation to the individual sister, supporting her through prayer, genuine interest and encouragement.

In fact, individual apostolates were not unknown in the history of the congregation but they had been carried out within the convent. When she was newly professed, Sister M. Ansgar Sheldon's artistic gifts had been encouraged and put at the service of the community. At Stroud where she had been in charge of the boarders, a wooden board upon which Sister M. Ansgar had painted a guardian angel holding aloft a pennant with the child's name, soon hung above each of the forty beds in the dormitory.[31] As early as 1942 the General Council was convinced of the apostolic opportunities this gift might offer and commissioned a series of prints of the Joyful Mysteries of the rosary, a thousand large-format sets being printed by Adams & Shardlow of Leicester.[32] A room was set aside at Stroud and the 'Picture Apostolate' thrived with exhibitions on a regular basis up and down the country.

Some years after her term as Prioress General ended, Mother M. Ansgar spent a year in Montpellier and some months in Bodø before moving to Portobello Road where she set up her studio and once again devoted herself fulltime to the Picture Apostolate. In 1972, at the age of sixty-five, she was elected prioress of Bodø and in Norway her artistic spirit flourished, drawing on the beauty of the natural environment which attracted her so much. Mother M. Ansgar moved into new media, employing acrylic paints and working appliqué, she received commissions for wall hangings for Lutheran churches and for the public hospital in Bodø and exhibited widely. The studio was also a place of welcome where many visitors came, not only to enjoy the sister's art, but to enjoy her conversation and profit by her counsel.

During the 1971 General Chapter, considering the involvement in the universities which had characterized the Order almost since its foundation, it was decided that the congregation should be involved in tertiary education. Sister Joyce Mary Webb had been appointed to the staff at Corpus Christi College in London after completing her studies there and remained until the college was closed. In February 1974 she was offered a post as principal lecturer at Mary Ward College at Keyworth, near Nottingham. This college had been established by the Loreto Sisters as a teacher training college as recently as 1967, but it enjoyed only an ephemeral existence, closing its doors in 1977 after a government White Paper reorganized Higher Education provision. Sister Joyce Mary then taught at Derby College of Higher Education.

Sister M. Jadwiga Świątecka accepted a post as lecturer in English at Christ Church College, Canterbury, an Anglican College of Education, in September 1973. Since it was too far to commute from Portobello Road, the community to which she was assigned and to which she returned regularly, Sister M. Jadwiga had to find her own accommodation, which proved to be as ecumenical as her work place. The address was suitably monastic: Lower Flat, Temple, St Augustine's College, Monastery Street. St Augustine's prepared Anglican ordinands, but part of the building was leased to the newly established Franciscan Study Centre run by Friars Minor and Conventual Franciscans. It also housed a community of Redemptorists who were still looking for a house of their own. Sister M. Jadwiga was able to enjoy Divine Office and meals in common, concelebrated Mass each day and even Benediction once a week.

Having lived in at New Hall, Cambridge, three years previously while studying for her doctorate, Sister M. Jadwiga was no stranger to an academic or ecumenical environment. At Canterbury, apart from one lapsed convert, she was the only Catholic on the staff, though there were a considerable number amongst the students. To these she acted as a sort of 'unofficial chaplain', putting them in touch with the chaplaincy at the University of Kent. Sister M. Jadwiga found Christ Church a particularly congenial working environment and she remained there for nineteen years.

Sister M. Cecily Boulding became the first woman to join the staff at Ushaw College near Durham. The seminary had a long tradition, having begun its life at Douai in northern France in 1568 and made its home at Ushaw in 1808. In such a venerable male institution, not everyone was pleased at the prospect of having women on the staff. But seminary education was beginning to change considerably at the time, and Ushaw had become a licensed college of the University of Durham in 1968. Numbers were already falling and candidates were more likely to be older with some work experience. Not all had a traditional academic background and Sister M. Cecily found she had to spend time on teaching basic study skills as well as systematic theology. Two years after she began to teach at Ushaw, Sister M. Cecily was invited to teach at the Dominican Summer School at Providence College in Rhode Island. She certainly felt at home working with Dominicans and was amazed at the number and variety of congregations of Dominican women whom she encountered at Providence, their differing external appearance, life styles and authority structures.

Perhaps even more significant was Sister M. Cecily's appointment to the Anglican-Roman Catholic International Commission in May 1983. ARCIC's function is to identify points of common ground in their theological understanding in such areas as the doctrine of salvation, the nature of the Church, and justification by faith. The first meeting of this second phase of ARCIC discussions was held in Venice in August the same year and Sister M. Cecily was the only non-cleric on the Catholic team, the only other woman being one of the Anglican members. Both the women found themselves reflecting on more than one occasion that it was clear it had not occurred to the men that a point under consideration looked different from a woman's point of view. The exchanges were frank and good-natured and one might tell a future cardinal he was speaking absolute nonsense without his taking offence.[33]

When Sister M. Cecily retired from teaching at Ushaw in 1996 the president, Monsignor Richard Atherton, wrote to the Prioress General that 'her work at this seminary will never be forgotten, nor our gratitude to the Dominican Order for putting her at our disposal'.[34] Since leaving Ushaw, Sister M. Cecily has been involved in further ecumenical work, not only with the Anglican Communion, but with the Faith and Order Commission of the World Council of Churches and with the United Reformed Church as well. She has served on the Theological Commission of Dominican Sisters International, continues to contribute to theological journals, give conferences, undertakes translations and is currently congregational archivist.

Another member of the congregation also enjoyed a long and happy association with a seminary. Sister M. Mildred [formerly M. Denis] Haden taught in several of the congregation's schools, including periods as headmistress at Brewood and Bridlington, always specializing in speech and drama. In 1967 she was invited to give a course of lectures in public speaking to the seminarians at Oscott College in Birmingham and was eventually appointed to the staff. She remained in charge of speech training, preparing future preachers, until her retirement in 1985. Although she also taught Jesuit novices and was an examiner for the English Speaking Board, Sister M. Mildred felt more at home at Oscott than anywhere and kept up with past and present students until shortly before her death in 1996. She was the first English Dominican Sister who requested to be cremated, and her ashes were interred at Oscott.

After St Rose's Convent School at Stroud closed the last principal, Sister Catherine Marie Keighley, registered for a degree in theology at the University of Bristol. After graduating in 1973, Mother M. Silvester Brennan invited her to share her enhanced knowledge of scripture with the sisters by means of a correspondence course on the readings from the breviary. Some years later Professor Kenneth Grayston, who had taught Sister Catherine Marie at

Bristol, approached Dom Aelred Baker of Prinknash Abbey with a view to setting up an extra-mural centre at the abbey. Since Dom Aelred did not feel able to take up the work alone, it was suggested that Sister Catherine Marie collaborate with him. Although the links with the University of Bristol lasted only a few years, this was the origin of Focus, an eight-week scriptural course offered by correspondence or by weekly classes at Prinknash. As numbers grew, peaking at eighty for the correspondence course – including a number of members of the congregation – and sixty for the Saturday classes, Sister M. Wulstan Gallini offered her services as administrative assistant for a number of years. Focus continues to offer an opportunity for continuing education in the faith to an appreciative audience and has broadened its scope in recent years to include courses in church history. Weekend retreats have been organized at Prinknash for participants, as well as outings to the British Museum and the Ashmolean in Oxford which provide students with a background in the social and religious history of the Near East in biblical times.

A further venture into providing education in the faith for adults was begun by Sister M. Valery Walker soon after she was assigned to the community in Hinckley in 1978. She was anxious to promote an appreciation of the works of St Thomas Aquinas both within the Congregation and beyond and received her own introduction to the writings of the 'Angelic Doctor' from Father Romuald Horn who was resident at the Priory in Hinckley at the time. A study group was set up in the parish at Hinckley and another in Bodø when Sister M. Valery was assigned there in 1981. After returning to England regular study weekends have been held attracting as many as twenty participants from a broad range of ages and social backgrounds. The weekends, each centred on a specific topic, benefited from Father Romuald's participation for many years, though in more recent times another of the Dominican friars, Father Thomas Crean has been collaborating in the work with Sister M. Valery.

From teaching in higher education, involvement in university chaplaincy work was a natural step. Since the 1990s sisters of the congregation have been involved in this very Dominican work, joining chaplaincy teams at the University of Leicester, De Montfort University in the same city, the University and the College of Further Education in Cambridge, Keele University and King's College in London. The needs and approach differ from one institution to another but there is always an element of faith education, of listening and support.

For nearly twenty years Sister M. Ninian Averill lived in a flat attached to the Dominican university chaplaincy in George Square, Edinburgh. After graduating with a Master's in educational psychology she took a post as educational psychologist with the West Lothian Education Authority having responsibility for special needs children.[35] In her early years in Edinburgh she also offered her professional skills to the work of the Cyrenians, a group founded by the Dominican Father Antony Ross to assist the marginalized to help themselves. Later Sister M. Ninian was involved with the Association for Family Therapy and the Association of Clinical Psychologists until she retired. At that point she set up the Siena Learning Centre for young people with learning difficulties and soon had nearly twenty clients on the books.[36] This work continued until Sister M. Ninian was assigned to Stroud in 1998.

Though several sisters retired from individual apostolates, new works were taken up by others. Before entering the congregation, Sister M. Teresa Billington had qualified as a physiotherapist in Manchester. After her profession of vows she worked for some years in this capacity at St Rose's Special School at Stroud. A chance meeting with a consultant, who had been one of her examiners in Manchester, resulted in the offer of a place to study medicine at Bristol. Mother M. Rupert Fitzpatrick, who was nearing the end of her term as Prioress General at the time, spoke to the General Council enthusiastically of the plan, and they voted in favour. Sister M. Teresa graduated in 1988 and has been working for a number of years in general practice.

Retiring from the active apostolate, whether corporate or individual, carries with it the challenge of detachment. Most sisters, however, tend to involve themselves in some sort of work as long as they are physically able. When Sister M. Oliver O'Connor retired from St Dominic's Primary School in Stone, she spent twelve years as bursar of St Mary's Home, keeping on until shortly before her death. Sister M. Germaine Higgins also spent her last years working in the Home, visiting and praying with the residents and caring for the rock garden. Over recent years sisters have continued to give private or group lessons in languages, scripture, calligraphy, embroidery and a range of other subjects and to lead prayer and meditation groups even when they have passed ninety years of age! Others have helped in local charity shops and have continued the traditional apostolate of visiting the sick and elderly, often those considerably younger than themselves.

Communities working in new ways

In the late 1960s the community in Newcastle-upon-Tyne was caught up in the whole process of urban regeneration instigated by the City Council. Since the threat of demolition and relocation had arisen, the General Council debated the closure of the Newcastle convent more than once. In the end it was decided to close the nursing home in July 1967 and to concentrate on developing the school.[37] The cottage in the grounds, formerly used as a nurses' home, became a hostel for students from Fenham Hall College, though they later moved into part of the convent itself. Although the road plan which had required the compulsory purchase of the Newcastle convent was abandoned, plans for the new convent in Helmsley Road went on apace. A new parish school catering for St Dominic's and Holy Name parishes was built on the site, along with a purpose-built nursery school.

In Newcastle the working relations with the Dominican friars were particularly close, and although the collaboration was not tightly structured, there were weekly meetings over supper shared by the two communities. The housing around St Dominic's church and as far as Walker and Byker had been swept away. Many elderly parishioners now found themselves living at a distance, unable to make the journey of more than a mile uphill to the church which had been a central focus of their social lives. The layout of the new flats did not really encourage social interaction and resulted in a sense of isolation which often led to clinical depression. Four sisters joined the local St Vincent de Paul Society and took part in extensive parish visiting, organizing parties and sing-along sessions to combat this loneliness.[38]

Since the nearest church, St Patrick's, had been closed, many of the local Catholics had quite simply lapsed in the practice of their faith; so when the new convent opened its chapel, it served as an unofficial Mass centre for sixty to seventy local Catholics. The sisters also ran the parish bookstall on Saturday mornings, served on the Parish Council, assisted in conducting a parish census and at various times gave shelter to battered or distressed wives. For some months a chronic alcoholic was taken on as a handyman and had made considerable strides towards rehabilitation by the time he left.[39]

For almost twenty years, Newcastle-upon-Tyne also became the centre for Sister Angela Mary Leydon's apostolate with the deaf. While teaching in the parish primary school at Fenham, she was caught up in an initiative begun by the Catholic bishops to improve the provision of catechetical instruction for deaf and hearing impaired children. After working as a volunteer, Sister Angela Mary was appointed co-ordinator of the programme based at the Diocesan Centre for the Deaf. In preparation for this new role, Sister Angela Mary undertook a four-month course in Dublin under the acclaimed Irish Dominican teacher of the deaf, Sister M. Nicholas Griffey. She then enrolled at the University of Newcastle and followed a two-year course, gaining a qualification as a teacher of the deaf. Sister Angela Mary spent fifteen years as co-ordinator of the centre in Newcastle and during this time attended international conferences and followed yet another course, this time in catechetics for the hearing impaired, in the Netherlands.

The work was not exclusively that of religious education. Recent technological developments have opened up access to information for deaf and hearing impaired people, from which they were almost entirely cut off thirty or so years ago. They were also cut off from active participation in the liturgy and to remedy this Sister Angela Mary began signing, and instructing others to sign, during Mass. At a time when the emphasis was on integrating deaf and hearing impaired people, and the use of sign language was being discouraged in some quarters, she could see it offered some obvious advantages. Sister Angela Mary also introduced drama into her work and formed a very successful choir. This choir sang at the Royal Festival Hall in London in 1987, at a concert to celebrate the silver jubilee of CAFOD, the guest of honour being the Brazilian Archbishop and champion of the poor, Dom Helder Camara.[40] In 1993 Sister Angela Mary was elected prioress at Stone, and subsequently Prioress General; in recognition for the work she had undertaken in Newcastle she was granted a Golden Service award by the Northumbria Deaf Children's Association. Soon after her term of office as Prioress General ended in 2007, she began working in sacramental preparation for the deaf and hearing impaired in Leicester.

At Stoke the long discussed plans for the reorganization of secondary education in North Staffordshire had begun to take shape by the mid 1970s. There were several permutations to the plan, which involved two Catholic grammar and four secondary modern schools. Under one these plans, the St Dominic's site would become a Sixth Form College, while under another, two single sex schools would be retained, along with two mixed comprehensives. The Christian Brothers then decided to withdraw St Joseph's College, Trent Vale, from the planned reorganization and continue as an independent school. In effect, this meant the Dominican

Sisters would have to give up their own school: an enormous sacrifice after more than 120 years. The final plan was for three mixed comprehensive schools at Longton, Tunstall and Newcastle-under-Lyme.

At the time there were over 1,000 pupils at St Dominic's School under the headship of Sister M. Edward [Anna Mary] House; it was academically successful and had an excellent spirit. Yet in a truly remarkable manner Sister M. Henry Yeaman, who had been a child at the school and spent most of her teaching life on the staff, sat on the Diocesan Schools' Commission and was able to convince governors and parents to accept the proposed restructure which would provide the best possible future for Catholic education in Stoke. Along with other members of the Commission she participated in the long series of interviews which eventually assured a place in the new schools for each member of staff.

When the new schools began functioning in 1981, Sister M. Edward was appointed Principal at St John Fisher's in Newcastle-under-Lyme, remaining until her election as Prioress General two years later. Sister M. Henry went as deputy principal to St Thomas More's in Longton, just 100 yards from the site of The Foley where Mother Margaret's sisters had first lived in the Potteries.[41] Here she soon felt entirely at home, but in 1986 she was asked to take Sister M. Mark's place as headmistress at St Dominic's Priory School at Stone. Although she was already living at Stone by this time, and commuting by moped to Longton, it was a great wrench for Sister M. Henry to leave Stoke and bring to an end 139 years of Dominican educational endeavour in the city.[42]

As the 1970s progressed there were also significant changes to the apostolic involvement of the sisters at Bodø. When Sister M. Pauline Bürling arrived in Norway in 1974, it was with the understanding that she would find a job for herself. In order to gain fluency in Norwegian she spent eight months with the Châtillon Dominican Sisters in Oslo and also gained a Norwegian qualification in Special Education. In May 1976 Sister M. Pauline, who had qualified as a speech therapist in London, presented herself to the local Director of Education in Bodø and soon after was offered a post as educational psychologist. Any apprehension at working in a secular context was soon overcome by the kindness of her new colleagues. Sister M. Pauline worked as part of a multidisciplinary team which included educational psychologists, teachers of the deaf and social workers. This involved a great deal of travelling, with diagnostic work and counselling parents and teachers.[43]

Sister M. Sunniva Cummins arrived in Bodø in 1978 and began

nursing in the local hospital only two weeks later. Over the course of twenty-five years she was much appreciated in hospital and town for her dedication to duty and her generosity. One area which she felt did not get the attention it deserved in the hospital was the care of the terminally ill. In order to develop this work, Sister M. Sunniva attended a course at St Gemma's Hospice in Leeds and subsequently there was a complete change in attitude in the nursing of the terminally ill in Bodø. Both sisters were conscious of how much they benefited from the foundations laid by the first sisters in Bodø; because the Dominicans were so well known, they were accepted and appreciated at once.

On 12 September 1978 the community in Bodø celebrated the silver jubilee of the Norwegian foundation, though the event was tinged with sadness by news of the death of Father Theodor Rusche. By this time the sisters were also taking a much greater part in the pastoral work of the parish, which was divided into three districts. Sister M. Carmel Daly took responsibility for the Lofoten Islands, four hours away by boat; Sister M. Sunniva took the southern area of 300 square kilometres centred at Mo-i-Rana – where Father Rusche had taken up residence in retirement – and Sister M. Pauline took the town district. The pastoral visits to the isolated areas of the parish involved the sisters in intensive catechetical instruction and preparation for the sacraments, seeking out and visiting newly arrived Catholic families and doing a good deal of listening and counselling. Since virtually no catechetical material existed in Norwegian, translations had to be made from English or German.

Another important role, played in a remarkably unobtrusive way by Sister M. Sunniva, was caring for the priests and giving some of them the encouragement they needed to engage more effectively with the needs of the parishioners. Bodø was growing rapidly at the time and the small number of long-standing families was joined not only by Norwegian Catholics from other parts of the country but by migrant workers from the Philippines, Sri Lanka and other parts of the world. A new presbytery was built in 1979 and two years later the sisters moved into a new convent, built in such a way that it could later be divided into two separate dwellings. A further break with the past occurred when the old convent and chapel were demolished to make way for the new church, which was consecrated in 1982. By the end of the decade it was clear that collaborators in the work were needed.

Preaching peace, working for justice

Another dimension to the work and mind set of the sisters was an increasing interest in social justice. Mother M. Silvester Brennan first made explicit mention of this theme after attending the Conference of Major Superiors in 1976. She recommended reading *The Catholic Worker* and urged the sisters to become more attuned to the struggle between good and evil.[44] Mother M. Rupert Fitzpatrick developed this interest further. In 1979 she issued a list of questions, with a strong social justice slant, to be asked of prospective parliamentary candidates before the general election. Later the same year, she was asked by the Justice & Peace Commission of the Bishops' Conference to appoint a sister to be responsible for bringing justice and peace issues to the notice of the members of the congregation and various sisters have filled this role since that time.[45]

While Sister M. Edward House was Prioress General, her letters to the congregation brought before the membership a whole host of moral issues in this area and encouraged a prophetic stand. It was not lip service, as the increasing involvement with Pax Christi and the Campaign for Nuclear Disarmament (CND) demonstrated. A circular letter in March 1984 asked the prayers of the sisters for a forthcoming meeting between Christian CND and the chairman of the Conservative Party, John Gummer. The increasingly public profile of English Dominican Sisters in the peace movement did not meet with universal enthusiasm, for there was a broad spectrum of political opinion in the congregation as in any group – Sister M. Edward clearly felt there was a need to emphasize that she would be with the CND delegation![46] A year later she would head a CND delegation handing in a letter to the Secretary of State for Defence, calling for positive and decisive action to halt the arms race.[47]

Neither did the Prioress General baulk at participating in a demonstration on Ash Wednesday 1987 when a prayer service was held in the middle of Whitehall and peace slogans were daubed on the walls of the Ministry of Defence.[48] Sister Máire Colette Ludden, who took on the role as link person for Justice and Peace, graduated with an MA in Peace Studies from the University of Bradford in 1989. Her interest in justice and peace was not purely academic as she was arrested during a demonstration at Aldermaston that year. The incident gained Sister Máire Colette a criminal record, cost her four hours in court, but not the ten days in Holloway Prison she had been expecting. She considered her involvement as a means of preaching the Good News and was grateful for the support she received from her Prioress General and sisters.[49]

In Leicester the International Hotel had been converted into a holding centre for refugees and asylum seekers and Father Duncan Campbell of Holy Cross Priory invited Sister M. Esther Selo to accompany him on visits to the residents, offering what help and advice they could. She remains in touch with some of those she met at the time, and her work was noted by David Blunkett, at the time Home Secretary, during a parliamentary debate.[50] In 1995 a Bosnian Muslim woman had arrived in the country with her daughter and infant son, who was in need of heart surgery. Some weeks after the operation they were thrown out of the temporary accommodation which had been provided for them, and when a local radio station put out an appeal for someone to take them in, St Catherine's offered assistance. The mother wished to return to her husband in Bosnia and it was only after several visits to the Croatian and Bosnian embassies that visas were obtained, travel arrangements made, financial assistance given, and the family was eventually reunited.[51]

Many other projects have received support through the distribution of the Prioress General's alms. Over the years these included: the Catholic Association for Racial Justice, charities working with the homeless, appeals for refugees in Ethiopia and Sudan, helping fund a workshop for the mentally disabled, granting an interest-free loan to a struggling student, charities for the physically disabled. In recent years, through membership of Dominican Sisters International, support has also been given to the Rosary Project through which work is provided for destitute Palestinian women making rosaries for sale throughout the Catholic world. The congregation also pledged, as a matter of social justice, to make its underutilized premises available for use by others. Local Quakers met for many years, first in a parlour and later in the community room at St Dominic's in Stone, and from 1988 until 1995 the Movement for a Better World had its offices in the part of the convent now housing the generalate.[52]

Continuing institutional involvement

In more recent years several more convents have closed. When the old convent at Stoke was converted into sheltered housing, a small group of sisters moved first to a house on the other side of Hartshill Road, and later to Priory House adjacent to the church. For several years a valiant trio of Sisters M. Paula Torley, M. Cuthbert Pattison and M. Guala Mason, all of them retired, animated the parish. They busied themselves in visiting the needy, taking Communion to the sick, caring for the sacristy and were indefatigable in making all sorts of goods for fund raising sales. For many years Sister M. Paula had been sending Catholic literature and raising money and collecting clothing and other items to send to the needy of the Diocese of Baroda in India. This soon became a common cause for the community and for the parish as well. Despite delicate health she visited India twice, in 1985 and 1994, travelled in ox carts and talked with the villagers in mud huts. After Sister M. Paula's death in 1998, much to the regret of the parish, the remaining sisters left Stoke. The link with the parish has been re-established since Sister M. Sunniva Cummins' return from Norway in 2007, though a member of the Stone community, she works as Parish Sister at Stoke.

The last Dominican principal of St Dominic's Priory School at Stone retired in 1994, and although two sisters have taught in the school since, none is currently employed there. A Board of Governors had been set up in 1990, but the appointment of a lay head required drawing up new instruments of government and clarifying the relationship between the Governors and the congregation who, as Trustees, are responsible for the buildings and overall management of the school. As with many private schools, financial stability depends very much on the economic climate and the rise and fall of enrolments. The school is obliged to justify its charitable status by providing scholarships and bursaries and opening its buildings to local groups. Though there are some who would question the involvement of the congregation in private education, the school enjoys and enviable academic record and continues the tradition of education and pastoral care in the Dominican tradition to a largely non-Catholic student body.[53]

In 1976 the new St Mary's Home was opened. It had been obvious for some years that the old building on Station Street could not serve the changing needs of care for the elderly. The planning process was led by the matron, Sister M. Antony McLoughlin, but the members of the Nursing Home's Commission were all involved in the process. When Sister M. Antony went to Rome for a year of study in 1980, Sister M. Aloysius Somers succeeded her as matron until 1986. Sister M. Conleth Lawless was the last Dominican Sister to be matron of the home. In 1997 the roles of matron and administrator were separated and Sister continued in the latter post with great vigour until retiring in 2010, by which time she was aged over eighty.

There have been further building works and the home enjoys

consistently excellent ratings for the standard of care provided. The pastoral care does not stop with the residents but extends to their families as well, particularly at the time of bereavement. With the cooperation of the staff, efforts are made to maintain contacts between the home and the town and to foster outside interests for the residents. When sisters in the infirmary at St Dominic's are in need of full nursing care, they are transferred to St Mary's Home and for some years now, the home has also welcomed Dominican friars and sisters of other congregations in need of care.

St Rose's Special School also continued to flourish over the last fifty years with student numbers increasing and boys being admitted for the first time in 1960. Each of the four sisters who succeeded one another in charge of the school during these years made her own particular contribution to the school's development. Sister M. Leonie O'Driscoll (1956–65) placed the school on a professional basis by ensuring fully qualified staff were employed; Sister M. Rupert Fitzpatrick (1965–9) worked hard to raise academic standards; Sister M. Ninian Averill (1969–73) brought the school more into the public eye through community outreach; Sister M. Quentin Colclough (1973–2003) oversaw a great deal of building and adaptation which provided the school with first-class accommodation. Sister M. Quentin still serves as a governor and to sit on a number of committees concerned with special education at local and national level.

Prenatal advances have resulted in the survival of very premature babies with severe handicaps, while at the same time there was a move to integrate the less disabled youngsters into mainstream schools. This has gradually changed the profile of the student population at St Rose's, but the school has kept pace with the changes this requires. A new kitchen and medical room were added as more consultants held clinics in school to avoid the necessity of children attending hospital outpatient departments. St Rose's became a centre of excellence in the provision of therapy, and a new building was erected to provide for physiotherapy, occupational therapy and speech therapy. The school was also a pioneer in the introduction of conductive education in Britain; employing conductors from Hungary, where the system had been pioneered, to train staff. Therapists were also given postgraduate training in Bobath techniques as newer research proved the benefits.

In the classroom technology was increasingly used to enable the children to access the curriculum and as the number of children without verbal speech increased the staff used signing and electronic aids to encourage the children to communicate. The school used Makaton signing and taught the system to many outside agencies. Integration with local schools increased, with children from St Rose's going to neighbouring schools for some subjects, and staff providing outreach sessions which enabled other children to remain in mainstream schools. The school is under a well-qualified lay head, though it is owned by the congregation. The Religious Education department is headed by Sister M. Julie Alves, who in a recent personal Ofsted evaluation was rated 'overall outstanding' in this role. St Rose's has achieved 'specialist status', bringing with it additional funding, and a certain amount of kudos, but also more work. It continues to provide an innovative approach to special education, for residential and day pupils from pre-school upwards, and includes a special residential unit for post 16 provision.[54]

Conclusion

During this period, it could be said that the English Dominican Congregation developed a more realistic view of itself and its capabilities. The sisters allowed themselves to let go of many of their traditional works and to seek out new ways of serving and preaching and to take on new works, collectively and individually. It was not always an easy or painless adjustment but the Second Vatican Council had called them to respond to 'the joys and the hopes, the griefs and the anxieties of the men [sic] of this age'.[55]

The current constitutions remind the sisters that 'Dominicans are always at the service of the Church in its mission to the contemporary world.'[56] There is certainly evidence that the congregation has made a concerted effort to address the major issues affecting contemporary society; either by keeping themselves well informed, giving moral and financial support or taking direct action. As their human forces have diminished, they have had to reassess possibilities and move towards collaboration, not just with other Dominicans, but with any and all whose aims are consistent with their own.

Notes

1. Stone, G100(i), Sister M. Edward House, Circular letter, Holy Week 1987.
2. Stone, G100(c), Mother M. Emmanuel Fuller, Circular letter, Easter 1946.
3. Ibid., *Norway*.
4. Nilsen, *Nonner i Storm og Stille*, p. 279.

5. Stone, Bodø Box 2, Sister M. Magdalen Curley, *Memoirs of the Arctic venture*, p. 9.
6. Ibid., p. 19.
7. Stone, Bodø Box 2, *Newsletters, 21*.
8. Stone, Bodø Box 2, Sister M. Alberta Barry, *Newsletters, 30b*.
9. Stone, Bodø Box 2, *Word*, August 1967.
10. Interview with Sister Patricia Mary England, 2008.
11. Conversation with Sister M Jadwiga Świątecka, February 2010.
12. Stone, G(xix), *Annals, 1956– 1965*, p. 154.
13. Stone, G100(f), *Report of the Schools' Council*, 10 May 1965.
14. Ibid., 1 May 1965.
15. Ibid., August 1972.
16. Stone, G2000/63, *Register of the Prioress General, January 1953–May 1959, Nursing*.
17. Stone, STM.3, *St Mary's Home file*.
18. Stone, STM.3, Sister M. Paula Torley to Mother M. Bonaventure Burke, 14 August 1962.
19. Stone, H2004–3, Brochures for the academic years 1963–4 and 1966–7. Sister Anne De Sousberghe was still living in 2010 at the age of 105.
20. Stone, H2004–3, Sister M. John of the White Sisters (Missionary Sisters of Our Lady of Africa), vote of thanks after meeting of Juniorate Mistresses, 23 May 1969.
21. Stone, H2004–3, Sister Anne Gregson, Provincial Superior of the White Sisters to Mother M. Silvester Brennan, 20 January 1967.
22. Conversation with Sister Nilda Pettanuzzo FC, February 2010.
23. *Each for All*, no. 8, spring 1970.
24. Interview with Sister M. Sunniva Cummins, 21 May 2010.
25. Stone, G2000/59, *Register of the Prioress General, June 1965–September 1977*, p. 63.
26. Stone, G100(g), Mother M. Silvester Brennan, Circular letter, 13 June 1970.
27. Ibid., 22 September 1970.
28. Gilda St Pierre is also known as Margaret James. *Each for All*, no. 10, Christmas 1970.
29. Stone, G100(g), Mother M. Silvester Brennan, Circular letter, April 1972.
30. Stone, G100(g), *Newsletter*, 2 December 1965.
31. E-mail from Rosemary Walters, pupil at St Rose's Convent School 1950–6, 27 February 2010.
32. Stone, G(xii), *General Council Book, February 1942–August 1948*, 1 May 1942.
33. *News Chronicle*, no. 8/9, February 1984.
34. Rev. Richard Atherton to Sister Angela Mary Leydon, 25 June 1996, reproduced in *Our News*, October 1996.
35. *News Chronicle*, no. 8/9, February 1984
36. Stone, G98c(iii), *Brief Report of the East Meeting, London Colney, 1–4 April 1991*, p. 3.
37. Stone, G2000/59, *Register of the Prioress General, June 1965–September 1977*, p. 39.

38. *Each for All*, vol. 1, no. 1, April 1968.
39. Ibid., no. 20, February 1975.
40. *News from the Houses*, October 1987.
41. *News Chronicle*, vol. 3, no. 5, Lent/Easter 1981.
42. Since the closure of the large convent in Stoke-on-Trent, Sister M. Henry had been commuting to Longton by moped. At her final assembly at St Thomas More, several hundred pupils sang a rousing chorus of *The Hell's Angel Nun* written in her honour.
43. Interview with Sister M. Pauline Bürling, 28 January 2010.
44. Stone, G100(g), Mother M. Silvester Brennan, Circular letter, 28 September 1976.
45. Stone, G100(h), Mother M. Rupert Fitzpatrick, Circular Letter, 1 August 1979.
46. Stone, G100(i), Sister M. Edward House, Circular letter, 8 March 1984.
47. Ibid., 27 May 1985.
48. Ibid., 11 February 1987.
49. *News from the Houses*, February 1989.
50. Stone, G100(j), Sister Angela Mary Leydon, Circular letter, 13 February 2003.
51. *Newsletter*, February 1995.
52. *News from the Houses*, August 1988.
53. Stone, G98a(iii), *General Chapter 2001, Report of the Administration of the Prioress General, 1995–2001*, p. 5.
54. Stone, G115(f), typescript of interview with Sister M. Quentin Colclough, for DSI 2002.
55. Pope Paul VI, Pastoral Constitution on the Church in the Modern World, *Gaudium et Spes*, 7 December 1965. http://www.vatican.va/archive/hist_councils/ii_vatican_council/documents/vat- ii_cons_19651207_gaudium-et-spes_en.html, accessed 21 October 2010.
56. *Rule and Constitutions*, 2009. Article 65, p. 32.

Chapter Ten

Making a start: Dominicans sharing mission

We should inspire one another and dream a little together. There should be a cross-fertilization of experience and insight, a sharing with one another that is creative. But more, I believe: we should also be collaborating in ministry. We have begun, but we are only scratching the surface.

Fr Damian Byrne, OP[1]

Introduction

Believing that 'the work of one is the work of all' is only a step away from accepting the need for collaborating in mission. By baptism, all Christians share the responsibility of proclaiming the Gospel message, and in common with all members of the Order of Preachers, the English Dominican Sisters have an obligation to share with others the insights gained through prayer and study. Beginning in the years immediately following the Second Vatican Council the Masters of the Order began to encourage collaboration between the different branches of the Order, while at the same time members of the laity were being encouraged to assume a more active role in the Church.

Collaborating with others and handing over works was not merely a consequence of the process of diminishment but a result of a renewed understanding of their own mission and an appreciation of the mission of others. The process began in small ways as the sisters sought to share buildings that had served a meaningful purpose in the past, but had now grown too large for them. It developed into collaborative working patterns because they were able to 'dream a little together' with others about what was possible in the future.

A new kind of poverty, or enrichment?: handing over works

Although the congregation continued its commitment to institutional apostolates, as numbers diminished, a conscious decision was made by the English Dominican Congregation to share its resources and to hand over to others those works it was no longer able to sustain. The process often began in a small, informal manner. After St Ann's School at Portobello Road closed, the premises were used for a pre-school play group and Rosary House provided the venue for a 'Welcome Club' for senior citizens. Later on the hall of Siena House provided a meeting place for a local Girl Guides' troupe, and yoga and other classes were also held there.[2] These activities, which supplied real needs and built links with the local community, continued until 1976 when the convent was closed and the community moved to Ealing. Sister M. Nicola Loeb, who was prioress at the time of the move, involved the entire community in the search for a new home. Estate agents might arrive to show the prospective buyer over a desirable property and find six or eight nuns seated in a row on a garden wall waiting! The convent at Portobello Road was then sold to the Spanish Institute of Emigration who established a school and cultural centre in the buildings.

At Stroud, once the small community had moved into St Rose's Special School, the old convent was stripped and the chapel deconsecrated. The chapel organ, which was extremely valuable, was removed, restored and reconstructed in the neighbouring parish church in 1981. The convent cemetery was also deconsecrated and the sisters buried there were re-interred at Woodchester. Finding a prospective buyer for the buildings was not easy. The school site was purchased by the Stroud District Council, who used the newer buildings as an adult training centre and erected a health centre on the old hockey field. In an act of architectural vandalism they demolished The Green, which had been built in 1642. Eventually the Matrix Company purchased the former convent and began a phased development of art and craft studios and alternative therapy units.[3]

When the community moved into the new convent in Newcastle-upon-Tyne at the end of 1972, they continued to provide accommodation for students. Sister M. Gemma Riordan was appointed warden of the hostel wing in 1975 and the residents found in her a good listener with whom they could talk freely. Some of the former students kept in touch with her until her death in 2004. By 1986 the numbers in both community and hostel had decreased and the five remaining sisters moved to a house in Granville Road. For a time the 'new' convent was leased to the Catholic Children's Society and subsequently sold to the Anchor Trust who developed it as a care home. The sisters eventually left Newcastle in 1993.

As the numbers at Stoke decreased, the community had retreated gradually into one wing of the convent. Here too much needed accommodation was provided for students and the rest of the building was given over for use as a hostel. By 1981 there were over thirty-five students in residence, many from overseas, with Sister M. Paula Torley acting as warden.[4] In the years immediately following the schools' reorganization the Hartshill site was used by St John Fisher School, while the junior department of the former St Dominic's became an independent primary school until its closure in 2010. In 1982 negotiations began for the sale of the convent at Stoke to the Coventry Churches Housing Association for conversion to sheltered housing. The development, named St Dominic's Court, comprised forty-four independent living units and is currently managed by ExtraCare Charitable Trust.

Four other Dominican houses have also been leased or sold to other agencies providing residential care. In 1980 the convent at St Marychurch was offered to the Margaret Clitherow Housing Association, a non-profit organization providing accommodation for the elderly, and the sisters moved into the annexe above the new laundry. On 25 April 1982 a Mass of thanksgiving was held and the church was packed with grateful but sad parishioners and two days later the sisters left.[5] Margaret Clitherow House is currently home to forty-two elderly residents but is still owned by the congregation. Almost thirty years after leaving the parish, the Dominican Sisters are still remembered with affection, their choir, opening onto the sanctuary of the church, preserved exactly as it was at the time of their departure.

In 1971 the old hall in the grounds of St Margaret's Home at Hawick was sold to Roxburgh District Council and in March the following year Myerslaw Court, offering sheltered accommodation for fourteen residents, was opened on the site. Sister M. Bede Tolson was appointed warden and gave unstinting service in this role for fourteen years. After a knee operation and several falls which turned her daily shopping trips for the residents into a painful ordeal, it was clear that she could not carry on. At the same time, Sister M. Hilary Woodward also retired after sixteen years as matron of the home. The decision was made to withdraw from St Margaret's at Hawick in 1986, though once again the process of finding a firm buyer was paved with difficulties, the buildings still serve as a residential care home.

At Kelvedon, the Mid-Essex Health Authority had announced its intention of terminating the contract with St Mary's Convalescent Home in June 1990.[6] The decision was made to adapt St Mary's as a nursing home and in little less than two years the necessary works had been undertaken and registration granted. However, in 1994 the decision was made to withdraw the community and the home was purchased by St Dominic's Residential Home Ltd who pledged to maintain its traditions, standards and philosophy.[7] The departure of the sisters from both these small towns was greeted with obvious regret by the local populations. In both Hawick and Kelvedon the sisters were surprised when so many people they did not know stopped them in the streets to say how sorry they were to lose them.

At Leicester St Catherine's Home had continued to serve the very needy and the building underwent considerable renovation, the remaining wards converted into one- and two-bed rooms. By the mid 1990s, the home accommodated forty-two chronically sick, terminally ill or physically disabled patients, all of whom were non-ambulant. Since for many of the residents, St Catherine's would be their last home, there was a strong emphasis on giving spiritual help and preparing them for death when the time approached.[8] The home fulfilled an obvious need; but with only one sister on the staff, the congregation's involvement could not be guaranteed in the long term. For some time the basement at St Catherine's housed a day nursery and was later transformed into the Emmaus Centre, which offered facilities for meetings and day conferences and consideration was given to alternative uses for the building.[9]

In 1997 an approach was made to the congregation by the Leicester Housing Association. They already managed residential care homes and were keen to acquire and continue running St Catherine's. Furthermore, they were keen to retain Sister M. John [M. Basil] Perks in her role as matron during the period of transition. They also wanted to buy the convent building and convert it into a residential training centre for workers involved in their other projects: with low-income families, the unemployed and people with learning disabilities. Meeting these needs was clearly in line with the congregation's ethos and meant a minimum of disruption for the residents; the decision was made to go ahead with the sale.[10] A small community continues to live in a house on the other side of Glenfield Road. In recent years Sister M. John has worked in the stroke unit of the University of Leicester Hospitals Trust where she has been involved in promoting the use of PAT (Pets as Therapy) dogs.

Schools also were handed on to others. In 1974 Mother M. Silvester Brennan announced to the community at Brewood the General Council's decision to close the convent there. St Dominic's School had grown significantly during the fifteen years of Sister M. Joan Isaac's headship and numbered 266 students at the time, though only a small minority were Catholics. Both Sister M. Joan and the Parents' Committee were determined to save the school, which was certainly financially viable and clearly filled a need.[11] With the full cooperation of the congregation, the Brewood Trust Ltd was incorporated in September the following year and the entire property was first leased and eventually sold to the Trust in 1983. A community of four sisters remained in Brewood until Sister M. Joan's retirement in July 1977.

The future of the community in Harpenden had also been under consideration for some time. After complicated negotiations the property in Southdown Road was sold and in February 1975 the community moved to a smaller house in Kirkdale Road. There were no longer any sisters teaching in the parish school and as numbers declined the decision was made in July 1978 to leave Harpenden, though the Dominican presence was maintained when the house was handed over to the Bushey Dominicans.[12]

At Harrow, though considerable efforts had been made during the previous twenty years to build up academic standards, St Dominic's School was in financial difficulties. With other Catholic secondary schools nearby, there seemed no option for St Dominic's to be incorporated into the voluntary sector. When the Local Education Authority adopted a development plan of high schools for eleven- to sixteen-year-olds feeding into sixth form colleges, the Archdiocese of Westminster decided to fall in line with this model. Negotiations began for the sale of the major part of the property to the Archdiocese for development as a Sixth Form College.

By this time the old convent required major renovation, and unable to face another winter without central heating, the local prioress took the unilateral decision to move the community into Mount Lodge.[13] After standing empty for ten years, the old convent was sold, the interior gutted and transformed into offices with the historic facade retained. Once final approval for the Sixth Form College was granted by the Department for Education, building work commenced and on 21 March 1978 Cardinal Basil Hume laid the foundation stone for the new building. That year was also the centenary of the foundation of the convent and a celebration was held in the summer. In his homily during the centenary Mass the Dominican Provincial, Father Jonathan Fleetwood, traced the school's response to changing times, emphasizing the necessity of adapting to new circumstances and the detachment this required.[14] In September 1979 the new St Dominic's opened with 289 students and soon acquired an enviable academic record. By 2010 the numbers had trebled; the school continues to stress the importance of individual human and spiritual development for its students and retains a proud consciousness of its Dominican origins.

Two years later the decision was made to close the convent at Mount Lodge. Of all the prospective owners, the most favoured by the community was the Purcell School of Music, already established in Mount Park Road, so it was a source of satisfaction to them that they secured the property. The sadness of departure was accentuated by the sudden death of a member of the community during the final week. It was emotionally exhausted group of sisters who gathered for the final community Mass which was celebrated in the beautiful chapel at Harrow, the date being the anniversary of the death of its founder, Mother Catherine Philip Bathurst.[15]

From almost the beginning the community at Stone, and many other Dominican houses as well, relied on the cooperation of local people who were employed in the convent. Today, with an ageing community and fewer sisters capable of carrying out support functions, their numbers are greatly increased: nurses and care assistants in the infirmary, cooks, cleaning staff, gardener and handyman. In the infirmary at St Dominic's there is twenty-four-hour care and in recent years a qualified manager has been appointed, leaving a sister free to concentrate on the pastoral needs of the resident sisters.

This cooperation with the lay helpers has extended to the stewardship of the congregation's goods. The Bursar General has always played an important role in ensuring the financial stability of the congregation, and the Prioress General and Council have always depended on the knowledge and support she can give. Since the more participative style General Chapter has been introduced, the members of the congregation are also more aware that the decisions they make almost always have a financial implication. As more and more legislation was passed regarding charitable status, trusteeship, health care, child protection, educational, and employment regulation, the task became increasingly complex. Sister M. Hugh Shayler, elected bursar at the General Chapter in 1965, took these changes in her stride and over a period of thirty years carried out the exacting responsibilities of the post with efficiency, friendliness and modesty.

Sister Joan Mary English followed her in the post with equal dedication from 1995 until she retired in 2001. The decision was then made to employ a professional accountant to take on the role of administering the finances, not only of the congregation in general, but subsequently of St Dominic's Priory School and St Mary's Home as well.[16]

The working relationship between the Dominican Sisters and those who have assisted them over the years has undergone a considerable change. From one of direction it has matured into one of cooperation and partnership. Many of those who share the congregation's mission, or work in the different convents, do so with enormous devotion and loyalty. There is room in this relationship not only for mutual respect, but for sincere friendship and gratitude.

Collaborating in mission

Addressing the General Chapter in 1965, the Dominican Provincial, Father Gerard Meath, insisted that the sisters should be prepared to adopt new ideas and be ready to serve the Church in whatever way was required. He also assured them that the brethren of the English Province of the Order would welcome the active cooperation of the sisters in their work.[17] The same year Father Bonaventure Perquin organized the first 'Dominican Day' which brought together members of the several congregations of Dominican Sisters working in England.

At the conclusion of the General Chapter of the friars held at River Forest near Chicago in 1969, the Master of the Order, Fr Aniceto Fernández, issued a letter to all the sisters of the Order. He called for a re-examination of the relationship between the brethren and sisters, urging them to take up their rightful place, collaborating with the friars in the apostolate of the Order.[18] This must have prompted Father Gerard Meath to invite Mother M. Silvester Brennan to address the friars assembled for the English Provincial Chapter in 1970. Having canvassed opinion from members of the congregation, Mother M. Silvester was well prepared. There was certainly a feeling amongst the sisters that the brethren were not as interested in the sisters, or as supportive as they had been in the past, and a conviction that the friars no longer advised women contemplating a religious vocation to enter the English Congregation. The sisters wanted regular, positive guidance, they were eager to know what the brethren were doing in terms of experimentation with the liturgy and conventual life, they wanted not just to 'get help' from them but to have closer contact. Mother M. Silvester reminded them that women religious no longer wished to be treated as 'dear daughters' but as persons in their own right, equals. She warned the capitulars to expect to be challenged by them, that the sisters could certainly produce some good ideas; in return, they would find the sisters their most enthusiastic audience.[19]

Clearly, the relationship did mature, for ten years later when responses were collated for a survey on relationships between the branches of the Order, the sisters were now reporting that, even if they did not see the brethren as often as they wished, when they did meet, relations were more free and casual. The old relationship of father-child had given way to much greater equality.[20] This is born out by a file of correspondence between the Prioresses General during these years and various members of the English Province. There is certainly mutual respect, warmth of feeling, considerable generosity on behalf of the sisters – a new washing machine for Spode House, the gift to a friar in Edinburgh of a motorbike no longer needed by one of the sisters, repeated financial gifts to the brethren working in Grenada – and sincere gratitude expressed on the part of the friars.[21]

An even stronger impetus was given to collaboration between the different branches of the Order during the time Father Vincent de Couesnongle was Master, between 1974 and 1983. Father Vincent admitted that he had a 'soft spot' for the sisters of the English Congregation as he had spent some months at Portobello Road in 1972, learning English.[22] In March 1975 a meeting of Dominican superiors from Britain and Ireland was held in Spode House at Hawkesyard and model constitutions were drawn up for the formation of a Dominican Association which continues to encourage the exchange of information and the development of cooperative ventures amongst its members.

From the mid 1960s several proposals for collaborative ventures between the friars and the sisters were made. In 1966 when the lease on a house owned by the friars adjacent to their priory in Cambridge was up for renewal, it was offered first to the sisters as a house of studies. Once the decision had been made to move out of the old convent at Stroud, Mother M. Silvester Brennan offered it to the brethren, hoping that some arrangement might be made with the diocese for them to exchange the parish of Woodchester for that of Stroud. She was anxious that the chapel remain consecrated and be used by a religious community. Neither of these plans could be brought to fruition. Ten years later Father Conrad Pepler, who managed Spode House conference centre at Hawkesyard suggested a mixed community of friars and sisters be established there to help with the administration, development of courses and assistance with domestic management. He specifically mentioned what a tremendous asset Sister M. Nicola Loeb would be to such an undertaking, and although the project did materialize, Sister M. Nicola did eventually work at Spode House. During 1982–3 she was appointed to assist Father Conrad and found it the most rewarding and enjoyable work that she had been asked to do.

The first formal collaboration between the brethren and the sisters of the English Congregation began in the summer of 1978. A request was made by Father Michael Platts, prior of Hinckley, the oldest continuous Dominican house in Britain at the time, for sisters to help in the parish which comprised the town and a large rural area. Since the brethren and sisters were to form a single working community this was not a formal foundation; the sisters were assigned to the community at Leicester. Sisters M. Beuno Crump, M. Joachim Maybrick and M. Valery Walker took up residence at 48 Charles Street and began work at once. They had not arrived too soon, as two of the five friars were hospitalized on the day they arrived! Eventually all the sisters were commissioned as Special Ministers of the Eucharist and each given responsibility for a district of the parish. They involved themselves in visiting the housebound and sick, preparing children for the sacraments, acted as sacristans, helped with the choir, organized study groups and set up a mothers' and toddlers' group. Each day they joined the brethren for the Divine Office and the midday meal over which parish matters were discussed and plans drawn up.[23]

The following year a fire broke out in the middle of the night in a factory behind the sisters' house; anxious for the safety of three elderly ladies in a neighbouring house, the sisters went immediately to their aid. In fact, the police had already moved them to the front of the house, the sisters spent the rest of the night keeping up their neighbours' spirits and making endless cups of tea for the police and fire fighters. The community was also involved in setting up fifty discussion groups in the parish as preparation for the Pastoral Congress to be held in Liverpool in 1980. One of the sisters also acted as religious consultant to Radio Leicester. By October 1982 the Hinckley group had grown to include five sisters and a second terraced house had to be purchased. A club for the over sixties was set up in the new parish hall, and prayer groups in preparation for the coming papal visit were organized.[24]

Fig. 22 First community Mass at the convent in Hinckley.

There was great sadness on the part of parishioners when the Provincial announced that the friars would be withdrawing from Hinckley in September 1989 and the sisters dispersed to other convents. By this time Sister M. Beuno had already been working for several years as pastoral assistant at Keyworth, on the outskirts of Nottingham. The area had developed very quickly and many of the local people had lost contact with the Church. During more than twenty years Sister M. Beuno animated every area of parish life. In 1984 a new church was opened at Keyworth and in 1990 another in neighbouring Cotgrave. At times there was no priest appointed to the parish and it fell to Sister M. Beuno to arrange for priests to supply Mass. It is hardly surprising that her golden jubilee of profession in 2008 was a great celebration and shortly afterwards her contribution to the parish was recognized by the award of a *Bene Merenti* medal by the Pope.[25]

Following the departure from Hinckley, the focus for collaboration between the friars and sisters moved to Holy Cross Priory in Leicester. Sister M. Terence Rogers had spent most of her religious life working as bursar in several convents, though her work of choice, at which she excelled, was visiting the poor and lonely; often those others would not be inclined to approach. Though living at St Catherine's Convent, she spent twenty years working in Holy Cross parish with the brethren and in 1997 was also awarded the *Bene Merenti* medal in recognition.

In 1992 a house was purchased in Lincoln Street, near the Priory, with the joint purpose of encouraging collaborative work with the friars and acting as a house of initial formation. Sister M. Jadwiga Świątecka, who had retired from her teaching position at Christ Church College Canterbury that summer, became a member of the Leicester University chaplaincy team, working with Dominican Father Fabian Radcliffe. The community was completed by Sister M. Antony McLoughlin, already working as a hospital chaplain in the City Hospital, and Sister M. Bertrand Buckley as housekeeper for the first two years.[26] Sister M. Felix Riley then joined the community and worked initially in a hospice day centre and with the Black & White Partnership. Since there was no Catholic chaplain at De Montfort University, she was soon involved in chaplaincy work in which she was greatly appreciated; she too received the *Bene Merenti* in 2000.[27] The house in Lincoln Street continued to be a centre for collaborative work until the sisters had to withdraw in 2007.

In several instances, individual sisters answered the call to collaborate with and assist other Dominicans. At the end of 1984, after a six-month wait for the necessary visa, Sister M. Rupert Fitzpatrick answered an appeal for help in a teacher training college at Blauwbosch in Zululand, where several Bushey Dominicans were teaching. For twelve months she saw at close hand the consequences of the apartheid system on the African peoples and learnt to admire their enthusiastic participation in the liturgy.[28] In 1995 Sister M. Justin Lane spent several months in the Ukraine teaching philosophy and theology to the Dominican students of the newly established house of studies in Kiev.[29] Sister M. David Burton responded to an appeal for someone to run the bookshop at Santa Sabina in Rome in 1992 and spent six years there.[30] After several years in England she spent some time working in the international guest house attached to the monastery of the Dominican nuns at Prouilhe and is currently living with the Italian Congregation of St Catherine of Siena, undertaking translation work for them.[31]

In England a member of the Dominican laity, Jean Terry, spent a year living with the community at Ealing while considering how best she might live out her Dominican vocation. In December 1991 there began eighteen years of collaboration between Joan and Sister M. Crispin Mitchell. Joan had purchased a property named Littlemead at Ashburton in Devon and together the two Dominicans welcomed guests in need of quiet time and private retreats. Within the first two months there were fourteen guests, and two converts had been received into the Church.[32] There was a network of members of the Dominican Laity in the west country, some of whom had been associated at one time with the convent at St Marychurch, and for them too, Littlemead became a meeting place. The sisters of the congregation also took advantage of the quiet surroundings and beautiful garden, a quarter of the membership having been to stay within the first three years.[33]

A new shoot? The joint noviciate

By the early 1990s there were a number of women making contact with the congregation, two of whom made application to enter. During the summer of 1991 both the General Council and the Formation Team devoted a great deal of time and energy to formulating a new plan for initial formation. For various reasons both the expected candidates withdrew their applications. But by this time the focus on formation had shifted quite radically.

A meeting of representatives of four Dominican congregations with houses in England was held at Rosary Priory, Bushey, in November 1991 to explore various means of collaborative action. Because of the age structure of the different groups it was considered important to bring together what the group termed 'the life-bearers' in each congregation in order to 'bring life to all'.[34] Over the next six months there were further joint meetings of both the General Councils and the Formation Teams of Bushey and Stone at which the idea of forming a 'new shoot' was developed. Almost all the women expressing an interest in Dominican life at the time had initially come to know the Order through the friars in Cambridge. They wanted, quite simply, to be Dominicans and the multitude of congregations of Dominican women seemed more of an obstacle than a help in fulfilling this desire. Perhaps with as much uncertainty as precision, the plan evolved whereby new candidates would not be called upon to make a choice of congregation but would be nurtured as a single group by the two congregations. They would be 'the responsibility of, responsible to, and at the call of the Dominican apostolate of preaching the gospel pursued by both congregations in the United Kingdom or, if they felt so called, to any of the congregations' missions overseas'.[35]

In the tranquil surroundings of Keswick in the Lake District a meeting of the two groups was held in September 1992 at which a document outlining the proposal was produced. This document was endorsed by the sisters attending the Easter Meeting of the English Congregation the following year. The joint Councils and Formation Teams continued to speak enthusiastically of the new shoot, despite the fact that a number of serious difficulties became apparent in the area of canon law. The initial canonical advice had certainly been less than thorough and further advice was sought from Father Malachy O'Dwyer, Procurator General of the friars.

Under the existing provisions of canon law it would have been impossible to receive or profess novices into a non-existent congregation, but setting up yet another congregation would seem to be against the principle of establishing the more unified expression of traditional Dominican life in England which the candidates sought. Neither was there any provision for a group of vowed apostolic women, as some had suggested or hoped, to make profession to the Provincial of the friars, as did members of the Dominican Laity. Placing themselves under the direct jurisdiction of the Provincial would hardly fit the long established principle for female congregations, of women governing women. The only solutions possible would be to obtain a dispensation from the canonical impediments that existed or to go through the process of setting up, with the required episcopal sanction, an 'association of the faithful' which would gradually develop into a canonically approved congregation.

Both congregations expressed their disappointment at the canonical advice given. The alternative of a joint noviciate would also pose problems. Would a competitive spirit arise? What would happen if there was a disagreement regarding the suitability of a novice between a novice mistress appointed from one congregation and the Prioress General of the novice's congregation? The possibility of the sisters formed in the joint noviciate initiating their own new shoot at a future date continued to surface in the meetings for some time. Any new shoot would inevitably result in the extinction of the collaborating groups but it is only in passing that any mention was made of the effect this would have on the remaining sisters who were so generously nurturing the new growth. Yet the new shoot applied only to the English region of the Bushey congregation, whose official title was the Congregation of St Catherine of Siena of Newcastle, Natal. In the African region, where almost half their sisters worked, local women would still be received into the congregation, though their formation would take place in the joint noviciate of four congregations belonging to the Federation of Dominicans of South Africa (FEDOSA).

Once the decision was made to go ahead with the joint noviciate, a suitable home had to be found and assignations made to form the new community. Some time would be needed for the community to knit together before the candidates arrived and the proposal was made to begin the joint community in the Bushey congregation's house in Tackley Place, Oxford in January 1994. Eventually a community of five sisters from Bushey and two from the English Congregation formed the first joint formation community. Sister Bertranda Mulryan of Bushey was appointed novice mistress and Sister Raymunda Jordan, who came to teach pastoral theology at Blackfriars, was elected prioress. Each of the sisters continued to have her own apostolate outside the noviciate. A programme of studies was designed to address the human, religious, intellectual and pastoral formation of the candidates. There was to be a common core of study but sufficient scope to allow for individual needs and development.

For the four impatient candidates the great difficulty was making, at such a late stage, the decision of which congregation to enter. They had met members and visited communities of both congregations, and there were different and contrasting things about each which attracted them. At the time they felt it was important that they should be together and all opted for Bushey. After a brief postulancy the four novices were clothed in the habit in September 1994. From the beginning they attended classes with the brethren at Blackfriars where they followed courses in biblical studies, church history, ecclesiology and pastoral theology as well as having classes at home on religious life and the vows.

There was input from the English Congregation with several sisters providing additional classes in New Testament, liturgy and human psychology. On the financial side as well, Stone gave support by contributing an equal share to the maintenance of the noviciate community. In December 1994 the novices spent a week at Stone where they benefited from talks on the history of the English Congregation and its antecendents by the archivist, Sister M. Hugh Shayler. They were very impressed by the sense of tradition at Stone and fitted in well enough to give the community there the sense of feeling some ownership of the joint noviciate. In fact, in many respects the novices appeared to have a more traditional approach to religious life than many well established members of either congregation. It was noted that they wanted greater structure to community life, more solemn choral recitation of the Office – in fact, they revived some of the traditional chant for Holy Week – and appeared less tolerant regarding the freedom exercised by some sisters not to wear the habit at all times. The minutes of the same Formation Team meeting also comment that there were rumours circulating concerning the novices' freedom to frequent pubs, perhaps pointing to an innovative balance in their approach to religious life![36]

Indeed the novices were conscious that some saw them as being 'pre Vatican II' in their approach. Two of them put together a document setting out their vision of Dominican religious life for women, in the context of the history of the Order and the situation in contemporary Britain, emphasizing that they wanted this vision to be and remain positive and forward looking, drawing on what was good from the past while leaving behind what was not. They were also quick to point out their own need for guidance from experienced religious in seeing this vision develop.[37] Never having experienced what might be considered the negative traditions of religious life in the pre-Conciliar era, the views they expressed were hardly surprising. In Sister Bertranda they were fortunate in having a novice mistress who could appreciate their enthusiasm, and the fact that the aspirations of the young at the end of the twentieth century were not the same as those of the 1960s.

It is perhaps not surprising, given this appreciation of the traditional aspects of Dominican life, that doubts about their initial choice of congregation surfaced in the minds of some of the novices. Two of them sought advice from one of the friars on this matter and his sage advice was to wait, even until after perpetual profession, before making such a move, so that there would be no doubt regarding the integrity of motive. In the event, one of the novices did decide to transfer to the English Congregation. In response, the Formation Team pondered whether this implied that something more than superficial differences distinguished the two groups; or whether it was a question of strengthening the novice's sense of identity.[38] For various reasons the novice in question did not make profession at the end of her noviciate, but the situation shows what a delicate matter dealing with all the possibilities of tension and upset in a joint noviciate could be.

By June 1995, despite the fact that the neighbouring house had been acquired, more room was needed for the noviciate, with two more novices expected: one for Stone and one for the Swedish vice-province of the Roman Congregation of St Dominic. Renovations were made to the Bushey congregation's convent at Boxmoor in Hemel Hempstead to accommodate the noviciate community and two Bushey sisters already working in the local school and parish. At Boxmoor, noviciate life developed quite happily, the novices commuting to Oxford to continue classes at Blackfriars. The first profession ceremony was celebrated in September 1996 and novices were received that month for both congregations. The following year a Dutch candidate for the King William's Town Dominicans, another South African congregation, made her noviciate at Boxmoor. Excursions a little further afield than Oxford sometimes enriched the novices' lives and appreciation of the Order. In April 1996 they benefited from a study week for Dominican women on the theme of 'Gender in Scripture' hosted by the Dominican nuns at Herne in Belgium. In 1998 Father Richard Conrad, novice master for the friars, organized a pilgrimage to 'St Dominic's Country' in the south of France and northern Spain for novices of the brethren and the sisters.

In 1997 Sister Raymunda submitted an account of her term as prioress. Leading a community of such strong personalities had been a challenge; at times she had found it difficult to harness all the competing energies and yet work towards a Dominican ideal of democracy. She was also struck by the strong sense of mission of the novices and the 'reforming spirit' with which some of them arrived. Keeping those in the house who were not involved directly in the work of formation from feeling excluded had also been difficult. But she had found trust and support from the community of varied backgrounds and nationalities and had enjoyed in particular the beauty of the liturgy achieved through patience and practice.[39] Sister M. Jadwiga Świątecka was elected to succeed Sister Raymunda, while Sister M. Pauline Bürling was appointed to follow Sister Bertranda as novice mistress.

For two years there were no candidates to the joint noviciate, though the two formation teams and General Councils continued to meet. With the imminent arrival of a candidate for the Bushey congregation in the summer of 2000 a review of the joint policy on formation was undertaken. During this process, evidence of differences in approach and ideology began to surface, and in May Sister M. Pauline felt compelled to hand in her resignation as novice mistress. Differences of opinion between good people of principle are not uncommon, even amongst saints, and the General Council of the Bushey congregation, while accepting her resignation, acknowledged Sister M. Pauline's valued contribution, commitment and integrity.[40] At about the same time Sister M. Jadwiga's term as prioress at Boxmoor ended and, since there was no member of the Stone congregation available to replace either sister in the formation community, the joint noviciate was suspended. In 2002, when the next candidate sought admission to the English Congregation, the decision was made to establish the noviciate at the newly opened house in Cambridge. This offered the advantage of sharing initial formation with the Dominican friars who had recently transferred their noviciate from Edinburgh to Cambridge.

Despite disappointment on both sides at the end of the joint noviciate, collaboration between the two congregations has continued. Both agreed that the experience had been a positive one, a judgement shared by the five professed sisters who had received their initial formation within it. In the future, given the age profile of both groups, it is possible that the bonds forged during initial formation will lead the sisters to work more closely. Perhaps, just beneath the surface, the possibility of new shoots is always there.

Collaboration and handover in Norway

The sisters in Norway had always appreciated the efforts made by the friars in giving retreats and conferences. Sisters from Bodø were welcomed in Oslo by the contemplative nuns and the Châtillon Dominican Sisters. During 1969 two friars, two Châtillon sisters and one English sister formed a working community at Trondheim for some years. After Sister M. Nicola Loeb's election to the General Council in 1989 the community at Bodø was reduced to three. Without the collaboration of other Dominicans, there was little chance of continuing the work. Since several of the Holy Family fathers working in northern Norway were Polish, consideration was given to asking a Polish Dominican congregation to collaborate with the work there, though this did not prove possible at the time.

Since there was an increasing population of Filipino migrant workers in the area, the Dominican Sisters of Quezon City were contacted, and after two Filipina sisters visited Bodø in May 1990, they agreed to accept the work.[41] Sisters M. Pauline Bürling and Angela Mary Leydon visited the Philippines soon afterwards to discuss the arrangements and in March 1991 Sisters Maria Fe Suberon and Cleopatra [Pat] Moreno arrived in Bodø. From the start, they threw themselves into the work with enormous courage, despite the distance and strangeness of life above the Arctic Circle. On her first Christmas, Sister Fe took the boat for the four-hour journey to the Lofoten Islands over exceptionally rough seas, making her act of contrition and thinking she would never see the Philippines again! It was the thought of the isolation of the small Catholic community on the Islands that gave her the courage to forget her seasickness and overcome her fears.[42] The Filipina sisters did not restrict their apostolic involvement to their compatriots;

apart from caring for their particular pastoral areas of the parish, they also found time to involve themselves in voluntary work with the Lutheran Church Mission to the City, visiting the elderly and working with the children's club.[43]

Although two associates of the Quezon City congregation came to live in the community for a year in 1998, no other Filipina sisters were available for the work in Norway after Sister Pat's departure in 2002. By this time the community was reduced to two: Sisters Anna Mary [M. Edward] House and M. Sunniva Cummins. For the next few years they were assisted on a temporary basis by a Swedish sister from the Roman Congregation, and by Sister Else-Marie Nordland – a native of Bodø and member of the Châtillon congregation's community in Oslo – and by lay volunteers. In 2005 the decision was made to withdraw from Norway, though every effort would be made to find other Dominicans to take on the work.[44]

Some years before, St Rose's Special School at Stroud had developed links with a similar school in Pampanga, in the Philippines. This school was run by the Dominican Sisters of Our Lady of Remedies, a congregation founded as recently as 1965 and numbering just over thirty members. When approached by Sister Angela Mary with the prospect of collaborating in Norway, despite their small numbers, they were eager to do so, as their own recent chapter had mandated them to work with the Filipino communities overseas. By August 2005 three Filipina sisters were resident in Bodø and for the next two years they shared the life and work of the community. In July 2007 the legal formalities of handing over the property in Bodø were completed and on 22 July a thanksgiving Mass brought the Norwegian mission of the English Dominican Congregation to an end.[45]

Finding new sisters: Dominican globalization

The collaboration with the Dominicans of Our Lady of Remedies, and two subsequent joint ventures with other Dominican congregations, would probably not have developed as quickly without the existence of Dominican Sisters International (DSI). The group had a slow genesis from two streams, a group of English-speaking Dominican superiors who would meet together in Rome after the gatherings of the International Union of Superiors General, and a similar networking group in Latin America. DSI was formed in May 1995 with the aim of mutual support amongst Dominican Sisters in living out their charism as women preachers, facilitating communication, working for justice and encouraging collaborative ventures. Eighty Prioresses General attended the inaugural gathering in Rome and the Master of the Order, Father Timothy Radcliffe, lent his support and put the facilities of the Dominican Curia at Santa Sabina at DSI's disposal. The organization represents more than 25,000 Dominican women and is divided into five geographical regions with a Co-ordinating Council elected with representatives from each.

From 2001 until 2007 Sister Angela Mary Leydon served on the Co-ordinating Council of DSI and travelled extensively, meeting other Dominicans across Europe and further afield, particularly in the English-speaking world.[46] She threw herself into this work with nothing short of zeal and her openness, sense of humour and genuine interest in others reached across boundaries of language and culture. In the opinion of Sister Margaret Ormond, the first International Co-ordinator of DSI, Sister Angela Mary was a 'consummate collaborator' whose contribution was vital to the creation and development of the group.[47] DSI contacts resulted in other sisters of the English Congregation lending their expertise to the International Theological Commission for Dominican Sisters, running courses for those responsible for the formation of sisters, and visiting both friars and sisters in Nigeria to assist the work of initial formation there. In the European region there have been meetings of younger Dominican sisters which have been a source of enrichment and encouragement for the two most recent members of the English Congregation.

Late in the 1970s a Dominican Sister from Hungary, Sister Margit Németh, spent several weeks staying with the community at Ealing. It was a joy for her to live in community and to wear again the Dominican habit which she had last worn as a novice at the time of the suppression of religious houses by the Communist government. After the fall of Communism, several of the sisters regrouped, and Sister Margit attended the 1989 General Chapter as an observer. Some years later the Hungarian Prioress General, Sister Dora Rauscher, approached Sister Angela Mary at a meeting of DSI asking if there was any possibility of receiving assistance with the formation of their young sisters. After years of living clandestinely, isolated from the rest of the Church, learning to live together as Dominicans, with only the experience of forty years earlier, was not easy. In August 1999 Sister M. Pauline Bürling visited the Hungarian sisters to give a series of talks on aspects of Dominican life, and returned full of enthusiasm for the manner in which Dominican life was thriving there.[48]

Sister Dora was anxious to send some of the young sisters to improve their English language skills, continue their theological education, and gain experience of established Dominican life. In a short time, the seeds of another collaborative venture were sown. These ideas developed at the same time as the possibility of establishing a house of formation in Cambridge was being considered. Since there were excellent facilities for English language study, one of the needs expressed by the Hungarian sisters, as well as ample choice for theological and other studies in the university and elsewhere, a foundation in the city seemed ideal. A house in Huntingdon Road was purchased and extended and the first two Hungarian sisters joined the community in 2002. Cambridge also served as the noviciate for the congregation, the first novice receiving the habit that September. The novices who have entered at Cambridge have shared their formation with the friar novices, both novice master and novice mistress giving classes.

Yet another collaborative venture developed with the Italian congregation of St Catherine of Siena. These sisters had made foundations in Pakistan, and in 1992 Sister M. Justin Lane had spent some time in Faisalabad giving classes in scripture to the novices. Several sisters came subsequently from Pakistan to study English and stayed with the community in Ealing. By 2005 the future of the house in Ealing was uncertain, though there was a strong desire to retain a house in London and to maintain the tradition of hospitality inherited from the Portobello Road convent. At the same time, the sisters of the Italian Congregation were contemplating a house of studies in England, particularly for their Pakistani, Nigerian and Ugandan sisters. By October that year sisters from Italy and Pakistan had joined the three English sisters in Ealing to form a core multicultural community which soon began to welcome student sisters of various congregations from Asia, Africa, Latin America and Eastern Europe for longer or shorter periods.[49] The increasingly restrictive practices of the Home Office in granting visas in the years since the terrorist incidents of 2001 and 2004 have put this mutually enriching collaboration at risk. Recent plans, which involve initiating work with the Dominican Sisters of the Holy Trinity from Mannarkkad in the Indian state of Kerala, still hang in the balance for this reason.

Conclusion

In the last twenty-five years there was a fundamental paradigm shift in the English Dominican Congregation. Its members moved from a subconscious expectation that trends would somehow be reversed and continuity assured, to a consciousness that this was highly improbable. Far from stopping the congregation in its tracks, this realization has enabled the sisters to hand over works they have nurtured for many years, and to continue to look for new ways of preaching the Gospel, both on their own and in collaboration with others.

Their work with the friars, other Dominican Sisters and members of the Dominican laity has given them a renewed sense of family and deflected the tendency to introspection. The process has been mutually enriching and their work, particularly the assistance they have given in the formation of other Dominican Sisters, shows that they still have much to give.

Notes

1. *To Praise, to Preach, to Bless*, p. 260.
2. *Each for All*, no. 14, Michaelmas 1972.
3. Stone, G2000/59, *Register of the Prioress General, June 1965–September 1977*, p. 49.
4. *Each for All*, vol. 3, no. 6, December 1981.
5. Stone, G2000/66, *Register of the Prioress General, September 1977–July 1983*, p. 71.
6. Stone, G100(i), Sister M. Edward House, Circular letter, 23 March 1990.
7. http://www.stdominicsrh.co.uk/, accessed 15 July 2010.
8. Stone, G98a(iii), *General Chapter 1995, Community Reports: St Catherine's Convent Leicester*.
9. G100(j), *Joint Statement of the Prioresses General*, April 1996, and Sister Angela Mary Leydon, Circular Letter, Ash Wednesday 12 February 1997.
10. Stone, G98a(iii), *General Chapter 2001, Report of the Administration of the Prioress General*, 1995–2001, p. 5.
11. Walters, *St Dominic's School Brewood*, p. 108.
12. Stone, G2000/66, *Register of the Prioress General, September 1977–July 1983*, p. 13.
13. Stone, G2000/59, *Register of the Prioress General, June 1965–September 1977*, p. 19.
14. *News Chronicle*, vol. 1, no. 1, Advent 1978.
15. Stone, HRW Box 2, Sister M. Matthew Morgan, *The last days of Harrow*.
16. Stone, G98a(iii), *General Chapter 2007, Report of the Administration of the Prioress General*, 2001–2007, p. 4.
17. Stone, G98a(ii), *Proceedings of the General Chapter, 5–18 June 1965, Account of the Chapter*.

18. Stone, G115(d), Fr Aniceto Fernández to the Sisters of the Order, 24 October 1968.
19. Stone, G115(d), rough draft of notes for address by Mother M. Silvester Brennan.
20. Stone, G115(e), *Responses to the International Symposium on the Dominican Family*, 1979.
21. Stone, G115(e), *Correspondence with the First Order, 1942–1993.*
22. Stone, G115(c), Fr Vincent de Couesnongle to Mother M. Rupert Fitzpatrick, 26 September 1977.
23. Stone, G98a(iii), *Proceedings of the General Chapter, 1–10 August 1983, Report of the Prioress General.*
24. *News Chronicle*, vol. 1, no. 2, September 1979.
25. Stone, Generalate current file, Sister M. Pauline Bürling, Circular letter, 29 October 2008.
26. *Newsletter*, March 1992.
27. Stone, G98a(iii), *General Chapter 2001, Report of the Administration of the Prioress General,* 1995–2001, p. 18.
28. *Our News*, vol. 6, no. 10, Easter 1985.
29. Ibid., April 1996.
30. Stone, G100(j), Sister M. David Burton, 24 October 1998.
31. Sister M. David Burton, e-mail to author, 17 March 2010
32. *Newsletter*, January/February 1992.
33. Ibid., February 1995.
34. Ibid., December 1991.
35. Stone, G2000/13a(i), *Statement of Discussion*, 19 May 1992.
36. Stone, G2000/13a(i), *Minutes, Joint Formation Teams Meeting*, 21 January 1995.
37. Stone, G2000/13a(i), Helen Alford and Samantha Rhydderch to Sister Angela Mary Leydon, April 1995.
38. Stone, G2000/13a(i), *Minutes, Joint Formation Teams Meeting*, 29 July 1995.
39. Stone, G2000/13a(i), *Report of Sister Raymunda Jordan's Administration as Priores*, 22 July 1997.
40. Stone, G2000/13a(i), *Joint General Council Meeting*, 5 July 2000.
41. Stone, G100(i), Sister M. Edward House, Circular letter, 26 June 1990.
42. Interview with Sister M. Pauline Bürling, 18 March 2010.
43. Stone, G98a (iii), *General Chapter 1995, Reports from the Communities: Bodø.*
44. Stone, G100g (j), Sister Angela Mary Leydon, Circular letter, 20 September 2003.
45. Ibid., 26 January 2001.
46. http://www.dsiop.org/, accessed 8 July 2010.
47. E-mail from Sister Margaret Ormond, 7 November 2010.
48. Stone, G98a(iii), *General Chapter 2001, Report of the Administration of the Prioress General,* 1995–2001, p. 21.
49. Stone, G98a(iii), *General Chapter 2007, Report of the Administration of the Prioress General, 2001–2007*, p. 11.

Chapter Eleven

Time past and time future

Time past and time future
What might have been and what has been
Point to one end, which is always present.
T. S. Eliot, *Four Quartets*[1]

Evaluating the past

In her review of the history of women religious in England and Wales during the nineteenth century, Carmen Mangion highlights the importance of the role these women played in building up an emerging Catholic Church.

> They provided a stable and consistent form of evangelisation that was, in some cases, a daily influence in Catholic lives. The practical nature of their philanthropic and evangelical work was the necessary link between the revivalist efforts of male preachers and the lives of Catholics practising their faith. Women religious were significant contributors to the growth of the nineteenth-century Catholic Church through their religious activism.[2]

English Dominican Sisters played a pioneering role in this work, even before the re-establishment of the English hierarchy. The early foundations at Coventry, Clifton, Stone and Stroud focused on a direct apostolate geared towards infusing life into a Catholic community which was isolated, introspective, and lacking in confidence. Having imbibed with enthusiasm the rich Catholic culture of Bruges, Mother Margaret Hallahan played a significant role in shaping a Catholic life based on sound instruction in the basic truths of the faith, and nourished by devotional and liturgical prayer. In practical terms this meant not only building a conventual infrastructure, but also providing financial support to struggling local churches. As we have seen, this 'peculiar kind of mission' was not always appreciated by members of the hierarchy, who expected women religious to respond to their agendas, rather than set their own. Congregations of women in simple vows were a novelty in the English Church and the process of negotiating boundaries and establishing their own identities took time.

During the nineteenth century Dominican Sisters in England responded to a number of urgent social needs. Foremost amongst these was that of education. They established or taught in a variety of schools, from small convent schools emphasizing cultural and social attainment, to large and overcrowded primary schools in working-class areas of industrial cities. In some the academic standards were high, and encouragement was given to the pupils to sit for public examinations and to develop professional careers; in others the acquisition of practical skills to fit girls for future employment was the principal aim. In all of these schools Catholic values and practice were reinforced by the network of guilds and sodalities directed by the sisters. In their homes, hospitals and orphanages the sisters also catered for the needs of the ill, disabled and dying at a time when the lot of the aged and infirm was very often one of insecurity and destitution. They displayed considerable adaptability, moving from one type of work to another as new needs arose. In the early years of the twentieth century this innovative approach continued in such works as St Rose's Special School at Stroud and the school for children with visual impairment at Portobello Road, London. At times the sisters were prepared to sanction working in areas forbidden to 'virgins consecrated to God' simply because an urgent need arose.

As the twentieth century progressed a greater degree of institutionalization is evident in both the manner of life and the works of the English Dominican Sisters. This reflected changing ecclesiastical and political outlooks, with centralization of authority and codification of canon law in the Church, and a greater degree of legislative intervention in education and social care provision on the part of the State. On the one hand, this led to a greater attention being given to professionalism; on the other to a certain loss of family spirit as structures became increasingly uniform and formalized. For the English Dominican Sisters this trend towards centralization culminated in the amalgamation of 1929. There is no doubt that the intention was to strengthen Dominican life for all. But the undue haste with which it was accomplished, the insensitive changes to the agreed terms and conditions upon which the sisters had voted, without any further consultation or consideration of their own views, did much to undermine the salutary aims Father Bede Jarrett had laid before the communities.

The firm commitment of the first Prioresses General of the new congregation to making these aims a reality is undeniable, but a certain sense of resentment, seldom admitted though clearly felt, festered beneath the surface for many years. This sense of malaise was almost certainly a contributing factor to the numerical decline which marked the newly formed congregation from the beginning. Although the necessity for retrenchment was acknowledged, there seemed to be a lack of courage on the part of the congregational leadership to withdraw from works until it was quite impossible to carry on. Perhaps there was a fear of being seen to fail, but this fear carried with it a considerable human cost in overtaxing the workers and moving them about constantly in order to fill gaps. The foundation at Bodø in Norway was more than an excursion into foreign missionary work; it was an affirmation that the congregation still possessed dynamism and enthusiasm, and perhaps more importantly, showed that its members had sufficient adaptability to work out new ways of living their Dominican vocation.

To those who entered the new English Congregation, particularly in the post-war era, the hurts and sorrows of the amalgamation were hardly comprehensible. In fact, if they sensed a certain lack of cohesion in the life of the congregation as a consequence, perhaps this made them more amenable to the changes that would be ushered in after the Second Vatican Council. There have been remarkable changes in the lives of the English Dominican Sisters since the Second Vatican Council, not all made easily and not welcomed with the same level of enthusiasm by all. Although the sense of being members of a large, disciplined and vigorous cohort may have gone, a sense of sharing in the fundamental Dominican work of preaching has emerged. There has been greater emphasis on allowing individual talents and abilities to determine the apostolic work undertaken. The ensuing emphasis on individual apostolates rather than institutional ones does carry disadvantages, as it can also result in a lack of cohesion and weaken the sense of corporate identity. It saw the sisters once again being pioneers as they moved into roles such as seminary teaching and parish administration. Those who have led the congregation have seen their role increasingly as one of service and the exercise of authority now has a distinctly human face.

Evaluating the contribution of the Dominican Sisters to the life of Church and society in the second half of these 165 years is more difficult. In terms of bricks and mortar they have left a significant architectural legacy. The churches built by Mother Margaret still provide a splendid sacred space for the celebration of parish liturgies and private prayer at Stone, Stoke-on-Trent, St Marychurch and Bow. In terms of spiritual patrimony, many congregations of Dominican Sisters were influenced by the particular ethos of the Stone congregation by making use of their constitutions, either adopting them for a time or adapting them to their own particular situations.

The involvement of women religious in the provision of health care and social services is acknowledged as lacking due recognition.[3] Without doubt, the impact of the sisters in education is more easily assessed. The family spirit fostered in the small convent schools, where many of the students were not Catholics, helped forge close bonds, and loyal gatherings of old students still occur even many years after some of the schools closed. But their impact was perhaps far greater in the maintained and Direct Grant schools. Though not consciously seeing themselves as agents of social change, educating the Catholic community, challenging the young to excel, contributed to social promotion and the emergence of a confident, well informed and intellectually able Catholic middle class.

Perhaps nowhere is this more obvious than at Stoke-on-Trent, where the sisters played a significant role in the development and education of the Catholic community. There remains a consciousness even in schools which have long since passed into other hands, such as those at Harrow and Brewood, of their Dominican legacy. The website *Friends Reunited*, where people share memories of their school days and reconnect with childhood friends, does not generally present the most positive image of teaching religious. Memories of English Dominican Sisters, however, are refreshingly positive. One comment shows that the sisters lacked any self-consciousness about having fun, recollecting two of them 'dancing the *Gay Gordons* together, black veils and white pinafores [sic] flying, despite their immense difference in height'. More significantly, others speak of the sisters as intelligent and kind, quite capable of coping with difficult teenagers and their constant questionings, able to take the pupils' part, 'definitely role models'.[4]

The pioneering work in Norway has also left its mark. When the sisters arrived, quite uncertain of what their role would be, a small wooden building served the triple purpose of convent, presbytery and chapel. By the time the sisters handed over their work in Bodø there was not only a whole complex of buildings but a large and thriving Catholic community which, two years afterwards, opened the only Catholic primary school north of the Arctic Circle. Building up and sustaining the scattered Catholic community from a handful of local families, into a united but multicultural membership of several hundred, was achieved largely through the efforts of the English Dominican Sisters. It is also worth mentioning that the general culture of the town still carries the imprint of Sister M. Ruth Earley's enthusiasm for ballet; the three schools of dancing in Bodø were all founded by her ex-pupils.

Ten years ago, in her essay in the collection published to mark the 150th anniversary of the re-establishment of the Roman Catholic hierarchy in England, Susan O'Brien lamented the fact that the contribution of religious sisters to the life of the Church through the individual apostolates of recent years is so little understood.[5] With further research, the personal contribution of a number of the English Dominican Sisters in various apostolates will doubtless show how positive their influence has been.

Looking forward to the future?

Even though she leads a congregation whose numbers have declined drastically, the amount of administrative responsibility falling on the shoulders of the present Prioress General and her Council, at an age when their contemporaries in secular life would have already taken retirement, is considerable. The sisters are now few in number and although there are two in their forties, there is none in the fifties and half are aged over eighty. There are small communities at Stroud, Leicester, Ealing and Cambridge but two-thirds of the sisters live at Stone.

Although there are two lifts in the convent, being on the slope of a hill, with more than one level to each floor and a Victorian obsession with steps, makes it a difficult home for an ageing community. Having been listed as an historical monument, any renovation of the fabric must adhere to strict regulations. Neither would it seem cost-effective to undertake the major works that would be necessary to make it more accommodating. Despite being one of the most ardent enthusiasts for the convent at Stone, the late Sister M. Barbara Pearce conceded that although Charles Hansom 'designed an excellent horse-drawn conveyance, these walls are hard on old flesh and bone'.[6] Within these limitations every effort is made to provide care for the elderly sisters with their varied needs, both in the infirmary within St Dominic's Convent and the neighbouring St Mary's Home, which cater respectively for those requiring partial or complete nursing care.

In one of the sessions at the 2001 General Chapter the sisters had been asked to express their feelings regarding the future. While one admitted to being 'devastated' that the congregation was now almost one-tenth the size it was when she entered, another noted that with smaller numbers, the trend is more easily reversed.[7] Even though vocations promotion has become a serious and organized business, many vocations promoters feel that the religious life, particularly for women, is not an option which is offered to the young for serious consideration. Even if some of their former pupils regarded the sisters as role models, few sisters in any congregation are involved in teaching in Catholic schools to project this model to the young. From being the public face of the Church less than fifty years ago, religious sisters have become almost invisible, despite the contribution they continue to make. There is a range of opinion as to whether the congregation should continue to seek and receive new members, but on the whole there is openness towards enquirers. Since 2002 there has been a congregational website, complete with an events blog, and considerable thought is being put into developing this resource, not merely as a point of enquiry for those considering a religious vocation, but also for promoting the history of the English Dominican Sisters.[8]

Margaret Hallahan reacted with dismay on several occasions when concern was expressed about the future of the congregation; to her the congregation meant nothing, it was the Order to which she was devoted. The collaboration with other Dominicans which has been such a major development in the life of the English Congregation in recent years has played a part in relieving anxieties over the future. So has the positive decision to make the congregation's resources available to others to carry forward the works and mission they began. They have become accustomed to the process of diminishment and have even seen positive elements in their decreased size and greater dependence. The English Congregation and its antecedents have a history of which today's sisters can well be proud. As in any history there have been difficulties and lost opportunities, but it has also been a record of fidelity to the fundamentals of Dominican life. There is no question that this particular expression of Dominican life deserves to survive, but no certainty that it will. What is certain is that, as long as they are able, the Sisters of the English Dominican Congregation will keep on preaching, praising and blessing and continue to carry on that 'peculiar kind of mission' that has been theirs from the beginning.

Notes

1. Eliot, *The complete Poems and Plays*, p. 172.
2. Mangion, *Contested Identities*, p. 133.
3. Walsh, *Roman Catholic Nuns*, p. 159.
4. http://www.friendsreunited.co.uk/ accessed 21 February 2010, St Dominic's High School, Stoke-on-Trent, Message Board, Teacher Memories.
5. O'Brien, 'Religious life for women' in *From without the Flaminian Gate*, p. 133.
6. Stone, *Notes & News*, November 1991.
7. Stone, G98a(iii), *Proceedings of the General Chapter, 3–15 August 2001*, p. 8.
8. http://www.stone-dominicans.org.uk/ accessed 22 July 2010.

Appendix 1

Major superiors

Stone: Congregation of St Catherine of Siena

Mother Margaret Hallahan, appointed December 1845
Mother M. Imelda Poole, appointed May 1868, elected November 1877
Mother Francis Raphael Drane, elected November 1881
Mother Agnes Philomena Dormer, elected April 1894
Mother Catherine de Ricci Wilson, elected April 1918

Stroud: Congregation of St Rose of Lima

Mother M. Catherine Sandys, appointed December 1857
Mother M. Austin Kenny, appointed August 1859
Mother M. Teresa Matthews, appointed June 1860, elected September 1865
Mother Rose Imelda Harrold, elected August 1901
Mother M. Pius Pretty, appointed April 1907, elected April 1913
Mother M. Reginald Elgar, elected May 1919
Mother M. Teresa Lamburn, elected May 1925

Leicester: Community of Our Lady Help of Christians

Mother M. Rose Corbett, appointed 1866
Mother M. Vincent Rosbotham, appointed 1885
Mother M. Lucy Hickey, elected May 1904
Mother M. Winefride Kane, elected June 1907
Mother M. Lucy Hickey, elected June 1911
Mother M. Winefride Kane, elected January 1917
Mother M. Ambrose Kilbride, elected December 1922

Mother M. Winefride Kane, elected 1925
Mother M. Ambrose Kilbride, elected September 1928

Harrow: Congregation of the Holy Rosary

Mother Catherine Philip Bathurst, no record of initial appointment or election
Mother M. Anne Claeys, elected December 1906
Mother M. Dominic Wilkes, elected December 1924

London: Congregation of St Vincent Ferrer

Mother M. Cecilia Marshall, appointed October 1896, elected November 1899

English Congregation

Mother M. Teresa Lamburn, elected August 1929
Mother Rose Imelda Raymond-Barker, elected June 1935
Mother M. Emmanuel Fuller, elected May 1941
Mother M. Aquinas Colgan, elected May 1947
Mother M. Ansgar Sheldon, elected January 1953
Mother M. Bonvaneture Burke, elected May 1959
Mother M. Silvester Brennan, elected June 1965, re-elected August 1971
Mother M. Rupert Fitzpatrick, elected August 1977
Sister M. Edward [Anna Mary] House, elected August 1983, re-elected March 1989
Sister Angela Mary Leydon, elected April 1995, re-elected August 2001
Sister M. Pauline Bürling, elected August 2007

Appendix 2

Houses of the English Dominican Sisters

Stone: Congregation of St Catherine of Siena

1) Coventry, March 1844–August 1846, the house was in Spon Street.
2) Bristol, August 1846–March 1848, the community lived first in a house in King Square, before moving to Queen's Square at the end of November 1847, the latter building is now used for offices.
3) Clifton, Park Place, March 1848–June 1876, afterwards transferred to the Stroud Congregation.
4) Bridgewater, July 1850–April 1851, the exact address is not known.
5) Longton, January 1851–February 1854, The Foley, King Street, has been demolished.
6) Stone, July 1853–to date.
7) Stoke-on-Trent, August 1857–November 1998, the convent was converted into sheltered accommodation in 1982; the community moved first to 123 Hartshill Road and in 1984 to Priory House adjacent to the old convent.
8) Leicester, February 1860–August 1860 and again November 1860–August 1861, the building in The Newarke has been demolished.
9) Rhyl, June 1864–August 1866, the exact address is not known.
10) St Marychurch, August 1864–April 1982, the convent buildings were converted into a care home, still owned by the congregation.
11) Walthamstow, 1866–December 1868, Walthamstow House, in Shernhall Street is now part of Holy Family Technology College.

12) Bow, December 1868–April1923, the convent buildings are currently divided into flats, commercial premises and an art studio.
13) Hawick, Scotland, January 1909–December 1986, the convent buildings are still operating as a residential care home.
14) Kelvedon, October 1919–December 1993, the convent buildings are, like those at Hawick, still operating as a residential care home.

Stroud: Congregation of St Rose of Lima

1) Stroud, 1857–to date. The convent buildings were converted into workshops and therapy rooms while the chapel stands empty. The community moved to the Special School premises.
2) London, 1866, became independent, see below under Leicester.
3) Newcastle-upon-Tyne, September 1879–November 1993. Began in Regent Terrace, moved within a number of years to Shieldfield Green. The Minories in Jesmond was acquired in April 1922 and the community remained there until December 1972. All these buildings have been demolished. In 1972 a purpose built convent opened in Helmsley Road, in May 1986 a final move was made to Granville Road.
4) Clifton, June 1884–December 1898. Former convent of the Stone congregation. The convent buildings were demolished soon after the Stroud sisters left, some of the school buildings still remain in a semi-derelict state (2010).
5) Erdington, July 1890–November 1984. First home The Limes, moved in 1895 to The Hollies in Orphanage Road, and to Norwood House on Sutton Road in 1913. All three houses have been demolished, the latter to make way for St Agnes' Grammar School, now a campus of Edmund Campion School. In 1965 the community moved to two houses in Silver Birch Road.
6) Cheadle, August 1898–June 1947, the convent remained in the hands of religious communities until the mid 1970s when it became a private house.
7) West Kirby, October 1912–December 1929, the convent in Park Road reverted to use as a private house.
8) Carisbrooke, September 1913–July 1915, Carisbrooke House was home to sisters of several congregations until the mid 1980s.

9) Brewood, January 1919–July 1977; Bargate House, still forms part of St Dominic's Independent School.

Leicester: Community of Our Lady Help of Christians

1) London, February 1866–71. First house, 52 Fortress Terrace in Kentish Town, now converted into flats. Subsequently moved to Maitland Park Villas, Haverstock Hill, demolished since the Second World War.
2) Kensal New Town, 1871–September 1875; exact address of house in Hazelwood Crescent not known.
3) Leicester, September 1875–to date. The community's first home was at Cambridge Terrace in Humberstone Road, now demolished, moving to Millstone Road at the end of the following year, the premises are currently the Rutland and Derby Arms public house. Another move was made in 1884 to Abbey Park Road and to London Road some years later. The move to Dane Hills was made in 1906. The former convent and home are a residential care home, the community living in a house in Glenfield Road.
4) Hinckley, 1876–92. The house was in London Road and has been demolished.
5) Washington, March 1892–July 1895, exact address unknown.
6) Bridlington, December 1894–July 1962. A move was made to the High Street in 1928, the building is still a convent of the Sisters of Mercy.
7) Leyburn, July 1895–April 1932, the building still forms part of the parish complex.
8) Easingwold, March–August 1896, exact address unknown.
9) Redcar, October 1896–December 1930, the house now flats.

Harrow: Congregation of Our Lady of the Rosary

1) Ghent 1868–83, the convent was sold to Franciscan Sisters and is still a Catholic School.
2) Harrow, October 1878–December 1980. Most of the convent buildings form part of St Dominic's Sixth Form College; the original convent is now an office block.
3) Kilburn, 1881–1919. The first house was in Quex Road; a move was later made to Mutrix Road before the move to West Hampstead. The former is now flats, the latter demolished.

4) Watford, 1882–April 1937. The Grade II listed building is currently a convent of the Sisters of St Mary of Namur.
5) Southsea, 1886. Dates and address uncertain, moved to Shoreham.
6) Shoreham, 1886–91. The house was in Buckingham Terrace and was handed on to the West Grinstead Dominicans when the Harrow sisters transferred to Bognor.
7) Bognor, 1891–June 1936. The building in Upper Bognor Road was demolished. Community and school transferred to St Leonards.
8) Sale, 1891–97, the former convent in Marlborough Road now a private house.
9) Beccles, 1897–1905, the house in Grange Road now flats.
10) West Hampstead, 1919–December 1931, moved from Mutrix Road; house now divided into flats.

London: Congregation of St Vincent Ferrer

1) Portobello Road, October 1896–December 1976. The former convent is now the Colegio Espanol Vicente Canada Blanch.
2) Dovercourt, September 1909–32. The former convent now a private home.
3) Haverstock Hill, April 1915–October 1916. Exact address uncertain.
4) Harpenden, May 1920–July 1978, initially at Bower's Cottage, acquired Harpenden Hall in October 1923, moved to Kirkdale Road in 1975; the convent was sold to the Bushey Dominicans. Harpenden Hall currently houses the District Council Offices.

English Congregation

1) St Leonards, 1936–July 1965. The house in Filsham Road was incorporated into the Convent of Our Lady. When the convent and school closed and were demolished in 1998 the former St Dominic's was converted into a nursing home.
2) Bodø, Norway, May 1953–July 2007. The convent was handed over to the Dominican Sisters of Our Lady of Remedies from the Philippines.
3) Shannon, Ireland, May 1965–September 1974.
4) Ealing, December 1976–to date
5) Hinckley, August 1978–September 1989.

6) Canterbury, August 1986–summer 1992.
7) Edinburgh, Scotland, October 1987–98. Leicester, Lincoln Street, 1992–September 2006.
8) Cambridge, Huntingdon Road, October 2002–to date.

Appendix 3

Sisters in group photographs

Plate 8. The community at Stroud in 1871.
In front: Sister M. Imelda Mayo. Seated: Sister M. Joseph Barry, Mother M. Teresa Matthews, Sisters Rose Columba Hawkins, M. Agnes Corcoran, M. Catherine Horn. Standing: Sisters Agnes Teresa Mayo, Catherine Teresa Broadway, M. Rose Pyle, M. Winefride Edmonds, M. Raymond McLaurin.

Plate 11. The community about to leave Stroud for London in 1866.
Seated: Mother M. Rose Corbett and Sister M. Joseph Barry. Standing: Sisters M. Vincent Nevin, M. Bernard Wathen, M. Columba Lound.

Plate 20. The Noviciate at Stroud, 1934.
Front: M Casimir Chases, M Francesca Lucas
Seated: M Andrea Kuss, M Leonie O'Driscoll, M Bonaventure Burke, M Conrad Harding, M Damian McGimpsey
Standing: M Cyprian Foulkes, M Alberta Graber, M Mark Bullough, M Ansgar Sheldon, M Adrian Vincent.

Plate 30. Temporary professed Sisters at Harrow, 1967.
Sisters M. Sebastian Shortland, M. Pauline Bürling, Marie Louise Lloyd, Margaret Mary [Anne Mary] O'Brien, Ann Joseph [Angela Mary] Leydon & M. Julie Alves.

Fig. 10, p. 131. The community at St Marychurch, 1896.
Seated: Sisters Rose Magdalen Fellowes, M. Barbara Butcher, M. Columba Fellowes, M. Austin Fogge, Ida Baptist von Wangenheim, Catherine Joseph Crawford, M. Paula Plumer, M. Winefride Dawes.
Standing: Sisters Stephana Exton, Francisca Bergen, M. Jordan Parke, Winefride Dow, M. Casimir Tozer, M. Sales Simmons, M. Hildegarde Lederer, M. Amy Beech, Placida Stephens, Catherine de Ricci Wilson, Agnes Vater , M. Hilda Cholemely.

Fig. 12, p. 183, Sisters at St Marychurch 1940.
In front: Sisters M. Mannes Hassall, M. Angela Kendal, M. Damian McGimpsey.
Standing: Sisters M. Cyril [M. Adelaide] Coulson, M. Cecilia Oddie, Agnes Raphael Sanderson, M. Edmund Lewis, M Gabriel Hartley.

Fig. 15, p. 215, the Noviciate at Stone, 1969.
Sisters M. Rupert Fitzpatrick (Novice Mistress), Catherine Mary Williams, M. Teresa Billington, unidentified Dominican friar, Rose Mary Lynch, Máire Patricia McKewon, M. Andrea Kuss (Prioress), Mother M. Silvester Brennan (Prioress General).

Fig. 21, p. 260, first Mass at Hinckley, 1978.
Sisters M. Joachim Maybrick, M. Valery Walker, M. Beuno Crump, Bishop James McGuinness, Sisters M. Hugh Shayler, M. Cuthbert Pattison, Mother M. Rupert Fitzpatrick, Fr Michael Platts.

Bibliography

Archival sources

As cited in the endnotes:
Birmingham: Archives of the Archdiocese of Birmingham.
Clifton: Archives of the Diocese of Clifton, Leigh Woods, Bristol
Edinburgh: Scottish Catholic Archives
EdinburghOP: Archives of the English Province of the Order of Preachers.
Nottingham: Archives of the Diocese of Nottingham
Rome: General Archives of the Order of Preachers, Santa Sabina, Rome.
Salford: Archives of the Diocese of Clifton.
Stone: Archives of the English Dominican Congregation, St Dominic's Convent, Stone.
West Grinstead: Archives of the Parish of West Grinstead, since transferred to the Archives of the Diocese of Arundel & Brighton.

Constitutions

Constitutions of the Sisters of Penance of the Third Order of St Dominic forming the Congregation of St Vincent to which is prefixed the Rule of St Augustine, s. n., London, 1913.

Constitutions of the Sisters of Penance of the Third Order of St Dominic, under the title of the Dominican Sisters of the English Congregation of Saint Catherine of Siena, Browne & Nolan, Dublin, 1931.

Coutumier des Dominicaines du Tiers-Ordre régulier de la Congrégation de Notre Dame de Grâce, Imprimerie Franciscaine missionaire, Paris, 1890.

Rule and Constitutions of the Dominican Sisters of the English Congregation of St Catherine of Siena, no publication details, 2009.

The Rule of St Augustine and the Constitutions of the English Conventual Sisters of Penance of the Third Order of St Dominic with the declarations and ordinances of the General Chapters, Thomas Richardson & Son, London, 1853.

The Rule of St Augustine and the Constitutions of the Sisters of Penance of the Third Order of St Dominic forming the English Congregation of St Catherine of Siena, James Stanley, Roehampton, 1889.

The Rule of St Augustine and the constitutions of the Sisters of Penance of the Third Order of St Dominic under the title of the Congregation of St Rose of Lima, Stroud, Gloucestershire, s.n., Stroud, 1897.

Published works

150 Jahre Institut St Dominikus Speyer. Dominikanerinnen 1852–2002, Institut St Dominikus, Speyer, 2003.

Ashley, Benedict M., *The Dominicans*, Liturgical Press, Collegeville, 1990.

Aubert, Roger, *The Church in a secularised Society*, *The Christian Centuries, Vol. 5*, Darton, Longman & Todd, London, 1978.

Beck, George Andrew (ed.), *The English Catholics, 1850–1950: essays to commemorate the restoration of the hierarchy in England and Wales*, Burns & Oates, London, 1950.

Boner, Kathleen, *Dominican Women: a time to speak*, Cluster Publications, Pietermaritzburg, 2000.

Boulding, Sister M. Cecily & Pearce, Sister M. Barbara, 'Mother Margaret Hallahan in Staffordshire', special issue of *Staffordshire Catholic History*, no date.

Brownlow, W. R., *Memoir of Mother Rose Columba Adams*, Burns & Oates, London, 1895.

Burley, Stephanie, *Chapel, Cloister & Classroom: reflections on the Dominican Sisters at North Adelaide*, St Dominic's Priory, North Adelaide, 1993.

Carpenter, H[ilary], 'Domenicane di San Vincenzo Ferrer' in Guerrino Pellecia & Giancarlo Rocca (eds), *Dizionario degli Istituti di Perfezione, 3: Conv-Fig*, Edizioni Paoline, Rome, 1973.

Champ, Judith, *William Bernard Ullathorne, 1806–1889: a different kind of monk*, Gracewing, Leominster, 2006.

Chaucer, Geoffrey, *The Canterbury Tales*, original text ed. F. N. Robinson, tr. David Wright, Folio Society, London, 1986.

Cleary, Columba, Murphy, Eleanora & McGlynn, Flora, *Being driven Forward: the story of Mother Rose Niland and the foundation of the Newcastle Dominican Sisters*, Dominican Sisters, Boksburg, 1997.

Clerkin, Rosemary, *A Heart for Others*, Sisters of the Sacred Hearts of Jesus and Mary, Chigwell, 1983.

Cnockaert, Lucienne, *Pierre-Joseph Triest, 1760–1836: le Vincent de Paul belge*, Publications universitaires de Louvain, Louvain, 1974.

Les congrégations Dominicaines du Tiers Ordre régulier, Letouzey & Ané, Paris, 1924.

Curran, Patricia, *Grace before Meals: food ritual and body discipline in convent culture*, University of Illinois, Urbana, 1989.

Cusack, Margaret, *The Truth about Convent Life: or the sad story of my life*, Marshall, London, 1894.

Darcy, Catherine C., *The Institute of the Sisters of Mercy of the Americas: the canonical development of the proposed governance model*, University Press of America, Lanham MD, 1993.

Darricau, Raymond & Peyrous, Bernard, *Father Noailles and the Association of the Holy Family: the Story of a Charism*, CLD, Chambray-lès-Tours, 1992.

Degnan, M. Bertrand, *Mercy unto Thousands*, Browne & Nolan, Dublin, 1958.

Doyle, Peter, *Mitres & Missions in Lancashire: the Roman Catholic Diocese of Liverpool, 1850–2000*, Bluecoat Press, Liverpool, 2005.

Drane, Francis Raphael, *The daily Life of a Religious*, Art and Book Company, London, 1897.

——, *Life of Mother Margaret Mary Hallahan, Foundress of the English Congregation of St Catherine of Siena of the Third Order of St Dominic*, Longmans Green, London, 1869.

Egar, Irene ffrench, *The Nun of Kenmare*, Mercier, Cork, 1970.

Eliot, T. S., *The complete Poems and Plays of T. S. Eliot*, ed. Valerie Eliot, Faber & Faber, London, 1969.

Finnegan, Frances, *Do Penance or perish: Magdalen Asylums in Ireland*, Oxford University Press, Oxford, 2001.

Flaxman, Radegunde Flaxman, *A Woman styled bold: the life of Cornelia Connelly, 1809–1879*, Darton, Longman & Todd, London, 1991.

Fontane, Theodor, *Von Zwanzig bis Dreissig : Autobiographisches nebst anderen selbstbiograph. Zeugnissen*, Deutscher Taschenbuch, Munich, 1973.

Foyle, Andrew, *Bristol*, Yale University Press, New Haven & London, 2004.

Gaine, Simon Francis, *Obituary Notices of the English Dominicans from 1952 to 1996*, Blackfriars, Oxford, 2000.

Geser, Fintan, *The Canon Law governing Communities of Sisters*, Herder, St Louis, 1938.

Gumbley, Walter, *Obituary Notices of the English Dominicans 1555–1952*.

Hamer, Edna, *Elizabeth Prout, 1820–1864: a religious life for industrial England*, Downside Abbey, Bath, 1994.
[Hampton], Mary Thomas, *The Lord may be in a Hurry: the Congregation of Dominican Sisters of St Catherine of Siena of Kenosha, Wisconsin*, Bruce, Milwaukee, 1965.
Hancock, Stephen H., 'From Hagiography to History': a critical re-examination of the first forty years of 'The Life' of Mother Margaret Hallahan and of its manuscript sources', in *Recusant History*, vol. 23, no. 3, May 1997, pp. 341–71.
Hanoteau, Marie-Émilie, *Une grande Nivelloise: Mère Gertrude (Justine Desbille) Fondatrice des Sœurs de l'Enfant-Jésus de Nivelles, 1801–1866*, Institut de l'Enfant-Jésus, Nivelles, 1985.
Harding, J. A., *The Diocese of Clifton, 1850–2000*, Diocesan Trustees, Clifton, 1999.
Harrison, Martin, *Hinckley St Peter's: Dominican revival, 1734–1958*, Samuel Walker, Hinckley, 1958.
Heimann, Mary, *Catholic Devotion in Victorian England*, Clarendon Press, Oxford, 1995.
Hill, Rosemary, *God's Architect: Pugin and the building of romantic Britain*, Allen Lane, London, 2007.
Hinnebusc, William A., *The Dominicans: a short history*, Dominican Publications, Dublin, 1980.
Horgan, Dominique, *Weavings: celebrating Dominican women*, Dominican Sisters, Dublin, 1988.
Hostie, Raymond, *Vie et Mort des Orders religieux*, Desclée De Brouwer, Paris, 1972.
Hughes, Philip, 'The English Catholics in 1850', in George Andrew Beck (ed.), *The English Catholics, 1850–1950: essays to commemorate the Restoration of the Hierarchy in England and Wales*, Burns & Oates, London, 1950.
Jarrett, Bede, *Letters of Bede Jarrett: Letters and other papers from the Dominican archives selected by Bede Bailey OP*, ed. Simon Tugwell, OP & Dom Aidan Bellenger, Downside Abbey, Bath, 1989.
Jégou, Marie-Andrée & Kogoj, Marija Jasna, *L'Union romaine des Ursulines: une marche vers l'unuité, 1900–1926*, Generalizia delle Orsoline, Rome, 1999.
Lancaster, Judith, *Cornelia Connelly and her Interpreters*, Way Books, Oxford, 2004.
Langlois, Claude, *Le Catholicisme au Feminine: les congregations françaises à supérieure générale au XIXe siècle*, Cerf, Paris, 1984.
Lawrence, C. H., *Medieval Monasticism: forms of religious life in western Europe in the Middle Ages*, 2nd edn, Longman, London, 1989.
McClelland, Maria G., *The Sisters of Mercy, popular Politics and the*

Growth of the Roman Catholic Community in Hull, 1855–1930, Edwin Mellen, Lampeter, 2000.

McClelland, V. Alan, 'The formative years, 1850–92', in V. Alan McClelland and Michael Hodgetts (eds) *From out the Flaminian Gate: 150 years of Roman Catholicism in England and Wales, 1850–2000*, Darton, Longman & Todd, London, 1999.

McClelland, V. Alan and Hodgetts, Michael (eds), *From out the Flaminian Gate: 150 years of Roman Catholicism in England and Wales, 1850–2000*, Darton, Longman & Todd, London, 1999.

McDonnell, Jeanette Clare, *Growing unto Christ: a Franciscan response in faith*, Webberley Printers, Stoke-on-Trent, 1988.

McKibben, Ross, *Classes and Cultures in England, 1918–1951*, Oxford University Press, Oxford, 1998.

McLeod, Hugh, *Religion and Society in England, 1850–1914*, Macmillan, London, 1996.

McNamara, Jo Ann Kay, *Sisters in Arms: Catholic nuns through two millennia*, Harvard University Press, Cambridge, MA, 1996.

Mainage,Th[omas], *La révérende Mère Saint Dominique de la Croix: Fondatrice et Prieure générale des Dominicaines de la Congrégation de Sainte Catherine de Sienne*, Téqui, Paris, 1929.

Mangion, Carmen M., *Contested Identities: Catholic Women Religious in nineteenth-century England and Wales*, MUP, Manchester, 2008.

Maynard, Jean Olwen, *150 Years of Mercy: a History of the Sisters of Mercy, Commercial Road, East London*, Sisters of Mercy, London, 2009.

Mortier, R[évérend] P[ère], *Bonne Mère ou la révérende Mère Chupin: Fondatrice de la Congrégation de Notre-Dame de Gâce*, Desclée de Brouwer, Lille, 1926.

Mullay, Camilla, *A Place of Springs: a History of the Dominican Sisters of St Mary of the Springs, 1830–1970*, Dominican Sisters, Columbus OH, 2005.

Newman, John Henry, *The Letters and Diaries of John Henry Newman*, ed. Charles Stephen Dessain, vol. 11, T. Nelson, London, 1961.

Newsome, D., *The Victorian World Picture*, J. Murray, London, 1997.

Nilsen, Else-Britt, *Nonner i Storm og Stille: Katolske Ordenssøstre i Norge id et 19. og 20. Århundre*, Solum, Oslo, 2001.

Noonan, Paschala, *Signadou: History of the Kentucky Dominican Sisters*, Brookville, Manhassett NY, 1997.

Norman, Edward, *The English Catholic Church in the Nineteenth Century*, Clarendon Press, Oxford, 1984.

Northey, Helen, *Living the Truth: the Dominican Sisters in South Australia, 1868–1958*, Dominican Sisters, Adelaide, 1999.

O'Brien, Susan, 'Lay-Sisters and Good Mothers: working-class women in English convents', in W. J. Sheils & D. Woods (eds), *Women in the Church: papers read at the 1989 Summer Meeting of the Ecclesiastical History Society,* Studies in Church History, Ecclesiastical History Society, Oxford, pp. 453–65.

——, 'Religious life for women' in V. Alan McClelland and Michael Hodgetts (eds), *From out the Flaminian Gate: 150 years of Roman Catholicism in England and Wales, 1850–2000*, Darton, Longman & Todd, London, 1999.

——, '*Terra Incognita*: the nun in nineteenth-century England' in *Past and* Present, vol. 121, 1988, pp. 110–40.

O'Sullivan, Deirdre, *Dominican Sisters of North Adelaide: their History and Spirituality, 1883–1983*, Dominican Sisters, North Adelaide, 1983.

Préteseille, Bernard, *Marie Poussepin: ou l'exercise de la charité*, CDL, Chambray-lès-Tours, 1989.

Prunty, Jacinta, *Lady of Charity, Sister of Faith: Margaret Aylward, 1810–1889*, Four Courts, Dublin, 1999.

Radcliffe, Timothy, 'The Mission of the Dominican Family' in *To Praise, to Preach, to Bless: Words of Grace and Truth*, Dominican Publications, Dublin, 2004.

Ranft, Patricia, *Women and the Religious life in premodern Europe*, St Martin's Press, New York, 1996.

[Raymond-Barker, M. Rose Imelda], A Dominican of Stone: *The Conventual Third Order of St Dominic and its development in England,* Burns Oates & Washbourne, London, 1923.

Roker, Penny, *Children of Mercy: the Story of the Schools of Our Lady's Convent, Abingdon*, Our Lady's Convent Senior School, Abingdon, 2000.

Sacred Heart Mere Street: School History, Sacred Heart School, Leicester, n. d. [1970s].

Sagarra, Eda, 'Theodor Fontane and the Petticoat Regiment' in *German Life and Letters*, vol. 58, no. 2, April 2005, pp. 124–5.

Scarisbrick, J. J., *Selly Park and Beyond: the Story of Geneviève Dupuis and the Sisters of Charity of St Paul the Apostle*, Sister of Charity of St Paul the Apostle, Birmingham, 1997.

Shaw, Pauline J., *Elizabeth Hayes: pioneer Franciscan journalist*, Gracewing, Leominster, 2009.

Sisters of the English Dominican Congregation of St Catherine of Siena, *A Treasure of Joy and Gladness: Mother Mary Cecilia Marshall OP*, Samuel Walker, Hinckley, 1948.

S. M. A., *A brief Account of the Life of Mother Mary Elizabeth Lockhart OSF and the Foundation of the Franciscan Sisters of the Third Order Regular of the Immaculate Conception*, Quick & Co. Printers,

London, 1958.
Smith, Richard, 'Elgar, Dot and the Stroud Connection' in *Elgar Society Journal*, vol. 14, no. 5, July 2006 & vol. 14, no. 6, November 2006.
Stephens, W. B. (ed.), *A history of the County of Warwick. Vol. 7, Coventry and the Borough of Warwick*, Oxford University Press, Oxford, 1969.
Sugg, Joyce, *Ever yours affly: John Henry Newman and his female Circle*, Gracewing, Leominster, 1996.
Vicaire, Marie-Henri, *Saint Dominic and his Times*, Darton, Longman & Todd, London, 1964.
Wall, Barbara Mann, *Unlikely Entrepreneurs: Catholic Sisters and the Hospital Market Place, 1865–1925*, Ohio State University Press, Columbus, 2005.
Walsh, Barbara, *Roman Catholic Nuns in England and Wales, 1800–1937: a social History*, Irish Academic Press, Dublin, 2002.
Walters, Jeremy, *St Dominic's School Brewood: a History, 1920–1995*, no publication details given.
Watts, John, *A Canticle of Love: the Story of the Franciscan Sisters of the Immaculate Conception*, John Donald, Edinburgh, 2006.
West, Elizabeth A., *One Woman's Journey: Mary Potter, Founder of the Little Company of Mary*, Spectrum, Richmond, Victoria, 2001.
Whitehead, Maurice, 'A View from the Bridge: the Catholic School', in V. Alan McClelland and Michael Hodgetts (eds), *From out the Flaminian Gate: 150 years of Roman Catholicism in England and Wales, 1850–2000*, Darton, Longman & Todd, London, 1999).
Wilberforce, Bertrand, *Memoir of Mother Francis Raphael Drane, O.S.D.*, Longmans Green, London, 1895.
Williams, Thomas Jay & Campbell, Allan Walter, *The Park Village Sisterhood*, SPCK, London, 1965.

Index